Practical Reflection

THE DAVID HUME SERIES
PHILOSOPHY AND COGNITIVE SCIENCE REISSUES

The *David Hume Series on Philosophy and Cognitive Science Reissues* consists of previously published works that are important and useful to scholars and students working in the area of cognitive science. The aim of the series is to keep these indispensable works in print.

PRACTICAL REFLECTION

J. DAVID VELLEMAN

THE DAVID HUME SERIES
PHILOSOPHY AND COGNITIVE SCIENCE REISSUES

 CSLI PUBLICATIONS

Copyright © 2007
CSLI Publications
Center for the Study of Language and Information
Leland Stanford Junior University
Printed in the United States
11 10 09 08 07   1 2 3 4 5

Library of Congress Cataloging-in-Publication Data

Velleman, James David.

Practical reflection / by J. David Velleman.

p. cm. – (The David Hume series)

Includes bibliographical references and index.
ISBN-13: 978-1-57586-534-8 (pbk. : alk. paper)
ISBN-10:   1-57586-534-3 (pbk. : alk. paper)
1. Act (Philosophy) 2. Agent (Philosophy) 3. Reasoning. I. Title. II. Series.

B105.A35V44 2007
128´.4 – dc22   2007007742
CIP

The *David Hume Series on Philosophy and Cognitive Science Reissues* consists of
previously published works that are important and useful to scholars and students
working in the area of cognitive science. The aim of the series is to keep these
indispensable works in print in affordable paperback editions.

In addition to this series, CSLI Publications also reports new developments in the
study of language, information, and computation. Please visit our web site at
http://cslipublications.stanford.edu/
for comments on this and other titles, as well as for changes
and corrections by the author and publisher.

For Kitty

CONTENTS

ACKNOWLEDGMENTS

Some of the ideas in this book were developed in my doctoral dissertation, which was supported by a Harold W. Dodds Fellowship from Princeton University and a Charlotte W. Newcombe Fellowship from the Woodrow Wilson National Fellowship Foundation. I wrote the book during my tenure as William Wilhartz Assistant Professor in the Department of Philosophy at the University of Michigan, a position established through the generosity of Edna and Norman Freehling. The first draft was completed during a year's leave from my teaching duties, which was funded partly by the philosophy department and partly by a research fellowship from the American Council of Learned Societies. Work on the book was also supported by my department with funds from the Denise Philosophy Endowment.

Portions of the book have been published before. Parts of chapters 1 and 2 appeared in "Practical Reflection," *Philosophical Review* 94 (1985): 33–61. Parts of chapter 4 appeared in "The Doxastic Theory of Intention," in *Reasoning About Actions and Plans*, ed. Michael P. Georgeff and Amy L. Lansky (Los Altos, Calif.: Morgan Kaufmann, 1987), 361–93. Parts of chapter 5 appeared in "Epistemic Freedom," *Pacific Philosophical Quarterly* 70 (1989): 73–97. I am grateful to the editors and publishers for their permission to reprint this material.

I would like to renew my thanks to my dissertation advisor, David Lewis, whose encouragement and advice were instrumental in launching my research on its present course. In writing the book, I have relied above all on comments and suggestions from Paul Boghossian, with whom I had the pleasure of discussing almost every part of the work as it progressed. I am also especially grateful to Rüdiger Bittner and Stephen Darwall, for extensive comments on early versions of the book, and to Alfred Mele, for a last-minute reading of the penultimate draft. Others to whom I am indebted for comments on the manuscript include: Michael Bratman, Harry Frankfurt, Allan Gibbard, Jaegwon Kim, Louis Loeb, Joseph Mendola, Peter Railton, Amélie Rorty, Nicholas White, and participants in a seminar that I taught on the philosophy of action during the winter of 1987.

I received excellent editorial and administrative assistance from Scott Dennis, Doreen Fussman, Sherri Kononetz, and Anne Webb. I am also indebted to John Brehm for the use of his computer program *PsX*.

Several people have sustained me with their love and friendship during my work on this book. If I have not already made my gratitude vivid to them on other occasions, such negligence can hardly be remedied here.

INTRODUCTION TO THE DAVID HUME SERIES EDITION *

Imagine that your arm becomes temporarily paralyzed. When you wake up each morning, the first thing you do is to check whether you have regained control of your arm. What exactly are you hoping to find?

Part of what you're hoping to find, no doubt, is that your arm moves. But movement by itself wouldn't be enough. Waking up to find your arm flapping around aimlessly wouldn't lead you to think that your control over it had been restored. You'd have to conclude instead that paralysis had given way to a spasm.

What you're hoping to find, then, is that your arm not only moves but moves when and where you want it to. But would movement in response to your desires be enough? You might of course be encouraged if you found your hand scratching an itch behind your ear; but if you subsequently found it grabbing food off someone else's plate, you wouldn't necessarily be reassured by the reflection that you had indeed wanted what he was eating.

The problem in this case, we might be inclined to say, is that although you wanted the food on someone else's plate, you also wanted to obey the rules of etiquette, and so grabbing the food wasn't something that you wanted to do on balance or overall. Your having control of your arm would require that the arm do, not just something that you wanted, but rather what you wanted on balance.

Yet how do you tell what you want on balance? If you have ever cast a speculative glance at the uneaten french fries on someone else's plate, you'll know that the contest between appetite and etiquette can be close. Surely, appetite might win out before you had realized that it was the stronger; indeed, you might realize that it was the stronger only by seeing it that it had won out, as evidenced by the movement of your arm. And then the thought that this movement reflected the balance of your motives would not convince you of your having regained control.

* This Introduction contains material from: my *precis* of *The Possibility of Practical Reason* (Oxford: Oxford University Press, 2000), published in *Philosophical Studies* 21 (2004): 225–38; "The Centered Self", published in *Self to Self* (New York: Cambridge University Press, 2006), pp. 253–83; and "What Good is a Will?", to appear in *Action in Context*, edited by Anton Leist and Holger Baumann (de Gruyter/Mouton: Berlin/New York). It has benefited from being discussed in a seminar conducted by Michael Smith at Princeton University in the fall of 2006.

Agency as a Way of Knowing

My description of these cases implicitly suggests that you still lack control of your arm in each case. How have I made this suggestion? I've made it by repeatedly casting you in the role of a spectator, who "sees" or "finds" that his arm is moving.

Many philosophers share the intuition that being a spectator is the dia-metrical opposite of being an agent. As one philosopher puts it, "Common to all experiences of loss of agency is the sense of becoming a spectator of one's own actions".[1] In the words of another philosopher, "[I]t seems as though someone has moved into your body and pushed you off the playing field up into the grandstand to be a mere spectator of yourself"[2]. This trope is almost universal in the philosophical literature about action and the will.[3]

---

[1] Brian O'Shaughnessy, *The Will; A Dual Aspect Theory* (Cambridge: Cambridge University Press, 1980), Volume 2, p. 36.

[2] Michael Kubara, "Acrasia, Human Agency and Normative Psychology," *Canadian Journal of Philosophy* 5 (1975) 215–32, p. 231.

[3] Examples include: "The agent is originating, the spectator is only contemplating" (Gilbert Ryle, *The Concept of Mind* [Chicago: University of Chicago Press, 2000], p. 54); "[O]ne's capacity to govern one's conduct is undermined .... One is reduced to a specta-tor." (Robert Audi, "Acting for a Reason", *Philosophical Review* 95 [1986] 511–46, p. 534); "The sense of autonomy is the sense that one is not merely a witness to one's life but rather fashions it from the world as one finds it (Gary Watson, "Introduction" to *Free Will* [Oxford: Oxford University Press, 2003], p. 1); "The agent must not be a mere bystander or onlooker of what happens" (Philip Pettit, *A Theory of Freedom; From the Psychology to the Politics of Agency* [New York: Oxford University Press, 2001], p. 10); "This makes it seem as if get-ting up from a chair is something that happens to a man, something to which he is at best a spectator" (Ilham Dilman, *Free Will; An Historical and Philosophical Introduction* [London: Routledge, 1999], p. 264); "I am not just a spectator of my life, but the real actor in it" (Ted Honderich, *How Free Are You? The Determinism Problem* [Oxford: Oxford University Press, 2002], p. 86); "One is not normally in a *passive* relationship which such features of one's be-havior, and is an agent who deliberates, decides, and acts out one's decisions, not a spectator of forces carrying one along" (Saul Smilansky, *Free Will and Illusion* [Oxford: Oxford Uni-versity Press, 2002], p. 207); "Thinking is not something that occurs to you, like the beating of your heart, something concerning which you are a mere spectator. Thinking is something you do" (John Heil, *Philosophy of Mind; a Contemporary Introduction* [London: Routledge, 1998], p. 73); "[I]n the experience of deliberation, we are not mere spectators of a scene in which ... contending desires struggle for mastery with ourselves as the prize" (P.F. Strawson, *Analysis and Metaphysics: An Introduction to Philosophy* [Oxford: Oxford University Press, 1992], pp. 134–35); "The thoughts that beset us. do not occur by our own active doing. It is tempting, indeed, to suggest that they are not thoughts that *we think* at all, but rather thoughts that we *find* occuring within us" (Harry Frankfurt, "Identification and Externality", in *The Importance of What We Care About* [Cambridge: Cambridge University Press, 1988], 58–68, p. 59); "When you determine yourself to be the cause of your action you must identify yourself with the principle of choice on which you act. ... In this kind of case, you do not regard yourself as a mere passive spectator ..." (Christine Korsgaard, "Practical Reasoning and the Unity of theWill", lecture II in the John Locke Lectures, MS); "It is sometimes said that Hume develops his moral theory from the standpoint of a spectator rather than an agent"

That this contrast seems so natural ought, on reflection, to seem odd. Why is *doing* so often contrasted with *seeing?* Why is the opposite of 'participant' so often 'observer' rather than 'abstainer' or 'absentee'?

This question is the starting point for one approach to the philosophy of action. If the essence of passivity with respect to an event is witnessing it, then perhaps activity with respect to an event consists in knowing about it in some other way. Maybe the distinctive relation that an agent bears to his own actions is an epistemic relation—a particular way of knowing. This approach was pioneered by Elizabeth Anscombe in her book *Intention*,[4] and it is the approach that I adopted in *Practical Reflection*.

I'll begin this Introduction, then, by summarizing Anscombe's view, as I now understand it. I now think that I didn't fully understand Anscombe when I wrote *Practical Reflection*, and so another task for this Introduction will be to set the record straight. Along the way, I will offer some modifications to the view laid out in the book, and I'll attempt to fill in some gaps.

According to Anscombe, the actions that one has a special way of knowing are intentional actions, because one's knowledge of them is embodied in one's intentions to perform them.[5] What one is doing intentionally is "known by being the content of [one's] intention" (sec. 30, p. 53). The notion that knowledge can be embodied in an intention requires explanation and defense, which Anscombe provides as follows.

We need to distinguish between two kinds of indicative statements about the future: expressions of belief, such as "I'm going to be sick," and expressions of intention, such as "I am going to take a walk" (p. 1). If someone responds to the statement "I am going to be sick" by asking, "Why would you do a thing like that?", he has misinterpreted the speech act, by failing to recognize it as an expression of belief rather than intention. Conversely, if someone responds to "I am going to take a walk" with "How can you tell?", he has failed to recognize it as an expression of intention rather than belief. The difference between these statements cannot lie in the former's being informative and hence potentially knowledge-conveying, since the latter is informative and hence potentially knowledge-conveying as well.

(Jerome B. Schneewind, *The Invention of Autonomy: A History of Modern Moral Philosophy* [Cambridge: Cambridge University Press, 1997], p. 361); "[O]ne may be conscious of what one is doing, not *qua* agent, but *qua* spectator" (M.R. Bennett and P.M.S. Hacker, *Philosophical Foundations of Neuroscience* [Malden, MA: Blackwell Publishing, 2003], p. 252). See also Al Mele, "Agency and Mental Action", *Mind, Causation and, World, Philosophical Persspectives* 11 (1997) 231–49, p. 238; Charles L. Griswold, Jr., *Adam Smith and the Virtues of Enlightenment* (Cambridge: Cambridge University Press, 1999), Index *s.v.* "spectator".

4 2d edition (Cambridge, MA: Harvard University Press, 2000).

5 I do not share Anscombe's view that all intentional actions are intended in the way that yields distinctively agential knowledge. See notes 7, 16, and 18, below.

As Anscombe puts it, "the indicative (descriptive, informatory) character is not the distinctive mark of 'predictions' *as opposed to* 'expressions of intention', as we might at first sight have been tempted to think" (p. 3).

The "indicative (descriptive, informatory) character" of a statement expressing an intention indicates that the statement expresses knowledge on the part of the speaker. When one says "I am going to take a walk", one lets the hearer know what one is going to do. One's assertion is meant to provide grounds on which the hearer will subsequently know that one is going to take a walk, and those grounds depend for their validity on the assertion's expressing one's own knowledge to the same effect. Hence an expression of intention must at the same time be an expression of knowledge—of something known, in other words, by being the content of the intention expressed.

In Anscombe's view, the underlying difference between "I am going to take a walk" and "I am going to be sick", given that both express knowledge on the part of the speaker, is that the latter expresses speculative knowledge, whereas the former expresses knowledge that is practical, in the sense that it causes the facts that make it true (p. 87). "I am going to be sick" expresses knowledge embodied in a belief that is caused by evidence of the speaker's becoming sick, whereas "I am going to take a walk" expresseses knowledge embodied in an intention that causes the speaker to take a walk. Both the belief and the intention embody knowledge because they are true and appropriately connected to the facts that make them true. The difference lies in the causal order of the connection. A belief amounts to knowledge if it is appropriately *caused by* facts, or evidence of facts, that make it true; an intention amounts to knowledge if it appropriately *causes* such facts.[6]

Anscombe calls knowledge of the latter sort "practical knowledge", crediting the phrase to Aquinas, for whom it described God's knowledge of His creation. God knows what the world is like, but not by dint of having found out; He knows what the world is like because it is just as He meant it to be. And His meaning it to be that way already constituted knowledge on His part of how it would be, or rather how it already was. What's more, this epistemic relation that God bears to the world—knowing how it is just by meaning it to be that way—is constitutive of his role as the world's inventor or designer. The designer of something is the one whose conception of the thing determines how it is, rather than vice versa, and determines this

---

[6] Here I am using the purposely vague term 'appropriately' to encompass whatever additional conditions are necessary to rule out various things that might defeat an attribution of knowledge. I am not trying to develop a precise epistemology for the knowledge embodied in intention, since the details of such an epistemology are not relevant to my purposes. All that's relevant is that the order of causation between facts and knowledge of those facts is reversed from that which is characteristic of speculative knowledge.

not by chance but by a mechanism reliable enough to justify his confidence in that conception as an accurate representation of the thing. To be the designer of something is to be the one whose conception of it has epistemic authority by virtue of being its cause rather than its concomitant or effect.

Anscombe's nod to medieval theology as her source for the term 'practical knowledge' suggests that she conceived of intentional action as a realm in which human beings exercise a minor share of divinity. We invent our intentional actions, just as God invented the world, and our inventing them consists in our framing a conception of them that has epistemic authority by virtue of being determinative of them. Hence intentional action is behavior that realizes the agent's knowledge of it, just as the creation realizes God's omniscience.[7]

EXPLAINING PRACTICAL KNOWLEDGE

But how can an agent's doing something be caused by his knowledge that he is going to do it? In the first two chapters of *Practical Reflection*, I offered a naturalistic account of this phenomenon, explaining how an agent's knowledge of his forthcoming action can be its cause. My explanation was based on some presuppositions about the structure of human self-awareness, but I didn't articulate them clearly. Let me articulate them now, by contrasting human self-awareness with that of a lesser creature—let's say, a cat.[8]

Now, a cat is conscious, I assume, and it has the sort of consciousness whose content can be put into words only with the help of the first person pronoun. A cat could never catch a mouse if it didn't have thoughts representing the world from its own egocentric perspective, thoughts with English-language equivalents such as "I'm gaining on it" or "I've got it." There is a sense, then, in which a cat has first-personal awareness. A cat can even have a reflexive awareness of a sort, as when it realizes that the tail it has been chasing is its own.

What a cat lacks, however, is a conception of a creature that it is. A cat is aware of the mouse that it is chasing, but it is not aware of there being a creature by whom the mouse is hereby being chased. When a cat

---

[7] Here 'intentional action' is Anscombe's term. My own view is that the category of intentional action is not a natural kind of behavior, because its boundaries are determined in part by norms of moral responsibility. See note 20, below.

[8] This section draws heavily on the work of John Perry. I discuss this work at length in an Appendix to "The Centered Self", pp. 275–80. See John Perry, "Self-Notions", *Logos*, 1990: 17–31; and "Myself and 'I' ", in *Philosophie in Synthetisher Absicht* (A festschrift for Dieter Heinrich), ed. Marcelo Stamm, editor (Stuttgart: Klett-Cotta, 1998), pp. 83–103. See also "The Problem of the Essential Indexical", *Nous* 13 (1979): 3–21.

recognizes its own tail, it merely forges a mental association between an object seen to its rear and a locus of sensation or motion at its rear end. It has no conception of being a creature chasing its own tail.

By contrast, when a person realizes that he's stepping on his own shoelaces, he attains more than a mental association between the sensation of treading on something with one foot and the sensation of being tripped up in the other. He has the concept of a particular person bearing the name to which he answers, sporting the face that looks back at him from the mirror, and doing the things that he is aware of doing—including, at the moment, stepping on his own shoelaces.

Of course, a cat is also aware of doing things, such as hissing at someone by whom it feels threatened. But a cat's awareness of its own doings never extends to the knowledge that they are being done by a creature in the world. It represents them from the perspective of the one doing them, without representing the creature occupying that perspective. Thus, even when a cat is aware of hissing at you, and even if it is hissing with the thought of scaring you away, it cannot be thinking that you will be scared of this hissing creature—scared, that is, of its hissing self—because it has no conception of being one of the world's creatures, and hence no sense of self. By contrast, if I tried to scare you away, I would be aware of confronting you with a person saying "Scram!", as would be manifest in that very utterance, since a person saying "Scram!" is intimidating precisely by virtue of manifesting the intention to be an intimidating person. I must therefore be able to understand what I'm doing as being done by the creature who I am.

Along with the ability to understand what I'm doing as done by that creature comes the possibility of finding it unintelligible in those terms. A cat can round on its own tail and wonder, "What is that thing up to?" But I can round on my entire self and wonder, "What is this creature up to?" As soon as the cat associates the waving motion that it sees to its rear with the motion that it is aware of making from its rear end, its puzzlement is over. It knows why the tail is waving, since it is now aware of waving it. It cannot go on with "Yes, but why am I waving my tail?" That question would be about the behavior of a tail-waving creature, which it has no cognizance of being. Self-puzzlement of this latter kind is possible only for a creature whose awareness of doing things results in an awareness of their being done by the creature who he is.

Now, perplexity is aversive: we try to avoid it, and when we have gotten into it, we try to get out. The aversiveness of this state is a reminder that we have intellectual drives. We do not passively receive knowledge; we gain it through cognitive activity, driven by intellectual motives. And the frustration of these motives is aversive, like the frustration of any fundamental drive.

A human being's intellectual motives are sometimes directed at the person who he is. The creature with whom he is aware of being identical naturally has a special salience for him—as the creature walking in his shoes, sleeping in his bed, eating his meals—and the doings of that creature therefore become the object of his intellectual drives. But the person's awareness of being identical with that creature opens up an obvious shortcut to knowledge about its doings. He must realize that doing things—that is, behaviors conceived from his perspective as the unrepresented agent—constitutes their being done by that creature, the same behaviors conceived objectively. And he must realize that seeking to know what it is doing—an intellectual activity conceived from his perspective as the unrepresented inquirer—constitutes that creature's striving for self-knowledge. Finally, then, he must realize that he can know what that creature is doing simply by doing what he conceives of it as doing, or as being about to do, since his conception will then turn out to be not only true but also justified, on the grounds of the creature's having this very intellectual incentive to bear it out. He tends to behave as he conceives of that creature as behaving, or as being about to behave, because he will then have, embodied in that conception, a knowledge of what that creature is doing; and that conception will have the reliability of knowledge because it is about a creature for whom the prospect of having knowledge embodied in it is an incentive to behave accordingly.

Strange as this psychological mechanism may sound, it has been copiously documented by social psychologists working in the area that is sometimes labeled self-consistency.[9] Research in this area has shown that people have a broad tendency to behave in ways that cohere with their own conceptions of themselves—of how they behave in general and of their motives on particular occasions. Potential voters are more likely to vote in an election if they have antecedently predicted that they are going to.[10] Children are more likely to be tidy if told that they *are* tidy than if told that they ought to be.[11] People behave angrily if they are led to believe that they are

---

[9] In writing *Practical Reflection*, I was unaware of this psychological research, which I later reviewed in a paper titled "From Self-Psychology to Moral Philosophy" (*Philosophical Perspectives* 14 (2000): 349–77; reprinted in *Self to Self*, pp. 224–52).

[10] Greenwald, A.G., Carnot, C.G., Beach, R., and Young, B., 1987. Increasing Voting Behavior by Asking People if They Expect to Vote. *Journal of Applied Psychology* 72: 315–18.

[11] Miller, R.L., Brickman, P., & Bolen, D., "Attribution Versus Persuasion as a Means for Modifying Behavior," *Journal of Personality and Social Psychology* 31 (1975): 430–41. See also Grusec, J.E., & Redler, E., "Attribution, reinforcement, and altruism: A developmental analysis," *Developmental Psychology* 16 (1980): 525–34; Eisenberg, N., Cialdini, R.B., McCreath, H., and Shell, R., "Consistency-based compliance: When and why do children become

angry—the more angrily, the more angry they are led to believe they are.[12] Shy people don't behave shyly if they are led to attribute the symptoms of their social anxiety to other causes.[13] And so on.

One team of researchers have observed that subjects' behavior can be influenced by the act-descriptions that they are antecedently prompted to frame, as if they have a tendency to fulfill antecedently framed descriptions of their forthcoming actions.[14] This tendency is cited by the researchers to explain how people know what they are doing—which is the very explanation that I have just offered, to the effect that people know what they're doing because they tend to do what they have just now thought that they are just about to do. The psychologists give this mechanism the label "act identification". And they invoke this mechanism, not only to explain how people generally know what they are doing, but also as a model for the process of acting on an intention: to frame an act-description and then fulfill it, they suggest, is just to form an intention and act on it.

Here, then, is the explanation of what Anscombe calls practical knowledge. Because I have an objective conception of the creature who I am, I can be puzzled by the behavior of that creature, but I can also avoid such puzzlement by first framing an idea of the creature's next action and then enacting that idea, a process that social psychologists have observed and have identified with the process of forming and acting on an intention. That

vulnerable?" *Journal of Personality and Social Psychology* 52 (1987): 1174–81; Eisenberg, N., Cialdini, R.B., McCreath, H., and Shell, R., "Consistency-based compliance in children: When and why do consistency procedures have immediate effects?" *International Journal of Behavioural Development* 12 (1989): 351–67.

[12] Schachter, S., & Singer, J.E., "Cognitive, social and physiological determinants of emotional state," *Psychological Review* 69 (1962): 379–99; Zillman, E., Johnson, R.C., & Day, K.D., "Attribution of apparent arousal and proficiency of recovery for sympathetic activation affecting excitation transfer to aggressive behavior," *Journal of Experimental Social Psychology* 10 (1974): 503–15; Berkowitz, L., & Turner, C., "Perceived anger level, instigating agent, and aggression," in *Cognitive Alteration of Feeling States*, ed. H. London & R.E. Nisbett (Chicago:Aldine, 1974), 174–89; Cantor, J.R., Zillman, D., & Bryant, J., "Enhancement of experienced sexual arousal in response to erotic stimuli through misattribution of unrelated residual excitation," *Journal of Personality and Social Psychology*, 32 (1975): 69–75; Zillman, D., "Attribution and misattribution of excitatory reactions," *New Directions in Attribution Research*, Vol. 2, ed. John H. Harvey, William Ickes, & Robert F. Kidd (Hillsdale, NJ: Erlbaum, 1978), 335–68.

[13] Brodt, S.E., & Zimbardo, P.G., "Modifying shyness-related social behavior through symptom misattribution," *Journal of Personality and Social Psychology* 41 (1981): 437–49.

[14] Vallacher, R.R., & Wegner, D.M., *A Theory of Action Identification* (Hillsdale, NJ: Erlbaum, 1985); Wegner, D.M., & Vallacher, R.R., "Action Identification," in *Handbook of Motivation and Cognition*, ed. Richard M. Sorrentino & E. Tory Higgins (New York: Guilford Press, 1986), 550–82; Wegner, D.M., Vallacher, R.R., Kiersted, G.W., & Dizadji, D., "Action Identification in the Emergence of Social Behavior," *Social Cognition* 4 (1986): 18–38; Vallacher, R.R., & Wegner, D.M., "What Do People Think They're Doing? Action Identification and Human Behavior," *Psychological Review* 94 (1987): 3–15.

intention will embody my knowledge of what I am doing, just as Anscombe contends.

This explanation of practical knowledge is the one that I laid out in Chapers One and Two of *Practical Reflection*. In presenting it here, I have filled in several gaps, but I haven't made any significant revisions. Let me turn now to a topic on which I think revision is needed.

INTENTION AND BELIEF

As we have seen, Anscombe contrasts intention with belief, and her claim that things can be "known by being the content of intention" seems to imply that they can be known without being believed. In *Practical Reflection* I chose instead to argue that intention is a kind of belief, and hence that practical knowledge, though embodied in intention, is also thereby embodied in belief. But the identification of intention with a kind of belief offends the intuitions of many philosophers, who think of cases such as "I am going to be sick" and "I am going to take a walk" as demonstrating that intention and belief are distinct.

In papers written after *Practical Reflection* I began to delve into the nature of these propositional attitudes, eventually figuring out how to describe the respects in which intention is like belief.[15] Like a belief that I am going to take a walk, the intention expressed by "I am going to take a walk" represents that proposition as true, and in doing so it aims get the proposition's truth-value right, by aiming to represent it as true only if it is true in fact. Like a belief, then, the intention to take a walk must be revised or withdrawn in the face of convincing evidence that one is not in fact going to take a walk. And one's actually taking a walk makes the intention a success at representing the truth, which can be awarded the title of knowledge if it was appropriately non-accidental.

This characterization of intention—as representing its content as true with the aim of doing so only if its content really is true—is all that I meant to convey in *Practical Reflection* by classifying intention as a kind of belief. In light of others' linguistic qualms about my use of 'belief', I would now be inclined to replace it with this explicit characterization.[16]

---

[15] These papers include "The Guise of the Good", *Nous* 26 (1992): 3–26; "The Possibility of Practical Reason", *Ethics* 106 (1996): 694–726; "On the Aim of Belief"; and the Introduction to *The Possibility of Practical Reason* (Oxford: Oxford University Press, 2000), a volume that contains the other papers as well.

[16] Note that, although I adopt Anscombe's view of intention as embodying practical knowledge, I do not agree with several other claims that she makes about intention. In particular, I do not believe that the mental state embodying practical knowledge is the state to which we refer when speaking of the intention with which someone acts: intending to take a walk and

DESIRE VS. DRIVE

Just as I now think that, in writing *Practical Reflection*, I was ill-advised to identify intention with a belief, I also think I was ill-advised to describe the intellectual motive behind practical knowledge as a desire. The term 'desire' is too suggestive of an attitude that has a well-defined object and is readily accessible to consciousness—an attitude that gives the subject a goal-in-view. When introducing this motive here, I described it instead as a drive, which is the description that I am now inclined to prefer.[17]

Here I am using 'drive' in something like the sense in which it is used in psychoanalytic theory. In this sense, 'drive' denotes a fund of labile psychic energy, often unconscious, which has a vague direction in itself but can be invested in various activities.[18] Consider, for example, the drive commonly known as aggression. A person can be full of aggression without there being anything in particular that he wants to do, not even something described as vaguely as "picking a fight" or "hitting something". He simply has a considerable fund of energy that can motivate bellicose behavior of many different kinds, toward many different objects, and whose constant presence in him may not be accessible to his awareness.

The motive behind practical knowledge might be described as an intellectual drive, or a drive to synthesize. It is a fund of energy that motivates various efforts to get the experienced world to hang together—to get the "blooming, buzzing confusion" that confronts one from birth to coalesce into an intelligible world. As one matures, this drive takes on progressively more determinate objects, motivating progressively more focused efforts to know and to understand. Some of these efforts, I believe, are aimed at knowing and understanding oneself, partly by getting oneself to coalesce into an intelligible piece of the world. But the drive behind this effort rarely obtrudes itself on one's consciousness and must therefore be inferred from its manifestations in one's cognitive activities.

Because I am no longer inclined to identify intention with a belief, and

getting up with the intention of taking a walk may involve two different kinds of intention. More importantly, I do not believe that every intentional action involves an intention of the practical-knowledge-bearing kind. Hence I do not accept Anscombe's thesis that every intentional action is an object of practical knowledge on the part of the agent. See also notes 7 and 20.

[17] For a more detailed discussion of drives, see my "Motivation by Ideal", *Philosophical Explorations* 5 (2002) 89–104; reprinted in *Self to Self*, pp. 312–29.

[18] Let me emphasize that I am borrowing only some elements of Freudian drive theory. I am not borrowing the model of stimulus reduction, for example, but only the notion of indeterminate motivational forces. Indeed, my conception of their indeterminacy is different from Freud's. Freud described drives as having determinate aims but being readily redirected toward other aims instead. I prefer to think of drives as having only inchoate aims.

the motive behind practical knowledge with a desire, I no longer endorse the specific form of reductionism that I advocated in *Practical Reflection*. The book attempts to reduce agency to psychological mechanisms constructed from the materials of belief-desire motivation. Were I writing the book today, it would still attempt to construct agency from more rudimentary materials, but those materials would not be belief and desire.

INTERPRETING ANSCOMBE

A fair amount of *Practical Reflection* was devoted to working out epistemological problems raised by practical knowledge. In working out those problems, I often used Anscombe as a foil, contrasting my solutions with hers. I now think that I misinterpreted her epistemology, and I'd like to take this opportunity to correct my interpretation.

Anscombe describes an agent's knowledge of intentional actions as "knowledge without observation", adding that it is not "founded on evidence". In this respect, she compares knowledge of intentional actions to knowledge of bodily posture:

> [A] man usually knows the position of his limbs without observation. It is without observation, because nothing *shews* him the position of his limbs; it is not as if he were going by a tingle in his knee, which is the sign that it is bent and not straight. Where we can speak of separately describable sensations, having which is in some sense our criterion for saying something, then we can speak of observing that thing; but that is not generally so when we know the position of our limbs. Yet, without prompting, we *can say* it. [pp. 13–14]

> It is not ordinarily possible to find anything that shows one that one's leg is bent. It may indeed be that it is because one has sensations that one knows this; but that does not mean that one knows it by identifying the sensations one has. [p. 49]

> If a man says that his leg is bent when it is lying straight out, it would be incorrect to say that he had misjudged an inner kinaesthetic appearance as an appearance of his leg bent, when in fact what was appearing to him was his leg stretched out. [p. 50]

These passages are best understood, in my view, as imprecise descriptions of the fact that, when it comes to the position of one's limbs, one is subject to perceptual appearances that involve no sensory qualities. The proprioceptive appearance that one's leg is bent is an appearance that doesn't feel like anything—like anything other than one's leg's being bent, that is. The appearance is empty of any sensations, such as pressure, tingling, and the like. Appearances without sensations are simply perceptual beliefs—proprioceptive beliefs, in the present case.[19]

Anscombe's claim is not that one is infallible about the position of one's limbs: she not only acknowledges but emphasizes the possibility of being wrong. Her claim is rather that when one's proprioceptive beliefs are true, they usually constitute knowledge, because they are connected in the right way with the facts that make them true. Anscombe is thus a reliabilist about proprioceptive knowledge. Her view is that one needs no sensory evidence on which to judge the position of one's limbs because the position of one's limbs generates proprioceptive beliefs via a mechanism that is generally reliable: the belief that one's leg is bent serves as a reliable indicator of the leg's being bent.

When I wrote *Practical Reflection*, I didn't read Anscombe as a reliabilist, and so my interpretation of her view about knowledge without observation was mistaken. In particular, I misinterpreted her reason for denying that knowledge of one's own intentional actions is "founded on evidence", as I shall now explain.

A mystifying part of Anscombe's view is her claim that what is known without observation can include, not just how one is moving one's limbs, or what one is thereby attempting to accomplish, but the fact that one is actually accomplishing it:

> I think that it is the difficulty of this question that has led some people to say that what one knows as intentional action is only the intention, or possibly also the bodily movement; and that the rest is known by observation to be the *result*, which was also willed in the intention. But that is a mad account . .
>
> Another false avenue of escape is to say that I really 'do' in the intentional sense whatever I think I am doing. E.g. if I think I am moving my toe, but it is not actually moving, then I am 'moving my toe' in a certain sense, and as for what *happens*, of course I haven't any control over that except in an accidental sense. The essential thing is just what has gone on in me, and if what happens coincides with what I 'do' in the sphere of intentions, that is just a grace of fate. .
>
> But this is nonsense too. [pp. 51–52]

Thus, Anscombe believes that if you are trying to shoot a bull's-eye, intend

[19] This interpretation implies that the second passage quoted above contains a slight error. Anscombe should not have said "it is because one has sensations [pl.] that one knows this." What she should have said is "it is because one has sensation [sing.] that one knows this." Proprioceptive appearances are received via sensory pathways, blockage of which, as in anesthesia, leaves one unable to judge the position of one's limbs. But the sensations conveyed by these same pathways are not intrinsic to proprioception.

to shoot one, and will consequently end up having shot one intentionally, then you already know without observation that you are shooting a bull's-eye, not just that you are intending or trying to do so or moving your limbs with that aim. But how can the content of your intention embody knowledge of whether the bull's-eye is going to be hit? How can you have knowledge of the intended outcome without observing it?

The answer that I attributed to Anscombe In *Practical Reflection* was drawn from her remarks about the distinction generally known as "direction of fit". Anscombe draws this distinction by saying, among other things, that if there is a discrepancy between one's intention and one's performance, then "the mistake is in the performance" rather than the intention (p. 5; p. 82): one's performance bears the responsibility of corresponding to one's intention, which consequently cannot be blamed for any lack of correspondence. Somehow, I imagined, relieving intention of responsibility for corresponding to the resulting action is thought by Anscombe to relieve the knowledge embodied in that intention of any need for evidential support.

I now think that Anscombe offers a very different reason, based on her reliabilism, for believing that knowledge of intended outcomes requires no evidence. Her reason is suggested by the following passage:

> 'Why are you pumping?' — 'To replenish the water supply'. If this was the answer, then we can say 'He *is* replenishing the water supply'; unless indeed, he is not. This will appear a tautologous pronouncement; but there *is* more to it. For if after his saying 'To replenish the water-supply' we can say 'He is replenishing the water-supply', then this would, in ordinary circumstances, of itself be enough to characterise *that* as an intentional action. (The qualification is necessary because an intended effect just occasionally comes about by accident.)
> [pp. 38–39]

The parenthetical remark at the end of this quotation indicates that, in Anscombe's view, one can bring about an intended result without doing so intentionally if the result comes about accidentally. Hitting the bull's-eye by luck doesn't count as hitting it intentionally, even if one intended to hit it.

Now compare the two passages just quoted, and notice that the concept of accident figures in the former passage as well. In that passage, Anscombe ridicules the view that what I do and know that I'm doing when I intentionally move my toe does not include my toe's actually moving. What's ridiculous about that view, according to Anscombe, is the implication that my toe's moving is accidental, "a grace of fate". Anscombe suggests that my toe's moving is part of my intentional action, and hence part of what I know without observation, because it is a reliable result of my intending to move my toe.

The lesson to be drawn from these passages is that the reliability of the connection between intention and movement is implicated in both the movement's being intentional and the intention's being knowledge, according to Anscombe's reliabilist epistemology. Speculative knowledge, which is caused by the facts, must be caused by them via some reliable mechanism; if knowledge can also be practical, by virtue of causing the facts, then it must cause them via a reliable mechanism as well. Unless an intention with the content "I'm going to move my toe" reliably causes my toe to move, it won't amount to practical knowledge. And this same reliable connection is necessary to the movement's being intentional; for if my toe moves accidentally, I will not have moved it intentionally, despite intending to move it. By contrast, if the intention "I'm going to move my toe" does reliably cause my toe to move, then the movement resulting from this reliable mechanism will be intentional, and the intention causing the movement will constitute knowledge—in both cases, because of the reliable connnection between the intention and the outcome that fulfills it.

Anscombe's view, then, is that the action's status as intentional and the intention's status as knowledge will tend to coincide, because they are constituted by the same reliable connection and undermined by the same failures of reliability. If your intention to hit the bull's-eye doesn't amount to knowledge of the fact that you're hitting it, the reason is probably that you can't reliably hit the bull's-eye; and in that case, your hitting it won't qualify as intentional, either. If your hitting the bull's-eye does qualify as intentional, then you must have a reliable way of hitting the bull's-eye, in which case your intention to hit it is reliably connected to that result and will probably amount to knowledge.[20] What you do intentionally, you also tend to do knowingly, because intentional action and knowledge are generally two ends of the same chain of reliable causation.

Although I now think that I misunderstood Anscombe when I wrote *Practical Reflection*, I still think that I was right to argue against her view that knowledge of intentional actions does not rely on evidence. As I argue

---

[20] What is done intentionally is not perfectly coextensive with what is known without observation. Whether something is done intentionally depends on the reasons for and against doing it—especially against. An unreliable but lucky marksman may not be credited with hitting the bull's-eye intentionally, but he may be blamed for hitting the President intentionally, simply by virtue of trying to hit the President and despite his lack of a reliable method for doing so. (This example is due to Gilbert Harman. Thanks to Gideon Rosen for reminding me of it.) In neither case does he know without observation that he is hitting his target. If his target is the President, then, what he does intentionally exceeds what he knows without observation. As I understand Anscombe, she believes that intentional action is invariably known without observation. On this point, among others, I believe that Anscombe is mistaken. See also notes 7 and 16, above.

in Chapter Two, this knowledge is "without observation" in the sense that it is not occasioned by evidence, but it can still rest on evidence that doesn't occasion it. I therefore prefer my evidentialist account to her reliabilism about an agent's knowledge of his intentional actions.

PRACTICAL REASONING

A second goal of *Practical Reflection*, after explaining practical knowledge, was to defend a theory of practical reasoning based on that explanation. This theory picks up where I left off, before my digression into Anscombe's epistemology, with the idea that an agent knows what he's doing by doing things that he has already identified.

The psychologists who have confirmed this phenomenon of "act identification" claim to have shown, furthermore, that we ordinarily seek to identify our behavior at a "high" or "comprehensive" level of description, representing our underlying motives and ultimate goals. They describe this tendency as a "search for meaning in action"[21] or "a human inclination to be informed of what we are doing in the most integrative and general way available."[22] These empirical findings support a further elaboration on Anscombe's view of practical knowledge.

With a now famous example, Anscombe pointed out that an agent often knows what he is doing under a series of descriptions each of which incorporates the answer to the question "Why?" directed at the same action under the previous description in the series. Why is he moving his arm? Because he is pumping water. Why is he pumping water? Because he is replenishing the water supply. Why is he replenishing the water supply? Because he is poisoning the inhabitants of the building. Why is he poisoning the inhabitants? Because he is assassinating enemy agents. With the exception of the first, purely physical description, all of the descriptions under which this person knows what he's doing are answers to the question why he is doing it as previously described.

The sequence from "moving his arm" to "killing enemy agents" displays a progression toward increasingly "high-level" or "comprehensive" act-descriptions. Hence if there is empirical evidence of "a human inclination to be informed of what we are doing in the most integrative and general way available", then it is evidence of an inclination to progress from rudimentary descriptions like the former towards comprehensive descriptions like the latter.

Thus, the goal toward which our cognitive processes are directed must

---

[21] Wegner & Vallacher, "Action Identification", pp. 555–56.
[22] Vallacher & Wegner, *The Theory of Action Identification*, p. 26.

be, not merely to register rudimentary, observable facts, but also to formulate them in "integrative and general" terms of the sort that convey understanding by answering the question "Why?". When directed at our own behavior, these processes must be oriented toward the goal of knowing what we are doing in the sort of comprehensive terms that indicate why we are doing it, by alluding to the relevant dispositions and circumstances. And the previously described shortcut to self-knowledge—the shortcut of doing what we think we are doing, or are about to do—is also a route to this "high level" self-knowledge. We can attain integrative knowledge of what we are doing simply by framing and fulfilling integrative conceptions of our own behavior, conceptions formulated in terms of the dispositions and circumstances that help to explain it.

In order to frame and fulfill integrative conceptions of our behavior, of course, we must be aware of a context with which to integrate it—projects and motives that we have (such as the project of poisoning enemy agents), emotions that we feel (such as hatred of the enemy), customs and policies that we follow (such as a policy of obeying orders), traits of character that we display (such as courage in the face of the enemy), all of which afford terms for understanding our behavior as more than mere bodily movement. These other aspects of our self-conception—projects, motives, emotions, customs, policies, traits of character—will provide the materials for integrative knowledge of what we are doing, provided that we do things appropriately integrated with them. The goal of a more comprehensive knowledge of what we are doing therefore militates in favor of doing things that can be understood as motivated by our desires, expressive of our emotions, implementing our policies, manifesting our characters, and so on.

Those aspects of ourselves and our circumstances which we could incorporate into an integrative conception of doing something turn out to coincide with what we ordinarily count as reasons for doing it. When giving our reason for doing something, we often cite a desire that motivated it, an intention or policy that guided it, an emotion or opinion that animated it, a habit or trait that was manifested in it, and so on. Examples of desire-based reasons are well known; here are some examples of reasons based on other considerations that provide an explanatory context for an action:

Why are you whistling?
Because I'm happy.

Why aren't you having any wine?
Because I don't drink.

Why worry about his problems?
Because I'm his friend.

Why are you shaking your head?
Because I think you're wrong.

Why do you have her picture on your wall?
Because I admire her.

Here already?
I'm punctual.

Reasons for doing something are facts that would provide an integrative knowledge of what we were doing, if we did that thing. Our cognitive processes favor framing and fulfilling a conception of ourselves as doing that thing, understood in the context of those facts, rather than other things for which we lack the elements of an equally integrative conception. Reasons for doing something provide a *rationale*, an account in which our doing it is seen to cohere with our psyches and our circumstances. Whereas acting on an intention is a matter of realizing practical knowledge of what we are doing, acting for a reason is matter of realizing more integrative practical knowledge, incorporating relevant facts that constitute reasons for acting.

NAVEL GAZING?

This conception of practical reasoning often strikes other philosophers as requiring a rational agent to devote too much attention to himself, when he should be attending to the world around him. I answered this criticism in *Practical Reflection*, but since it continues to arise, I want to repeat my answer here.

Consider a case in which your attention is properly focused on something outside yourself. If you look up from reading *Felix Holt* and say to yourself, "What a genius she was!", your thought is explicitly about the author George Eliot; but in articulating this thought, you express an attitude that lends intelligibility to various further thoughts and actions on your part. Suppose that your next thought is "I wonder what else she wrote" (or perhaps just "What else did she write?"). The rational connection between your thoughts is that admiration of the sort expressed in the first thought naturally leads to curiosity about its object, as reported (or expressed) in the second. This connection cannot be discerned in the explicit content of your thoughts. There is no rule of inference leading from the premise that George Eliot was a genius to the conclusion that you wonder what she wrote in addition to *Felix Holt*. Unless the first of these thoughts is understood as expressing an attitude held by the thinker of the second, they amount to a *non sequitur*.

The only way to make the logic of these thoughts explicit would be with

further, reflective information—"I admire the author of *Felix Holt* as a genius, and so I am moved to wonder what else she wrote"—which describes
a psychologically intelligible transition of thought. Yet to articulate this
reflective information to yourself would be to shift the focus of your attention, from the author whom you admire to your own attitude of admiration.
And this shift would make your admiration less rather than more evident,
because admiring someone entails attending to her rather than yourself.
"I admire the author of *Felix Holt*" would be a less admiring thought, a
thought less expressive of your attitude, than "She was a genius." Articulating your awareness of admiring Eliot would therefore leave you less
vividly aware of admiring her than articulating thoughts expressive of that
admiration, which would be thoughts about Eliot.

Thus, explicit reflection is often self-defeating. Reflective reasoning is
best left implicit, in the background, so that the attitudes that are its objects
can be revealed more clearly in explicit thoughts about other things. Hence
the fact that your thoughts prior to acting are not explicitly about yourself
is no evidence that their logic is not reflective. Thoughts that are explicitly about other things may yet be structured by what they reveal about
yourself—as in "What a genius she was! I wonder what else she wrote."

Note that this response to the present objection points to a flaw in the
traditional philosophical method of studying practical reason. The traditional method is to construct an argument-schema that will both represent
the explicit content of, and illustrate the rational connections among, the
thoughts leading up to an action performed for reasons. Aristotle's practical syllogism was the first attempt to construct such an argument-schema,
and many other attempts have followed. In my view, however, the rational
connections in an agent's deliberations are connections of reflective intelligibility, and such connections tend to hold, not between the contents of
the agent's explicit thoughts (e.g., "What a genius she was!"), but rather
between the self-attributions that remain in the background, implicitly registering the attitudes that his explicit thoughts express (e.g., "I admire the
author of *Felix Holt*"). Because these unarticulated self-attributions provide
the logical structure of the agent's thinking, they contain the agent's reasons
for acting, in my view; but because they remain unarticulated, they cannot
be represented by the same argument-schema that represents the agent's
explicit thoughts.

In sum, an agent's reasons for acting are not the things that he says to
himself before acting. That he doesn't saying anything about himself to
himself before acting doesn't prove that his reasons for acting are not considerations conducive to self-understanding.

REASONS AND VALUE

This account of practical reason is still unpalatable to most philosophers, who insist that reasons for acting must show there to be some *value* in acting—something good or desirable about the action for which they are reasons. I do not believe that practical reasoning is fundamentally about value: it is about making sense.

In Chapter 10 of *Practical Reflection* I tried to make a concession to the conventional view, by saying that an action's making sense is our measure of its value. I thus claimed that my view merely reverses the order of explanation between value and intelligibility: whereas other philosophers think that an action makes sense if and because it is good, my view (I said) is that an action is good if and because it makes sense.

I now regard this concession as a mistake. What has value, I now think, is what it makes sense to value, where the verb "to value" is a placeholder for some particular appreciative response. That is, something is valuable by virtue of being desirable, admirable, lovable, inspiring, amusing, or whatever; and it's desirable if and because it makes sense to desire, admirable if and because it makes sense to admire, and so on. There is no such thing as having value merely as such, without being what makes sense to value in some specific way. Practical reasoning, as I conceive it, doesn't recommend any particular appreciative response to the action that makes most sense; it merely recommends that the action be performed. We can characterize its recommendation as saying that the action would be a good thing to do, but 'good' in this context doesn't ascribe value; it merely recommends.

Of course, to recommend that an action be performed is to recommend that it be performed in preference to others, and hence that it be preferred, in a thin sense of the word that implies behavior but no particular attitude. If being preferred in this behavioral sense is conceived as a way of being valued, then recommending an action as a good thing to do can be interpreted as ascribing value, after all. But the value thus ascribed to the action that makes most sense is not a value that overrides or outweighs the other, more substantive values attaching to alternative actions. That is, practical reasoning doesn't recommend performing the intelligible action *rather than* the admirable or desirable one. Those substantive values are already subsumed under the assessment of intelligibility. Practical reasoning recommends desiring the desirable, as that which makes sense to desire; admiring the admirable, as that which makes sense to admire; and so on. And then it recommends doing that which makes sense to do in light of what one desires, what one admires, and so on. Other values are thus taken into account in any verdict of intelligibility.

The standard of intelligibility is a standard of coherence. It requires an agent to find that action which is explanitorily most coherent with his values, commitments, motives, habits, customs, practices, and personality. The agent's values, commitments, and so on have no standing to challenge this overall reconciliation, because it already subsumes them.

There may be cases in which one fails to muster a desire for that which makes sense to desire, or admiration for that which makes sense to admire; and practical reasoning will not necessarily recommend pursuing what one doesn't in fact desire, or emulating what one doesn't in fact admire, despite their being desirable or admirable. But even in these cases, the considerations that make something intelligible to desire may independently make it intelligible to pursue even without that desire; or they may render intelligible a desire to desire it, and that second-order desire may make the thing intelligible to pursue, with the aim of learning to desire it. If one still doesn't desire it, one's recalcitrance in that respect may cast doubt on whether desiring it really made sense, in the first place, and hence whether the thing really was desirable, after all. I believe that these results correspond to our intuitive practical judgments.

The thing to remember when considering my view is that practical reasoning, as I conceive it, is fundamentally holistic, because its aim is understanding. It seeks that total configuration of self and behavior which makes the most sense overall. Philosophers are accustomed to framing examples of practical reasoning in terms of a few, atomistically enumerated reasons for or against an action, and when such examples are fed into my conception of practical reasoning, the results can easily seem out of whack. But the examples always turn out to have been underdescribed for the purpose of testing a mode of reasoning that is fundamentally holistic.

Some have suggested, for example, that practical reasoning as I conceive it should count an agent's admitted vices, such as laziness, as a *prima facie* reasons for undesirable actions, such as procrastinating. But why does the agent in such a case think of himself as lazy rather than laid-back or easygoing? Isn't that self-description indicative of reflective disapproval, perhaps arising from a perception that his laziness conflicts with many of his own ambitions and values? And don't those conflicts often cloud the question which courses of action he has sufficient enthusiasm to undertake, and hence which courses would make sense for him? In the context of a self-conception that includes a self-attribution of laziness, the way to make best sense to himself may be, not to procrastinate, but to look for more robust and reliable sources of motivation, which can decisively resolve the resulting conflicts and, with them, the confusion about what it makes sense to do. This resolution may not be needed by an agent who has no ambitions or values to be frustrated by his laziness; but such an agent is more likely to describe himself, and to be described by others, as laid-back or easygoing. And the rational course for an easygoing agent may well be to go easy.

Remember, too, that the intelligibility of an action is not the reason for recommending it, much less a reason for doing it, according to my view. Reasons for recommending or taking the action are to be found in the concerns and commitments in light of which it makes sense, which jointly make up the agent's entire evaluative and motivational point-of-view. And an action that makes sense in light of all the agent's values and motives surely has some claim to count, from his perspective, as a good thing to do.

INTRODUCTIONS

Let me close by noting the main difference between this Introduction and the Introduction that appears as Chapter 1 of *Practical Reflection*. In that original Introduction, I argued that questions in the philosophy of action should ask how the phenomena of agency are possible, and that answers should describe ways in which those phenomena might possibly be realized, irrespective of whether they are so realized in fact. The philosophy of action should therefore set about describing possible agents, without concern for whether they are real. I still favor that approach to the subject in principle, but I have given it up in practice, as is evident from my appeal to emprical psychology in this new Introduction. On that empirical basis, I now believe that *Practical Reflection* describes not just possible agents but actual human agents—in other words, us.

I gave up my earlier approach for reasons both strategic and philosophical. The strategic reason was that other philosophers simply weren't interested in merely possible agents—or, at least, not possible agents of the kind I described. If I wanted anyone to take an interest in my account of agency, I found, I would have to show that it was plausible as an account of human agency. The philosophical reason for giving up the approach of describing merely possible agents is that I now think it to be incompatible with the aspirations of the project that occupies the last two chapters of the book. Those chapters seek to explain the rationality of being moral, and there really is no point in explaining why morality would be rational for merely possible agents, without explaining why it really is rational for us. I am no longer satisfied with the explanation given in those chapters, but I have left them unchanged, since they still provide a rough approximation of the explanation that I would give today.[23]

---

[23] For a recent attempt at that explanation, see my *How We Get Along* (MS).

PRACTICAL REFLECTION

INTRODUCTION

THE IMAGE

What do you see when you look at your face in the mirror?

The obvious answer is that you see your face looking in the mirror. But this obvious answer fails to acknowledge the fact that a face looking in the mirror is actually doing two things—trying to see itself and presenting itself to be seen. Sometimes these two activities are visibly distinct. When you examine a mole on your chin, for example, you don't just lower your gaze until it lights on that part of your reflection; you also jut out your chin, until it intercepts your reflected gaze. In this case, there's no mistaking the fact that the face in the mirror is both seeking itself and showing itself simultaneously. Yet even when your face just stares out at you, flatfooted, it bears the same two aspects: it is both eyeing you, in order to see you, and facing you, in order to be seen.

This book is about the nature of a rational agent. Its thesis is this: If you want to know what a rational agent might be like, just look in the mirror.

THE QUESTIONS

To the deliberately naive eye of philosophy, the very possibility of action can be puzzling. The source of puzzlement, I think, is commonsense behavioral psychology—our practice of explaining human actions, including our own, in terms of the agent's desires, beliefs, habits, emotions, traits of character, and the like. From commonsense psychology comes the conception that we hold of ourselves as agents, and this conception often seems to be at odds either with experience or with itself.

The primary problem is that psychological explanation seems to be a kind of causal explanation. The language of motivation is permeated by causal imagery—not just the paler metaphors of inclinations, urges, and impulses, but also more vivid pictures, of pressure and release, kindling and quenching, tension and slack. These images color how we experience our own motives, with the result that we actually feel our desires to be exerting pressure or emanating heat.

3

Yet we don't regard our actions as the mere effects of motivational causes. Acting on a desire doesn't feel like catching fire or bursting at the seams. What's missing from the purely causal picture of agency is a locus of rational autonomy, a conscious self who can reflect on his[1] desires as grounds for acting rather than causes—as advisory rather than coercive—and can then decide whether to act on them. We certainly feel autonomous in this sense even as we also feel the causal power of our motives. One puzzle is how we can accommodate both feelings in a single conception of ourselves.

Another puzzle generated by the causal image of motivation has to do with our knowledge about our actions. We usually know what we're doing, and we seem to know it quite spontaneously, without having to discover it. We feel as if we're inventing what we do and hence that we don't have to find it out. But if our actions are caused by our motives, then they must follow a predetermined course that isn't really ours to invent: we aren't the authors of our actions but merely spectators. How, then, can we have spontaneous knowledge of them?

---

[1] Some readers may take offense at my use of 'he' to denote the arbitrary person. Let me assure these readers that I share their goal of inclusiveness in language and differ with them only about the means to that goal. My view is that traditional usage in this case makes English more inclusive, not less.

The rule governing traditional usage is that when 'he' denotes the arbitrary person, its gender is purely grammatical, not semantic, and hence carries no implications as to the referent's sex. So understood, 'he' no more denotes a man, because of being masculine, than the German 'die Person' or the French 'la personne' denote a woman, because of being feminine.

The alternative practices that are currently recommended as inclusive—such as saying 'he or she' or alternating 'he' with 'she'—actually threaten to rob the language of its capacity for gender-neutral reference to persons. These practices imply that 'he' by itself excludes women; which implies that the grammatical and semantic gender of English pronouns are inseparable; which implies that a speaker of English cannot refer pronominally to the arbitrary person at all, but only to the arbitrary woman or man. If this view ever comes to govern English usage, the language will become quite awkward for anyone who wishes to discuss persons in abstraction from their sex.

This book is about agency, which is an important aspect of personhood. The concepts of agency and personhood do not just include both genders; they are blind to the question of gender altogether. I therefore feel compelled, in discussing agents and persons, to rely on the only personal pronoun in English that is similarly gender-blind—namely, 'he'.

I am not insensitive to the drawbacks of this usage. Obviously, the use of 'he' as the genderless pronoun entails the risk that the word will be misunderstood, on occasion, as semantically masculine. Furthermore, the choice of 'he' as the genderless pronoun may be traceable to some prejudice on the part of our linguistic ancestors, such as a belief that the classic specimen of humanity is male. I regret both of these possibilities, but I think that their unpleasantness is outweighed by the value of having a generally recognized means for referring to the arbitrary person. I comfort myself with the thought that we manage to live with many other words that are equally flawed, both by ambiguity and by politically suspect etymology.

A HUNCH

My aim is to develop a theory of agency that explains and perhaps resolves our puzzlement about these questions. The guiding hunch behind my theory is that the former, metaphysical questions should be subordinated to the latter, epistemological ones. I suspect that we shall understand how autonomy can coexist with causality only when we have understood how spontaneous self-knowledge can, because autonomous agency is rooted in self-consciousness.

That's why I say that a rational agent might resemble what you see in the mirror. I don't just mean that self-scrutiny reveals a possible image of agency because you happen to be an agent. I mean that the very activity of self-scrutiny, which is what you see your reflected self engaged in, might be what makes you an autonomous agent in the first place.

Now, the idea of studying the nature of agency in terms of an agent's self-knowledge is not original with me. It is central to much of the work that has been done in the past thirty years in the philosophy of action, beginning with Elizabeth Anscombe's *Intention* and Stuart Hampshire's *Thought and Action*. When I refer to Hampshire and Anscombe in subsequent chapters, it will be primarily for the purpose of registering my disagreements with them, but the critical tone of my remarks should not be misunderstood. I wouldn't be so interested in noting the places where I think that these philosophers stumbled if I weren't following directly in their footsteps.

THE THEORY'S STATUS

Before I outline my theory of agency, let me carefully define its status, lest the theory be misread. The status of my theory can be defined in one word: hypothetical. It describes, as I have said, what a rational agent might be like.

Readers unfamiliar with philosophy, as well as some philosophers, may wonder why I would develop a purely hypothetical theory, about what rational agency might be, rather than a theory about whether rational agency actually exists and what it actually is. The answer is that between a theory of what such a phenomenon might be and a theory of what it actually is lies a gap that would have to be closed by empirical rather than philosophical inquiry. Whether human beings are in fact rational agents and, if so, how rational agency is realized in them—these questions have an empirical component that calls for methods of inquiry beyond the competence of a philosopher. Philosophical methods are suited to questions of a different sort, questions about whether the world could possibly be as we conceive it in some respect, and how we conceive it.

Examples of the former sort of question are these. Is knowledge, as we conceive it, possible? Could anything possibly have value as we conceive it? Could we possibly be free in the sense in which we conceive ourselves to be? Such questions are not raised and are unlikely to be answered by empirical discoveries. The philosophical debate about free will, for example, isn't sparked by scientific evidence suggesting that human beings are in fact unfree. The philosophical debate is sparked by the claim that human beings cannot be free, because nothing can be—that is, because freedom, as we conceive it, is simply impossible. One way to settle this debate would be to show how people could be free, by providing design specifications, so to speak, for a hypothetical free agent. Such a showing would still leave open the questions whether people are in fact free and, if so, whether their freedom is realized in accordance with the proposed specifications; but those questions are for the social sciences rather than for philosophy to answer. The philosophical question would have been answered once human freedom had been proved a possibility.

Of course, we cannot usefully consider whether the world could be as we conceive it in some respect unless we know how we conceive it to be. Here is a second kind of question for which philosophical methods are appropriate—namely, questions about our concepts. The program of conceptual analysis has come under suspicion, for various philosophical reasons, but efforts at conceptual elucidation and clarification are still perfectly in order. And sometimes the kind of elucidation that our concepts require is precisely the kind that would be provided by hypothetical instances. For example, we sometimes fear that we don't know what we mean by the word 'free' precisely because there's nothing we can imagine that would count as a free action or a free will. We begin to suspect that our textbook definitions of freedom are empty in the sense that we have no idea what an instantiation of them would be like. In such a case the task of elucidating a concept coincides with that of showing its realization to be possible. Describing a hypothetical case of freedom both illustrates what we mean by 'freedom' and settles the question whether freedom, so conceived, could ever exist.

My hypothetical theory of agency is meant to answer questions of these two kinds. Let me elaborate on this point by narrowing my attention, for the moment, to a few elements of the theory.

We sometimes talk about reasons for acting as favoring or recommending or prescribing the actions for which they are said to be reasons. Philosophers express this feature of reasons by saying that reasons have *normative force*. We also think of rational agents as being self-directed, self-controlled, self-governing, or—as philosophers say—*autonomous*. Finally, we tend to think that personal self-governance is connected with, perhaps even constituted by, the capacity to appreciate and act on the recommending force of reasons.

One question to ask about these elements in our conception of rational agency is what they mean and, indeed, whether they have any substantive meaning at all. Aren't phrases like 'rational force' and 'personal governance' just empty metaphors? I think that this question can be answered by hypothetical instances illustrating what would count as referents of these phrases. If one can identify a kind of force that would exemplify our conception of normativity, and a kind of personal constitution that would exemplify our conception of autonomy, then one will have shown what kind of descriptive work these concepts can do. And if one's hypothetical examples of normativity and autonomy are phenomena that would be connected in the appropriate way, then one will have illustrated what we have in mind in conceiving of autonomy and normativity as connected.

Another question to ask about concepts such as 'normative force' and 'autonomy' is whether they are compatible with our concept of motivational causality. If a creature were caused to act by his motives, wouldn't he thereby be disqualified from acting on the recommendation of reasons or manifesting a capacity for self-control? Here again hypothetical instances can answer our question. For if one can describe a motivationally driven system that would be reason-guided and autonomous, one will thereby have demonstrated that these features of agency aren't mutually incompatible. Design specifications for a hypothetical agent can therefore settle the philosophical question while leaving open the empirical question whether human beings are in fact built to the proposed design.

Although philosophical questions can thus be answered by a purely hypothetical model of agency, the model must not become too far removed from reality. After all, concepts such as those of reasons for acting and autonomy have been formed in response to human phenomena. In particular, they have been formed for the purpose of describing what our deliberations and actions appear to be like from the perspective of commonsense introspection. Although the question whether we actually are reason-guided or autonomous may be open, the question whether we seem or feel reason-guided and autonomous is not, since these concepts have been framed precisely for the purpose of describing how our practical life appears. Any adequate elucidation of these concepts must therefore elucidate them as describing the appearances, though not necessarily the reality, of our practical life. Design specifications for a hypothetical agent must describe a creature whose life would seem like ours; they must describe a creature who might be us, for all we can tell from ordinary experience. Otherwise, they won't add up to an illustration of what we have in mind when, on the basis of that experience, we conceive of ourselves as acting for reasons or as being self-governed.

In order to keep myself within this latter, phenomenological constraint, and in order to make the reading easier, I shall not present my theory in explicitly hypothetical terms. Instead of presenting my theory as the design for a hypothetical agent, I shall speak as if we are rational agents and as if I am stating the true explanation of how rational agency works in our case. I shall present the theory in this manner solely for reasons of expository convenience, however. My private view, of course, is that we probably are rational agents and that my theory may well explain how our instantiation of rational agency works; but this view is strictly private and is not defended here. What I present as the explanation of how we are rational agents is in fact intended as an explanation of how creatures like us could be.

Perhaps the easiest way to keep the status of my theory in mind would be to read words such as *agent*, *subject*, and *person* as enclosed in invisible quotation marks, indicating that they name imaginary creatures of a race conveniently homonymous with ours. I call these creatures "you" and "me," not because they are numerically identical with us, but only because they are our counterparts in a "human" race—a race to which we might belong, for all we can tell from everyday experience, and whose members would be rational agents in the same sense of the concept that we ordinarily apply to ourselves.

The Theory

In order to lay the groundwork for my conception of agency, I shall begin, in part 1, by trying to explain "your" knowledge about "your" actions. (But from here on, I'll leave the quotation marks to the reader's imagination.) I shall argue that intellectual self-scrutiny follows the model of visual self-scrutiny, as described above. Just as your efforts to see your face in the mirror are aided by your reciprocal efforts to make it visible; so too, I shall argue, your efforts to understand your conduct are aided by your reciprocal efforts to make it intelligible. You don't just try to make sense *of* yourself, you also try to make sense *to* yourself. Hence your practical self-understanding is the product of a collaboration that you carry on with yourself, as both the subject and the object of understanding.

The same can be said about your practical self-awareness—your knowledge of the *what* of your actions rather than the *why*. For whenever you try to mind what you're doing, you reciprocate by trying to do what you have in mind. You don't just look where you're going, you also go where you're looking. Your concurrent awareness of your conduct thus results from a collaboration between the subject and the object of that awareness.

In part 2, I shall develop this explanation of self-knowledge into a rudimentary theory of agency. I cannot summarize the entire theory here, but I can perhaps hint at one of its major themes. I shall argue that when a person expects himself to act, he prompts himself to meet that expectation, much as his looking for himself in the mirror prompts him to meet his own gaze. Hence a person's grounds for thinking that he'll do something can be that he'll do it in order to intercept this very thought.

The result, I shall claim, is that reflective predictions defy the apparent incompatibility between foreknowledge and autonomy. Predicting the course of someone's conduct usually seems to imply that it's predetermined and hence not for him to decide. But when he predicts a course for his own conduct, on the grounds that he is thereby prompting himself to follow that course, he implies the reverse. For he implies, quite rightly, that he would have followed a different course if only he had predicted a different course, and hence that his course is being decided by his prediction. His prediction therefore embodies rather than precludes his autonomy—and all because self-scrutiny is a collaboration between the viewer and the viewed.

In part 3, I shall expand this conception of agency so that it eventually accounts for an agent's autonomy over his distant future, over his preferences, and even over his traits of character. In expanding my conception of autonomy, I shall also try to overturn the traditional conception of deliberation. Traditionally, deliberation has been conceived as reactive—that is, as our calculation of how to cope with a given predicament. But if my conception of autonomy is anywhere near the truth, then our predicaments aren't given at all: we invent them, and their invention is the primary task of deliberation. Hence deliberation, according to my theory, is creative rather than reactive. The perennial practical question is not "How shall I solve my problem?" nor even "What's my problem?" but rather "What shall my problem be?"

In part 4, I shall show how an autonomous agent, as I conceive him, is capable of having values, including the values that are ordinarily thought to constitute morality. My account of values begins as an essential component in my theory of agency. For I locate an agent's autonomy in his capacity for deliberation, and deliberation essentially involves value judgments. In order to vindicate my account of autonomy, then, I must show how it captures the evaluative aspect of deliberation.

Although my discussion of values originates within my theory of agency, however, I hope that it may interest the reader in its own right. It is an attempt to map out, in an admittedly rough hand, a skeptical justification of morality. I shall argue that moral judgments are false, and yet that they are perfectly in order, because they have a worthy purpose other than stating the truth. Their other purpose, I argue, is to consummate that practical reasoning by which we constitute ourselves as autonomous agents.

REDUCTIONISM

As the foregoing outline reveals, my model of rational agency is reductionist in some respects. I argue that deliberation could consist in self-scrutiny and that intentions could consist in reflective beliefs. I thereby envision reducing practical reasoning to a kind of theoretical reasoning, and practical conclusions to a kind of theoretical conclusion.

Fearing that my reductionism will be misunderstood, I want to devote the remainder of this brief introduction to an explanation of its purpose.

First, I urge the reader not to interpret the arguments supporting my reductive definitions in a way that would render those arguments viciously circular. My defense of the definitions will often rely on motivational explanations and predictions. That is, I shall make assertions to the effect that if you had such-and-such desires and beliefs, then you would be moved to do so-and-so; or that if you did this, then your motive would probably have been that. The reader may be tempted to assume that these assertions are elliptical, as they might be if made in ordinary discourse. For when we say that a person was moved by particular desires and beliefs, we sometimes mean that he reflected on those motives, recognized them as reasons for acting, and consequently decided to act on them. Thus, talk of motivation often serves in ordinary discourse as a shorthand way of describing deliberation and decision.

For my purposes, however, this shorthand must be avoided, since it would introduce intolerable confusions. After all, deliberation and decision are precisely the phenomena that I hope to prove compatible with motivational causality. My goal is to demonstrate that being caused to act by desires and beliefs is consistent with deciding to act for reasons. My project would thus be shortcircuited by a terminology in which 'motive' already meant "reason" and 'being moved' already meant "deciding."

I therefore ask the reader to take my motivational predictions and explanations at face value. When I speak of someone as being moved by various attitudes, I have a strictly causal process in mind, a process that doesn't yet involve the intervention of a deliberating intelligence. I am trying to explain how the deliberating intelligence might get into the act.

Furthermore, I ask the reader not to assume that my reductionism springs from the same intellectual impulses as other reductionist theories. Often philosophers try to reduce a concept because they regard it as somehow suspect or unmanageable. They think of 'mind' as a less respectable concept than 'body', for instance, or of 'value' as less tractable than 'fact', and so they try to define the one in terms of the other. These philosophers tend to be not just reductionists but also, in a sense, conceptual eliminativists: they regard the target concept as an intellectual embarrassment that should be denied an independent role in our thinking. For them, reductive definition is therefore an end in itself.

I am not a conceptual eliminativist. I do not wish to stop conceiving of intention as a peculiar mental state, or of deliberation as a peculiar mental process. Why, I virtually revel in their peculiarities. My only claim is that the peculiarities of intention can best be appreciated as those by which a peculiar kind of belief would be set apart from other beliefs, and that the peculiarities of deliberation can best be appreciated as those which would distinguish a peculiar kind of theoretical reasoning. Hence my modeling intention on belief, and deliberation on reflective theorizing, is not an attempt to eliminate the practical as a distinct category but to make the category stand out.

But how can I tell that I am indeed setting practical thought into proper relief? Why not design a model in which intention and deliberation would be phenomena sui generis, wholly different from belief and theoretical reasoning rather than peculiar species thereof? My answer is that my reductive model puts us in a position to understand the possibility of the very phenomena that make our practical life so puzzling—that is, the various manifestations of autonomy and spontaneity that seem to be at odds with the causal image of motivation. For me, then, reductive definition is not an end in itself but rather a means to explaining the possibility of agency.

Compromises

As I have said, this book is an attempt to describe a way that the world of action might be, as far as we can tell from commonsense experience. I try to make this possible world seem real—I mean, really possible—by filling in as much detail and color as I can. I try to show that the life of my hypothetical agent would be like ours in many respects, large and small, so that our being like him will strike the reader as a genuine possibility.

One unfortunate side effect of my efforts is that the theory may also strike the reader as, shall I say, too much to swallow. The theory includes accounts of such significant phenomena as self-knowledge, reasons for acting, freedom and autonomy, intentions and plans, value and morality, as well as more mundane phenomena such as vertigo, insomnia, or absentmindedness. On the one hand, I want my accounts of these phenomena to hang together, so that they add up to a description of a coherent possibility, of something comprehensible as a way that the world might be. On the other hand, making these accounts hang together entails leaving the impression that they cannot be pulled apart. Consequently, when the reader cannot imagine a particular phenomenon's being as I imagine it, he may feel compelled to reject the entire theory.

Yet elements of the theory are indeed separable from the whole. For example, the account of self-knowledge in chapters 1 and 2 is quite independent of subsequent chapters. Many of my arguments about the reduction of intentions to beliefs, in chapters 3 and 4, are independent of the particular motivational model by which I propose to accomplish that reduction. My account of free will in chapter 5 may depend on the reduction of intentions to beliefs but, once again, doesn't depend on the particular way in which the reduction is carried out here. And so on.

Nevertheless, I make little effort to alert the reader to the seams in my theory. The reason is that I am trying to construct a hypothetical model of our practical life, as it appears to us, and our practical life appears seamless. I encourage the reader to plunder my view for enhancements to his own, but I'm afraid that he'll have to do so without my assistance.

PART ONE

AN AGENT'S SELF-KNOWLEDGE

ONE

SELF-UNDERSTANDING

A MOMENT OF REFLECTION

You are walking up Fifth Avenue. All of a sudden you realize that you don't know what you're doing. You can see that you're walking up Fifth Avenue, of course: the surroundings are quite familiar. But the reason why you're walking up Fifth Avenue escapes you, and so you still don't know what you're doing. Are you walking home from work? Trying to catch a downtown bus? Just taking a stroll? You stop to think.

I assume that you have gone through moments like this, when your own conduct perplexes you—when you stop and ask yourself, "What am I doing?" These moments of reflective puzzlement are rare, of course, but they are revealing. How you behave in moments of reflective puzzlement sheds light, first of all, on why such moments are so rare—why you almost always know what you're doing. More importantly, your response to reflective puzzlement illuminates the nature of rational agency, by shedding light on a hitherto neglected connection between reasoning and action.

I shall thus draw two morals from my story about your walk up Fifth Avenue. The ultimate moral of the story, which won't begin to emerge until chapter 3, will be that practical reasoning is a kind of theoretical reasoning, and that practical conclusions, or intentions, are the corresponding theoretical conclusions, or beliefs. The kind of theoretical reasoning that I shall identify as practical is the kind that you are struggling with in my story when you reflect on why you're walking up Fifth Avenue. In order to demonstrate the practical nature of such reflection, however, I shall have to draw another moral, about the peculiar way in which reflective reasoning works. I shall therefore begin, in this chapter and the next, by examining how you usually come to know what you're doing.

REFLECTIVE KNOWLEDGE

You usually know what you're doing in at least two senses. First, you know some prima facie descriptions of your conduct—descriptions that venture little by way of interpretation or explanation. In this sense you know what you're doing even as you walk up Fifth Avenue in my story, since you do know that you're walking up Fifth Avenue. Of course, you never know every such description of your conduct, and sometimes you believe descriptions that are badly mistaken. You may know that you're walking up Fifth Avenue, for instance, but not that you're stepping under a falling safe; or you may believe that you're walking up Fifth Avenue when you're actually headed downtown.[1] Still, you almost always believe some prima facie description of your conduct, and the description you believe is usually adequate for commonsense purposes.[2]

The other sense in which you usually know what you're doing is the sense in which you don't in my story. What you don't know in that story is an interpretive or explanatory description of your conduct— a description like "walking home" or "taking a stroll" that would reveal some of your motives[3] and hence explain why you're walking up

---

[1] These remarks should make clear that I do not individuate actions in the way recommended by Alvin Goldman in chapter 2 of *A Theory of Human Action* (Princeton, 1970). Goldman would say that if, in walking up Fifth Avenue, you are stepping under a falling safe, then you are performing two actions. Goldman would therefore have to say that most of the actions you perform, you perform unwittingly. I prefer to say that although you don't know most of the true descriptions of the actions you perform, you do know most of those actions under some description. I heartily endorse the critique of Goldman offered by G.E.M. Anscombe in "Under a Description," *Nous* 13 (1979): 219–33.

In individuating actions, I follow the practice recommended by Donald Davidson in "The Logical Form of Action Sentences," in *Essays on Actions and Events* (Oxford, 1980), 109–10.

[2] What are "commonsense purposes," and when is a description adequate for such purposes? I don't think there is a general answer to these questions. Although you almost always know when you are *doing something*, that description is almost never adequate. Although you almost never know the biochemical and microphysical details of your actions, such descriptions are almost always unnecessary for the purposes of common sense. Between these two extremes, no generalizations can be drawn.

[3] I want to remain as neutral as I can on various questions about motives—what they consist of, how an agent recognizes them, and how recognizing them enables him to explain his actions. However, there are some senses of the word 'motive', and some assumptions about motives, from which I must dissociate myself.

For one thing, I do not assume, with Gilbert Ryle, that automatic or inadvertent actions are not ascribable to motives: "[W]hen we say that someone acts in a certain way from [a motive], we mean by implication to deny that the action was merely automatic. In particular we imply that the agent was in some way thinking or heeding what he was doing. . . . [T]he class of actions done from motives coincides with the class of actions describable as intelligent" (*The Concept of Mind* [New York, 1949], 110–11). See also Betty Powell, *Knowledge of Actions* (New York, 1967), 9: "[I]t seems obvious that what a man does inadvertently he does not do . . . 'with a motive'." Here Ryle and Powell are

Fifth Avenue. Such thorough ignorance of your motives for acting is rare.[4]

Both sorts of knowledge may elude you on some occasions, when motives of yours produce behavior without your being aware of it under any description at all. For instance, you may know only that you are pondering a problem in philosophy, even as you are also shredding a piece of paper on your desk. Or you may feel that the mosquito bite on your shin is bleeding and only then realize that you have been scratching it.

But these occasions are exceptional: most of the time, you can give both prima facie and explanatory descriptions of your conduct. The first question I shall raise is how you come to have this knowledge. How do you manage to know what you're doing and why you're doing it?

---

expressing an intuition that I simply do not share. I suspect that they are using the phrase 'acting for a motive' to mean what I and others mean by the phrase 'acting for a reason'.

My views on motivational explanation are similar to those outlined by Richard Brandt and Jaegwon Kim in "Wants as Explanations of Actions," *Journal of Philosophy* 60 (1963): 425–35; and by Paul M. Churchland in "The Logical Character of Action-Explanations," *Philosophical Review* 79 (1970): 214–36. I am not entirely sure to what extent these views about motivation are essential to my theory of agency.

[4] Readers of the psychological literature might think that this assumption is refuted by the experiments surveyed by Richard Nisbett and Lee Ross in chapter 9 of their book *Human Inference: Strategies and Shortcomings of Social Judgment* (Englewood Cliffs, N.J., 1980). Those experiments reveal that people's explanations about themselves are often mistaken. Perhaps, then, one should conclude that, contrary to my assumption, people cannot usually explain what they're doing.

But no: to draw this conclusion would be to misinterpret both my assumption and the empirical data. To begin with, the research reviewed by Nisbett and Ross does not focus primarily on people's explanations of what they are doing; it focuses instead on their explanations of their moods, judgments, and preferences. The few experiments that test reflective explanations of actions, rather than of attitudes, are ones in which the experimenters "go to unusual lengths to confuse subjects about the true causes of their behavior." Nisbett and Ross concede that such experiments "say little about the degree of accuracy to be expected [in reflective explanations] under less stage-managed conditions" (206).

Furthermore, even if Nisbett and Ross's conclusions held for reflective explanations of actions, as well as of attitudes, they would not refute my initial assumption about agents' self-understanding. Nisbett and Ross conclude, first, that people's reflective explanations are drawn from a commonsense theory of human behavior in general and, second, that this commonsense theory often proves inadequate when compared with the theories of experimental psychologists. But I assume nothing about the scientific adequacy of commonsense psychology. All I claim is that people can almost always explain their actions to the satisfaction of commonsense psychology, whatever its merits or flaws. The question I shall address below is how people manage to apply this commonsense theory to themselves with such ease and immediacy that they seem not to be theorizing at all.

Possible Explanations of Self-Knowledge

One way of obtaining such knowledge would be to examine yourself in action. By sensing muscle contractions and simply watching your limbs, you could compile some account of your outward behavior. And you could trace that behavior back to its motives introspectively, by noting and interpreting your inner thoughts and feelings.

But these methods of inquiry appear to be largely superfluous. You seem to know how you're using your limbs without having to see or feel yourself use them, and you seem to know your motives for acting without having to reflect on yourself in the act. Thus the reflective knowledge that almost always attends your actions almost never appears to derive from the evidence of the actions themselves.

Consider the following example, which is borrowed from Elizabeth Anscombe's *Intention.*[5] When you write something on the blackboard, you seem to know what you're writing without having to read it. Your audience will follow your hand, collecting the words that it leaves in its path, but you already know the words without having to take them in, because you're the one writing them. If I took hold of your hand, with the chalk in it, and used it to write something on the board, you might still be able to tell the words without looking, by feeling the lines and curves over which I was leading you. But when you're doing the writing, your thoughts don't similarly grope along after your hand. Your thoughts don't follow your hand at all; they lead it. And the consequence seems to be that you have a very different knowledge of what you're writing.

Reflection on such examples has led Anscombe and other philosophers to suspect an intimate connection between an agent's self-knowledge and the nature of agency itself. To the question "How do you know what you're doing?" the most obvious reply is "Well, I'm the one who's doing it!"—which suggests that doing something is a special way of knowing about it. Anscombe's hope, and mine, is that if we study this way of knowing about something—the way that consists in doing it—we'll learn what doing something really is.

"Knowledge without observation." Anscombe, and those who follow her, describe the apparent connection between knowledge and action by saying that one's own actions are things that one "knows without observation."[6] Other philosophers have branded this description false; I would call it simply misleading.

---

[5] (Ithaca, N.Y., 1963), 53, 82.
[6] *Intention*, esp. 49ff. See also Stuart Hampshire and H.L.A. Hart, "Decision, Inten-

Objections to the claim that you know your actions without observation rest on cases in which you're quite sure about what you're doing but then turn out not to be doing it. You just know, for example, that you're opening the window—but then you aren't, because the window is nailed shut, or your arm has gone limp. Your belief that you're opening the window is not perceptibly different on this occasion from the like belief on other occasions—that is, until it turns out to be false. But then how can you tell on those other occasions that the like belief isn't false, short of seeing it come true? This question moves some commentators to conclude that in order to know that you're doing something, you need to see yourself succeed at doing it.[7]

But I think that the wrong lesson is being drawn here from the possibility of error on the agent's part. A correct lesson would have to be either far more radical or far more conservative. One might note, for instance, that seeing yourself open the window wouldn't put an end to the possibility of error. After all, the sight of your opening the window might be a dream, the work of an evil genie, or an hallucination insinuated by computer into a potted brain. Perhaps, then, the lesson to draw is not that an agent's self-knowledge requires observation but that knowledge of any kind is impossible.

Yet claims about an agent's self-knowledge aren't meant to be proof against radical skepticism. When I say that you usually know what you're doing, I don't mean that you're absolutely and incorrigibly certain; I mean that you know by ordinary standards of evidence. And when other philosophers say that you know your actions without observation, they mean—or, at least, ought to mean—that observation

---

tion and Certainty," *Mind* 67 (1958): 1–12; Stuart Hampshire, *Thought and Action* (London, 1959), and *Freedom of the Individual* (Princeton, N.J., 1975); P. F. Strawson, *Individuals* (London, 1959), 111–12; A. I. Melden, *Free Action* (London, 1961), chapter 4; contributions by Brian O'Shaughnessy and Keith Donnellan in "Symposium: Human Action," *Journal of Philosophy* 60 (1963): 365–445; H. P. Grice, "Intention and Uncertainty," *Proceedings of the British Academy* 57 (1971): 263–79; David W. Hamlyn, "Self-Knowledge," in *The Self; Psychological and Philosophical Issues*, ed. Theodore Mischel (Totowa, N.J., 1977), 192; Lawrence H. Davis, *Theory of Action* (Englewood Cliffs, N.J., 1979), chapter 4; Anthony Kenny, *The God of the Philosophers* (Oxford, 1979), 35; Brian O'Shaughnessy, *The Will: A Dual Aspect Theory* (Cambridge, 1980), 1: 12 and passim; George M. Wilson, *The Intentionality of Human Action*, vol. 31 of *Acta Philosophica Fennica* (Amsterdam, 1980), 110ff.; John R. Searle, *Intentionality* (Cambridge, 1983), 90; Powell, *Knowledge of Actions*, 90.

[7] See, e.g., O. R. Jones, "Things Known Without Observation," *Proceedings of the Aristotelian Society* 61 (1961): 129–50; Goldman, *Theory of Human Action*, 98–99; C. B. Martin, "Knowledge without Observation," *Canadian Journal of Philosophy* 1 (1971): 15–24; Arthur C. Danto, "Action, Knowledge, and Representation," in *Action Theory*, ed. Myles Brand and Douglas Walton (Dordrecht, 1976), 17.

isn't necessary for knowledge that meets equally ordinary standards. By stricter standards, observation wouldn't be sufficient.

A more suitable lesson to draw from the possible sources of error about your actions is that your knowledge of those actions rests on background knowledge about your surroundings and abilities. In order to know that you're opening the window, you have to know that it's a window and that you can open it. These items of knowledge aren't the sort that you get without observation, but they don't necessarily require observation on the present occasion. Surely, you can know that something is a window, and that you're capable of opening it, without putting yourself and it to the test here and now: you can know these things, to the appropriate standard of evidence, on the basis of past observation. And if you already know that the thing before you is a window that you can open, then you needn't see yourself opening it in order to know that you're doing so.

I therefore disagree with both sides of the debate about knowledge without observation. On the one hand, your knowledge of what you're doing requires a background of observational knowledge; on the other hand, it still doesn't seem to require observation of the action in question. For if you know from past observation that something is a window and that you can open it, then the further knowledge that you *are* opening it doesn't seem to arise by means of further observation. Having learned, at some point, that the object at hand is a window you can open, you don't similarly learn that you're opening it. Your initial discoveries—"Lo, a window!" and "Works fine, I see"—aren't followed by another discovery: "Why, I'm opening it!"

The question therefore remains why knowledge of what you're doing seems to require only so much observational input. At each moment there are various alternative actions that have been shown by past observation to be within your power. Yet if you perform one of these actions, you'll feel as if you know so without any further observation. Your knowledge of having various actions within your power will be superseded by the knowledge of performing a particular one, seemingly without any additional reflection on your part. But how? Of all the things that you know you can do, how can you come to know, without looking, which one you're actually doing?

Trying.   One is tempted to respond that all you know without observation here is what you're trying to do.[8] For given the premise that you're in a position to do something, all that's needed in order to es-

---

[8] This point is made by Goldman, *Theory of Human Action,* 99.

tablish that you are in fact doing the thing is the further premise that you're trying to. Hence the input that advances you from a knowledge of what you can do to a knowledge of what you are doing must be an awareness of what you're trying to do. And there is nothing odd, one is tempted to add, about the assumption that your awareness of what you're trying to do is nonobservational, since trying to do something is an inner, mental state of the sort that's immediately accessible to its subject.

Now, I am inclined to agree that the noteworthy component of an agent's self-awareness is indeed his awareness of what he's trying to do.[9] But I do not believe that what's noteworthy about this knowledge can be explained by the mere accessibility of its object. For one thing, commonplace instances of Freudian repression indicate that what you're trying to do can sometimes elude your efforts at introspection. For another thing, even when your trying to do something lies open to introspection, it doesn't automatically make itself known. Just remember the cases of your walking up Fifth Avenue or distractedly scratching your shin—cases in which you are trying to do something and yet remain unconscious of trying to do it. These cases indicate that trying to do something is not a self-reporting state, a state of the sort whose very existence entails your knowing about it. At most, the accessibility of this state amounts to your being able to tell what you're trying to do, upon reflection. And yet in the ordinary case, you seem to know what you're trying to do without reflecting—indeed, without having to "tell" at all. You don't think of yourself merely as being able to tell what you're trying to write on blackboard, for example. If asked, "Can you tell what you're trying to write?" you'd retort, "I don't have to *tell*: I know already." Your practical self-awareness therefore seems odd even for awareness of an introspectible state of mind.

At this point, I think, the phrase "knowledge without observation" becomes inadequate to the task of characterizing the experience of practical self-knowledge. It becomes inadequate because observation is not the only thing that one seems to dispense with on the way to the knowledge in question. Anscombe says that one has observational knowledge of something if "we can speak of separately describable sensations, having which is in some sense [one's] criterion for saying [it]."[10] By this definition, you can certainly be said to have nonobservational knowledge of what you're trying to do, since you don't detect

---

[9] At this point I shall offer no systematic account of trying. I'm content to say that trying is whatever makes the difference between being in a position to do something and doing it.

[10] *Intention*, 13.

what you're trying to do by some separably describable sensation, like a tingle or an itch. But to say only this much is surely to say too little. The point is rather that you don't seem to detect what you're trying to do at all—whether by a separately describable feeling or otherwise. Your knowledge of what you're trying to do not only appears independent of your feeling characteristic tingles or itches; it even appears independent, say, of your directly intuiting what you're trying to do—an experience that wouldn't be separably describable and hence wouldn't entail observation, in Anscombe's sense. In short, your knowledge of what you're trying to do seems to preempt not just observation but any method of discovery whatsoever.

Another way of seeing why "knowledge without observation" is inadequate to convey the apparent character of an agent's self-knowledge is to note the wide variety of phenomena that Anscombe regards as objects of nonobservational knowledge. According to her, an agent has knowledge without observation not only of his intentional actions but also of many involuntary bodily movements, as well as the mere position of his limbs.[11] Yet there are significant differences between how you know what you're doing, or trying to do, and how you know that your knee has flexed at the tap of the doctor's mallet or that your arm is bent. I am inclined to say that the latter are things that you feel, though not by separately describable sensations, and I am quite confident in saying that you must at least notice them. But what you're trying to do is something that you usually seem to know without feeling it, without even having to notice.

Here I do not mean to imply that your knowledge of what you're trying to do is never a discovery. Sometimes the true aim of your conduct dawns on you quite slowly. All I am claiming is that such is not the normal case and that the difference is not that in the normal case the aim of your conduct dawns on you quickly. Normally, what you're trying to do isn't something that dawns on you or occurs to you at all.

The hypothesis of early warning. We might think that the reason why you needn't find out what you're trying to do is that you usually know already, having known before the attempt ever began. And we might be tempted to explain this advance knowledge by saying that you usually get advance notice, before you try to do anything, of what motives you have and what they will move you to attempt.

Let us suppose, for the sake of this explanation, that desires and beliefs are directly introspectible states of mind. If so, then you can

---

[11] *Intention*, 13–16.

easily tell what you want and what you believe. What the present explanation suggests is that you can also tell how these attitudes are inclining you to behave and hence that you are in a position to know in advance what you will try to do. This explanation has the virtue of accounting not only for your knowledge of the attempt itself but also for your knowledge of the motives behind it.

One problem with this explanation, however, is that introspective access, once again, is insufficient to account for the experienced character of your self-knowledge. After all, desiring and believing, like trying, are not self-reporting states, even though they may be introspectible. To be sure, some beliefs and desires do obtrude themselves on your attention by giving rise to occurrent thoughts and feelings. The vast majority are more reticent, however, and you cannot easily poll those tacit attitudes simply by reflecting on what you want and believe in general. Open-ended reflective inquiries like "What do I want?" and "What do I believe?" are apt to be met with silence. Successful introspection on these attitudes usually requires that you first propose a topic and then ask yourself what you think or feel about it. "What do I believe about this?" and "How do I feel toward that?" are the questions that most readily elicit a reply.

But then how can you be certain, or even reasonably likely, to have noted the motives of your forthcoming action before they move you to perform it? If introspection has a relatively narrow focus, then how does it happen to focus, from one moment to the next, on just those attitudes which will enable you to identify and explain your next action?

One way of answering this question would be to suppose that desires and beliefs usually give rise to conscious manifestations just before producing an action. Perhaps these attitudes emit occurrent thoughts and feelings whenever they're on the verge of unleashing their motivational potential. Some philosophers have proposed such an account, but I find it at odds with ordinary experience.[12] Many actions that are performed out of desire are not preceded by any pangs, twinges, or yearnings. You want something and you try to get it, without experiencing any conscious manifestations of the operative desire.

Furthermore, the conscious feelings that rise to the surface from a desire do not guarantee your immediate recognition of it. Feeling a desire is not the same as recognizing it introspectively. Often you feel

---

[12] See, for example, Alvin Goldman's claim that motives are occurrent beliefs and desires (*Theory of Human Action*, chapter 4). Anscombe expresses the opposing view on page 17 of *Intention*.

a vague pang or yearning without knowing what it's a pang of or a yearning for. Since these feelings do not fully disclose the attitudes from which they arise, they would not by themselves enable you to identify and explain your forthcoming action. In order to learn that much from your feelings, you would first have to diagnose the attitudes beneath them. And if you were relying on that diagnosis for prior knowledge about your impending action, then you would have to arrive at the diagnosis before the action began.

Yet your mind isn't constantly racing to identify the attitudes beneath your feelings. When you get an inchoate sense of longing—of wanting something, you know not what—you don't feel that you must hurry to pinpoint your desire before it precipitates an action. And if you make no special effort to identify your desires before they produce action, the question remains how introspective access to your motives could account for your awareness of each action as it begins.

A more serious problem with the present hypothesis is that, like the preceding hypothesis about introspective access, it fails to account for the apparent spontaneity with which you know what you're doing. Although it portrays you as getting advance notice of what you'll do, rather than as waiting to see, it still portrays your knowledge as a discovery. It suggests, in effect, that you feel each action coming, like a sneeze. But when you know what you're doing, the reason doesn't seem to be that you felt the action coming. Rather, it seems to be that you know, and indeed already knew, without finding out at all.

Thus, your knowledge of what you're trying to do seems to be knowledge that you originate—spontaneous knowledge, as I call it. Yet you sometimes fail to know what you're trying to do, and indeed fail to find out upon inquiry. The question is how something can be known spontaneously on some occasions if, on other occasions, it can't even be discovered.

"Practical knowledge." This question has a commonsense answer that lacks philosophical clarity but at least helps to identify the phenomenon that seems to need explaining. When you know spontaneously what you're trying to do, the reason, according to common sense, is that the action was your idea to begin with: it's what you had in mind to do. And when you fail to know what you're trying to do, the reason is that the action wasn't your idea—not in the sense that it was someone else's idea instead but merely in the sense that it wasn't something you had in mind.

But how could your having an action in mind constitute knowledge? Your idea of doing something is indeed spontaneous, in the sense that you come up with it on your own. But its very spontaneity seems inconsistent with the claim that it embodies knowledge. For if you invent this idea, what grounds could you possibly have for taking it as an accurate representation of anything that's actually going on? And if you have no grounds for taking it as an accurate representation of an actual event, how can it qualify as knowledge about your conduct?

Some philosophers, Anscombe among them, have answered this question by saying that the knowledge contained in the idea of doing something is a unique kind of knowledge that simply doesn't require grounds. According to these philosophers, a person's conception of what he's doing, or of what he's going to do, constitutes "a kind of . . . knowledge to which the notion of evidence is irrelevant."[13]

These philosophers try to save the commonsense psychology of self-knowledge by elevating it to the status of epistemology. Common sense claims that your knowledge of what you're doing is contained in your idea of doing something—an idea that you invent without consulting evidence. Since this claim is about how you come into possession of self-knowledge, it's a claim of cognitive psychology. What the philosophers say in support of the claim, however, is that knowledge of your actions doesn't require evidential grounds; and this statement belongs to epistemology, since it's about how self-knowledge is to be justified. According to these philosophers, you can invent a conception of your action without consulting evidence, in practice, because your conception of what you're doing requires no evidential support, in principle.

I believe that this explanation of practical self-knowledge is mistaken, for reasons that I shall discuss in due course.[14] In order to analyze the mistakes involved, however, I must first offer an alternative explanation of practical self-knowledge—an explanation that saves the commonsense description of such knowledge without making epistemological exceptions in its favor. I shall argue that although your knowledge of what you're doing is something that you invent spontaneously, without consulting evidence, it is nevertheless subject to the usual requirements of evidential support. How a spontaneous invention can satisfy those requirements will be subject of the next two chapters.

Summary and proposal. My account will in fact encompass more than an agent's awareness of what he's doing; it will also encompass his ability to understand his action, in terms of the motives behind it.

[13] Hampshire and Hart, "Decision, Intention and Certainty," 1. Among the philosophers cited earlier, in note 6, I would list Anscombe, Grice, Kenny, and Melden as agreeing, or likely to agree, with Hampshire and Hart.

[14] Chapter 2, 61–64; chapter 3, 102–5.

These are two different kinds of knowledge, each presenting a slightly different philosophical problem. Let me summarize what seems to call for explanation in each of them.

An agent's ability to explain his actions is not spontaneous in the sense I have just defined. You usually know about the attitudes that are moving you because you have introspectively recognized them on some occasion. Unlike your action, then, your motives are discovered. What's puzzling about your knowledge of these motives, I have suggested, is not how you manage to know about them but how you usually manage to know about them before they become relevant to the anticipation or explanation of your conduct. The question, in other words, is one of timeliness rather than spontaneity.

Your awareness of what you're doing is also timely, of course, since you usually know what you're doing even as you start to do it. But in this case, the question of timeliness is eclipsed. Your tendency to know about your actions before they're available for inspection seems like a consequence of your ability to know about them without inspection, period; and so the foremost question is one of spontaneity.

I propose to explain an agent's self-knowledge in a way that accounts for both its timeliness and its spontaneity. I shall explain why, in the normal case, you already know what you're doing, or at least what you're trying to do, without ever finding out; and why you tend to have equally timely, though not necessarily spontaneous, knowledge of the motives behind your action. My goal is to explain these features of an agent's self-knowledge without having to exempt such knowledge from the ordinary requirements of justification.

Before beginning, however, I should warn the reader that my account of an agent's self-knowledge is bound to seem backwards, at least initially. The best way to figure out how an agent knows about his actions, I believe, is to figure out how he'd react if he *didn't* know. If you want to see why an agent usually has reflective knowledge, I say, first look at how he would get such knowledge if he didn't have it to begin with. Unfortunately, this method requires me to imagine a situation that doesn't usually obtain—namely, the situation in which an agent doesn't know what he's doing or why he's doing it. I shall often speak of an agent as if he is in the dark about his own conduct, and at such times the reader is likely to wonder whether *I'm* in the dark about the most obvious features of agency. The answer is that those features of agency are the very ones whose presence I'm trying to explain, but I'm trying to explain them by showing how an agent would remedy their absence.

Hence my interest in the story of your walk up Fifth Avenue, in which you suffer a lapse of self-knowledge. By interpreting and embellishing that story, I shall examine how you react when you don't know enough about your actions, and I shall thereby arrive at an account of why you usually do.

The Response to Reflective Puzzlement

Consider what happens, then, when you're walking up Fifth Avenue and realize that you don't know why.

One thing that happens is that you ask yourself, "What am I doing?" Another is that you stop doing it. I suggest that these two developments are connected. The connection between querying your conduct and stopping it is that they are two bits of behavior that share a common motive. Asking yourself what you're doing, of course, manifests a desire to know what you're doing. My suggestion is that stopping does, too.

Now, the desire to know what you're doing has probably miscarried in the antecedent to my story. That is, until you realize that you don't know what you're doing, you have probably been walking along absentmindedly, paying little attention to what you're doing and hence showing little desire to know. When the desire to know what you're doing reasserts itself, it moves you to ask. But then it does more. When you can't think of what you're doing, the desire to know restrains you from doing it; for wanting to know what you're doing is a motive against doing something once you become conscious of not knowing what it is. One of your motives for stopping, then, is the same desire that motivates your question.

Your motive. Let me be more precise about the motive I have in mind. To begin with, you obviously want to know more than a prima facie description of your conduct, since you already know such a description when you ask what you're doing. I therefore assume that having a name for your conduct isn't enough: you also want an explanation. The operative desire is not just to know but also to understand what you're doing.[15]

Furthermore, the desire I have in mind is the desire to understand whichever action satisfies the description 'what you're doing'. To that description, the desire delegates the job of selecting which action is to be understood. Yet the action thus selected is to be understood under

---

[15] For the moment I shall treat an agent's desire to understand his actions as a desire to know his proximate motives for acting. Of course, different agents may want different kinds of reflective explanations, or may have different intellectual standards. I discuss these differences on pp. 39–40.

a more informative description than 'what you're doing'. Your desire is, not to be capable of answering the question "Why am I doing what I'm doing?", but rather to be capable of answering a question like "Why am I walking up Fifth Avenue?", given that walking up Fifth Avenue is what you're doing. More generally, you want it to be the case that you have an answer to some question of the form "Why am I doing x?", where x has been replaced by a description co-referential with, but more informative than, the description 'what you're doing'.[16]

Now, for you to understand any action that satisfies the description 'what you're doing' is the same as for no action to satisfy that description unless you understand it. You can therefore fulfill the desire in question by two coordinate means—both by understanding anything that you're up to and by not being up to anything that you don't understand. Whether you make sense of things that you are doing or you are doing things that make sense to you, the outcome will be that you understand what you're doing, in the desired sense.

I do not mean to deny that you have desires to understand actions selected by other descriptions, or actions selected directly, all descriptions aside. You may have a desire to understand your present action precisely because it's a case of your walking up Fifth Avenue, such walks being a matter of special interest to you. Or you may want to understand an action glimpsed in the reflecting surface of a store window, no matter whose action or what action it may be. These desires aren't the desire that I have in mind, but in positing that one, I do not mean to deny that you may have these as well. All I claim is that these desires are not the whole of your interest in understanding your conduct. Even if you want to understand your current action because it's a case of your walking up Fifth Avenue, I claim, you also want to understand your walking up Fifth Avenue because it's your current action—because it's what you're doing. And these two desires are not at all the same.

The difference between these desires emerges most clearly in how they move you when you realize that you can't say why you're walking

<hr/>

[16] Of course, there are always many descriptions that can replace x in this formula. If one regards each description as corresponding to a distinct action, then one will think that there are many actions satisfying the description 'what you're doing'; and so one will think that the desire to understand whatever satisfies this description is, in fact, the desire to understand many actions. But as I have already explained, I do not regard each description of your conduct as corresponding to a distinct action. Hence I regard the desire to understand whatever satisfies the description 'what you're doing' as the desire to understand a single action and to understand it under any of the more specific descriptions that it happens to satisfy. See note 1.

up Fifth Avenue. The desire to understand that action because it's a case of walking up Fifth Avenue moves you to scrutinize it more closely. So does the desire to understand the action because it's what you're doing. But this latter desire, having made you scrutinize what you're doing, also makes you wish that you weren't doing something so inscrutable. Not having taken your walk up Fifth Avenue wouldn't have helped to satisfy the former desire, which embodies a curiosity about such walks per se; but the latter desire is the desire to understand such walks only if you happen to be taking one and, if you aren't, to understand whatever you happen to be doing instead. If you weren't doing something so puzzling as walking up Fifth Avenue, you might have a better chance of understanding whatever you *were* doing. The desire to understand whatever you're doing therefore moves you not only to ask what you *are* doing but also, when no answer emerges, to wish that you weren't doing it.

Another important point about the desire I have in mind is that it's not the desire to understand, once and for all, whatever you're doing *now*; it's the desire to understand, at any moment, whatever you're doing *then*. The distinction here depends on the relation among the tenses of the verbs in the phrase 'wanting to know what you're doing'. On the one hand, the tense of 'doing' may be interpreted as coordinate with that of 'wanting', since your desire may be to understand what you were doing at the onset of the desire itself. If so, you are wondering about what you were doing just now—that is, when you started wondering. On the other hand, the tense of 'doing' may be coordinate with that of 'to understand', since your desire may be to understand your actions while you are performing them. The latter desire is what I have in mind.

Again, I do not mean to deny that you may have both desires. That is, you may want to compile an explanation of your present action and store that explanation for future reference. All I claim is that you also want your understanding to stay abreast of your actions: you want to understand them in succession, each one as it is performed.

Your desire therefore motivates more than the wish that you weren't now doing something that puzzled you. What you're now doing is only part of the conduct you want to understand: it's the part that you want to understand now. There's always another part that you want to understand next—namely, whatever you'll be doing next. And you needn't just wish for that part of your conduct to be something other than a walk up Fifth Avenue; you can make it something other than a walk up Fifth Avenue, simply by curtailing your walk. Hence the desire to keep abreast of whatever you're doing, having moved you to ask what you're doing, now moves you to stop doing it.

From the perspective of this desire, the rewards of having stopped are immediate. You have not only stopped doing something you can't understand but also started doing something you can. A moment ago you were walking up Fifth Avenue, without knowing why. Currently, you're refusing to go on without knowing why—and no wonder. Your motive for refusing to go on is evident to you; for you've just expressed it to yourself by asking, "What am I doing?" Since you're aware of wanting to be capable of explaining your conduct, you can understand refusing to go on with conduct that you can't explain. That's what you're currently doing—and so you have your explanation.

Note, finally, that the desire in question here is not the desire to have explanations of your actions pass continually before your mind; and yet what passes before your mind will sometimes determine the desire's behavioral effects. On the one hand, all you really want is to understand your actions in the dispositional sense—in the sense of being able to explain them if you try. What matters is having access to the relevant explanations rather than an active awareness of them. On the other hand, the desire to be capable of explaining your present conduct will never move you to curtail that conduct unless you realize that you can't explain it. So long as you don't know that you don't understand what you're doing, the desire to understand what you're doing won't move you to stop. And the most common way of learning that you don't understand something is to experience puzzlement in the course of a conscious attempt to explain it.[17] Thus, although conscious insight is not the object of your desire, conscious bafflement may be what triggers the desire's inhibitive force. The reason why you halt your walk up Fifth Avenue is not simply that you can't explain it but that you try to explain it and realize that you can't.

Alternative responses.   Under some circumstances, of course, you might not have stopped walking. If you had remembered at least that you were heading somewhere—that you had some destination or other—you might have hoped to remember your destination when it came into view. And the hope that you would remember where you

---

[17] Although conscious puzzlement is often what conveys a knowledge of your inability to explain something, it is not a necessary component or concomitant of that knowledge. Sometimes you just know that you can't explain something, and you know it without experiencing anything in particular. Such implicit knowledge, when combined with your desire for self-understanding, is sufficient to restrain you from unintelligible courses of action.

were going, when you got there, might then have moved you to keep going.

But in that case walking on would not have been a puzzling thing to do. As you proceeded up Fifth Avenue, you would have known why— namely, in order to find out the purpose with which you had walked that way to begin with, and perhaps also in order to give that purpose, now temporarily forgotten, a chance of being fulfilled. You are well acquainted with your desire for the fulfillment of your purposes in general, and the desire to know the purpose of your walk up Fifth Avenue was just revealed to you by your conscious experience of puzzlement. Hence the continuation of your walk, unlike the initial walk, would have been motivated by desires that you knew.

In fact, however, your walking on, in this case, would not really have been a straightforward continuation of your initial walk. Instead of simply going home or catching a bus, as you had initially been doing, you would now have been looking for a reminder of what you had initially been doing, with the hope of resuming that course of action once you'd been reminded.[18] You would therefore have been doing something rather different. Even in this case, then, you would have suspended your puzzling conduct, in a sense, though without suspending your outward movements.

Similarly, you might have walked on simply out of an urge to savor the incongruity of the moment or to watch events unfold. But once again, you would not then have been continuing the conduct whose motives escaped you. Rather, you would have been shifting to a significantly different line of conduct, such as savoring the moment or playing spectator to the course of events, and your motives for pursuing these lines of conduct would have been clear to you.

As you walked on, in some of these cases, you might even have said to yourself, "I don't know why I'm doing this." But you wouldn't have meant it literally. You would have meant something like "I don't know why I started walking, and now I'm continuing out of nothing more

---

[18] Note that unless some reminder of your initial motive is in the offing, walking on is unlikely to help you understand your initial walk at all. In particular, you cannot hope, by watching yourself walk on, to detect the motive for your initial walk. For as you walked on, you would be manifesting different motives—in particular, the desire to be reminded of your initial motive, a desire that is not itself the initial motive of which you hope to be reminded.

Hume makes just this point in *A Treatise of Human Nature*, ed. P. H. Nidditch (Oxford, 1978): "[S]hould I endeavour to clear up . . . any doubt in moral philosophy, by placing myself in the same case with that which I consider, 'tis evident this reflection and premeditation would so disturb the operation of my natural principles, as must render it impossible to form any just conclusion from the phaenomenon" (xix).

than curiosity" or "I've forgotten why I came this way, but let's see what happens."[19] In short, you would have been expressing puzzlement only about the initial—now past—portion of your walk. You would not have meant that the present continuation of your walk continued to mystify you, as if to say, "Now, here's a perfectly baffling piece of behavior for you." If continuing up Fifth Avenue had been baffling to you, you wouldn't have continued.

I'll wager that you never find yourself expressing simple, ongoing bafflement at an ongoing piece of behavior. The reason is not, as some would claim, that you always know which motives you're acting on, just by virtue of acting on them. The reason is that your desire to understand what you're doing restrains you from going on with behavior once you realize that you don't know your motives for it.

REFLECTIVE UNDERSTANDING

This response to reflective puzzlement suggests an explanation why you usually understand your actions even as you undertake them. The explanation, briefly, is that actions you understand are usually the only ones you undertake.

On the surface, this explanation has a simple and familiar structure. All it says is that your efforts at making sense *of* a particular agent usually succeed because of his reciprocal efforts at making sense *to* you. What could be simpler than to explain that you understand someone partly because he's trying to make himself understood?

Well, in this case, plenty. For in this case, the explanation is not just that the agent tries to be understood but also that his efforts to be understood are inseparable from your efforts to understand him. The reason is that, in this case, the person understanding and the person understood are one and the same person—namely, you—and their motives are numerically identical. Your wanting to understand him is identical with his wanting to be understood by you, since you are identical with him (and you know it). Hence what moves you to make sense of him is identical with what moves him to make sense to you. No sooner do you try to grasp what he's doing than he tries to do what's within your grasp.

[19] The remark "I don't know why I'm doing this" can mean other things as well. It can mean, "I've lost my original motives for this behavior and now I'm continuing by habit or inertia"; it can mean, "I know my motives for this behavior and I don't like them"; it can mean, "My motives for doing this are far more charitable than you deserve." But it almost never means, literally, "I have no idea of what I am up to right now, even as I speak."

Unfortunately, this complication is only the first. Here's another. If you want to understand someone who's trying to be understood, then one of the things you must understand about him is that he's trying to be understood. And if he desires to be understood by you, then his so desiring is one of the things that he must make you understand. The collaboration between you and the agent therefore becomes complicated indeed, and these complications are further compounded by the convergence of these two roles in a single person.

Of course, you aren't conscious of carrying on such a complicated collaboration with yourself. Indeed, you aren't even conscious of occupying distinct roles as the person understanding and the person understood. But recall here that I am trying to explain your self-knowledge by imagining you in an unusual state of ignorance, and reflective ignorance does tend to divorce your acting and reflecting selves. When you find that you can't understand what you're doing, you suddenly face a choice between stepping back into passive reflection and pressing blindly on with action, and so these two roles are finally presented to you as distinct. I distinguish between these roles, then, because I am presenting them as they appear to you from the perspective of reflective ignorance.

The split between your active and reflective roles disappears when you once again understand what you're doing, but the split disappears, I believe, for the very same reason that your self-understanding returns. When you understand your actions again, the reason is that your two personas are once again working together—the one striving to understand the other, the other striving to make himself understood. And when a collaboration works so smoothly, the collaborators seem to fuse. In either role, you're so used to working with yourself in the other role that you and your alter ego lose your distinct identities. As we often say of close collaborators, you work as one person.

Let me apologize in advance for these complications, since I don't know how to eliminate them. The most I can do, I'm afraid, is to beg the reader to bear with me as I now resume the circuitous tale of a reflective agent—an agent who makes sense *of* himself by making sense *to* himself.

The Explanation

My story resumes with the sequel to your walk up Fifth Avenue. Now that you have stopped walking, what will you do next?

I suggest that you won't do anything until you can think of something understandable to do. Most of the steps that you could take next are steps for which you don't know of any motives. If you let yourself initiate such a step, you might subsequently recognize your motives for it, but recognizing your motives would take a moment, during which you'd already be doing something without knowing why.[20] What's worse, you'd have no assurance of recognizing your motives at all. What if you started to act and no motives came to mind? There you'd be, unable to account for your actions again.

Taking a step whose motives you don't already know might thus lead you back into the predicament you have just managed to escape. You are better off refusing to do anything, while you try to think of motives for doing something—that being the only action for which you already know of motives, and hence the only understandable thing for you to do, until you can think of motives for doing something else. For on the one hand, you already know that what moved you to curtail your walk was that you turned out to be ignorant of its motives. You are therefore aware of your motive for refusing to do anything unless you're conscious of knowing motives for it, and so that refusal, at least, is an action that you understand. On the other hand, simply refusing to do anything at all, without looking for motives for doing something else, would not be understandable, since it would be inconsistent with other motives of which you're aware. You know that you have numerous desires that favor actions other than simply warming the pavement here on Fifth Avenue, and you're aware of wanting those desires, whatever they are, to be fulfilled. This latter, second-order desire favors your trying to figure out what the former desires are; for until you identify those desires, any steps toward fulfilling them would strike you as potentially baffling, and so you'll be inhibited from taking any steps toward their fulfillment. Your desire to fulfill those desires, whatever they are, opposes allowing your ignorance of them to paralyze you indefinitely. Hence that desire is a motive for trying to identify your other desires. It is also a desire of which you're already aware. The one thing that you currently know of motives for doing, then, is trying to figure out what else you have motives for doing.

One clue to your other desires, of course, is your recent behavior, which indicates that some of them recently favored your walking up Fifth Avenue. Indeed, these are probably the desires whose fulfillment you would best be able to promote here and now—if only you knew

[20] What's more, many motives lead you to focus your attention outside yourself, on matters other than your own motives for acting. Hence letting yourself take a step at the behest of some unknown motive might, for all you know, lead to your being distracted from the task of detecting it. If so, you may not get around to detecting the motive until after you've finished acting on it—which will be too late, from the perspective of your desire to keep abreast of your actions.

what they were, so that you could promote their fulfillment without baffling yourself all over again. You may therefore continue to reflect on the motives for your walk up Fifth Avenue, not out of autobiographical curiosity, but in order to figure out what to do next. If this line of reflection fails, however, you will give up on your walk and try to identify motives for doing anything at all.

Now suppose you realize that you're aware of desiring something and of believing a particular step to be the best way of promoting it. That step will then be doubly attractive. You want something, first of all, and believe that the step will promote it. Even if you were unaware of having this desire and belief, they would incline you toward taking the step, but you might then take it without knowing why. My current supposition, however, is that you not only have these motives but also know that you have them, and know that you know. Hence you would understand taking the step that they are inclining you to take, and you know that you would understand it. The step in question therefore becomes all the more attractive to you, as a means to the self-understanding that you desire.

Your desire to understand whatever you're doing thus favors or opposes actions in proportion to their seeming intelligibility, thereby reinforcing or suppressing your other motives for these actions. It holds you back from actions that you perceive as potentially baffling and urges you on in actions that you perceive as potentially making sense. How you perceive an action in this respect depends, of course, on whether you think that you know of motives for performing it. The desire to understand your actions therefore restrains you from actions for which you aren't confident of knowing motives and encourages you in actions for which you are. It thereby detracts from the sum of motivational force in favor of the former actions while adding to the sum of motivational force in favor of the latter. And the result, presumably, is that you tend to avoid the seemingly unintelligible actions and to perform the seemingly intelligible ones.

Of course, your confidence in knowing motives for a particular action may be misplaced, and in that case, the desire for self-understanding may encourage you to take an action that you won't, in fact, understand. But nothing I have said is meant to imply that your self-understanding is guaranteed. I am the last one who would posit an infallible mechanism of self-understanding. What I am seeking to explain is how your self-understanding can be fallible and yet so unfailing.

My explanation is that your actions are screened in advance for their apparent intelligibility and that the appearance of intelligibility is a fair indicator of the reality. For if you feel able to explain an action, you usually have good reason. Perhaps you have consciously tried and succeeded at identifying your motives for the action, or they have just been brought to your attention spontaneously, or they are familiar to you from similar occasions in the past. Without these or comparable grounds for thinking that you could explain an action, you probably wouldn't think so; and so if you think that you can explain an action, you probably can. Consequently, the desire for self-understanding usually ends up favoring actions that you really do understand, by favoring the ones that you think you do; and similarly, it ends up opposing actions that you really don't understand, by opposing the ones that you think you don't.

The point, in any case, is not that you're especially prescient in estimating whether you can explain particular actions; it's rather that your estimate, however rough, helps to determine which actions you're inclined to perform, with the result that explaining the actions you do perform is not just a matter of hit or miss. The actions that get performed tend to be the ones that have passed the test of seeming explicable; and although seeming explicable is an imperfect test of being explicable, an imperfect test is better than none. My claim is that this imperfect test accounts for your impressive ability to explain your actions—which, though impressive, isn't perfect, either.

For the moment I want to disregard the imperfections, in both your self-understanding and the mechanism that accounts for it. I shall therefore adopt a vocabulary of success, by speaking of actions for which you're aware of knowing motives, for example, instead of saying that you merely think you know of motives for them. I adopt this manner of speech as a useful idealization and not in order to deny the possible discrepancies between your real and your apparent knowledge. I shall return in later chapters to a discussion of those discrepancies.[21]

Thus idealizing, I arrive at the following explanation of why you usually needn't infer your motives from your actions or hurry to identify them before they make you act. The reason is that you have an additional, intellectual motive for performing only those actions for which you're aware of knowing motives. Consequently, you needn't infer your motives from your actions, because you're deflected away from acting on motives that remain to be inferred, toward acting on motives that you already know; and you needn't hurry to identify your

---

[21] See chapter 4, 137–38, and chapter 9, 251–53.

motives before they make you act, because they're unlikely to make you act unless you've already identified them.

Questions

Now, this explanation is bound to raise various questions, all of which I hope to answer eventually. My answers to some questions won't emerge until chapter 3, I'm afraid. At present, I shall consider only the questions that I regard as most urgent—namely, the ones directed at the assumption that you want self-understanding.

Do you really care about self-understanding? The assumption that you want self-understanding may seem questionable, to begin with, because you rarely feel such a desire. You aren't continually pining for reflective insight or dreading reflective puzzlement. You feel no suspense over whether you'll understand your next action, and no relief or gratification when you do. How, then, can I claim that you want self-understanding, when the feelings that would be symptomatic of such a desire are absent?

My reply is simply to point out that many desires influence your behavior without being felt. I assume, for example, that you have an abiding desire to avoid pain and that this desire continually guides your conduct. Cross a street, lean on a fence, light a match, bite into a cherry, and your actions are being shaped and modified by your desire not to get hurt. Yet even as you perform these actions, getting hurt rarely crosses your mind. You do not live in continual dread of pain or in continual relief over having avoided it. The desire to avoid pain thus guides your conduct subliminally.

Indeed, this desire's behavioral effects may be what spare you from feeling it. The times when you feel how much you want to avoid pain are the times when you're in pain or directly threatened with it. And those times are rare precisely because the desire not to get hurt is always at work, steering you out of hurt's way. By doing its motivational job so well, this desire manages to stay in the background.

So it is with your desire to understand what you're doing. When you don't understand what you're doing, your desire for self-understanding makes itself felt plainly enough. But you usually do understand what you're doing, and hence don't feel how much you want to, precisely because that desire is continually at work, unobtrusively nudging you toward conduct that you understand. How often you feel the desire is therefore no indication of how often it influences your actions.

Experience has taught me that my answer to this particular objection, though usually accepted, is rarely assimilated. Whenever I speak

of the desire for self-understanding, readers continue to imagine desir-
ous feelings—hungerings and thirstings for self-understanding, of a
sort that no sane agent ever felt. I must therefore beg the reader to
remember that I am positing a largely subliminal desire, which troubles
the agent's consciousness only when it is thwarted and otherwise
guides him in silence.

If you want self-understanding, why don't you aim at it?   The claim
that you want self-understanding may still seem questionable, however, because almost none of your actions are aimed at attaining that
end. You almost never set your sights on self-understanding; so how
can I claim that you want it?

Here I reply that some ends are best attained by indirection—by actions aimed at the attainment of other ends.[22] Such is the case with self-
understanding, since the best way of attaining it is usually by pursuing
those ends whose pursuit you best understand.

Actions aimed primarily at promoting your self-understanding
might actually undermine it, since they wouldn't themselves be particularly understandable—except, of course, on those rare occasions
when your conduct has perplexed you. Then, as we have seen, it makes
sense for you to drop everything and reflect. Otherwise, however, de-
voting yourself entirely to reflection is not a particularly understandable thing to do; and effort spent on making sense of your conduct
would be wasted if such effort itself made no sense.[23]

If while you were engrossed in self-analysis, your career or marriage
were going to ruin, you would have to ask yourself—with redoubled
puzzlement—"What am I doing?" After all, you're aware of knowing
that you want a successful career and a successful marriage, and so
you're aware that if you aimed at professional or marital success, you
would understand your conduct and thus stand to gain, not only
professional or marital success, but self-understanding, to boot. Since
aiming at these other ends strikes you as a fully effective means to self-

---

[22] This point is often made about happiness as an end. See, e.g., Henry Sidgwick, *The
Methods of Ethics* (Indianapolis, 1981), 136ff.

[23] See Hamlyn, "Self-Knowledge": "[G]enuine self-knowledge presupposes that we
must *be* ourselves and not be in the position of standing back from ourselves in any way.
We shall be in that position either if we insist on regarding ourselves theoretically all the
time or if, under the influence of a theory, we concentrate our consciousness and attention on one part of ourselves" (194). For a related point, see: "Someone who has true
insight into himself needs to be aware of what he is to others, but he does not need to be
looking over his shoulder all the time to see how others are regarding him; to do so
would inhibit a concern for and commitment to what he is engaged in and thus one of
the essential conditions of self-knowledge proper would be missing" (174).

understanding, your desire for self-understanding favors your aiming at them, although it may also favor, as an equally effective means, your aiming at self-understanding directly. Your desires for the other ends, however, favor only your aiming at those ends and not your aiming at self-understanding, since you don't think that aiming at self-under-standing would yield, as byproducts, a promotion at the office or a reconciliation at home.

Hence if you're aware of knowing about desires for ends other than self-understanding, then your desire for self-understanding will incline you in the direction of those other ends at least as much as it inclines you in the direction of self-understanding itself, whereas your desires for the other ends will always incline you toward those ends alone. Your motives will therefore seem on balance to favor your pursuing those other ends, and so pursuing those other ends will be the only action that you feel prepared to explain, after all.[24]

You will therefore regard the pursuit of your other ends as intelligible and the pursuit of self-understanding as potentially puzzling. How could you ever explain seeking self-understanding at the expense of your career or marriage, when you could attain it by attending to them instead? The best way to understand what you're doing will be to pursue your professional and marital ends—and you'll know it. Consequently, your desire for self-understanding won't favor the direct pursuit of self-understanding, after all; it will favor only the pursuit of those ends whose pursuit you're prepared to explain.

Thus, your desire to understand your conduct is not to be measured by your apparent dedication to that end. This desire attains its object by indirection—by bolstering other motives and letting them take the lead.

What kind of self-understanding do you want? My claim that you want self-understanding would indeed be questionable if it carried undue assumptions about the kind of self-understanding that you want; but it doesn't. Naturally, I have illustrated my explanation of self-understanding with a particular case, in which an agent seeks and attains self-understanding of a particular kind. But I am willing to concede—indeed, eager to affirm—that different agents seek and attain different kinds of self-understanding.

When the *National Enquirer* tells us that Inquiring Minds Want to

---

[24] You'll know that if you did something other than that which seemed to be favored by the balance of your known motives, you would have to assume that you did it under the influence of motives still unknown—in which case, you would have to concede ignorance of your motives for doing it.

Know, we are suddenly reminded that not all inquiring minds want the same thing. The difference is not just that some but not others want to know about the latest doings of Elvis Presley's ghost; it's also that some but not others regard ghosts as a possibility, and knowledge about them as something to be found in the *National Enquirer*.

The point here is that even if all people have the same concept of the truth, different people have different conceptions of what the truth might contain and how to tell whether they have discovered its contents. Consequently, their intellectual appetites tend to be satisfied by different cognitive outcomes. Among those who want self-understanding, some won't feel that they can explain an action unless they have a Freudian diagnosis of it, complete with cross references to the master's own cases; others will find an action intelligible so long as it resembles the behavior of a fictional character with whom they identify; and yet others will go by their horoscopes. I have chosen as my example an agent with more mundane intellectual tastes—an agent who favors commonsense explanations couched in terms of familiar motives.

I shall continue to use this and similar examples, since they are most likely to reflect the experience of my readers. I state here, once and for all, that these examples are not intended to exhaust the possibilities. My explanation of self-understanding doesn't assume that everyone wants the same kind of reflective knowledge. All it says is that everyone wants reflective knowledge of some kind; and it explains how they manage to attain the object of their desire.

What about self-deception?   Another reason for questioning my claim that you want self-understanding is that you probably try to avoid acknowledging the motives behind some of your actions. Reflective knowledge is frequently an object of aversion. How, then, can I assume that you always desire it?

I agree that people are often afraid of knowing the truth about themselves. But this aversion coexists with the desire that I have in mind.

When we say that someone is afraid of the truth about himself, we mean, not that he wants to avoid believing anything that may be true about him, but that there is something about him that he wants to avoid believing and it happens to be true. He's not afraid of self-knowledge per se—that is, of being able to name and explain his actions. Rather, he's afraid of a particular name or explanation, which turns out to be the one that, in the circumstances, would furnish the content of self-knowledge.

There are therefore two respects in which the fear of self-knowledge fails to present direct opposition to the desire that I have posited. To begin with, the fear is narrower in scope than the desire. The agent is averse only to knowing about particular actions, and this aversion would amount, at most, to a local reversal of the desire to have such knowledge by and large. But it doesn't even amount to that, because the object of the aversion differs in kind from the object of the desire. What the agent wants, according to my explanation, is self-knowledge described merely as such, irrespective of its content; whereas what he fears is the content of self-knowledge in a particular case. His desire is for something in the shape of the true account of his conduct; his aversion is to the stuff of which the true account would be made.

Clearly, these two attitudes exist side by side. Even as a person recoils from a particular item of self-knowledge, he's still attracted to the idea of self-knowledge in the abstract. He'd still like to know and understand what he's doing; he'd simply like to avoid the particular self-descriptions that such knowledge would currently entail. Here is a conflict of a familiar kind, between the desire for an end and an aversion to the necessary materials or means.

I suspect that if the aversion to self-knowledge didn't encounter a conflicting desire, it wouldn't motivate self-deception at all. For suppose that an agent was not only averse to the particulars of the truth about an action but also indifferent to self-knowledge per se. In that case, he would simply ignore the action in question, omitting to account for it at all. Dissatisfied with the content of knowledge about the action, he would be perfectly willing to make do with ignorance. The result would be, not self-deception, but merely self-ignorance. In reality, however, an agent who dislikes the truth that's available usually supplies himself with a plausible substitute, and he does so precisely because he also dislikes reflective ignorance. He feeds himself a bogus account of his conduct in order to pacify his appetite for self-knowledge without having to swallow the unpalatable truth.[25]

Here let me add that self-deception is not always motivated by an aversion to a particular truth: sometimes it's motivated by an affection for a particular falsehood. An agent sometimes indulges in a fiction about himself, not because the truth is unacceptable, but simply because the fiction is so appealing. In such cases, the motive for self-deception operates much like the ordinary motive for self-inquiry. That is, just as an agent's desire for genuine self-understanding inclines him

[25] Of course, it is a serious philosophical question how a person can placate himself with a story that he knows to be false. But I am not concerned here with this, the central question of self-deception. I am concerned not with the method of self-deception but with the motives for it—and in particular, whether those motives are incompatible with the desire for self-understanding.

toward actions that fit genuine explanations that he already knows, so his desire to maintain a particular pretense about himself inclines him toward actions that fit the pretense.

(Note, by the way, that this analogy provides another means of describing the mechanism of genuine self-understanding. We are all familiar with the practice of living out a fantasy. We can now see that self-understanding results from a corresponding practice, which might be called living out the truth.)

In any case, the question arises, once again, whether an agent who is bent on living out a fantasy still wants genuine self-understanding, too. And once again, I don't see why he shouldn't. As before, the motive for self-deception isn't diametrically opposed to the desire for self-understanding. It isn't the desire to believe falsehoods per se; it's the desire to believe particular things, which happen to be false.

Admittedly, the desired beliefs, being false, pose an obstacle to the goal of genuine self-understanding. But wanting things that would stand in the way of one's goals is hardly unusual. The self-deceiving agent suffers a familiar kind of conflict among his desires, and his self-deception is an attempt to evade this conflict, by having it both ways. One of the attractions of self-deception is a smug sense of self-knowledge—a satisfaction in which the self-deceiver indulges undeservedly but with no less relish than the honest self-inquirer.

No matter how self-deception is motivated, of course, the balance of motives, where self-deception occurs, will be different from the one that I have posited in my explanation of self-understanding. But in such cases there is no self-knowledge to explain. I readily concede that these cases are exceptions to my theory, since they are exceptions to the explanandum as well. All that I have tried to establish here is that cases of self-deception do not undermine my claim that you want self-understanding. And I have established this much simply by showing that the desire for self-understanding coexists with the motives for self-deception.

What about understandable misbehavior?   My claim that you want self-understanding may also seem to be undermined by this simple observation, that when you find yourself falling into some unfortunate pattern of behavior, knowing your motives for it is no consolation. If you ask yourself why you keep making sophomoric wisecracks in front of your senior colleagues, you may suddenly realize that you're trying to discredit yourself in order to punish your father for demanding that you become a success. But does this knowledge reconcile you to the offending behavior? The next time you feel a wisecrack coming on, will its greater intelligibility now move you to welcome it or to deliver yourself of it with any less self-loathing? Hardly. How, then, can I claim that you have a motive in favor of actions that you understand?

My answer here is two-fold. On the one hand, I believe that understanding your obnoxious behavior does render it, though no less obnoxious, at least less unsettling to you. Previously your little outbursts were doubly unpleasant, since they not only offended but also perplexed you; now they are at least intelligible, though admittedly still offensive. My claim that you want self-understanding does not entail that every intelligible action will be wholly attractive to you, no matter what its potential drawbacks. All my claim entails is that intelligibility will make an action somewhat more attractive—or, as in this case, somewhat less unattractive—than it otherwise would have been.[26]

On the other hand, I believe that cases like the present one involve significant complexities that I'm not currently in a position to analyze. I shall return to them later, first in chapter 7 and again in chapters 9 and 10. All I can do at the moment is to point out that if you regard your behavior as unfortunate, then you probably know of significant motives for refraining from it, and that if you know of significant motives for refraining from the behavior, then the intelligibility of continuing it is questionable. You may know your motives for acting the fool, but the realization that you hate yourself for it should make you ask, "Why do I go on?" Thus, the cases in question aren't necessarily cases in which an action is undesirable despite being fully intelligible.

What the present objection shows, I think, is not that you lack a desire for self-understanding but that the self-understanding you desire entails more than a mere awareness of some motive or other for what you're doing. How much more it entails is a question that I shall have to postpone.

Do you want self-understanding for its own sake? Note that my explanation of self-understanding presupposes not just that you want self-understanding but that you want it for its own sake. Yet one can easily imagine other desirable ends to which self-understanding would be a means, and one may therefore ask whether you want self-understanding as a means to these other ends rather than as an end in itself.

I have already assumed, for example, that you want your desires to be fulfilled. But when you don't understand what you're doing, your

[26] Of course, the explanation of your behavior may dismay you. But this possibility falls within the scope of my comments on self-deception. That is, understanding your conduct per se is still preferable to being baffled by it, but the contents of self-understanding, on this occasion, are not as you would have preferred.

actions often fail to fulfill the desires that motivate them. Suppose that you walk up Fifth Avenue out of a desire to reach a particular destination. If you then forget why you're walking up Fifth Avenue, you become more likely to take a wrong turn and to find yourself in a place where you have no desire to be. Conversely, knowing what you're doing helps you to do it in such a way as to secure the desired outcome. Self-understanding is thus desirable as a means to desire-fulfillment.

Why, then, do I posit a desire for self-understanding in itself, when your desire for self-understanding might be explained as subordinate to other desires? Let me answer this question by inviting you to join me in a thought experiment.

Imagine that all your endeavors, though perfectly successful, were like your walk up Fifth Avenue, taking you by surprise and leaving you baffled. Imagine always being sure that your conduct was promoting some desired outcome and yet never knowing what the desired outcome was. Imagine, in other words, living in a perpetual state of self-puzzlement but without any of its attendant inconveniences. I think that once you have conjured up such a life, you will find it undesirable, to say the least, and that the absence of inconveniences won't ameliorate the prospect. In this life you would be hemmed in by unknowns at every turn, since your every turn would itself be an unknown. Your own trajectory through the world would strike you as a strange phenomenon. What could be more upsetting?

I therefore assume that you have a desire for self-understanding and that this desire is not entirely subordinate to your desire for desire-fulfillment. No doubt, you want self-understanding as a means to other ends, but you also want it as an end in itself.

Maybe the reason why I do not hesitate to posit such a desire is that I am inclined to regard having intellectual motives, in general, as necessary to having an intellect at all. The traditional division of mental faculties tends to mislead us into thinking that Reason (as Hume would call it) is an inert calculating machine that could in principle exist in a creature who had no intellectual passions—that the intellectual faculty is all gears and no springs. We therefore imagine that one could have the capacity to understand the world and yet have no desire to understand it. However plausible this view may be at first, it strikes me, upon closer inspection, as quite bizarre. Doesn't our ability to understand things depend upon, and indeed partly consist in, preferences among possible cognitive outcomes? Our ability to understand doesn't seem like a dispassionate capacity to recognize good explanations whether or not we care about having them; rather, it depends on our liking some explanations more than others, on our finding some explanations more satisfying or more pleasing. The ability itself thus seems to require motivational forces. If we weren't drawn to some hypotheses, as offering comprehension, and put off by others, as threatening confusion, we might not have a capacity to theorize at all. I therefore suspect that claiming intellectual apathy may be incompatible with claiming intelligence.

Of course, the desire to understand oneself, in particular, is hardly essential to intelligence. The essential motive is more likely to be, say, a desire to make sense of one's world. But one's self is the core of one's world and is therefore bound to fall within the focus of any general inquisitiveness. How, then, could you, intelligent creature that you are, lack a motive for making sense of your own behavior?

How badly do you want self-understanding? Even if one grants my assumption that you have an intrinsic desire to understand your actions, one may still object that I have attributed an implausible degree of strength to that desire. One may think that your desire for self-understanding is at most a faint inclination, whereas I have made it sound like an inexorable drive. How can I assume that you want self-understanding so badly?

My answer is simply that I don't. My explanation of how you understand your actions doesn't presuppose that your desire to understand them is especially strong. My explanation requires only that your desire for self-understanding be strong enough to detain you temporarily from acting on other desires, until you find an intelligible course of action, and that it be strong enough to tip the balance of motives in favor of some action that you find intelligible. Neither of these tasks requires great strength.

The former task—that of detaining you from acting until you find an intelligible action—doesn't require that your desire for self-understanding be stronger than your desire for any other end. For even when you want an end very badly, your pursuit of it can be postponed by relatively minor concerns, simply because your desire for the end, though strong, is not especially urgent. Of course, if what you want is to attain the end without delay, then only a stronger desire can restrain you; but in most cases, what you want is to attain your end sooner or later, and so you can be temporarily deflected from pursuing it in order to secure results that you desire less strongly but more immediately. Since self-understanding is something that you continually want here and now, it is just the kind of thing that can briefly distract you from ends that you desire more.

The latter function of the desire for self-understanding—that of tip-

ping the motivational balance in favor of intelligible actions—also
doesn't require that it be stronger than your other desires. In order to
prefer intelligible actions to unintelligible ones, you needn't desire intelligibility more than anything else. You need desire it only enough to
make up the differences between your other motives for the actions
available to you. The intelligibility of an action is almost never its main
attraction; it's simply enough of an added attraction to sway you from
any unintelligible actions toward which you might otherwise have
been more inclined.

Finally, let me reiterate that my explanation doesn't require that
your desire for self-understanding be strong enough to perform its
tasks at all times without fail. Sometimes you have an urgent impulse
that makes you do something that baffles you; sometimes you become
so engrossed in a course of action that you find yourself unable to explain its issue; sometimes, in short, you find yourself asking "What am
I doing?" What I have sought to explain is why you understand what
you're doing most of the time, given that you can sometimes fail to
understand it.

CONCLUSION

Note that I have explained why you tend to know of motives for your
actions, but not why you tend to know which motives you're acting
on—that is, which of all the motives known to you are behind your
current action. My answer to the latter question is roughly this. The
reason why you know which motives you're acting on is that you know
what you're doing and (for reasons that I *have* explained) you know
your motives for doing it. The question how you know which motives
you're acting on is thus replaced by the question how you know what
you're doing. That question will be my next concern.

TWO

SELF-AWARENESS

What has occupied me thus far is your self-understanding, or your ability to explain what you're doing. I have not yet discussed your ability simply to name what you're doing—to give a prima facie description of your action. The latter ability is also a form of self-knowledge, which I shall call practical self-awareness.[1] Its explanation is the topic of this chapter.

What needs explaining in the case of practical self-awareness is that its crucial component seems to come without observation or inference. You do need to discover, or to have discovered in the past, what you're capable of doing. But among the many things that you're capable of doing, which one you're actually doing doesn't dawn on you as a further discovery. You don't find out what you're doing; in the normal case, you already know, because doing it was your idea, to begin with. Your practical self-awareness therefore seems to constitute spontaneous knowledge, generated from within, not discovered from without.

My explanation of practical self-awareness and its spontaneity will be analogous to my explanation of practical self-understanding. The reason why you usually know what you're doing without having to find out, I shall argue, lies in the motivational effects of your desire to know.

REFLECTIVE SURVEILLANCE AND
ITS DRAWBACKS

My explanation must therefore begin with the assumption that you want not only to understand actions if you perform them but also to know, in the first place, whether you are in fact performing them.[2] This

---

[1] Note that I am using the term 'awareness' for knowledge that is dispositional in form. In particular, being aware of what you're doing consists in being able to name your current action, not necessarily in having the name of that action before your mind.

[2] See my characterization of the former desire (chapter 1, 27–30) for distinctions that also apply to the latter. In particular, I shall assume that your desire to know what you're doing is the desire to know about any action that satisfies the description 'what you're

latter desire played no part in my story about your walk up Fifth Avenue, because my story began at a point when you already knew that
you were walking up Fifth Avenue. Until then, however, you could
have been ignorant of your very movements as well as their motives.
And I assume that you want to avoid, not only being puzzled by the
actions of which you're aware, but also being unaware of your actions.

Of course, you can learn of your movements simply by paying attention to them. If only you watch out for your next move, you can ensure
that you'll make no move unawares. Unfortunately, what you learn in
this fashion would often be too little or too late.

Suppose that after stopping your walk up Fifth Avenue, you turn
and walk back downtown. A moment's observation will tell you that
you're turning and walking back, but a moment's observation will take
a moment, during which you won't know what you're doing. As you
bestir yourself, as you raise your foot, you won't yet know that you're
turning around; as you swivel your hips, you may see that a turn is in
progress, but you won't yet know how sharp a turn; and in general,
the beginnings of an action won't immediately suggest its prima facie
description.

Reflective surveillance would be adequate, of course, if you could be
content with identifying your conduct in minute stages. As soon as you
stir, you'll be able to tell that you're stirring; as soon as you lift your
foot, you'll be able to tell that you're lifting it. But surely such knowledge is not enough to satisfy you. As you stir, you're not just stirring:
you're starting some larger action, such as walking back downtown,
which will occupy more than an instant. Surely, you want to know
what larger action you're starting, and you want to know as soon as
you start it. The problem is that you won't learn so much so soon
simply by watching yourself act.

REFLECTIVE FORESIGHT

What can prevent your actions from outrunning your awareness is
your forecasting them in advance. Instead of waiting to see what larger
action you'll start next, you can try to anticipate it, so that when you
start something, you'll already know what sort of action it will turn

---

doing'—though, of course, to know about it under some more specific description. I
shall also assume that this desire is not a desire to know, once and for all, what you're
doing now but rather a desire to know, at any moment, what you're doing then. Furthermore, I shall assume that the desire in question is for dispositional knowledge—that
is, for the ability to say what you're doing, if you try. Finally, this desire is just as un-
obtrusive as your desire to understand what you're doing, and for the same reasons.

out to be. If you thus anticipate your actions, you will never find yourself falling behind in your knowledge of them. Your desire to stay abreast of what you're doing is therefore a motive for bringing it about that you foresee what you're going to do next.

Now, you might try to foresee your forthcoming actions by looking for clues that foreshadowed them. Your present thoughts and feelings, your long-established aspirations, the exigencies of your situation, your past record of behavior—all shed light on your future conduct. Unfortunately, the light they shed is often dim or deceptive. If you had to rely on behavioral forecasting, in the present state of that art, you'd often expect to do one thing and then find yourself doing another.[3]

Two Means to Reflective Foresight

Fortunately, however, you needn't rely on such reflective forecasting. Reflective foresight, like reflective understanding, can be reached by two coordinate paths—both by the right sort of inquiry and by the right sort of action. On the one hand, you can anticipate what you're going to do; on the other hand, you can do what you already anticipate. Either way, by the time you do something, you will have anticipated doing it.

The desire to know what you're doing therefore disposes you to undertake only those actions which you're aware of expecting yourself to perform. Until there is something that you consciously expect to do next, the desire to know what you're doing restrains you from so much as stirring. Stirring at such a time would amount, in your eyes, to starting an action that you might not identify until it was well underway— during which time you wouldn't know what you were doing. The desire to know what you're doing therefore opposes your doing anything. But once there is something that you consciously expect to do next, you know that you'll regard your next move as the beginning of that action and hence that if you begin that action, you'll know from the outset what you're doing.[4] At this point, the desire to know what you're doing favors the action that you're aware of expecting. You also know, however, that if you happen to begin a different action, you'll first mistake it for the expected one, and then you'll have to identify it

[3] I discuss this possibility at greater length in chapter 4, 137–38ff.
[4] Here one might think that I am claiming more than I'm entitled to. I say that if you begin the action that you expect, you'll know from the outset what you're doing. One might think that I am entitled to say, not that you'll *know* what you're doing, but only that you'll have a true belief about it. For I haven't shown that the expectation you fulfill will be appropriately justified, and so I haven't shown that it will satisfy the criteria of knowledge. I ask the reader to withhold this objection briefly. It will be answered later.

from scratch—not knowing, in the meantime, what you're doing. The desire to know what you're doing therefore favors the expected action only and continues to oppose any others.

In short, you can bring it about that you know what you're doing, as soon as you're doing something, if you bring it about that you have anticipated doing precisely that which you end up doing; and to have anticipated doing precisely that which you end up doing is the same as to end up doing precisely that which you have anticipated. Doing all and only the things that you've anticipated will therefore have the result that you know what you're doing. The desire to know what you're doing therefore moves you to do whatever you're aware of anticipating and restrains you from doing anything else.

Note that the desire for self-awareness, like the desire for self-understanding, interacts with your self-knowledge indirectly, through your beliefs about it. Just as your desire for self-understanding will move you to do things that you think you understand, even if you don't really understand them; so, too, your desire for self-awareness will move you to do things that you think you expect, even if you don't really expect them. But there is this difference. You can utterly fail to understand something despite thinking that you understand it, but you cannot entirely fail to expect something that you think you expect, since to think that you expect something is already, in some sense, to expect it. Of course, you may on occasion speak of being surprised or disappointed by something that you mistakenly thought you expected, but what you mean in such a case is that you found yourself inadequately braced for the ostensibly expected outcome, not that you found yourself unable to identify it. All that your remark implies, then, is that thinking you expected the outcome turned out to be quite different from actually expecting it insofar as concerns how you were prepared to feel and to act about it. As for how you were prepared to describe the outcome, however, your apparent expectation was just as good as a real one. For whether you actually expected the event under a particular description or merely believed that you did, you would still have been prepared to apply that description when the event arrived.

Hence whether you do what you expect or what you only think that you expect, you'll still end up knowing what you're doing, in the sense that interests me. I shall therefore feel free to gloss over the distinction between actual, conscious expectations and merely apparent ones. When I speak about what you expect, I shall assume that you're aware of expecting it, and I shall ignore whether that awareness is entirely accurate in respect to your emotional preparedness for the outcome in question.

Thus simplified, my argument can be summarized like this. Your desire to know what you're doing moves you to do whatever you expect to do next and restrains you from doing otherwise. It thereby ensures that whatever you do, you will already have anticipated—which is a means of ensuring that you know what you're doing.

Ancillary Means

But wait. Simply foreseeing which action will be your next one may not be sufficient for practical self-awareness. True enough, if you foresee that your next action will be to walk downtown, then as soon as you know that you've started doing something, you'll know that walking downtown is what you've started doing. But you might start doing something without knowing that you'd started doing anything at all. Suppose, for instance, that you take several steps before it ever dawns on you that you're no longer standing still. By the time you realize that you're doing something—and hence that you're walking downtown—you will have already been walking downtown, without knowing that you were doing so. Your return trip will have been gathering speed even as you were still waiting for it to begin. Once again, you will have missed the boat.

The first ancillary means. This problem, at least, self-surveillance can help you to avoid. As we have seen, you cannot immediately see what you're doing simply by watching yourself do it. But if you already know *what* you're going to do, then you will be able to see *that* you've started doing it, so long as you're watching at the time. Hence you can bring it about that you know from the outset what you're doing if you bring it about, not only that you will have anticipated your next action, but also that you'll be paying attention when it begins.

As before, there are two coordinate paths to the result that you're paying attention when you start doing something: you can pay attention until you're doing it, or you can not do it until you're paying attention. Of course, the latter path is the more efficient. For if your next action might start at any moment, then in order to ensure that you're watching when it starts, you must watch yourself constantly; but if your next action won't start until you're watching, you can let yourself be distracted without fear of missing anything.[5] Your desire to know

---

[5] Young children quickly learn a corresponding lesson at the playground. When they first start climbing on the jungle gym, for instance, they try to make Daddy watch constantly, lest he miss one of their tricks. But they soon figure out that if they want Daddy to see a trick, they should wait to do it until he's watching.

what you're doing therefore favors postponing your next action until you're ready to see it begin.[6]

But ensuring that you'll see yourself start an action is not the only way of ensuring that you'll know when it starts. There is yet one more path to self-awareness, which I shall illustrate by reverting to your adventures on Fifth Avenue.

The second ancillary means.   When we last saw you, you had just anticipated that your next move would be to walk downtown. Suppose, now, that you became convinced not just that walking downtown was what you'd do next but also that you'd start walking then and there. In that case, if you had started walking then and there, you would have started at a time when you had just noted that you were just about to start. Since your action would thus have been immediately preceded by the expectation that it would immediately follow, it could hardly have caught you by surprise.

Conversely, if you hadn't immediately started walking, your staying at rest might not have registered for a moment—a moment during which you would have been confused about what you were doing. Of course, your staying at rest would not thus have taken a moment to register if you had waited to see whether you'd start. But waiting to see whether you'd start would have required a different frame of mind from being convinced that you would.[7] Once you formed a firm expectation of starting immediately, that expectation could not have been immediately disappointed without some confusion.

Seeing yourself start your next action is thus not the only thing that can prevent your being caught unawares when the action starts; another is starting the action just after you've become convinced that it's just about to start. And once you have become convinced that your

---

[6] Of course, your lack of attention won't deter you from acting if you're unaware of it: unless you know that you're not ready to see yourself act, you won't be moved to wait until you are. And sometimes when you're oblivious of yourself, you're oblivious even of your own oblivion. Such are the occasions when your conduct can get away from you. On other occasions, however, you knowingly direct your attention away from your own actions; and on these latter occasions, you can indeed be moved to postpone your next action until you're aware of paying attention once again.

[7] This point depends on the view that expectations aren't thoughts, or mental assertions, but dispositional states. Being sure that you're going to act is not a matter of saying to yourself emphatically, "I'm going to act." Rather, it's a state that disposes you to think and feel and do various things. One of the things it disposes you to think is "I'm going to act"; one of the things it disposes you to do is to look no further into the question whether you're going to act. Hence it disposes you not to notice right away if your expectation isn't borne out.

next action is just about to start, starting it immediately is the only thing that will prevent the converse surprise.

Your desire to know what you're doing therefore filters your actions in the following, rather complicated way. Until there's something that you expect to do next, this desire restrains you from doing anything. Once there's something that you expect to do next, it decisively restrains you from doing anything else, and it tentatively restrains you from doing even what you expect, either until you're paying attention or until you've just become convinced that you're just about to do it. Then the desire to know what you're doing encourages you to begin the expected action.

Here, then, is the kernel of my explanation for practical self-awareness. The reason why you usually know what you're doing, I contend, is that you simply don't do anything unless, first, you have already anticipated doing it next and, second, you have either just become aware of being just about to do it or just started paying attention to what you're doing. Your inhibition against doing anything you haven't expected to do next, or aren't prepared to see now, ensures that no action of yours will catch you unawares—which is the same as ensuring that you know what you're doing.

Objections

This explanation requires much elaboration and defense. In particular, the question arises how you ever expect to do anything next or to start anything now, given that you're restrained from doing anything until you expect to. I shall answer this question presently, in this and the following section, but first I want to introduce some other possible objections.

Repeats. My explanation of practical self-awareness raises many of the same questions as my explanation of practical self-understanding. In particular, the reader may be skeptical about the desire I have posited—in this case, the desire for self-awareness—on the grounds that one rarely feels such a desire or takes aim at its object. My answer to this question has the same form as it had in chapter 1,[8] although some of the details in the present case will not emerge until later.

What will emerge in due course is that the desire for self-awareness is almost never an agent's primary motive for an action. Rather, this desire tips the balance among the agent's other motives, promoting its object by steering the agent toward actions aimed at the objects of

[8] See 37–39.

other desires. What the agent expects himself to do, and is therefore encouraged to do by his desire for self-awareness, is to take some action in pursuit of an end other than self-awareness. And he is thereby spared the need to feel his desire for self-awareness or to aim at its fulfillment. Because the agent is subtly inhibited from unanticipated actions and subtly inclined toward the actions that he anticipates, he rarely has to face the unpleasantness of reflective ignorance or to consider how it can be avoided. His not feeling the desire for self-awareness and his not aiming at its object are therefore evidence of the desire's influence rather than of its absence.

Thus, my explanation of practical self-awareness must not be read in an unduly rationalistic sense.[9] When I say that an agent wants to know what he's doing, and that this desire moves him to do what he expects, I do not mean that he consciously thirsts after self-awareness and deliberately bears out his expectations in pursuit of that end. I mean that his pursuit of other ends is selectively inhibited or encouraged by a largely unnoticed desire—in ways that have yet to be fully explained.

Apparent counterexamples.   I have claimed that expecting an action causes your desire for self-awareness to reinforce your motives for it. This claim may appear to be refuted by ordinary experience. Consider the times when you realize, in the heat of an argument, that you're about to raise your voice. This realization doesn't move you to raise your voice; on the contrary, it often restrains you. Similarly, the expectation that you're about to step into the path of oncoming traffic causes you to recoil. How can I account for the failure of these expectations to encourage the actions that they represent?

My answer is twofold. To begin with, I doubt whether the cases that are initially called to mind by the foregoing descriptions actually involve expectations of acting. What you usually realize in the heat of an argument, I think, is not that you are going to raise your voice but rather that you're going to raise it if you go on speaking—that you'll start shouting if you don't shut up. And the realization that you'll start shouting if you don't shut up is not a positive expectation of shouting, any more than it's an expectation of shutting up. Hence its failure to make you shout, rather than shut up, should be no surprise.

Of course, one can always call different cases to mind—cases in which you do positively expect to raise your voice or to step into traffic. And one can point out that in such cases, although you regard

[9] See my general comments on this problem in the Introduction, 10–11.

the expected actions as beyond physical recall, your expectation still makes you rebel against them in spirit. Why, one might ask, doesn't your desire for self-awareness move you to embrace these actions once you see them coming?

Here my answer is that your desire for self-awareness is simply overwhelmed by countervailing motives that are also aroused by your expectations. The descriptions under which you come to expect these actions are descriptions under which you have strong motives against performing them. Although you want to win the argument, you don't want to raise your voice, and although you want to cross the street, you don't want to step into traffic. Consequently, the realization that what you're about to do is to raise your voice, or to step into traffic, arouses powerful motives against doing it, and these motives overwhelm any attraction that the action might have gained by virtue of being expected.

Yet one would be wrong to conclude that being expected has lent these actions no attraction at all simply because that attraction has been outweighed. Surely, if you're going to start shouting, you'd prefer not to be startled by your own voice, and so an expectation of shouting makes your shouting somewhat less undesirable than it otherwise would have been. The overall effect of your expectation is still inhibitive, but only because it arouses your aversion to shouting as well as your inclination to do what you expect. Similarly, you'd rather step into traffic knowingly than unawares, but since you'd rather not step into traffic at all, the knowledge that you're going to is more alarming than it is encouraging. Thus, cases in which you realize that you're about to do something undesirable do not disprove my claim that an action is made more desirable by virtue of being expected, and so they cannot disprove my claim that the expectation of doing something gives you some additional motive for doing it.

Failures. Even if you expect to do a thing, of course, you may be incapable of doing it. Your expectation may remove a motivational obstacle to the performance—namely, your inhibition against doing something without knowing what—but it cannot remove physical obstacles. Expecting to open the window won't overcome a temporary paralysis of the arm or an unseen nail in the sash. Hence you sometimes fail to do what you expect. One might therefore object that your expectation of acting cannot constitute knowledge, as I have claimed. You don't really know what you're going to do, one might think, until you see whether anything prevents the expected action. Until the possibility of failure is ruled out, your expectation of acting must amount to something less than knowledge.

This objection simply disregards the standards of justification that I laid down in chapter 1.[10] When I say that your expectation of acting constitutes knowledge, I do not mean that it is incorrigible or absolutely certain. I mean that it is sufficiently justified to count as knowledge, by ordinary standards, if it turns out to be true. Naturally, you mustn't expect to do something if you have no reason to believe that you can or if you have good reason to believe that you can't. But on any occasion there are usually many actions of which you justifiedly believe yourself capable. And if you then turn out to be capable of those actions in fact, then you are said to have known that you were capable of them, even though you might in principle have been mistaken. Similarly, if you expect to perform one of those actions and you do in fact perform it, then you can be said to have known that you were going to, despite any residual possibility of error.

Justification.   Yet in order for your expectation to qualify as knowledge, even by ordinary standards, it would have to be justified. And the expectation in question seems to be one for which justification is necessarily unattainable. For how could you ever have grounds for expecting an action whose very occurrence would remain unlikely until you expected it? You would never have justification for forming this expectation unless you'd already formed it, and so you could never justifiedly form it, in the first place.[11]

My answer to this objection has two parts. On the one hand, I shall point out that as soon as you consciously expect an action, your expectation is fully justified, by your awareness of expecting the action and of being inclined to do what you expect. Your expectation is therefore not only true but also appropriately justified, and so it qualifies as knowledge. On the other hand, the evidence by which you justify your expectation necessarily includes your having that expectation, and this evidence was lacking until the expectation was formed. You therefore must have formed the expectation in the absence of sufficient evidence for it, but I shall argue that you were perfectly within your rights to do

---

[10] See 19–20.

[11] See Grice, "Intention and Uncertainty": "For if my going to London is to depend causally on my acceptance that I shall go, the possession of satisfactory evidence that I shall go will involve possession of the information that I accept that I shall go. Obviously, then, I cannot (though others can) come to accept that I shall go on the basis of satisfactory evidence; for to have such evidence I should have *already* to have accepted that I shall go" (274).

so. The reason is that in forming an expectation of acting, you needn't rely on evidence. You can rely instead on your tendency to do what you expect.[12]

REFLECTIVE METHODOLOGY

Let me begin with the latter claim—namely, that your inclination to do what you expect entitles you to form reflective expectations in the absence of evidence. This claim will come to the fore in future chapters, especially chapter 5, where it will be discussed and defended at length. Here I shall provide it with a preliminary defense.

The Extent to Which You Must Follow the Evidence

Note first what my claim does not say: it doesn't say that your inclination to do what you expect entitles you to expect any action whatsoever, regardless of the evidence. For as I have already mentioned, your expectation of doing something cannot overcome physical obstacles to your doing it; and I should add that there may be motivational obstacles that it cannot overcome, either.

For example, your inclination to do as you expect wouldn't make you dance naked down Fifth Avenue, even if you expected to. True, if you expected to dance naked down Fifth Avenue, then the prospect of doing so would have the added attraction that you would know what you were doing from the very first pirouette. But the attraction of knowing what you were doing wouldn't be strong enough to outweigh the deterrent of looking like a fool—not to mention catching a cold. Hence even if you expected yourself to dance naked down Fifth Avenue, you wouldn't, and so you had better not expect to.

Generally speaking, then, if you have an aversion to a particular action, your expecting that action may not give you a sufficient motive for taking it. Indeed, merely lacking any other motives for an action may prevent you from bearing out an expectation of performing it, since your motive for bearing out such expectations may not by itself be sufficient to make you resist your motives for alternative actions. In forming such expectations, then, you must look out for evidence against the probability of your fulfilling them. You may not expect yourself to do something if you find evidence that you can't do it or that you won't do it even if you expect to.

---

[12] Of course, in order to rely on your tendency to do what you expect, you must know about that tendency. I shall henceforth assume that you do. I discuss this assumption in the final section of this chapter and in chapter 3, 85–90.

The Extent to Which You May Exceed the Evidence

Yet to avoid expecting anything that the evidence rules out is not the same as to insist on expecting only what the evidence rules in. After you have eliminated the actions that you couldn't or wouldn't perform even if you expected to, there will usually remain several alternative actions that you would and could perform if you expected to, and the prior evidence doesn't dictate which of these actions to expect.[13]

The reason is that there are usually several different actions toward which you're antecedently inclined, each inclination being capable of prevailing over the others if it is reinforced, while the others are suppressed, by your inclination to do what you expect. At any moment you have various sets of motives, favoring various alternative actions. Which action you take will of course depend on which one is favored by the strongest set of motives.[14] But the way to anticipate which action you'll take is not to ascertain which set of motives is antecedently the strongest, since the motives that are strongest before you form an expectation are unlikely to be strongest thereafter. What's strongest before you form an expectation is your inhibition against doing anything until there's something that you expect to do—an inhibition that will be lifted when you form an expectation. And the motives that are currently second-strongest, next to that inhibition, will not necessarily become the strongest when the inhibition is lifted. For when you form an expectation that dispels your inhibition *against* acting, the same

[13] This statement might seem inaccurate. Suppose that before you form an expectation of acting, there is conclusive evidence about which action you'll expect. If there is also conclusive evidence that the action you'll expect is one that you'd perform if you expected to, then the evidence prior to your expectation might seem to dictate which action you ought to expect: you would seem obliged to expect the very action that, according to the evidence, you're going to expect.

But the evidence in question here does not dictate which action you ought to expect. For you cannot go wrong by forming a different expectation from the one that, according to the evidence, you're going to form and hence fulfill. If you do manage to defy the evidence by forming a different expectation, you'll fulfill the expectation you form instead of the one currently indicated by the evidence.

I discuss this issue at greater length in chapter 5.

[14] Let me remind the reader at this point of remarks that I made in the Introduction about how my motivational explanations should be interpreted (10–11). When I say that the action you take will be the one that's favored by the strongest motives, I do not mean that you will necessarily *decide* to act on those *reasons* which consist in your strongest motives for acting. I have in mind a perfectly causal mechanism, in which the strongest forces are necessarily the ones that prevail. I think that your being such a mechanism is compatible with your deciding to act for reasons that aren't your antecedently strongest motives. How this is possible is a question that I discuss in this and subsequent chapters.

expectation will also alter your remaining motives *for* acting, by causing your desire for self-awareness to favor whichever action you expect
and to oppose the alternatives. If you come to expect the action that's
currently favored by your third- or fourth-strongest set of motives, the
resulting boost to those motives, and the corresponding brake on all
the others, may propel the former motives—your motives for the expected action—into first place. Hence what you will be most inclined
to do once you have an expectation is not necessarily the same as what
you would now be most inclined to do if only you weren't inhibited by
the lack of one. What you'll be most inclined to do once you have an
expectation will depend on what you expect.

Of course, your third- or fourth-strongest sets of motives wouldn't
become your strongest if their initial disadvantage was too great to be
redressed by the addition of your motive for doing what you expect.
An expectation can't alter the balance of your motives if they're already too far out of balance. But if the motives favoring several alternative actions are all of moderate strength, then any of those alternatives can indeed become the favorite by being expected. No matter
which action you expect, your motives for it will then gain the advantage and produce the action, thus bearing out your expectation.[15]

The upshot is that whenever you have moderate motives for various
actions, you can expect any one of those actions before you have found
evidence that you will in fact perform it. All you need to find before
expecting an action is evidence that you'll perform it if you expect to.
And this evidence is of a sort that you can usually find in reference to
many different, mutually incompatible actions. Among these actions,
your prior evidence is neutral. It doesn't identify any one of these actions as the action to expect; rather, it identifies all of the actions
equally as candidates for expectation, each on a par with the others in
its likelihood of being performed if expected. Yet the neutrality of the
evidence doesn't require you to remain neutral in your expectations.
Even though your evidence doesn't favor expecting one of the actions
instead of the others, you can go ahead and form a determinate expectation. For as soon as you expect to perform one of the actions instead

[15] My argument here is analogous in some respects to Charles Taylor's claims about
self-description. See his "Responsibility for Self," in *Free Will*, ed. Gary Watson (Oxford, 1982), esp. 122ff.; see also Taylor's "What is Human Agency?" in *The Self: Psychological and Philosophical Issues*, ed. Theodore Mischel (Totowa, N.J., 1977), 103–
35. Taylor says that an agent's description of his motives *alters* his motives. I say that it
gives rise to a *new* motive, which helps to determine which of the others takes effect. See
also Jon Elster's interpretation of Taylor in *Ulysses and the Sirens: Studies in Rationality
and Irrationality* (Cambridge, 1979), 106.

of the others, the expected action will thereby become the one that you're going to perform.

Similarly, you can exceed your current evidence when you expect to start your next action immediately. The only evidence you have, in most cases, is that you'll start your next action immediately *after* starting to pay attention or expecting to act immediately. Such evidence doesn't pinpoint the moment at which your next action will be imminent, and so it doesn't pinpoint the moment at which you should think so. Again, however, the neutrality of your evidence doesn't require you to remain neutral in your expectations. At any time you like, you can think that your next action is imminent; for whenever you think so, it will be.

The Extent to Which Your Expectation Is Justified

Note that your evidence on these questions remains inconclusive only until you draw a conclusion. No sooner do you form a determinate expectation than it becomes better justified than the alternatives. Given the prior evidence that you would perform an action if you expected to, the additional evidence that you expect to perform it clinches the case for so expecting. Given the prior evidence that your next action will be imminent whenever you think so, the additional evidence that you now think so clinches the case for so thinking.

Your reflective expectations therefore rest on evidence, but on evidence from which they aren't derived—from which they couldn't have been derived, in fact. Your evidence about what you'll do includes, most crucially, your awareness of expecting to do something, and it is therefore incomplete until there's something that you consciously expect. Your expectation couldn't have been derived from the relevant evidence, since that evidence wasn't complete until the expectation had already been formed. Once there is something in particular that you consciously expect to do, however, your evidence that you'll do it becomes complete, and that evidence then supports your expectation. Similarly, your evidence about when you'll start to act is incomplete until you think you're about to start; and so you cannot think so in response to prior evidence. Once you consciously think that you're about to start, however, you thereby complete the evidence that you are, and that evidence supports your thought.[16]

---

[16] Here I am glossing over one important issue—whether you know about your inclination to do what you expect. Unless you're aware of this inclination, you cannot possess the evidence that justifies your expectations of acting. I shall discuss your awareness of this inclination in chapter 3.

How Psychology Gets Confused with Epistemology

The necessity of expecting one's actions before possessing the requisite evidence helps to explain one rather puzzling response that philosophers have made to the question of practical self-knowledge. Stuart Hampshire and H.L.A. Hart have claimed that knowledge of one's own actions is "a kind of . . . knowledge to which the notion of evidence is irrelevant," and other philosophers have tended to agree.[17]

I suspect that those who regard evidence as irrelevant to an agent's self-knowledge are simply confusing the grounds for a belief with the occasion for it.[18] Because an agent's reflective expectations aren't derived from evidence, these philosophers assume that they cannot rest on evidence. But they can.

An illustration. This confusion is nicely illustrated in the following passage from G.E.M. Anscombe's *Intention*: "[W]hen a doctor says to a patient in the presence of a nurse, 'Nurse will take you to the operating theatre', this may function both as an expression of his intention . . . and as an order, as well as being information to the patient; and it is the latter in spite of being in no sense an estimate of the future founded on evidence. . . ."[19] To be sure, the doctor's assertion could not have been elicited by evidence; for until he said that the nurse was going to take the patient to the operating theater, the nurse wasn't going to. Anscombe therefore infers that the doctor isn't giving "an estimate of the future founded on evidence." But the doctor's assertion is indeed founded on evidence. His evidence for telling the patient, "Nurse will take you to the operating theater," is that the nurse is herewith getting implicit instructions to do so and that nurses tend to understand and obey such instructions.

Note that the doctor might have misjudged either part of his evidence. This nurse might not have been as obedient as the doctor thought, or the doctor might have forgotten that "operating theater" was used in this hospital as an ironic euphemism for the morgue. If the

---

[17] "Decision, Intention, and Certainty," 1. See also Hampshire, *Freedom of the Individual*, chapter 3; and Grice, "Intention and Certainty," 266ff.

[18] I think that Gilbert Harman offers a similar diagnosis of the comment by H. P. Grice that I quoted earlier in note 11. Harman says, "The problem arises from supposing that the justification of a belief represents a way that someone might reach that belief as a conclusion" ["Practical Reasoning," *Review of Metaphysics* 29 (1976): 448, n. 8]. Harman expands on this point in "Willing and Intending," in *Philosophical Grounds of Rationality: Intentions, Categories, Ends*, ed. Richard E. Grandy and Richard Warner (Oxford, 1986), 363–80.

[19] P. 3.

patient had then found himself being taken to the morgue, he would
have been entitled to complain that the doctor had given him information that rested on faulty evidence.

Although the doctor's assertion thus rests on evidence, that evidence
wasn't there to elicit his assertion, since it wasn't there until the assertion itself was made. Before the doctor made the assertion, then, he
didn't have evidence that it was true; all he had was evidence that it
would be true if he made it. And he had similar evidence about various
other assertions, many of them inconsistent with the one he actually
made; for there are many mutually incompatible actions of which any
one would have been forthcoming from the nurse if only the doctor
had said so. The evidence prior to the doctor's assertion was thus
insufficient to dictate what he should assert, and yet whatever he asserted would thereby have come to rest on sufficient evidence. Hence
Anscombe would have been right if she had said that the assertion
wasn't occasioned by evidence, but she was wrong to infer that it lacks
evidential foundation or grounds.

Similarly, the claim that an agent's reflective expectations aren't
grounded on evidence is just a mistaken inference from the fact that
evidence doesn't occasion them. Before an agent anticipates his next
action, the evidence doesn't dictate which action to anticipate; for
there are several incompatible actions of which he'll perform whichever one he anticipates. But once he anticipates which action he'll perform, his anticipation rests on evidence. His evidence for anticipating
the action includes his prior motives for it, his anticipation of it, and
his motive for doing as he anticipates. Because this evidence includes
the very conclusion that it supports, it couldn't have elicited that conclusion, but evidence needn't have elicited a conclusion in order to support it.

The epistemological issue.   Now, some philosophers believe that rationality requires a belief to have been formed in response to evidence,
not just supported by evidence once it has been formed. These philosophers seem to recognize the distinction between a belief's occasion
and its grounds, but they claim that the rules of justification are indifferent to that distinction.[20] I disagree.

[20] See S. I. Benn and G. F. Gaus, "Practical Rationality and Commitment," *American
Philosophical Quarterly* 23 (1986): 256–57: "[R]ational beliefs are caused by the rea-
sons which are their grounds." Benn and Gaus not only endorse this view themselves but
also attribute it to Bernard Williams ["Deciding to Believe," in *Problems of the Self*
(Cambridge, 1973), 136–51]. I shall discuss Williams's views later, in chapter 4.
   See also K. W. Rankin's discussion of the self-faith-healer—that is, the person who

Surely, the rules of justification are designed to provide a method of maximizing the proportion of truths to falsehoods among one's beliefs (within the constraints of other rules about the range of issues on which one ought to hold beliefs at all).[21] This purpose may well require a rule that one shouldn't retain a belief unless one has evidence of its truth. But does it require a rule that one shouldn't *form* a belief without *prior* evidence? I say no—at least, not if one has evidence that the belief would be true if one formed it. Why would rules designed to help one arrive at the truth forbid one to form a belief that would be true? What errors would one be avoiding by refusing to form a belief that wouldn't be erroneous?

Here I am subscribing to a view put forward, most famously, by William James. James writes: "There are . . . cases where a fact cannot come at all unless a preliminary faith exists in its coming. *And where faith in a fact can help create the fact*, that would be an insane logic which should say that faith running ahead of scientific evidence is the 'lowest kind of immorality' into which a thinking being can fall."[22] I

---

heals himself by forming a self-fulfilling belief in his own recovery ("The Non-Causal Self-Fulfillment of Intention," *American Philosophical Quarterly* 9 [1972]: 279–89). Rankin says: "A doctor, who has insight into the therapeutic effect that his assurance of recovery has upon his patient, can anticipate the patient's recovery in a rational way on the basis, among other things, that the patient has accepted his assurance. On the other hand, the self-faith-healer is not assured until he commits himself to the anticipation of his recovery. His anticipation consequently cannot have a complete rational basis" (284). Here Rankin's reference to "rational basis" seems to contain the relevant confusion between occasion and grounds. Note, furthermore, that Rankin has credited the doctor with more rationality than he should. Rankin says that the doctor can anticipate the patient's recovery on the grounds of the patient's having accepted his assurance. But on what grounds did the doctor *give* his assurance, before the patient had accepted it?

A very similar confusion between grounds and occasion appears in G. J. Warnock's discussion of promises (*The Object of Morality* [London, 1971], 101ff.). Warnock claims that a promise is a kind of prediction that doesn't require evidence. What Warnock should have said is that although a person's promise of doing something is not derived from prior evidence that he is going to do it, making the promise must give him evidence for expecting so. Surely, one is not permitted to make a promise if, having made it, one still won't have grounds for expecting its fulfillment.

[21] To speak simply of maximizing the proportion of truths among one's beliefs would not be correct. If that were the point of the rules in question, they would instruct one to hold beliefs on a lot of useless but obvious questions and to avoid holding beliefs on crucial but controversial ones.

[22] "The Will to Believe," in *Essays on Faith and Morals*, ed. Ralph Barton Perry (New York, 1962), 56. Unfortunately, James fails to make an important distinction between those beliefs which are immediately self-fulfilling and those which are initially false but fulfill themselves in the end: "*Do you like me or not?* . . . Whether you do or not depends, in countless instances, on whether I meet you half-way, am willing to assume that you must like me, and show you trust and expectation. The previous faith on my part in

would add that forming a self-fulfilling belief isn't really "running ahead" of the evidence: it's running *toward* the evidence—that is, toward evidence that will consist in the belief itself. For if faith in a fact can help create the fact, then the faith can constitute decisive evidence in its own favor. Such faith is justified as soon as it exists, and to rule it out would indeed be an insane logic.[23]

An agent may therefore form an expectation about his forthcoming action without being prompted by evidence. Although the agent's expectation of acting is a conclusion to which he jumps before the evidence is complete, he jumps with the assurance that the conclusion will achieve verity even as he lands.

How Reflective Expectations Get Formed

The question remains why the agent would ever jump to such a conclusion. What would attract him to a conclusion for which the evidence still remained to be completed?

What attracts him, in most cases, is simply the prospect of making the conclusion true by jumping to it. Here again the agent resembles the doctor in Anscombe's story. The doctor doesn't wait for evidence to tell him what the nurse is going to do. He wants the nurse to take the patient to the operating theater, and he wants the patient to know where he's being taken. The doctor realizes that he can prompt the desired action and convey the desired knowledge simultaneously, by uttering a self-fulfilling prediction. He therefore ventures into the prediction without being drawn by prior evidence.

So, too, the agent is moved by the prospect of simultaneously

---

your liking's existence is in such cases what makes your liking come. But if I stand aloof, and refuse to budge an inch until I have objective evidence, until you shall have done something apt, as the absolutists say, *ad extorquendum assensum meum*, ten to one your liking never comes. How many women's hearts are vanquished by the mere sanguine insistence of some man that they *must* love him!" (54–55). Here James suggests that he is justified in believing that he already *is* liked, because that belief will eventually cause him to be liked. Yet surely James must recognize that until his belief has the desired effect, it will be false. I would therefore say that it is not warranted. What would be warranted in this case is, not the belief "You like me," but rather the belief "You're going to like me"—provided, of course, that the latter belief would have the same happy influence as the former.

[23] David Pears discusses the validity of self-fulfilling beliefs in *Motivated Irrationality* (Oxford, 1984). At one point, he denies their validity: "It is the normal function of beliefs to aim at independent truth rather than at truth depending on their own existence. It would, therefore, be possible to argue that, when a belief is formed because it will make itself true, its formation is irrational . . ." (40). At another point, however, Pears seems to endorse the validity of self-fulfilling beliefs (146).

prompting a particular action and making it known.[24] He has desires that favor his performing some action, and he wants to know about whatever action he performs. Both sorts of desire favor his drawing the self-fulfilling conclusion that he will act on those very desires, since this conclusion will both prompt[25] the desired action and constitute the desired self-knowledge. By reaching his conclusion the agent will manage both to do what he wants and to know what he's doing. He therefore doesn't wait for evidence to drag him to the conclusion; he jumps, creating his evidence as he goes.[26]

Note, then, that an agent will ordinarily come to expect the action for which his antecedent motives are strongest. And yet the reason why he comes to expect this action is not that it's the only one that he would be justified in expecting. As we have seen, the agent would be perfectly justified in expecting any one of several other actions, for which his antecedent motives are weaker, since his motives for any one of those actions would become the strongest if only he expected to perform it. The reason why he comes to expect the action for which his motives

[24] Here again, I assume that the agent knows about his tendency to do what he expects. See note 12.

[25] I shall often speak of the agent's expectation of acting as "prompting" him to act. What I mean by this is just that the agent's expectation will initiate a shift in the balance of his motives, which will consequently cause him to act. For the full motivational story behind this "prompting," see 49–50, 58–59.

[26] Indeed, we can redescribe Anscombe's characters so that their roles correspond more closely to the roles played by the reflective agent. Imagine Anscombe's vignette as taking place in a hospital whose staff is especially sensitive to the disorientation often experienced by hospitalized patients. The physicians and nurses in this hospital want every patient to know and understand what's happening to him at every stage of his treatment and convalescence. Hence before moving or examining or treating a patient, they make sure that he's told what to expect, and once a patient has been told what to expect, they try not to confound his expectations. Each member of the staff has therefore learned that he can influence the behavior of his colleagues simply by predicting that behavior to a patient within the colleagues' hearing. On the one hand, his colleagues are inclined not to do anything to a patient until they know that the patient has been told to expect it; on the other hand, they are inclined to do to a patient whatever they know he's been told to expect. Thus whenever a member of the staff wants a colleague to move, examine, or treat a patient, he need only tell the patient, in the colleague's hearing, that the colleague will do so. The colleague, moved by concern for the patient's grasp of his situation, will be inclined to act accordingly.

Of course, the concern felt by a staff member's colleagues for a patient's cognitive well-being won't be sufficient to make them do just anything. For instance, they would rather confuse a patient than kill him, and so they won't be inclined to bear out potentially fatal predictions. However, among the actions that they're predisposed to take, they will be further disposed to take whichever action the patient expects. A member of the staff will therefore be able to influence his colleagues' choice of actions by predicting that choice to the patient within their hearing.

are already strongest is that although he would be equally justified in expecting other actions, he prefers to expect this one and he feels justified in expecting it if he prefers.[27] And the reason why he prefers to expect this action is that because he anticipates performing whichever action he expects, his motives for performing an action become motives for expecting it, with the result that he most wants to expect whichever action he most wants to perform—which is the action for which his antecedent motives are strongest.

From the agent's perspective, expecting an action is a means of getting himself to perform it and to do so with self-knowledge. Naturally, he is moved to adopt such a means to whichever action he prefers to perform. Hence an action's being favored by the strongest antecedent motives makes it, not the action he *has* to expect, but the action he *wants* to expect, given that he may expect whichever action he wants. His antecedent motives do not dictate his expectation; they motivate it.

Spontaneous Self-Awareness

I believe that I have now explained the felt spontaneity of an agent's self-awareness. As I have said, an agent's self-awareness feels spontaneous in the sense that he knows what he's doing without having discovered it. He seems to know what he's doing because doing it was his idea to begin with.

The foregoing arguments have spelled out how such knowledge arises. The agent invents what he's going to do by voluntarily adopting one of several mutually incompatible conceptions of his forthcoming action. Thereafter he needn't find out or notice or feel what he's doing; he already knows, since his action ensues in accordance with his conception of it. And although he has formed this conception of the action at will, it rests on a solid basis of evidence and fully deserves his credence as a true representation of what he's doing. Thus does an agent fabricate self-awareness.

[27] At this point, some readers will object that the agent wouldn't feel free to expect what he prefers, since one cannot form a belief at will. My reply is that one can form a belief at will—at least, that is, when the proposition believed in is one whose truth depends on one's believing it.

This is the possibility that Bernard Williams ignores in "Deciding to Believe." According to Williams, a person cannot hold a belief unless he regards himself as thereby "aiming at truth," and a person cannot so regard himself if he adopts his beliefs at will. What Williams misses is that a person can indeed regard himself as aiming at truth in beliefs adopted at will, provided that the beliefs are such that they will be true if he adopts them. I discuss this issue at greater length in chapter 4.

The Locus of Spontaneity

In chapter 1, I said that the spontaneity of an agent's self-awareness is confined to his knowledge of what he is trying to do.[28] My present account agrees with this earlier statement, though not in the way that one might have expected. I do not say that the agent spontaneously comes up with the idea of trying to do something. Trying is rarely what the agent has in mind. The idea that an agent comes up with, according to my account, is the idea of *doing* something, since his expectation is an expectation of acting, not trying. Nevertheless, the agent's expectation is spontaneous only to the extent that he jumps to it without evidence, and as I have explained, he does need some prior evidence before he can jump. Before expecting himself to do something, he needs evidence that he is capable of doing it and that he is already inclined to do it to the point where he would do it if he expected to. What the agent then jumps over without any further evidence is the gap between being ready and able to do something, on the one hand, and actually doing it, on the other; and 'trying' is our name for this gap. Trying is what transforms ability and willingness into action, and this transformation is precisely what the agent takes for granted when expecting to act. Thus, the agent doesn't spontaneously come up with an awareness of what he's trying to do per se. Rather, he comes up with an awareness of what he's doing, and that awareness is spontaneous insofar as it encompasses what he's trying to do.

The Nature of Spontaneity

Having pinpointed the extent to which an agent's self-awareness is spontaneous, I want to pinpoint the respect in which it's spontaneous—the precise nature of its spontaneity. I shall do so by contrasting my explanation of practical self-awareness with a familiar explanation of self-awareness in another realm. The latter explanation may not be true, but it is at least intelligible, and its intelligibility is all that I need, since I am using this explanation only for the sake of contrast.

The explanation that I have in mind has to do with a person's knowledge of his beliefs. It says that when you want to know what you believe about a particular matter, you just say "I believe . . ." followed by the first thing that occurs to you on the subject, and this unreflective utterance, made either aloud or in your head, turns out to be a reliable report of what you believe. The explanation assumes that some un-

[28] Pp. 20–22.

known psychological mechanism enables you to give vent to your beliefs simply by letting the words come.

Now, this story implies that your knowledge of your beliefs is embodied in self-justifying statements. For according to the story, you don't have sufficient evidence about what you believe until you say to yourself or to others that you believe something, whereas once you say that you believe something, your saying so provides reliable evidence that you believe it, given the proven reliability of your unreflective avowals. Hence these unreflective avowals of belief are portrayed in the story as being justified by evidence from which they couldn't possibly have been derived—namely, the evidence of your making them. Indeed, they are portrayed as not having been derived from any evidence at all, since their very reliability is supposed to depend on your letting them come unpremeditated.

If this story were true, it would explain the tendency among philosophers to claim that one knows one's beliefs without evidence. That claim would be unmasked as another instance of the confusion between occasion and grounds—as a mistaken inference, from the fact that avowals of belief aren't derived from evidence, to the false conclusion that they don't rest on evidence, either.

What interests me here, however, is that the self-justifying statements posited by the story, though very similar to expectations of acting, would not have the same kind of spontaneity. That is, even if you did let avowals of belief come to you without evidence, you still wouldn't be making them up. You wouldn't be inventing your beliefs in the way in which you invent your next action when you anticipate its performance. An explanation of the difference will help to clarify the sense in which expectations of acting are spontaneous.

The difference can be analyzed as a difference between two different ways of thinking what you like. The sense in which you can think what you like about the content of your beliefs, according to the foregoing story, is that you are justified in holding the first thought that comes to you. This thought can be described as the one that you "like" because it's what you're initially inclined to think on the subject. You like it in the same sense in which an unsystematic bettor is said to "like" a horse in the next race; that is, you've got a hunch that it's a winner. On the question of what you're going to do, however, you can think what you like in a very different sense. Here you can think what you like in the sense that you will be justified in holding that thought which you want to come true. And wanting a thought to come true is quite different from being initially inclined to think that it is. Your license for anticipating your next action is a license not just to stick with your first hunch but to engage in wishful thinking.[29]

A reliable mechanism for venting your beliefs would not entitle you to wishful thinking about what you believe. The reason is that the avowals of belief issuing from such a mechanism, though self-justifying, would not be self-fulfilling: they would be reliable effects rather than reliable causes of what they reported. Consequently, you would still have to let the words come, because uttering different words wouldn't lead you to have a different belief. By contrast, expectations of acting justify themselves precisely because they tend to produce the action expected. You can therefore choose from among several mutually incompatible expectations of acting, since any one of them will come true if you choose it. The consequence is that you can choose the expectation whose truth you most desire.

What makes an agent's self-knowledge spontaneous, then, is that it is licensed wishful thinking. And the agent's thoughts are licensed to be wishful because they are self-fulfilling.

COMPLICATIONS

This concludes my explanation of an agent's self-knowledge. In chapter 1, I argued that the reason why an agent usually knows of motives for his action even as he begins it is that he rarely begins any action until he knows of motives for it, and that he rarely begins an action without knowing of motives for it because he wants to understand what he's doing. In this chapter, I have argued that the reason why an agent usually knows what he's doing, without having discovered it, is that he usually acts in conformity with a prior expectation of acting, and that he usually acts in conformity with a prior expectation because he wants to know what he's doing.

As I have said, my explanation of practical self-knowledge resembles Elizabeth Anscombe's, in some fairly general respects. I shall discuss

---

[29] Grice seems to think that "licensed wishful thinking" is an impossibility ("Intention and Uncertainty," 263). Harman seems to agree. He says, "[W]ishful thinking is precisely thinking that something is so because one wants it to be so where one is not justified in believing the corresponding conditional proposition" that the thing will be so if one believes it ("Willing and Intending," 374). In short, Grice and Harman seem to regard wishful thinking as, by definition, unlicensed.

I concede that wishful thinking is usually unlicensed, but I don't see why its being so should be part of its definition. Wishful thinking is just thinking that something is so and thinking so because one wants it to be so. Such thinking is sometimes licensed, as in the cases that I have been discussing.

the similarities and differences in the next chapter.[30] Before ending this chapter, however, I want to introduce some complications to my explanation, complications that I have hitherto omitted because the explanation was already complicated enough. Readers who wish to be spared any further complications for the moment are invited to skip the rest of this chapter.

Habit

Thus far I have been discussing actions that are motivated by desires. But many actions owe less to the agent's desires than to his habits, and a course of action that is initiated by desires often consists in a series of shorter actions linked together by habit. For instance, if I want to get ready for bed now, this desire may move me to start my bedtime routine, but once I start, the routine takes over. That is, once the desire to get ready for bed has moved me to climb the stairs, I proceed to wash and undress out of habit, not out of specific desires to wash and undress. How do the mechanisms of self-knowledge interact with such habits?

Habitual actions and habitual expectations. To begin with, I think that the mechanisms of self-knowledge reinforce habits just as they reinforce desires, but they do so in an especially mechanical way. The reason is that habitual action is usually accompanied by habitual knowledge.

For example, I not only have a bedtime routine but also know that I have one. And this reflective knowledge is different from the knowledge that I acquire when a particular motive comes to my attention on a particular occasion. That is, I don't suddenly realize tonight that the force of habit stands ready to convey me through a specific series of preparations for bed. I have long had the habits that guide me through these preparations, I have long known that I have these habits, and so I have become accustomed to having a simple explanation for the actions that follow upon my decision to get ready for bed.

I have therefore acquired a further habit—namely, the habit of relying on my longstanding knowledge of my bedtime habits. As soon as I start getting ready for bed, I habitually dispense with any further reflection on the causes of my behavior until I've slid between the sheets. I still want to understand what I'm doing, and so I still want to do only that which I'll understand. But I needn't continue to make sure that I know of a motive before I allow myself to act. For I know from long

[30] Pp. 102–5.

experience that once I've mounted the stairs at night, I can entrust my behavior to the force of habit and let my mind wander, without fear of puzzling consequences.

By relying on another kind of habitual knowledge, I can similarly let down my guard against performing actions that are unexpected. Countless repetitions of the same bedtime routine have given me the habit of anticipating each step along the way. As I reach the top of the stairs, I habitually expect that I'll next place my watch on the bedside table; as I lay down the watch, I habitually expect that I'll next walk to the bathroom; as I reach the bathroom, I habitually expect that I'll next fetch the dental floss from the cabinet; and so on.[31] I have therefore acquired the further habit of relying on these habitual expectations to keep me abreast of my habitual behavior. Upon initiating my preparations for bed, I habitually dispense with any further efforts to keep track of what I'm doing. I still want to know what I'm doing, as soon as I'm doing it, and so I still want to do only that which I already expect myself to do. But I needn't continue to make sure that I have my next action in mind before I allow myself to act. For I know from long experience that the congruence between my cognitive and behavioral habits will spare me from reflective surprises.

Note that my habitual expectations still reinforce my behavioral habits in guiding me through my successive tasks. For I still want to do what I expect, and so an expectation of performing the next task will help the force of habit to make me perform that task next. But even if my expectations were somehow interrupted, my actions might still proceed, since I have dropped my guard against performing unexpected actions. The result is that the times when I'm in the midst of an habitual course of action are the times when I am most likely to find myself acting absentmindedly.

---

[31] Note that these expectations may be entirely dependent upon habit. If you asked me at midday about my usual preparations for bed, I probably wouldn't be able to recall their precise order. I would have to go through the motions—or imagine that I was going through the motions—in order to reconstruct my routine. Then I would know, as I pretended to take each step, what my next step would be. The reason is that I have no standing beliefs about the order in which I wash and undress; what I have are habits of believing, as I take one step, that I'm going to take the next.

See William James, *The Principles of Psychology* (1890; reprint, New York, 1950): "Few men can tell off-hand which sock, shoe, or trousers-leg they put on first. They must first mentally rehearse the act; and even that is often insufficient—the act must be *performed*. So of the questions, Which valve of my double door opens first? Which way does my door swing? etc. I cannot *tell* the answer; yet my *hand* never makes a mistake. No one can *describe* the order in which he brushes his hair or teeth; yet it is likely that the order is a pretty fixed one in all of us" (1: 115).

Furthermore, I can sometimes find myself in the midst of an habitual course of action that I didn't expect to initiate. If I have to fetch something from my bedroom early in the evening, for example, climbing the stairs may send me into my bedtime routine.[32] Five minutes later, as I am diligently brushing my teeth, I notice that it's only 8:30 and wonder what I'm doing. What has happened, of course, is that climbing the stairs in the dark triggered not only my bedtime routine but also my associated habit of relying on my habitual expectations to keep me abreast of its progress. I therefore proceeded out of habit to expect my bedtime routine instead of whatever I originally expected to do upon reaching the top of the stairs, and so I knowingly got ready for bed, despite my original expectation of doing something else.

In sum, when behavior runs by habit, the mechanisms of self-knowledge do likewise, and the results are not always ideal. I shall therefore segregate the topic of habitual action from the rest of my discussion, resuming it periodically, but always dropping it in order to discuss the less mechanical operations of the reflective agent.

Another form of habitual self-knowledge.   Finally, let me point out that habits may also be incorporated into the mechanisms of reflective knowledge themselves. Although your original and fundamental motive for doing what you expect is your desire to know what you're doing, that motive is likely to be reinforced, in time, by a habit. As you repeatedly fulfill conscious expectations of acting, you get into the habit of responding to such expectations by fulfilling them. Each reflective expectation then becomes a cue to which compliance is your habitual response. And insofar as this habit is conducive to self-awareness, your desire for self-awareness encourages you to maintain it.

In doing what you expect, then, you are usually acting out of a desire that's reinforced by a habit that's sustained by that very desire. Because this arrangement is so complex, and because it wouldn't be initiated or sustained without the appropriate desire, I shall go on speaking as if your pursuit of self-awareness is driven by the desire alone. The imaginary agent of my theory will therefore pursue self-knowledge far more purposefully and far less mechanically than his counterpart in reality. I hope that this discrepancy will be accepted as another useful idealization.

[32] James offers a similar example: "Very absent-minded persons in going to their bedroom to dress for dinner have been known to take off one garment after another and finally to get into bed, merely because that was the habitual issue of the first few movements when performed at a later hour" (*Principles of Psychology,* 1: 115).

Interactions

If an agent's self-scrutiny is anywhere near as convoluted as I have portrayed it until now, then it will turn out to be even more convoluted by far. The mechanisms of reflective awareness and understanding that I have posited, if they exist and if the agent has any inkling of them, must reinforce one another and feed back into themselves in many complicated ways. Here I shall begin to trace some of those convolutions, but the most intricate of them will have to be left for subsequent chapters.

Understanding the effects of reflective expectations. Recall that an agent's desire to understand what he's doing moves him to do what he is aware of understanding. I initially said that an agent is aware of understanding an action so long as he's aware of knowing motives for performing it. But the agent's self-understanding now appears to be more complex, since he seems to understand that he has motives for several different actions, among which he'll perform whichever action he consciously expects.[33] The action that he would understand performing is therefore, not just any action for which he knows of motives, but that action whose motives he is aware of reinforcing by consciously expecting to perform it. He would be puzzled as well as surprised to find himself performing an action that he hadn't thought he expected. For he knows that he's usually inhibited from doing anything that he doesn't consciously expect.

Consciously expecting an action is therefore necessary not just to the agent's thinking that he would be aware of the action, if he performed it, but also to his thinking that he could explain it. An action's seeming intelligible to him thus depends on his awareness of expecting it, and so his desire for self-understanding provides a further motive for doing only that which he consciously expects.

Understanding the effects of reflective understanding. Now suppose that the agent's self-understanding encompasses not only the effects of his reflective expectations but also those of his reflective understanding. Suppose, in other words, that he knows he's usually inhibited from doing anything that he isn't aware of understanding.

In that case, the agent won't expect himself to do anything unless he thinks that he's aware of understanding it. But as we have just seen, he

[33] For the sake of precision, I shall temporarily resume referring to the agent's awareness of expecting an action. For the sake of simplicity, I shall once again dispense with these references at the end of the present section.

won't think that he understands an action unless he is aware of expecting it. Here, then, is another respect in which the evidence for expecting an action isn't present until the agent has already formed the expectation. The agent has no grounds for expecting to perform an action unless he thinks that it will pass the test of seeming intelligible to him, but he knows that an action won't seem intelligible to him unless he is already conscious of expecting it.

As before, however, the agent simply forms the expectation before the evidence is present. He can expect to perform any action for which he is aware of knowing motives, in the confidence that once he is aware of expecting to perform it, he will also be aware of understanding its performance and will therefore be further moved to perform it, not only by his inclination to do what he expects, but also by his inclination to do what he understands.

Expecting what one will understand.   Furthermore, the agent's desire for self-understanding favors his expecting that action which he thinks he has the strongest motives for thus prompting himself to perform. Here's why.

The agent wants to perform an action that he'll understand, he knows that he'll perform whichever action he consciously expects, and so he also wants to expect an action that he'll understand—lest he expect, and hence be prompted to perform, an unintelligible action. Of course, the agent will understand the action he performs as having been prompted by his conscious expectation of performing it, and he may therefore seem to be assured of understanding whichever action he consciously expects. But what if the agent doesn't know why he expected the action he's performing rather than the others that he would have performed instead if he had been conscious of expecting to perform them? He would know that he was performing this particular action because he had prompted himself to perform it, by consciously expecting to, but he wouldn't know why he had expected to. Hence he wouldn't know why he had prompted himself to perform the action, and so he wouldn't really know why he was performing it, after all. In order to ensure that he performs an action that he'll understand performing, the agent must expect an action that he'll understand expecting.

Now, the agent knows that he may expect whichever action he prefers to expect and hence that which action he expects will depend on his preference. That is, he knows that the way to explain which action he expects will be to cite, not his evidence for expecting it, but his preference for expecting it. He also knows that he prefers to expect whichever action he most wants to prompt himself to perform; for he knows that any motive for prompting himself to perform an action yields a motive for expecting it, in light of his knowledge that consciously expecting an action is a means of prompting himself to perform it. The action that he thinks he prefers prompting himself to perform is therefore the action that he thinks he would understand expecting. And since the action that he thinks he would understand expecting is the one that he thinks he would ultimately understand performing, his desire for self-understanding moves him to expect the action that he thinks he has the strongest motives for prompting via such an expectation.[34]

Of course, the agent's motives for prompting himself to perform an action will be nearly the same as his motives for performing it, since most of the possible motives for doing something will also be motives for getting himself to do it, and vice versa. There may be exceptions, however.

On the one hand, there may be brute impulses that would move one to act if one could but will not move one to take prior, instrumental steps that would pave the way for action. Physiological hunger, for instance, though capable of impelling one to eat whatever's available, may not be capable in itself of motivating steps preparatory to the act of eating. Such hunger would be a motive for eating but not for forming the expectation that would prompt one to eat. On the other hand, one may want to take credit for having tried to get oneself to do something—say, to fulfill an obligation—without caring whether one actually does it. In that case, one will have a motive for forming the expectation that would prompt an action, without having a motive for performing it.

Ordinarily, however, an agent will find that he has the strongest motives for prompting himself to do that which he has the strongest motives for doing. And that will be what he thinks he would understand doing, partly because it will be something that he's aware of knowing

---

[34] What if the agent is mistaken in his belief that he prefers to prompt a particular action? Even so, this belief (or rather, his awareness of it) will make his prompting the action seem understandable, thereby causing his desire for self-understanding to favor his prompting it. And this additional motive for prompting the action may shift the balance of motives, thus altering the agent's preference. Even if the agent didn't initially prefer to prompt the action, he may now prefer to prompt it, precisely because prompting it makes sense to him, in light of the belief that he prefers to. Hence the agent's belief that he prefers to prompt the action may actually induce that preference, even if he didn't already have it. The agent is therefore in a position to form self-fulfilling beliefs about his preferences. This is one of the complications that I shall discuss in later chapters.

powerful motives for doing and partly because it will be what he's aware of knowing powerful motives for prompting himself to do.

Summary.   What has begun to emerge, I hope, is that two intellectual motives—the desire to know and the desire to understand what one is doing—introduce subtle complications into the motivational forces governing one's actions. An agent who has these motives still does what he most wants to do, but he no longer does it just because he wants to. Rather, he does it because of a sequence such as this.

- He realizes that it's the action that he most wants himself to perform.
- This realization makes him think that he would understand both prompting himself to perform the action and performing it—which reinforces his preference for prompting himself to perform it.
- He therefore forms the conscious expectation of performing the action, in order to prompt himself to perform it.
- His consciousness of expecting to perform the action, and of his belief that it's the action he most wants to perform, confirms his belief that he would know and understand what he was doing if he performed it.
- Hence his expectation of performing the action reinforces his original motives for performing it—as well as the motivational force of his awareness of understanding it, in light of those motives—to the point where he performs it.

Let me reiterate that the foregoing arguments do not exhaust the complications. They are, if you like, a taste of complications to come.

CONCLUSION

Perhaps this would be a good time for me to remind the reader of the remarks I made in the Introduction about the logical status of my theory.[35] Although I have been propounding an explanation of practical self-knowledge as if it were the one true explanation, all I am entitled to claim, and all that I am interested in claiming, is that mine is a possible explanation, consistent with the evidence of commonsense observation and introspection. My thesis is that practical self-knowledge could arise as I have described, as far as we can tell from ordinary experience.

[35] Pp. 5–8.

The point of establishing hypothetical claims of this kind is that they can settle philosophical questions, which are characteristically about the realm of possibility. In the present case, the question is whether the spontaneity of our practical self-knowledge is compatible with our being governed by motivational causality. How could we avoid having to find out what we're doing and why we're doing it if our actions were the products of a psychological mechanism?

I have now explained how we could know these things without having to find them out, despite our being motivational systems. I have thereby demonstrated that spontaneous self-knowledge is indeed compatible with motivational causality. Whether we actually are motivational systems of the kind that I have described is beyond the power of philosophy to establish. I have simply tried to make the possibility as plausible as I could.

PART TWO

ASPECTS OF AGENCY

THREE

PRACTICAL REASONING

THE REFLECTIVE AGENT

When reflecting you go on two feet. You adjust your self-conception to fit your behavior, you adjust your behavior to fit your self-conception, and thus you proceed by alternate strides in intellection and intelligibility, prediction and predictability. Anticipating what you will do, doing what you anticipate; making sense *of* yourself, making sense *to* yourself—such are the steps to self-knowledge.

Purpose of the Next Five Chapters

In the previous two chapters I reconstructed these steps in such minute detail, I'm afraid, that I failed to convey their natural cadence. The result would have been similar, of course, if I had tried to reconstruct your walk up Fifth Avenue as a study in body mechanics. My account of reflective knowledge sounds about as much like the ordinary person's self-awareness as a physiological account of human locomotion would sound like an ordinary stroll.

In the next five chapters, I shall try to breathe some life back into my account of the reflective agent. I shall try to convey what it would be like to think and act in the ways I described in chapters 1 and 2. What it would be like, I believe, is exactly what it *is* like to be an autonomous agent; for in my opinion, the characteristic phenomena of autonomy and agency would be produced by the reflective mechanisms that I have described. My ultimate hope, then, is to develop the foregoing theory of self-knowledge into a model of autonomous agency.

Objections to the Preceding Chapters

The latter hope may strike you as ironic, since you may already have dismissed my theory of self-knowledge precisely because it seemed to explain an agent's self-knowledge at the expense of his autonomy. When I claimed that you predict how you will act, for example, you may have wanted to respond that how you will act is rather a matter that you decide. Deciding how to act is a way of claiming control over your actions, you may have thought, whereas predicting how you'll act is a way of denying that control. The point of making a reflective prediction is ordinarily to characterize a future action of yours as an unintended mistake or failure of will. "I'll probably trip on my way to the podium," you say, or "I just *know* I won't be able to hold my tongue." By adopting the forecaster's tone about these actions, you imply that you view them through the eyes of a spectator, and so you implicitly deny being their author. My claim that you're continually predicting your forthcoming actions may therefore have seemed to imply that you're continually disavowing them.

Indeed, my views on self-prediction may have struck you as only one symptom of a larger problem. After all, the distinction between predictions and decisions has traditionally been regarded as one aspect of a larger distinction, between theoretical and practical reasoning, and my views on reflective prediction are part of a larger picture, in which I portray an agent as reasoning about his actions theoretically. You may well have disliked this whole picture of the agent as reflective theorist, not just the detail about self-predictions. Not only did I say that an agent predicts rather than decides about his actions; I also said that his motives give him evidence about his actions, instead of reasons for acting, and I said that he cites his motives in order to explain his actions, not in order to justify them. In each case I described the agent's reasoning as theoretical, and in each case my description may have seemed to rob the agent of his very agency. Theoretical reasoning, you may have thought, casts the agent as a bystander at his own actions, taking a passive attitude that would be unthinkable for any agent worthy of the name.

My reflective agent may even have struck you as a case of what Sartre calls *mauvaise foi*, or bad faith.[1] According to Sartre, an agent manifests bad faith by pretending that he is inevitably determined to do the things he does; and the agent often tries to maintain this pretense by choosing to perform actions that he has previously identified as inevitable, as if he could thereby prove that they actually were. By sticking to a purportedly predetermined course of action, Sartre says, the agent emulates a machine, just so that he can claim that his actions proceed mechanically rather than by choice. Such an agent is in bad faith because his actions, as well as his very pretense of having no choice about them, are freely chosen.

Wouldn't Sartre accuse my reflective agent of this pretense? I say that self-knowledge requires performing those actions which one has already predicted; Sartre says that bad faith involves performing those actions which one has already labelled as predetermined. What's the

[1] *Being and Nothingness*, trans. Hazel E. Barnes (New York, 1956), 29–70.

difference? Surely the reflective agent, in purposely being predictable, is pretending to be a machine.

Finally, my reflective agent may be charged with a corresponding pretense in his capacity as inquirer. Just as an agent who is guilty of bad faith misrepresents the nature of his actions, so the reflective agent seems to misrepresent the nature of his self-knowledge. For despite all of his supposed self-analysis, the agent I have described never knows his true self. He doesn't act like himself and then size up his actions; no, he tailors those actions to fit his reflective preconceptions. Hence he doesn't simply act; he puts on an act—a pretense of being the sort of agent he thinks he is. The only reason why he succeeds in predicting and explaining his conduct is that his conduct has always been rigged to bear out his predictions and explanations. His predictive and explanatory success would therefore seem to be not a sign of true self-knowledge but a sham.

Plan of the Next Five Chapters

I shall organize the next five chapters around these objections to my account of self-knowledge, beginning with the last. I shall first show why the reflective agent of chapters 1 and 2 has genuine self-knowledge; I shall then show why his theoretical perspective on his actions doesn't deprive him of a practical perspective; I shall show, consequently, why such an agent is not in bad faith; and finally, I shall show that my theory of self-knowledge, far from denying an agent's autonomy, actually explains it.

GENUINE SELF-INQUIRY

My first task, then, is to answer the objection that a reflective agent, as I have portrayed him, has only the pretense of self-knowledge. I believe that this objection rests on an imprecise analogy between reasoning about one's own behavior and reasoning about the behavior of others.

A Canon of Psychological Inquiry

A student of human behavior must ordinarily take precautions against influencing the behavior he studies. If an observer lets on what he expects of his subject, and his subject takes the hint, then the observer cannot claim to have seen the subject as he really is: all the observer has seen are his own preconceptions reflected in the subject's behavior. The current objection to my account of reflective knowledge is that it portrays the reflective agent as violating this canon of psychological inquiry—as influencing the subject's behavior and then claiming to have seen how he really behaves.

Note, however, that an observer would be permitted to influence the behavior he observed so long as he took his influence into account. His observations would be perfectly valid if they were treated as observations of the subject taking hints from an observer. The problem when one person observes another is that he usually wants to see how his subject behaves when not under an observer's influence.[2] His purpose is to characterize the subject as he is when he's being himself, and a subject isn't being himself when he's taking hints from someone else. Observations of the subject being influenced by an observer would therefore be irrelevant to the observer's purpose, though potentially valid in themselves.[3]

But here the analogy with reflective inquiry fails. In observing oneself, one sees the only person in the world who can fall under one's influence and still be himself. One doesn't want to know how this subject would behave if he weren't under the eye of this observer; for then he wouldn't be what he naturally is—namely, a self-observant person. Nor would one want to see this subject act as if he didn't care whether this observer knew or understood what he was doing; for then he wouldn't be influenced by a motive that is perfectly natural to him—namely, the desire to know and understand himself.

Suppose that you could shield your behavior from the effects of your reflective inquiry by watching yourself, as an experimental psychologist would, from behind a one-way glass. The self you saw through that glass would no longer be the self you wanted to observe. As the

[2] Usually but not always. Consider my efforts to know and understand what my colleagues are doing. On the one hand, I may think that my colleagues behave in interesting ways, and I may want to know about those particular ways of behaving. If I have this desire, I shall want to watch my colleagues without exerting any influence on them—lest the behavior I see turn out to be different from the behavior I want to study. On the other hand, I may want to know and understand whatever's going on in my department. Then my desire will move me to influence my colleagues if I can; for if I can get them not to surprise me or baffle me, I'll be better able to know and understand what's going on. Of course, I shall then have to acknowledge that what's going on is partly the result of my influence; otherwise, I won't truly understand it. But that's precisely the point that I shall be making in the text.

[3] Thus, the reason why an interviewer must usually take care not to ask leading questions is not that leading questions are intrinsically invalid. Leading questions would be appropriate for an interviewer to ask if he wanted to know how far respondents could be led. Usually, however, an interviewer wants to know what his respondents genuinely believe, and he must therefore elicit responses that reflect their opinions rather than his. The interviewer wants to hear the respondents speak for themselves, and people aren't speaking for themselves when they're mouthing responses suggested by an interviewer.

agent in front of the glass, shielded from the effects of your own reflective inquiry, you would be quite willing to do something even if you couldn't think of a motive for doing it, since your frustrated efforts to detect your motives would be concealed behind the glass, where they couldn't affect your actions. You would be equally willing to do something even if you had no idea of what you were going to do, since your actions would be insulated from your efforts at self-prediction, too. In short, you would be willing to let unidentified motives propel you in unforeseen directions. Would you then be behaving like yourself—like the person whose behavior you want to observe?

No. If you want to see how you behave when you're being yourself, then you need to see how you avoid doing things that would surprise or baffle you, and how you do things that strike you as likely and sensible things to do. And you won't see such behavior if you try to observe it without influencing it, simply because it is, in essence, behavior influenced by reflective observation. Your behavior is characteristically affected by your observing it, and so observing your characteristic behavior cannot require that you not affect it.

A Canon of Reflective Inquiry

What you can be required to do, however, is to take the effects of your reflective inquiry into account. If your actions are influenced by your efforts to know and understand them, then you had better know how, or you won't understand them, after all. If you do acknowledge the effects of your self-inquiry, however, then the inquiry will not be invalidated.[4]

---

[4] A similar point is made by David Pears in a recent discussion (*Motivated Irrationality*, 34) of how a person's confidence of success can be self-fulfilling:

> If the belief is 'I shall succeed', and if it actually produces that effect, then . . . it will make itself true in the end. On the other hand, if the belief is 'I would succeed even if I had no belief in my own success', then, like the majority of beliefs, it cannot make itself true. . . .
>
> The [first] belief is simply 'I shall succeed' and the agent calculates that it will make itself true and he is right. So he has a perfectly rational plan for achieving what he wants, namely success, and he does not have the irrational idea of founding his belief on the situation that exists before its formation. This, therefore, is a rational kind of faith and not the self-deceptive kind. But again, things turn out differently for the second belief, 'I would succeed even if I had no belief in my own success'. For this belief is in the same position as the majority of beliefs: it ought to be founded on independent evidence, which does not include the existence of any degree of belief in success. But, in fact, the independent evidence goes against the belief. It is, therefore, irrationally formed and so it certainly qualifies as the self-deceptive kind of faith.

My hypothesis. I believe that an agent does understand the influence of self-inquiry on his conduct. He is aware of being reluctant to take action without first knowing what and why, and he is aware, conversely, that knowing the what and the why of an action encourages him to take it. I therefore hypothesize that a reflective agent understands the effects of his reflections.

I have already made use of this hypothesis, without stating it so boldly. For instance, when I have said that an agent feels free to expect whichever action he prefers, because he'll perform whichever action he expects, I have been assuming that he knows about the effects of his reflective expectations. When I said in chapter 2 that an agent would find it difficult to understand performing an action he didn't think he expected, or expecting an action that he didn't think he preferred to prompt,[5] I assumed that he understood not only the effects of his reflective expectations but also their causes. And when I said that an agent couldn't expect to perform an action he didn't think he understood, I assumed that he understood the effects of reflective understanding as well. In explaining an agent's self-knowledge, then, I have relied on the hypothesis that a reflective agent knows how his reflections affect his actions.

What now moves me to state this hypothesis explicitly is that it would acquit the reflective agent of contaminating his inquiry. In acting, he may well be putting on an act for the benefit of his observing self; but if he understands, in observing, that he's seeing an act put on for his benefit, then this convoluted collaboration between actor and observer may still yield genuine self-knowledge.

I am not yet in a position to say what, if anything, lends my hypothesis plausibility. I shall eventually try to make it look plausible, by showing how much it would explain, if it were true; and I shall try to show how its truth could, in turn, be explained. My aim, in short, will be to find a niche in commonsense psychology for the notion that when an agent inquires into his own behavior, he acknowledges the behavioral effects of that very inquiry.

An agent's reflective conclusions. For the moment, however, let me just state how such an acknowledgement can be embodied in an

---

The only difference between Pears's point and mine is this. He is pointing to the irrationality of *denying* the self-fulfilling effects of one's self-confidence, whereas I am pointing to the necessity of *acknowledging* them. I should note here that Pears goes on to cast doubt on the foregoing account of self-fulfilling belief.

    5 For an explanation of how I am using the word 'prompt', see note 25 of chapter 2.

agent's reflective conclusions.[6] What must an agent think about himself if he knows how that self is being influenced by what he thinks?

Well, if an agent knows that his motives rarely produce an action until he's aware of knowing about them, then when he's aware of learning about his motives, he must realize that he's thereby priming them to make him act. That is, his recognition of motives for acting must encompass its own tendency to reinforce them. His conclusion must be—not just "I have these motives for that action"—but rather "I have these motives, which are hereby being primed to produce that action."

If the agent also knows that he rarely performs an action unless, in addition to consciously knowing motives for it, he also expects it to be the next one he performs;[7] then in expecting an action to be his next one, he must expect it to issue not only from his motives for it, and from his conscious knowledge of them, but also from this very expectation. That is, his expectation of acting must encompass its own role in causing the expected action. What the agent must expect is that his motives for the action, already reinforced by his conscious knowledge of them, will herewith be further reinforced to the point of making him perform the action next: "Because I have these motives for doing this, because they have been primed by this awareness of them, and because those predispositions will hereby be reinforced, I'll do it next."

Moreover, the agent's expectation of acting must encompass the fact that it has been caused by his motives for getting himself to act. For if the agent realizes that of the various actions for which he has antecedent motives, he'll be prompted to perform whichever one he expects; if he therefore realizes that he may expect whichever one of these actions he prefers expecting and that he will prefer expecting whichever action he prefers prompting himself to perform; if he realizes, finally, that he'll have an even greater preference for expecting an action if he thinks he'll understand expecting it, in light of his preference for thereby prompting its performance—then he must regard his motives for prompting the action, and his awareness of knowing about them, as motivating his expectation. The agent must conclude, not just that his motives for the action, and his conscious knowledge of them, will herewith be reinforced to the point of making him perform it, but also that his motives for thus prompting the action, and his conscious

---

[6] Here and elsewhere I use the word 'conclusion' equivocally, to denote both the attitude of belief and the proposition believed. To my knowledge, none of my arguments depends on this equivocation.

[7] As in the preceding chapter, I shall assume that expecting an action entails knowing that one expects it.

knowledge of them, are herein making him *expect* it. More concisely: "Because I have these motives for getting myself to do this (and I know it), I'm hereby reinforcing those predispositions to the point where I'll do it next."

Finally, if the agent knows that once he's set on performing some action next, his becoming certain of immediately performing it usually leads immediately to its performance; then if he does become certain of immediately performing it, what he becomes certain of must be that he'll do so partly out of this very certainty. That is, his expectation must once again encompass its own role in causing the expected action. The agent must conclude, "I'll do it herewith."[8]

An agent's reflective thoughts. What convoluted beliefs! How can I think that an ordinary reflective agent—a man in the street, literally minding his own business—would ever arrive at such convoluted beliefs?

Let me reply by emphasizing that I have been characterizing the reflective agent's beliefs, not his thoughts. I do not imagine for a moment that anyone ever says to himself, "Because I have these motives for

---

[8] The conclusions involved here may seem problematic, since their content cannot be specified without the use of demonstratives such as 'herewith' or 'this very conclusion'. These demonstratives refer to the agent's conclusions, and so the only way to eliminate them would be to refer to those conclusions by specifying their content instead. But when we try to specify the content of those conclusions, the demonstratives reappear. In order to specify the content of the agent's conclusions without the use of demonstratives, we would have to replace the demonstratives in our specification with demonstrative-free specifications of the conclusion's content. Any attempt at such a specification would therefore lead in a vicious circle.

However, there is independent reason to think that many of the belief-states that we cite as motives cannot be assigned demonstrative-free content. Consider the belief that moves the notorious Heimson to impersonate David Hume. Like Hume, Heimson believes "I am David Hume." The demonstrative 'I' in the content of this belief-state is as hard to eliminate as 'this very conclusion' in the belief-states I am discussing. See John Perry, "Frege on Demonstratives," *The Philosophical Review* 86 (1977): 474–97; and "The Problem of the Essential Indexical," *Noûs* 13 (1979): 3–21. See also Hector-Neri Castañeda, *Thinking and Doing: The Philosophical Foundations of Institutions* (Dordrecht, 1975), chapter 6; David Lewis, "Attitudes De Dicto and De Se," *The Philosophical Review* 88 (1979): 513–43; Steven Boër and William Lycan, "Who, Me?" *The Philosophical Review* 89 (1980): 427–66; Roderick Chisholm, *The First Person* (Minneapolis, 1981); Myles Brand, *Intending and Acting: Toward a Naturalized Action Theory* (Cambridge, Mass., 1984), chapter 4.

Note that when these authors describe a belief as "self-referring" or "*de se*," they often mean that the belief is about its subject, the believer. The beliefs that I am discussing, however, are not only about the believer but also about themselves, the beliefs. Such beliefs are self-referring or *de se* in a different—and, I think, more precise—sense.

getting myself to do this (and I know it), I'm hereby reinforcing those predispositions to the point where I'll do it next." The quotation marks here and throughout the preceding section are not meant to indicate that anyone speaks the enclosed sentences, even to himself, even subconsciously. What the quotation marks indicate is that the enclosed sentences express the content of beliefs—mental states that need not actually attain linguistic expression, ever.

I suspect that very little of any reflective conclusion emerges in articulate thought. All that an agent usually says to himself, I imagine, is "This is what I'll do." Yet as he says "This is what I'll do," he believes that he's saying what he likes and getting himself to do what he says. (He believes this, I say; he doesn't say it. The problem is that in order to assert that he believes it, *I* have to say it, whereupon I seem to imply that he says it, too.[9])

Recall Anscombe's story about the doctor who tells a patient, in the presence of a nurse, "Nurse will take you to the operating theater." This doctor isn't saying all that he believes on the subject; indeed, he isn't saying all that he hopes to convey. Surely he believes and hopes to convey something like this: "Because I want the nurse to take you to the operating theater; because I want you to know where you're being taken; and because I know (and I know that you know) that nurses tend to do whatever they hear a doctor tell a patient that they'll do, provided that he seems to speak from motives like these and seems to know that they've heard him—I'm hereby telling you (loudly enough to make clear that I know the nurse has heard me) that the nurse will take you to the operating theater, so that the nurse will now do so and you'll know it."

No doctor has ever spoken or thought these words (except for one Doctor of Philosophy, and I don't count). All Anscombe's doctor says—all he needs to say—is, "Nurse will take you to the operating theater." As he says these words, however, he and his listeners have a commonsense grasp of what's going on. All of them know that the nurse wouldn't be taking the patient to the operating theater if the doctor hadn't said so, and all of them know that the others know it.

---

[9] John Searle encounters the same problem when he tries to explain how visual experiences represent themselves as the results of the objects perceived: "The sense . . . in which the visual Intentional content is self-referential is not that it contains a verbal or other representation of itself: it certainly performs no speech act of reference to itself! Rather, the sense in which the visual experience is self-referential is simply that it figures in its own conditions of satisfaction. The visual experience itself does not *say* this but *shows* it; in my verbal representation of the Intentional content of the visual experience I have said it" (*Intentionality*, 49).

Hence they know that the doctor is basing his prediction, not on prior evidence, but rather on his confidence that uttering such a prediction will move the nurse to make it come true. Indeed, they know that the doctor expects the patient, not just to believe what the doctor is saying, but to believe it on the grounds that the doctor is saying it out of confidence that he can thereby move the nurse to make it come true. And they know that the nurse is inclined to make it come true partly because the nurse understands that the doctor expects the patient to believe it on the grounds of the doctor's confidence in the nurse's inclination to make it come true.

What convoluted beliefs!

Well, they're convoluted to say, but not to believe. Just put yourself in the shoes of the doctor, the nurse, or the patient, and you'll find that you have all of the aforementioned knowledge. Similarly, if you can put yourself in the shoes of the reflective agent (which ought to fit you, if I'm not mistaken), you will find that you can tell yourself "I'll do this" with an intuitive grasp of the motives and grounds for what you're saying. That is, you can tell yourself "I'll do this" in the awareness that the expectation thus expressed will reinforce your motives for acting, and your conscious awareness of those motives, to the point where you'll act; and that those motives, and your conscious awareness of them, moved you to form the expectation for precisely that purpose.

In the next chapter, I shall be in a position to offer a far more perspicuous formulation of an agent's reflective predictions. In the meantime, my present, convoluted formulation will have to do. This formulation should be sufficient, at least, to refute the objection that is currently under discussion—namely, that the reflective agent invalidates his inquiry by allowing it to influence its subject. If my formulation of the agent's predictions is correct, then his inquiry takes account of its own influence, and so it isn't invalidated. I therefore dismiss the current objection.

PRACTICAL REASONING

Let me return, then, to an earlier objection, which was that I have portrayed an agent as an onlooker to his own actions rather than as their author, because I have portrayed him as reasoning about those actions theoretically instead of practically. My reply to this objection will be that the reasoning I have attributed to the agent really is practical, although it is theoretical, too. The reasoning in question is, in my view, a peculiar mode of theoretical reasoning, whose peculiarities just amount to the fact that it constitutes practical reasoning.

This view will be my main thesis for the rest of the book; I can only begin to defend it in this chapter. First, I shall argue that the agent's reflective reasoning, as I have described it, does not cast him in the role of bystander or spectator to his own actions and consequently isn't theoretical in the sense that would be most disturbing. Next, I shall argue that the reasoning I have described can conclude with an action or with an intention to act, just as practical reasoning is ordinarily thought to conclude. Finally, I shall briefly outline how my identification of reflective theoretical reasoning with practical reasoning will be defended in subsequent chapters.

Factual Fictions

The term 'theoretical reasoning' is rich in implications—all too rich, I think. In its barest sense, it refers to reasoning whose goal is knowledge and whose typical outcome is, at least, justified belief. But the term also reflects a particular view of how knowledge and justified belief are attained. The word 'theoretical' is descended from the Greek word for looking or contemplation, and it still retains some color of this ancestral image, suggesting that knowledge is a passive reflection or perception of the truth.

A related image survives in the terms with which we refer to the truth and its opposite: 'fact' and 'fiction'. The word 'fact' usually denotes a true proposition. Its origin, however, is in the Latin word meaning "that which is done." The etymologically precise use of 'fact', then, is the lawyer's use, denoting the completed act in reference to which evidence is sought and a finding made. The term therefore invites us to think that reasoning about the facts, and hence reasoning about what's true, must be a process of finding or discovering that which is already done or antecedently fixed. Like legal findings, factual judgments must come after the fact.

The word 'fictional' carries the same implication, in contrapositive form. Etymologically speaking, the word simply means "made up" or "fabricated." But in common parlance it is taken to denote statements that aren't true and don't even purport to be. Thus, just as 'fact' implies that the truth is something antecedently existing that we must try to find, so 'fiction' implies that if we fabricate something rather than find it, then it must not be true. Both terms join with 'theoretical reasoning' in suggesting that our pursuit of the truth must be a matter of passively registering preexistent features of the world.[10]

Now, the two preceding chapters have largely been devoted to dis-

---

[10] For a discussion of these and related issues, see W. C. Kneale, "The Idea of Invention," *Proceedings of the British Academy* 41 (1955): 85–108.

solving the view that's crystallized in these bits of ordinary language. I have tried to show that we can sometimes obtain the truth by making it up, simply because our inventions are self-fulfilling. I have argued that our understanding of what we're doing is not the product of detective work about a deed that's as good as done; rather, it's something that antedates the deed and, in fact, guides us to do it. Similarly, I have argued, our awareness of what we're doing is not the reflection of an antecedent truth; it is rather a self-fulfilling expectation adopted, on the promise that it will be true if adopted, from among alternative expectations that bear the same conditional promise of coming true. The theme of all these arguments has been that not all of our knowledge results from our registering settled facts: some of it is contained in true and reliably justified fictions.

The agent's self-knowledge is constituted by fictions especially insofar as it is spontaneous, in the sense explained at the end of chapter 2. As I explained there, the agent's self-knowledge is spontaneous because it isn't dictated by prior truths about what the agent is going to do. Rather, there are several possible stories about what the agent will do, each of which would be true if he adopted it, and he adopts the one he prefers, precisely in order to make it come true. Hence the agent doesn't just report the news about himself; he doesn't even *make* the news and then report it. He *makes up* the news in advance, relying on himself to act accordingly.

Thus, the reflective reasoning that I have attributed to an agent is theoretical only in a thoroughly inoffensive sense. It's theoretical in the sense that it aims at knowledge and yields, if not knowledge, then at least justified belief. But it isn't theoretical in the sense of being contemplative, reactive, or passive. The agent's reasoning about what he's doing and why doesn't alienate him from his actions by casting him in the role of bystander, onlooker, or commentator; quite the reverse. The agent's reflective reasoning casts him in the role of inventor, creator, and author. For he attains his awareness and understanding of what he's doing by making up a story in the confidence that he will then be moved to live it out.

Concluding with an Action

The reasoning by which an agent attains self-knowledge is not just theoretical, then, but also practical. Indeed, I think that it's practical in a more technical sense than I have yet explained—that is, in the Aristotelian sense that it concludes with an action.[11] Here is why.

---

[11] See *De Motu Animalium* 7.

When a person reasons theoretically about his actions, I have claimed, he acts so as to facilitate his reasoning; in fact, he reasons in a way that relies on his acting so as to facilitate his reasoning. His reasoning thereby comes to incorporate his actions.

Consider, for instance, how an agent regulates his beliefs about what he is about to do. If he were forming a belief about what someone else was about to do, he would compile evidence until he had enough to indicate the truth of a determinate conclusion, and then he would draw the conclusion whose truth was indicated. But when forming a similar belief about himself, he compiles only enough evidence to indicate a set of alternative conclusions each of which he would be moved to make true if he drew it, and then he draws whichever conclusion he likes, in the confidence that he'll thereby be moved to make it true. In short, he arrives at a belief that's true *of* his action partly by relying on himself to perform an action that's true *to* his belief.[12]

Performing that action thus becomes an indispensable phase of the agent's intellectual strategy. The action is not a byproduct of the agent's reasoning; it's the step on which all the preceding steps have relied and without which they would fall flat. The agent's procedure for forming true beliefs about his actions doesn't end with his forming a belief; on the contrary, that procedure includes his forming a belief only as a prelude to the further step of making it true. Making the

[12] G.E.M. Anscombe proposes a similar account of "practical truth" in the last two paragraphs of "Thought and Action in Aristotle," in *New Essays on Plato and Aristotle*, ed. Renford Bambrough (London, 1965), 143–58. Note, however, that my account of practical reasoning does not rely on the appropriateness of calling an action true. Rather, it relies on the appropriateness of regarding an action as an integral step in a strategy for attaining true belief. (Anscombe's notion of practical truth is discussed at length by David Pears in chapter 8 of *Motivated Irrationality*.)

Also relevant here is John Searle's discussion of "direction of fit" [*Intentionality*, 7ff.; and *Expression and Meaning* (Cambridge, 1979), 1–27]. Searle distinguishes between different illocutionary acts, such as asserting and promising, in terms of whether the act is supposed to conform to the world or the world to the act. He then draws a similar distinction between different propositional attitudes, such as beliefs and intentions. I disagree with Searle insofar as I claim that beliefs can sometimes have the same direction of fit as orders or promises rather than assertions. That is, there are beliefs that "are not supposed to match an independently existing reality but rather are supposed to bring about changes in the world so that the world matches [their] propositional content" [*Intentionality* 7]. I agree with Searle insofar as I claim, below, that such beliefs, by virtue of their direction of fit, constitute intentions.

Finally, See G. J. Warnock's discussion of promises in *The Object of Morality* (London, 1971), 101ff. Warnock says that the obligation to keep one's promises is just the obligation of veracity, applied in the reverse of the usual direction. That is, it's the obligation to ensure correspondence between one's words and the facts by bringing the facts into correspondence with one's words rather than vice versa.

belief true is the final step in his reasoning. In this sense, he concludes with an action.

The agent's procedure for arriving at an explanation of his action can also be said to conclude with the action. His procedure is not to discover an explanation for whatever he happens to do; his procedure is rather to discover an explanation for doing something and then to do that thing. In this procedure, coming up with an explanation is only the first step, a step that wouldn't be taken except in preparation for a second, practical step—namely, performing the action explained. Again, the agent's reasoning concludes with an action.

Concluding with an Intention

To show that a kind of reasoning can terminate in action is not, of course, to show that it does the entire job of practical reasoning. Sometimes an agent's practical reasoning stops short of producing an action and produces instead a mere intention of acting, because the time for action itself has not yet arrived. And even when deliberation produces an action immediately, the action is usually thought to be accompanied or imperceptibly preceded by an intention. Reasoning that's practical must therefore be able to yield an intention, as a temporary surrogate for action or a penultimate step toward it.

The penultimate step toward action in my story, however, is the agent's self-fulfilling expectation of acting. And surely, one is tempted to say, expecting to do something is different from intending to do it.

Well, is it? What exactly is the difference between an intention to act and an agent's reflective prediction?[13]

What's the difference between intention and prediction? The most salient feature of the agent's reflective prediction is that it represents a future action. But then, an intention does, too. Intending to perform an action entails conceiving of it—as is most evident, perhaps, when an intention contains a misconception. For instance, Oedipus intended to marry Jocasta but not to marry his mother, even though those actions were one and the same. His intention thus contained a mistaken representation of the action he intended to perform. Yet his intention couldn't have *mis*represented the intended action unless it represented it in the first place. Hence an agent's reflective prediction, in representing a forthcoming action, is no different from an intention.

---

[13] The theory of intention that I present in this section was derived from the work of H. P. Grice ("Intention and Uncertainty") and Gilbert Harman ("Practical Reasoning"). However, neither Grice nor Harman subscribes to the theory as I develop it here. I shall elaborate on the theory, and its sources, in the next chapter.

Of course, an intention not only represents a forthcoming action but also tends to bring about the action that it represents.[14] Forming the intention to do something is a step toward doing it, a way of getting oneself to do it. But then, so is making the corresponding prediction. As we have seen, when an agent predicts that he will perform an action next, he thereby prompts himself to perform it next. Hence the agent's reflective prediction, like an intention, tends to bring about what it represents.

Perhaps the difference is that an agent's intending to do something is normally to be explained by his wanting to do it, whereas his predicting that he'll do something is to be explained by his having evidence that he will. But no. For as we have seen, what an agent expects to do depends primarily on what he wants to do, not on the evidence. An agent's evidence about what he'll do usually shows only that among the many things that he has motives for doing, he'll do whichever one he expects to. The agent therefore expects whichever one of these actions he wants to expect, and he wants to expect whichever action he wants himself to perform. Hence he usually predicts that he'll do something because he wants himself to do it, and so his predicting that he'll do something, like his intending to do something, is to be explained by his desires.

To be sure, the agent isn't entitled to expect himself to do something unless he has reason to believe that he'll do it if he expects to. But there is no difference here, either, since the corresponding requirement applies to intentions. An agent isn't entitled to intend to do something unless he has reason to believe that he'll do it if he intends to. For instance, when an incorrigible procrastinator announces the intention of finishing his projects today, we assume that he is being either insincere or overconfident. That is, we assume either that he doesn't truly intend to finish today or that if he does intend to, he is guilty of disregarding the evidence, which shows that he won't. We tend to think that the procrastinator isn't entitled to form the intention of finishing because he has no reason for expecting that he'll carry it out. Intentions

[14] Compare Alvin I. Goldman's definition of volitions as "conscious occurrences which are, or express, propositional attitudes, and . . . have the following property: each has a tendency to cause an event which satisfies or fulfills its propositional content" ("The Volitional Theory Revisited," in *Action Theory*, ed. Myles Brand and Douglas Walton [Dordrecht, 1976], 68). In the same volume, Arthur C. Danto describes intentional action as "a representation on the one side, and a piece of operant behavior on the other, with the former causing the latter and the latter satisfying the former" ["Action, Knowledge, and Representation," 24]. Elsewhere, K. W. Rankin characterizes intentions as "self-fulfilling anticipations" ["The Non-Causal Self-Fulfillment of Intention," *American Philosophical Quarterly* 9 (1972): 279–89].

are therefore answerable to the evidence, just like reflective predictions.

Finally, an agent's expectations not only bring about the expected action, and issue from the agent's desire to bring it about, but also depict themselves as doing so. Here again, they resemble intentions. First of all, the content of an agent's intention of doing something cannot be merely that he's going to do it, because of some impetus or other; it must be that he is going to do it partly because of this very intention.[15] If the agent could intend to do something, without intend-

---

[15] See Harman, "Practical Reasoning," 440–48; and *Change in View: Principles of Reasoning* (Cambridge, Mass., 1986), chapter 8; Searle, *Intentionality*, chapter 3; David Pears, "Intention and Belief," in *Essays on Davidson: Actions and Events*, ed. Bruce Vermazen and Merrill Hintikka (Oxford, 1985), 75–88.

Harman believes that some intentions do not represent themselves as bringing about the intended action. He calls these "negative" intentions, because they are mostly intentions *not* to do things, although the content of such intentions can of course be rephrased in positive terms. Harman's example of negative intention is the case in which I intend not to go out tonight even though I believe that I wouldn't have gone out anyway. In this case, according to Harman, my intention doesn't present itself as causing me not to go out.

The problem here is that Harman doesn't describe the case with sufficient precision. Although he says my intention is not "responsible" for my staying in tonight, he also says that it "settles that issue," so that I can make alternative plans [*Change in View*, 80]. But surely, if I were already certain of not going out, then there would be no issue to settle, and I could make alternative plans without forming an intention of not going out. Just imagine an inmate of a maximum security prison saying, "I intend to stay in tonight." This remark would be ironic: the prisoner isn't in any position to intend on staying in, precisely because there is no question of his going out and hence no outcome for his intention to influence.

A better way to describe the case that Harman seems to have in mind would be to say that I think myself unlikely to go out in any case, but I want to make sure. I form my intention in order to rule out an eventuality that I already regard as unlikely. In this case, however, I regard my intention as further reducing the probability of my going out and hence as raising the probability of my staying in, which is the intended outcome. I may not want to call the intention "responsible" for my staying in; but I do think that I will stay in partly because of the intention—that is, partly because of its having raised the probability of my staying in. Here I am making a causal judgment of a familiar statistical variety.

(Statistical causal judgments are a complicated issue. Note, in particular, that my intention needn't raise the *overall* probability of the intended outcome in order to be regarded as helping to cause it. Christopher Peacocke presents cases in which I can regard my intention as partly causing an outcome even though my forming the intention made the outcome less probable than it otherwise would have been ["Intention and *Akrasia*," in *Essays on Davidson*, ed. Vermazen and Hintikka, 70–71]. In these cases, the intention triggers one mechanism that raises the outcome's probability, but it also blocks another mechanism that would have raised the outcome's probability even more. If the outcome occurs, the intention can still be regarded as one of its causes. Of course, this causal

ing to do it partly because of so intending, then he could intend to do the thing unintentionally—which he can't.[16] And if his action isn't in fact caused by his intention, then it usually turns out to be something other than what he intended, as is illustrated by examples like this:

> Betty intends to kill someone. She aims her gun and, at the crucial moment, a noise startles her, leading her to contract her finger so that she shoots and kills him. . . . Although she intends to kill him and does kill him, she does not do what she intends. For her intention to kill him is the intention that that very intention will lead her to pull the trigger at the crucial moment; and that does not happen.[17]

Such examples demonstrate that intentions, like reflective predictions, not only bring about the actions they represent but also represent themselves as doing so.

---

judgment still relies on the notion that the intention has raised the probability of the outcome—not overall, but in some restricted context. The intention has raised the outcome's probability *given* that the other potential causes have been blocked.)

[16] Of course, an agent can intend to bring it about that he does something unintentionally. But then the *bringing about* is, and is intended to be, intentional, even if the *doing* isn't.

[17] Harman, "Practical Reasoning," 445. In fact, the content of the intention probably specifies the manner in which the intention will lead to the action. For as Harman goes on to say, "If Betty's intention makes her nervous and nervousness causes her to pull the trigger, her intention leads her to pull the trigger but not in the intended way; so she does not do what she intends . . ." (ibid.). Similar cases are discussed by Searle, *Intentionality*, chapter 3; R. M. Chisholm, "Freedom and Action," in *Freedom and Determinism*, ed. K. Lehrer (New York, 1966), 28–44; Goldman, *Theory of Human Action*, 55ff.; Donald Davidson, "Freedom to Act," in *Essays on Actions and Events*, 63–81; Harry Frankfurt, "The Problem of Action," *American Philosophical Quarterly* 15 (1978): 157–62; Christopher Peacocke, "Deviant Causal Chains," in *Midwest Studies in Philosophy*, no. 4, ed. Peter A. French, Theodore E. Uehling, and Howard K. Wettstein (Minneapolis, 1979), 123–55; Lawrence Davis, "Wayward Causal Chains," in *Action and Responsibility*, ed. Michael Bradie and Myles Brand (Bowling Green, Ohio, 1980), 55–65; Wilson, *Intentionality of Human Action*, 116ff.; Dorothy Mitchell, "Deviant Causal Chains," *American Philosophical Quarterly* 19 (1982): 351–53; Brand, *Intending and Acting*, 17ff.; Michael H. Robins, "Deviant Causal Chains and Non-Basic Action," *Australasian Journal of Philosophy* 62 (1984): 265–82; Irving Thalberg, "Do Our Intentions Cause Our Intentional Actions?" *American Philosophical Quarterly* 21 (1984): 249–60; Alfred R. Mele, "Intentional Action and Wayward Causal Chains: The Problem of Tertiary Waywardness," *Philosophical Studies* 51 (1987): 55–60; and "Are Intentions Self-Referential?" *Philosophical Studies* 52 (1987): 309–29.

If intentions consist in the agent's reflective expectations—as I shall argue in the text—then my account of those expectations specifies the manner in which an intention ordinarily causes the intended action, and hence the manner in which it ordinarily represents itself as causing the action.

Secondly, when an agent forms an intention, he normally regards it as a manifestation of his motives for acting. For in order to regard the intention as *his* intention, he has to regard it, not as a product of extraneous forces or as a mere psychological glitch, but as an expression of his desires. And the desires that he regards his intention as expressing are his motives for performing the intended action. He therefore regards his intention as arising from, and giving effect to, his motives—which are the two things that reflective predictions represent themselves as doing.

In sum, I can see no difference between an agent's reflective predictions and his intentions to act. I therefore conclude that there is no difference between them and no distinction, either. Intentions to act, I believe, are the expectations of acting that issue from reflective theoretical reasoning. These are self-fulfilling expectations of acting that are adopted by the agent from among potentially self-fulfilling alternatives because he prefers that they be fulfilled, and they represent themselves as such.[18] Henceforth I shall summarize the relevant features of these expectations by saying that they are, and represent themselves as being, self-fulfilling expectations of acting that the agent adopts out of a desire for their fulfillment. What I have now argued is that these features of the expectations cast them in the role of the agent's intentions to act.

Let me hasten to add that the commonsense distinction between intentions and predictions survives in my account, but it survives as a distinction between two different kinds of prediction, one of which has monopolized the name. The term 'prediction' is ordinarily applied to future-tense beliefs that have been derived from preexisting evidence. Ordinary instances of prediction are therefore different from intentions, which rest on evidence from which they couldn't have been derived. But this difference doesn't show that intentions aren't predictions; all it shows is that, as predictions, they're out of the ordinary. They differ from ordinary predictions in their psychological relation to

[18] According to Stuart Hampshire, a person is logically precluded from predicting his own actions, because any attempted reflective prediction would unavoidably turn into, and be preempted by, an intention: "The short and sure method of ending the uncertainty [about one's future action], namely, actually deciding what to do, would be irresistible and unavoidable" [*Thought and Action*, 110; see also 129ff.]. My view coincides with Hampshire's insofar as I regard intention as containing information about one's future; my view differs from Hampshire's, of course, in that I regard intention as consisting in, rather than precluding, a prediction.

(Note that Hampshire's grounds for denying that one can predict one's *actions* are somewhat different from the grounds on which he and others deny that one can predict one's *decisions*. I discuss the latter argument in chapter 5, 164–66.)

the evidence, but they are future-tense beliefs that rest on evidence, and so they still deserve to be called predictions.[19]

In everyday speech, of course, 'prediction' can be presumed to denote its ordinary instances, despite the existence of other predictions—just as 'cat' is presumed to denote domestic felines despite the existence of other, more exotic cats. Consequently, when someone says, "I'm about to lose my temper," we can sensibly ask, "Is that an intention or a prediction?"—just as we can ask, when presented with a feline, "Is that a lynx or a cat?" The fact remains that we won't be trying to distinguish between something that simply is a prediction and something that simply isn't. Rather, we'll be trying to distinguish, among predictions, between ordinary and exotic specimens.

In particular, we'll be asking, "What made you think you'd lose your temper? Was it that you wanted to lose it and knew that you could get yourself to lose it by thinking so? or was it that you had antecedent evidence that you'd lose it whether you thought so or not?" In neither case do we expect the agent to say that his statement expressed anything other than it seemed to express—namely, a prediction, of one sort or another, that he was about to lose his temper. Rather, we expect a clarification of the grounds, the occasion, and the content of what is in either case a prediction.

Intentions as commands. My theory of intention can be read as a variation on a familiar theory that identifies intentions with commands issued by the agent to himself.[20] According to the latter theory, intending to do something consists in telling oneself, "Do it!" My theory of intention is quite similar. For although I do not identify intentions with commands, I do identify them with expectations whose utterance would convey commands.

Anscombe's hospital story has already illustrated how the utterance of an expectation can convey a command. Let me alter the story

---

[19] Anscombe uses the term 'estimates of the future' to denote future-tense beliefs or assertions based on evidence; she thinks that estimates of the future are obviously different from intentions, or expressions thereof; and she uses the term 'predictions' as a broader term that encompasses both (*Intention*, 1–7). In her terminology, my claim would be that intentions are not only predictions but also estimates of the future.

[20] Proponents of this theory include Hector-Neri Castañeda (*Thinking and Doing*, 42–43, 155) and Anthony Kenny, *Action, Emotion and Will* (London, 1963), 216–20. For the pros and cons of comparing intentions to commands, see David Pears, "Predicting and Deciding," *Proceedings of the British Academy* 50 (1964): 206–8; R. M. Hare, "Wanting: Some Pitfalls," with "Comment" by D. F. Pears, in *Agent, Action and Reason*, ed. Robert Binkley, Richard Bronaugh, and Ausonio Marras (Toronto, 1971), 81–97, 108–27; and Bruce Aune, *Reason and Action* (Dordrecht, 1977), 66–67.

slightly in order to highlight the similarity between such commands and intentions. Suppose that the doctor had spoken not to the patient but directly to the nurse, saying, "I expect you to take this patient to the operating theater." In that case, as in the original story, the doctor would have been issuing an implicit command. The import of his utterance would have been roughly this: "I expect you to take this patient to the operating theater, and I expect this because, in saying so, I'm implying that you had better take him there so that I won't be fouled up by a mistaken expectation."

Now suppose that the doctor had addressed his statement to himself rather than to the nurse. His reflecting self could have said to his acting self, "I expect you to take this patient to the operating theater"—meaning, "You had better take him there so that we won't be fouled up by a mistaken expectation." In that case, the mental state that the doctor was expressing would have constituted an intention, according to my theory.[21]

The Problem of Practical Reasoning

I conclude that an agent's reflective theoretical reasoning can not only terminate in an action but also reach that terminus by way of an intention to act. I therefore conclude that an agent's reflection deserves to be called practical reasoning. Much remains to be said in defense of this conclusion, since it is bound to arouse many and various objections. The most obvious objection, I think, is that reflective theoretical reasoning doesn't have the same topic as practical reasoning. The reasoning I have characterized is about what one *is* doing, or will do, whereas practical reasoning is about what *to* do, what one ought to do, or what would be the best thing to do. How can I claim that reasoning on the first topic can do the work of reasoning on the second?

My answer to this objection will emerge only gradually, I'm afraid, and won't be completed until the end of this book. In defense of my

---

[21] Cf. David Pears's remarks on direction of fit [*Motivated Irrationality*, 139]. Pears asks, "[H]ow can [a] sentence have the task of fitting [a] fact and, at the same time, have the task of inducing the fact to fit it?" He then argues that sentences with such a dual direction of fit are indeed possible and that philosophers who deny their possibility are paying undue attention to the distinction between statements and commands: "The assumption, that it is incoherent to suggest that there might be two opposed directions of fit between a single pair of items, has dominated this topic for the last twenty-five years. The model has been a social one: you tell someone that such and such is the case or you tell him to make it the case, but you cannot get a single atomic sentence to perform both these functions simultaneously." As Anscombe's example shows, you *can* get a single sentence to perform both functions simultaneously, because one and the same utterance can constitute both an assertion and a command.

apparent dilatoriness in this regard, let me say that any theory of practical reasoning needs to answer two questions, and they cannot both be answered at once. I have simply chosen to answer first the question that other theories of practical reasoning answer second—or, more frequently, not at all.

One question that we want a theory of practical reasoning to answer is what sort of mental operations are involved in our figuring out what to do. The other question is what sort of mental operations are responsible for the nature of agency—for freedom of choice, for self-governance, for rationality, and so on. After all, the reason why our bodily movements amount to the actions of autonomous agents must have something to do with the fact that those movements are under the control of our intellects.[22] The question is therefore what it is about the operations of our intellects, in controlling our behavior, that makes us agents.

An answer to this latter question ought to address the former question as well, and vice versa. Surely, the mental operations in virtue of which our movements involve free actions ought to be the same operations that constitute our figuring out what to do. 'Practical reasoning' is just the term that we give to whichever mental operations serve both of these functions.

Most theories of practical reasoning begin by examining the methods by which an autonomous agent figures out what to do. Some of them go on to examine how these methods of figuring out what to do make the agent autonomous. I have chosen to begin with the latter question and work my way toward the former. I shall try to show how a particular mode of reasoning can make an agent autonomous; then I shall try to show that the reasoning in question constitutes the agent's figuring out what to do.

Conclusion

Thus far in this chapter I have dispensed with the objection that the reflective agent, as I describe him, would attain only the pretense of self-knowledge, and I have introduced my theory of practical reason-

---

[22] Here I am not committing myself to any particular theory about the metaphysics of action. I don't care whether actions are identical with bodily movements, or with the mental causes of bodily movements, or with the movements and causes taken together, or what have you. I'm merely saying that our capacity for acting has something to do with the intelligent governance of our behavior. For discussions of the metaphysics of action, see Donald Davidson, "Agency," and "Logical Form of Action Sentences," in *Essays on Actions and Events*, 43–61, 105–48; and Jennifer Hornsby, *Actions* (London, 1980).

CHAPTER 3

ing, in response to the objection that my agent's attitude to himself
would be too theoretical. In answering the first objection, I showed
how the reflective agent's self-knowledge could be formulated so as to
represent its own effects. I then characterized some of the resulting self-
referential beliefs as practical conclusions, in the form of intentions to
act.

Much remains to be said, pro and con, about this theory of intention
and about the theory of practical reasoning of which it is a part. Before
I say any of it, however, I would like to tie up two loose ends from this
and the preceding chapter.

PRACTICAL KNOWLEDGE

In chapter 2 I promised to explain how my account of an agent's self-
knowledge squares with Elizabeth Anscombe's. Now that I have introduced my theory of intention, that promise can be fulfilled.

The reason why I had to introduce my theory of intention before I
could discuss Anscombe's account of self-knowledge is that according
to Anscombe's account, a person knows what he's doing, or at least
what he's trying to do, by virtue of intending to do it. I can now agree
with Anscombe on this score, since I have identified the agent's intentions with the self-fulfilling expectations that contain his practical self-
awareness. I agree with Anscombe further in saying that this self-
knowledge is not acquired by observation, although I go even further,
by saying that it is not, strictly speaking, acquired at all. And finally, I
agree with Anscombe in regarding the agent's self-knowledge as practical knowledge in the sense defined by Aquinas—that is, as knowledge
that is "the cause of what it understands."[23]

My differences with Anscombe are not many, but I think that they're
significant. For one thing, I attempt to explain how a piece of knowledge might cause its object—a matter that Anscombe leaves obscure.[24]

[23] *Summa Theologica* Ia IIae, Q3, art. 5, obj. 1, quoted by Anscombe in *Intention*, 87;
see also 1–5; 56–58. Arthur Danto criticizes Anscombe's views on practical knowledge
in "Action, Knowledge, and Representation." D. M. Armstrong denies that a mental
state can qualify as knowledge if it causes its object: "The essential point of a 'faculty of
knowledge', is that it should, in respect of what is known, be passive to the world. If the
'reflection' is achieved by our mind moulding the world, we are not knowing but creating. (Although there may be a model here for God's knowledge of his creation)" (*Belief,
Truth and Knowledge* [Cambridge, 1973], 181). Armstrong doesn't explain why God
can have practical knowledge while mortal creators cannot. The analysis of God's
knowledge as practical is pursued by Kenny, *God of the Philosophers*, 35.
[24] Indeed, I doubt whether Anscombe takes the word 'cause' seriously. The connection

More importantly, I attempt to explain how a mental state that causes its object can still qualify as knowledge in a reasonably familiar sense, whereas Anscombe's account of an agent's self-knowledge leaves it looking not just causally perverse but epistemically mysterious.

The bone of contention here is what justification an agent needs to have for his conception of what he's doing. I have already discussed Anscombe's view that this conception, being contained in the agent's intention, doesn't in fact rest on evidence. Anscombe denies that it rests on evidence, I have argued, because it isn't and couldn't have been derived from evidence and because she fails to see that it can rest on evidence from which it couldn't have been derived.

But my present interest is not in repeating the debate over whether an agent's conception of his action is in fact supported by evidence. Rather, I want to discuss the epistemological implications of Anscombe's belief that it isn't. For if the agent's conception of what he's doing isn't supported by evidence, then it cannot qualify as knowledge unless it is exempt from the usual demand that knowledge have justification. Anscombe is therefore obliged to argue that practical knowledge not only lacks evidential support but also doesn't require it and hence cannot be faulted for lacking it.[25]

The reason why practical knowledge doesn't require evidence, according to Anscombe, is that it is embodied in the agent's intention, and an intention is not responsible for being true. The point here is not to deny that an intention is capable of being true. For insofar as an intention says that the agent will perform some action, its content is susceptible of truth or falsity; indeed, coming true is the object of the intention. Anscombe's point here has to do with how the intention is supposed to come true—namely, through the agent's being subsequently true *to* his intention, instead of through its being antecedently true *of* him. If any discrepancies arise between what an agent intends and what he does, then "the mistake is in the performance" rather than in the intention.[26] In this respect, Anscombe argues, an intention is like a command. Both an intention and a command are meant to achieve conformity with the world, not by conforming themselves to it, but rather by obliging the world to conform itself to them.

Now, Anscombe seems to believe that if an agent's conduct is an-

---

that she posits between the agent's knowledge and his action seems conceptual rather than causal. See *Intention*, 87–88.

[25] For another discussion of the these implications, see Jones, "Things Known Without Observation," 137ff.

[26] *Intention*, 5, 82. Here Anscombe is quoting Theophrastus, *Magna Moralia*, 1189b 22.

swerable for conferring truth upon his intention to do something, then it must also be answerable for conferring truth upon his knowledge of what he's doing, since that knowledge is identical with his intention. In its capacity as an intention, the agent's conception of his action needn't conform itself to the action, and Anscombe therefore infers that it needn't do so in its capacity as the agent's knowledge of the action, either. And if the agent's knowledge of his action needn't conform itself to the action, she reasons, then how can it require evidence of that conformity?

Look at it this way. Anscombe points out that an intention isn't required to track the facts, precisely because the facts are responsible for tracking it. She then figures that if a piece of knowledge consists in an intention, then it can't be required to track the facts, either. And knowledge that needn't track the facts needs no evidence of being on the right track.

The best illustration of this view, and of its flaws, is once again the hospital example. What interests Anscombe about this example is that the doctor's instructions to the nurse and his information to the patient are contained in one and the same utterance, "Nurse will take you to the operating theater." As I have already noted, Anscombe claims that even in its capacity as information to the patient, this statement isn't founded on evidence. The question, for present purposes, is how a factual statement can stand without evidential support.

What Anscombe is committed to saying about the doctor's statement is this. The doctor's statement requires no evidence because it constitutes instructions to the nurse, and ensuring that the content of those instructions comes true is the nurse's responsibility, not the doctor's. In its capacity as a command, the doctor's statement makes the nurse answerable for making it come true. According to Anscombe's reasoning, then, the doctor isn't answerable for the truth of his statement, and so he doesn't need any evidence for it.

I think that this application of Anscombe's theory shows why the theory is wrong. The problem is that responsibility for the truth of a representation cannot be assigned independently of the role that the representation plays. The nurse is indeed answerable for fulfilling the doctor's statement insofar as it conveys instructions, but the nurse does not thereby become answerable for its accuracy as information to the patient. The doctor has undertaken to inform the patient about the next step in his treatment; the doctor is obligated not to misinform the patient about these matters; and so the doctor is answerable for the truth of what he says. The doctor therefore requires evidence for his statement. Fortunately, he has the requisite evidence, as I have shown in the previous chapter. The doctor's evidence for his statement has escaped Anscombe's attention only because it isn't evidence from which the statement could have been derived.

The same goes for an agent's conception of what he's doing. Insofar as that conception serves as the agent's intention, the agent's conduct bears the burden of making it true. But insofar as it serves as information—as the agent's knowledge of his forthcoming conduct—it bears responsibility for being true, and it must be able to vouch for its truth by means of evidence. Fortunately, the requisite evidence is present, as I have also shown in the preceding chapter. Here, too, I have argued, the evidence has escaped Anscombe's attention because the agent's conception of his action isn't and could not have been derived from it.[27]

I hope that I have thereby made an agent's self-knowledge seem worthy of the name. My view, in effect, is that practical knowledge does track the facts—like a hunter. That is, practical knowledge flushes its quarry, making the facts come out in a particular way, and then leads its target, firing at the spot where they're going to come out. This mode of tracking is different from theoretical reasoning, which takes aim only after the facts have come to rest; but it is not simply a matter of firing blindly and then blaming the quarry for not being hit.[28]

PRACTICAL THINKING

Finally, I do not want to end this chapter without reemphasizing a distinction that I drew near the start—namely, the distinction between an agent's reasoning and his thoughts. The self-referential belief that I

[27] A corollary of the present argument is that Warnock's account of promising is also mistaken. Warnock claims that promises are predictions to which the obligation of veracity applies in the opposite of the normal direction—that is, as an obligation to bring the facts into conformity with one's utterance rather than one's utterance into conformity with the facts. I would say that insofar as a promise is meant to convey information about the promisor's future actions, the responsibility for its truth cannot just be delegated to his future self. For suppose that a person has no present grounds for believing that if he promises to do something, he will actually do it. In that case, he is not entitled to make the promise; and if he does make it, he is not only going to *become* guilty of breaking the promise; he is *already* guilty, because he has made a promise that he is not entitled to make. Hence the obligation of veracity never devolves entirely upon the acting rather than the uttering self.

[28] See K. W. Rankin's "Critical Notice" on *Intention* in *Mind* 68 (1959): 261–64: "The distinction . . . between practical and theoretical knowledge is that the latter comprehends only predictions of the sort which should have a sufficient basis in what has happened up to the present moment. . . . Practical knowledge on the other hand comprehends predictions which cannot have a sufficient basis in what has happened up to the present, simply because the intention expressed by these predictions cannot enter into the calculation" (264). Rankin continues, "This opens the door, of course, to the subject of free will, but it is an incomplete sort of enquiry into intention that does not." I attempt to cross the threshold of this topic in chapter 5.

have now identified with the agent's intention to act is the one of which I previously noted that the agent needn't express it in words, even to himself, or that if he does express it, he needn't express it completely. I can now summarize that point by saying that an agent's intentions needn't be represented in his thoughts.

The same goes for all steps of practical reasoning, the premises as well as the conclusions. When I say, for instance, that the necessary grounds for an intention include evidence about the agent's motives, I don't mean to imply that an agent must make mental remarks to himself about his motives before he is entitled to form an intention. In order to have justification for the expectation that constitutes an intention, the agent must know the relevant information about his motives, and in order to ensure against forming an unjustified intention, he must be aware of what he does and doesn't know, but he can know something, and be aware of knowing it, without reciting it to himself.

In general, then, when I claim that intentions issue from reflective theoretical reasoning, I don't mean that they are necessarily preceded by a reflective monologue. I mean that forming intentions is a step in the process by which an agent comes to know and understand what he is doing or will do. I mean that an agent ordinarily forms intentions in such a way that the predictions in which they consist are justified, and in such a way that he can explain why he's forming them.[29] And I mean that intentions are therefore formed in accordance with theoretical norms—the norms governing the prediction and explanation of behavior. But an agent needn't talk to himself about predicting and explaining his behavior in order to form intentions that embody self-knowledge and self-understanding.

Of course, if we wish to discuss a person's reasoning, we must state the contents of his premises and conclusions, and we must state what logical relations he believed to obtain among them. But we shouldn't be deceived by this necessity into assuming that the reasoning under discussion consisted in similar statements rehearsed in the reasoner's head.

Sometimes, of course, an agent does think through some of the reflections that support an intention. He may ask himself, "What do I feel like doing?"; make a mental list of his options, taking note of his

[29] In ordinary theoretical reasoning, to see how a conclusion is justified is to understand why one is forming it. In reflective theoretical reasoning, however, one would be justified in forming any one of several incompatible conclusions, and so seeing what justifies a particular conclusion isn't enough for an understanding of its formation: one must also understand why one is forming that particular conclusion instead of the others that would have been equally justified if one had formed them.

feelings toward each of them; make some remark to himself about what he most wants to do; and only then decide to do it. But at other times the thoughts that precede the formation of an intention are not reflective at all. An agent may simply ask himself how to attain some end, and after figuring out the appropriate means, he may immediately intend to adopt them. Or he may ask what his obligations are and, upon answering, form the intention of fulfilling them. These inner discussions aren't about how to predict and explain the agent's behavior. But then, they don't express all of the reasoning that the agent is doing at the time.

In fact, thinking through one's instrumental and normative reasoning is often what enables one to do reflective theoretical reasoning without thinking. When an agent asks himself how to attain some end, for instance, he shows himself—in case he didn't already know—that he wants to attain it. And when he tells himself that some action is the appropriate means, he shows himself that he believes so. Thus the agent's inner discussion demonstrates, but doesn't state, that the action under discussion is one for which he has motives—namely, the desire and belief manifested by his mental question and answer.

Indeed, if the agent's inner discussion is carried on at the center of his attention, then he will end up, not only with a knowledge of the motives manifested in that discussion, but also with an awareness of having that knowledge. For he will have seen himself listen to the discussion, so to speak, and so he can hardly help knowing that he's aware of the desires and beliefs revealed therein. The resulting self-knowledge will therefore be conscious, and it will consequently be capable of combining with the desire for self-understanding to influence the agent's behavior.

An agent's practical thoughts thus convey more than they say. Their express topic may be simply how to attain a desired end. And yet the agent might have found the means to his end without holding an inner discussion on the subject. By rehearsing his means-ends reasoning on the stage of conscious thought, however, he manages to learn not only how to attain his end but also that he has the motives for thus trying to attain it, and that he knows about those motives.

The agent's next thought may express his intention to implement the means that he has discovered. This practical conclusion doesn't rest solely on the premises that he has consciously stated; rather, it rests on all he has learned by consciously stating those premises—including reflective information about his motives and his knowledge of them. His intention is the belief that under the impetus of those known motives, he will hereby empower those same motives (or some future motives) to make him act.

Of course, if we confuse thinking with reasoning, we shall assume that a transcript of the agent's practical thoughts would fully represent his practical reasoning, with all of his premises and his entire conclusion. And since the agent's practical thoughts display no ordinary logical connections, we won't be able to explain how his premises support his conclusion unless we posit extraordinary connections—a practical logic, under which beliefs about the means to desired ends can support an intention to act. We shall thus be tempted to elevate the patterns of practical thinking into a logic of intentions, distinct from the logic of beliefs. But this temptation will indeed be due to a confusion, since the agent's premises and conclusions don't necessarily appear in a transcript of his thoughts, and the connections between them cannot be surmised from the patterns in which he thinks.

Now, I believe that practical reasoning does follow extraordinary patterns—in particular, the pattern of jumping to a preferred conclusion in order to make it true. But the pattern of reasoning is not its logic. The order of theoretical reasoning, for instance, is the order in which beliefs are formed, which is a psychological matter. But beliefs aren't necessarily formed in order of logical dependence—premises first, conclusions following. Often we adopt a conclusion and then look for evidence, or reject evidence once we see which conclusion it supports.[30] Logical order is something that we try to attain in our beliefs, but we don't attain it by forming beliefs in their logical order.

Practical reasoning differs from theoretical reasoning in that it involves jumping to conclusions and then acting so as to fulfill them. But these steps are taken in pursuit of knowledge, a knowledge whose logic is nothing out of the ordinary.

[30] Gilbert Harman makes this point in "Logic and Reasoning," *Synthese* 60 (1984): 107–27. However, Harman confines logic to deductive logic, whereas I would regard it as encompassing inductive evidential relations.

FOUR

INTENTIONS

I have identified intentions with self-fulfilling expectations that are motivated by a desire for their fulfillment and that represent themselves as such. The explanation and defense of this identity statement is the business of the present chapter.

OBJECTIONS

My theory of intention borrows freely from the work of other philosophers, especially H. P. Grice and Gilbert Harman.[1] Objections that have been raised against their work may therefore count against my theory as well. My first task will be to answer some of those objections.

Are There Intentions?

The most fundamental objection to the approach that I share with Grice and Harman would be that we attempt to attach the word 'intention' to a distinct mental state where no distinct state exists. Those who would press this objection think that the phenomena of practical life can be explained without recourse to any mental states other than the beliefs and desires that have traditionally been conceived as motivating action. These philosophers are happy to use the word 'intention' to convey summary information about an agent's motives, but they insist that the word does not refer to a distinct, additional state of mind.[2]

---

[1] Grice, "Intention and Uncertainty"; Harman, "Practical Reasoning," "Willing and Intending," and *Change in View*, chapter 8.

[2] The staunchest opponent of intention was Ryle, who argued against what he called "the myth of volitions" in chapter 3 of *Concept of Mind*. Anscombe seems to have denied the existence of intention when she said that "an action is not called 'intentional' in virtue of any extra feature which exists when it is performed" (*Intention*, 28; see also 42, 47, 52). But other aspects of Anscombe's theory seem to require a distinct state of intention, and I therefore suspect that in the passages cited she is denying only that intention involves a characteristic feeling or conscious event. Donald Davidson denied the existence of intentions categorically when he said, "The expression 'the intention with which James went to church' has the outward form of a description, but in fact it is syncategorematic and cannot be taken to refer to an entity, state, disposition, or event" ("Actions, Reasons, and Causes," in *Essays on Actions and Events*, 8). But Davidson

I may sometimes sound like a proponent of this view, since I say that intention is nothing but a kind of belief. But in saying that an intention is a belief, I do not mean to say that it is just one of the agent's motives. The belief with which I identify an agent's intention is not among the beliefs that would ordinarily be cited by the classical theory of motivation. Intention, as I characterize it, consists in a belief above and beyond the agent's ordinary motivating beliefs and plays a very different role in producing his action. Those who regard the theory of motivation as sufficient to explain the phenomena of action will therefore reject my reductionist theory of intention.

The ordinary-language approach.   I can well understand why some might think that we can dispense with the concept of intention as a state distinct from ordinary motives. The reason is that the concept is usually expected to serve purposes to which it is unsuited. The traditional assumption is that a philosophical theory of intention will provide a unified analysis of the various expressions in which the word 'intention' or its cognates appear. An account of the state called intention is thus expected to explain what we're talking about when we describe an agent as intending to do something, as doing one thing with the intention of doing another, and simply as doing something intentionally. But some of these expressions resist analysis in terms of intention or are analyzable in other terms, and the concept is consequently branded superfluous.

The idea that intention was supposed to figure in the analysis of intentional action is what led Gilbert Ryle to ridicule intention as a myth.[3] As Ryle pointed out, if we analyze intentional action as action caused by an intention, then we face an infinite regress, since forming an intention is itself something that's done intentionally. Hence positing a distinct state of intention for the purpose of analyzing intentional action is absurd.

When it comes to analyzing the concept of acting with an intention, as opposed to that of intentional action, a distinct mental state turns out to be simply unnecessary. To say that someone does one thing with the intention of doing another is just to say that his motive for the former action is a desire to accomplish the latter. The intention with

---

later retracted this statement (see p. xiii and the essay "Intending," in the same volume). Goldman's *Theory of Human Action* analyzed the concept of intentional action without invoking the concept of intention. But Goldman's later paper "The Volitional Theory Revisited" posits distinct entities called volitions.

   [3] In Ryle's terminology, the myth was that volitions would play a role in the analysis of voluntary action.

which a person acts therefore turns out to be nothing other than his motivating desire.

Planning.   In short, if the only reason for positing a state of intention is to further the analysis of intentional action, or of acting with an intention, then there is no valid reason for positing it at all. But analyzing these expressions isn't the right reason for positing a state of intention. The right reason is simply that the classical theory of motivation by itself is inadequate to describe our practical life. Something is missing from the theory that posits only motives for acting, and 'intention' is the word for it.

The theory of motivation betrays its inadequacies most clearly on the subject of our attitudes toward future actions. We continually plan to do things in the future, and our plans cannot be analyzed in terms of our current motives in relation to the actions planned. One of the most important features of plans, as Michael Bratman has pointed out, is that they settle our course in a way that enables us and those around us to count on our performing particular actions in the future.[4] Yet our motives for acting cannot settle our future actions in this way. On the one hand, our present motives cannot extend their influence into the future: our conduct on future occasions will be determined by the motives we have then, not the ones we have now. On the other hand, planning a future action is not simply a matter of predicting that our future motives will determine us to perform it. Indeed, we often plan to do something precisely because we foresee that in the absence of a prior commitment, our future motives won't bring it about. Hence a plan is neither a premature inclination to act nor a prediction of our future inclination; it's something else, and that something else—that mental commitment to act—is what we call an intention.

Once we recognize this state of mind in our long-range plans, we can see it in our short-range decisions as well. We often decide, or are decided, upon an immediate course of action in a way that clearly resembles our commitment to a future course. This state is typically formed at the close of deliberation: it settles the practical question, leaving us nothing further to deliberate. We can also form this state without deliberating, in which case it *fore*closes deliberation rather than closes it. We tend to speak as if this mental commitment to an action is more than a motivational state: to be most inclined toward an action is not yet to be decided upon doing it. The apparent differ-

4 See Michael Bratman, "Taking Plans Seriously," *Social Theory and Practice* 9 (1983): 271–87.

ence can best be explained in terms of the mental state that is required, in any case, to account for long-range plans.

Although long-range planning is the case that forces us to acknowledge the existence of intention, it is not, in my view, the simplest case, and so it isn't the appropriate case to analyze first. I have therefore begun with immediate intention, and I shall continue to confine myself to it in this chapter, postponing the topic of long-range planning until chapter 8.

The ambiguity of 'intention'.   Note that the state of being decided upon one's next action, which I shall call an immediate intention, is different from the intention with which one acts. The latter is an agent's ultimate motivating desire, or the object of that desire, which is also called the agent's goal. The intention with which the agent is said to act is just the intention of attaining his goal, and attaining his goal is often something that the agent can desire but cannot be decided upon, since whether he attains his goal may not be sufficiently within his control for him to decide. An unskilled marksman may fire his gun out of a desire to hit the target and thus, in one sense, with the intention of hitting it; but he cannot be decided upon hitting it, because the issue of his hitting or missing is not sufficiently within his control to be settled by his deliberation. And since he cannot be decided upon hitting the target, he cannot intend to hit it in the sense of 'intend' that denotes the state of being decided.[5]

The words 'intention' and 'intend' are thus ambiguous.[6] They are used to denote, on the one hand, the agent's attitude toward outcomes that are settled, from his perspective, at the close of deliberation and, on the other hand, his attitude toward outcomes whose pursuit is the topic of his deliberation but whose attainment is not thereby settled. In other words, they are used to denote both plan-states and goal-states of the agent. I am interested in only the former sense of these words, and so I shall use them exclusively in that sense, except when quoting or paraphrasing others.

In ruling these terms ambiguous, I am giving up, once and for all, on the project of finding a unified analysis for the expressions in which

[5] The difference between intention and goal is noted by Annette C. Baier in "Act and Intent," *Journal of Philosophy* 67 (1970): 649ff. Baier's remarks are endorsed by Hector-Neri Castañeda in "Intentions and Intending," *American Philosophical Quarterly* 9 (1972): 140.

[6] This ambiguity is explicated by Harman in "Willing and Intending" and chapter 8 of *Change in View*. However, Harman seems to think that the noun 'intention' and the verb 'intend' gravitate toward opposite poles of the ambiguity. On this point, I don't share Harman's intuitions.

they appear. Some philosophers refuse to give up. As Anscombe puts it, "Where we are tempted to speak of 'different senses' of a word which is clearly not equivocal, we may infer that we are in fact pretty much in the dark about the character of the concept which it represents."[7]

I don't see how Anscombe can be so sure that the word 'intention' isn't equivocal. I would have thought that the best criterion of its being equivocal was precisely whether we are tempted to posit two senses for it. No doubt, there is some unity in the word's meaning, but that unity needn't be at the level of philosophical interest.

Consider a term like 'responsibility', which is from the same conceptual neighborhood. This term, too, has many uses. We call an official's duties his responsibilities, we wonder whether a criminal bears responsibility for his actions, and we praise a solid citizen for acting responsibly. These uses of the term do have something in common, but what they have in common is an ancestral metaphor—the metaphor of answering for an action. And this metaphor invites different interpretations when set in different expressions, yielding literal meanings that are significantly different for philosophical purposes. A person can bear responsibility for actions that aren't in fulfillment or violation of any responsibilities, or he can fulfill his responsibilities without bearing any responsibility for doing so. We are therefore forced to conclude that the term is equivocal.

Similarly, the different uses of the word 'intention' all hark back to a common metaphor—the stretching or aiming of one's mind. But since there are many senses in which the mind can be pictured as having a direction or aim, this unifying metaphor doesn't yield a unitary meaning for the term.

Does Intention Entail Belief?

My greatest debt to Grice's and Harman's work on intention is the thesis that intending to do something entails believing that one will do it. This thesis has other adherents,[8] but it is far from universally accepted.

---

[7] *Intention*, 1.

[8] Adherents include John Austin, *Lectures on Jurisprudence; Or the Philosophy of Positive Law* (London, 1911), 1: 421, 435–36; Sir John Salmond, *Jurisprudence* (London, 1930), 393 (quoted by J. A. Passmore in a symposium with P. L. Heath entitled "Intentions," *Proceedings of the Aristotelian Society, Supplementary Volumes* 29 [1955]: 132); Pears, "Predicting and Deciding," 197–98; "Intentions as Judgements," in *Philosophical Subjects: Essays Presented to P.F. Strawson*, ed. Zak van Straaten (Oxford, 1980), 222–37; *Motivated Irrationality*, 124; and "Intention and Belief," 75–88; Wilfrid Sellars, "Thought and Action," in *Freedom and Determinism*, ed. Keith Lehrer (New York, 1966), 126ff.; Roderick Chisholm, "The Structure of Intention," *Journal of*

Davidson's objection. Donald Davidson, for one, has attempted to refute it, in a well-known article entitled "Intending."[9] Davidson offers counterexamples that purport to show an agent intending to perform a difficult task without necessarily believing that he will succeed. For instance, Davidson claims that "in writing heavily on this page I may be intending to produce ten legible carbon copies," and yet "I do not

---

Philosophy 67 (1970): 646; Rankin, "Non-Causal Self-Fulfillment of Intention," 281; Robert Audi, "Intending," *Journal of Philosophy* 70 (1973): 387–403; Jaegwon Kim, "Intention and Practical Inference," in *Essays on Explanation and Understanding*, ed. Juha Manninen and Raimo Tuomela (Dordrecht, 1976), 249–69; Monroe C. Beardsley, "Intending," in *Values and Morals: Essays in Honor of William Frankena, Charles Stevenson, and Richard Brandt*, ed. Alvin Goldman and Jaegwon Kim (Dordrecht, 1978), 163–84; Wayne Davis, "A Causal Theory of Intending," *American Philosophical Quarterly* 21 (1984): 43ff.; and Benn and Gaus, "Practical Rationality and Commitment," 261.

Stuart Hampshire thinks that intending to do something entails believing that one will *try* to do it and that success is at least a possibility (*Thought and Action*, 102, 107–8, 112, and especially 134). A similarly modified version of the belief thesis is accepted by Jack Meiland, *The Nature of Intention* (London, 1970), 18; and Davis, *Theory of Action*, 75ff. For objections to this modification, see Audi, "Intending," 388–89.

Note the difference between the thesis that intention entails belief and the (perhaps more familiar) thesis that belief entails intention. The latter thesis says that if a person expects particular consequences to flow from an action that he intends, then he also intends those consequences, whether or not he desires them. (See, e.g., Sidgwick, *Methods of Ethics*, 202. For the opposing view see, e.g., Anscombe, *Intention*, 42.) Obviously, to say that foreseen consequences are intended is not the same as to say that intended consequences must be foreseen.

9 *Essays on Actions and Events*, 92. See also "Reply to David Pears," in *Essays on Davidson*, ed. Vermazen and Hintikka, 211–17. For a useful discussion of Davidson's theory of intention, see M. Bratman, "Davidson's Theory of Intention," in *Essays on Davidson*, 13–26. (A somewhat longer version of the same paper appears in *Actions and Events*, ed. Ernest LePore and Brian McLaughlin [Oxford, 1985], 14–28.) Others who have disputed the thesis that intention entails belief include: Irving Thalberg, "Intending the Impossible," *Australasian Journal of Philosophy* 40 (1962): 49–56; David L. Perry, "Prediction, Explanation and Freedom," *Monist* 49 (1965): 237; Castañeda, *Thinking and Doing*, 41–42, and his replies to Michael Bratman and Bruce Aune in *Agent, Language, and the Structure of the World: Essays Presented to Hector-Neri Castañeda, with His Replies*, ed. James E. Tomberlin (Indianapolis, 1983), 395–409, 435–40; Colin McGinn, *The Character of Mind* (New York, 1982), 94; Michael Bratman, "Intention and Means-End Reasoning," *Philosophical Review* 90 (1981): 254–56, and "Two Faces of Intention," *Philosophical Review* 93 (1984): 384–85; Brand, *Intending and Acting*, chapter 6; Peacocke, "Intention and *Akrasia*," 69; and Hugh J. McCann "Rationality and the Range of Intention," *Midwest Studies in Philosophy*, no. 10, ed. Peter A. French, Theodore E. Uehling, Jr., and Howard K. Wettstein (Minneapolis, 1986), 191–211. Although Bratman thinks that intending to do something doesn't entail believing that one will do it, he also thinks that intending to do something while believing that one *won't* do it is irrational ("Castañeda's Theory of Thought and Action," in *Agent, Language, and the Structure of the World*, ed. Tomberlin, 159ff.).

know, or believe with any confidence, that I am succeeding."[10] From such examples Davidson concludes that intending to do something doesn't necessarily entail believing that one will do it.

One of Harman's counterarguments.   Harman offers several persuasive counterarguments.[11] He points out, for instance, that if we wish to concede the difficulty of a task, we don't say that we intend to accomplish it; we say that we intend to try. The reason is precisely that claiming the intention of accomplishing the task would imply that we were confident of success. Indeed, sounding this note of confidence is often the point of stating an intention. For instance, an Olympic athlete may declare that he intends to win a gold medal, in order to convey that he's not merely intent upon victory but also confident of it. Of course, he may be expressing confidence that he doesn't feel, or he may feel confidence to which he isn't entitled; but then, he may also be expressing an intention that he doesn't or isn't entitled to have. Unless Davidson meant to express similar confidence about making ten carbon copies, he should have expressed the intention only of trying to make them.

An objection to Harman's counterargument, with my reply.   Harman's counterargument relies on the assumption that an agent can have the intention of trying to do something and yet lack the intention of doing it. Some philosophers share this assumption,[12] but others disagree.

David Pears has argued that the intention of trying to do something is no different in content from the intention of doing it. Pears's argument is this: "[I]f I were asked whether I had done what I intended to do when I had tried and failed, I would give a negative answer."[13] Hugh McCann has argued, somewhat similarly, that trying to do something entails intending to do it and hence that an intention to try has as its object something that entails the intention to succeed.[14]

The proper response here, I think, is that Pears and McCann are falling prey to the ambiguity of 'intention'. If one tries or intends to

[10] "Intending," 92. Similar cases are offered by Brand, *Intending and Acting*, 149ff.

[11] In "Willing and Intending." Harman repeats these arguments in *Change in View*, chapter 8. Other arguments against Davidson's claim that intention is independent of belief appear in Pears, "Intention and Belief."

[12] E.g., Bratman, in "Two Faces of Intention," 387; and Davis, "A Causal Theory of Intending," 44.

[13] "Intention and Belief," 86.

[14] "Rationality and the Range of Intention," 196ff.

try, then success is ordinarily one's goal,[15] and it is therefore what one intends, in one sense of the word. But it isn't what one intends in the sense of one's being decided upon it, since one wouldn't have needed to speak of trying if one could simply have decided to succeed.[16]

Now, if Davidson doesn't know whether his attempt to make ten carbon copies will succeed, then he cannot have decided or be decided upon making them. He can still intend to make them, in the sense that he can have making them as his goal. But the most that he can intend in my sense—that is, the most that he can be decided upon—is to try. Hence Davidson's example is not one in which he intends to do something, in my sense of the word, without believing that he will.

Another of Harman's counterarguments.   Harman offers a further reason for dismissing supposed examples of intention without belief. He argues that in some cases in which an agent is thought to intend an action without expecting to perform it, he doesn't really intend the action but seems to, because he ends up performing it intentionally. Yet one can do something intentionally without having the intention of doing it, Harman argues,[17] and so the fact that one can do something intentionally without having expected to do it doesn't prove that intention can exist without belief.

Here I would add that the gap between what's done intentionally and what's intended is sometimes due to the ambiguity in the meaning of 'intention'. One is often said to have done something intentionally because doing it was one's goal and hence what one intended, in one sense of the word.[18] Yet I am using the word 'intention' to denote the

[15] There may be cases in which one tries or intends to try but doesn't have success as a goal. For instance, one may try to swing "through" the approaching tennis ball without hoping to succeed. Harman discusses these cases in "Willing and Intending," 370.

[16] One wouldn't have needed to speak of trying, but one would still need to try. For even when one can do something at will, one won't end up doing it if one doesn't try to. Of course, we might say that one can do the thing "without trying," but we wouldn't be speaking literally. That is, we wouldn't mean that one can succeed without ever making an attempt. All we would mean is that one's attempt was bound to succeed, and so there would be no point in talking about it as an attempt rather than as a success. (For the same reason, there would be no point in intending it as an attempt, either.)

[17] Harman defends this claim in "Practical Reasoning" and "Willing and Intending"; he discusses related issues at length in "Rational Action and the Extent of Intentions," *Social Theory and Practice* 9 (1983): 123–41. (The latter paper is the basis for chapter 9 of *Change in View*.) The claim is also defended by Georg Henrik von Wright, *Explanation and Understanding* (Ithaca, N.Y., 1971), 89–90; Davis, *Theory of Action*, chapter 4; and Bratman in "Two Faces of Intention." It is disputed by McCann in "Rationality and the Range of Intention."

[18] Not all cases of intentionally bringing about a result are cases in which the result

state of being decided upon an action, and as we have seen, doing something can be one's goal even when one isn't in a position to be decided upon doing it. The upshot is that one can intentionally accomplish things that one was never in a position to intend, in my sense of the word. Thus, Davidson will end up making his carbon copies intentionally if he makes them at all, since he has the goal of making them. But we cannot infer, from the fact that he may end up making his copies intentionally without expecting to make them, that he intends something he doesn't expect; for he can end up doing something intentionally without (in the relevant sense) intending to do it.

A third counterargument of Harman's. Here is another reason that Harman offers for dismissing supposed examples of intention without belief. He points out that apparent discrepancies between an agent's intentions and his beliefs may be due to differences in the precision with which the attitudes in question are expressed. Just as a person can be said to intend an action even though he concedes that his attempt at it may fail, so he can be said to expect the action despite the same concession. That is, he can admit the possibility of failure and still be said to believe that he'll succeed. Hence Davidson's doubts about whether he'll make ten carbon copies should not prevent him from saying that he still believes he'll make them, any more than they prevent him from saying that he intends to. Davidson can of course reject this characterization of his belief, arguing that if he admits the possibility of failure, then all he believes, strictly speaking, is that he'll make the copies if he can. But then, Harman argues, equal precision should be introduced into the characterization of his intention. If the claim that Davidson expects to succeed should be qualified, on the grounds that what he expects, strictly speaking, is to succeed if he can, then the claim that he intends to succeed should undergo the same qualification. Speaking with equal strictness, what Davidson intends is to make ten carbon copies if he can, and so his intention still corresponds to his belief.

An objection to this counterargument. Davidson objects to the suggestion that his counterexamples involve intentions whose precise expression would require such qualifications. On the one hand, he contends that if intention did entail belief, then "I intend to do it if I can" would convey no more or less than "I intend to do it," since nobody

---

was one's goal. Sometimes a result is said to be intentional because one acted despite being aware that the result might occur and that its possibility was a reason against acting.

uttering the latter would be thought to believe, and hence to intend, that he would do the thing even if he couldn't. On the other hand, Davidson would also reject the suggestion that he should say something more specific, like "I intend to make ten copies if this paper isn't too thick." For according to Davidson, if precision required an agent to mention one condition that he considered necessary to the intended outcome, then it would require him to mention all such conditions— which it clearly doesn't. Thus Davidson would argue, for instance, that if precision required him to say "I intend to make ten copies if this paper isn't too thick," on the grounds that he doesn't believe he'll succeed if it is, then precision would also require him to say "I intend to make ten copies if I'm not struck by lightning, or kidnapped by terrorists," and so on, since he doesn't believe that he'll succeed in any of those circumstances, either. But the latter statement, having been qualified to death, would tell us little about what Davidson intended. He therefore concludes that precision doesn't require him to mention any such conditions. In his view, an agent who states an unqualified intention of doing something but doesn't expect to do it need not be omitting anything from his statement of intention.

A reply to the objection.   One problem with this objection is that even if it was valid, it would apply not just to statements of intention but to statements of belief as well, thus frustrating Davidson's attempt to drive a wedge between the two attitudes. Davidson claims that he intends to make ten carbon copies but that he doesn't believe he will. But Davidson would surely admit to believing that he'll make the copies if he can, and then his own objections should persuade him to drop the qualifier "if I can" and to admit that he believes simply that he'll make the copies. For if the qualifying phrase "if I can" would have added nothing to Davidson's statement of intention, then it would add nothing to his statement of belief, either, and for the same reason—namely, that nobody would take him to believe that he'd make the copies even if he couldn't. And if the phrase "if I can" were no more necessary to a precise statement of intention than other, superfluous phrases such as "unless I'm struck by lightning," then why would it be more necessary to a precise statement of belief? Thus Davidson's reasons for making an unqualified statement of intention would also favor an unqualified statement of belief, thereby removing the discrepancy between his beliefs and intentions.

Of course, Davidson shouldn't remove the qualifier "if I can" from the expression of his belief. But this just goes to show that there's something wrong with his reasons for removing it from the expression of his intention. Indeed, Davidson's essay subsequently provides an example that shows what's wrong.[19] Consider the following passage:

> I intend to eat a hearty breakfast tomorrow. You know, and I know, that I will not eat a hearty breakfast tomorrow if I am not hungry. And I am not certain I will be hungry, I just think I will be. Under these conditions it is not only not more accurate to say, 'I intend to eat a hearty breakfast if I'm hungry', it is *less* accurate. I have the second intention as well as the first, but the first implies the second, and not vice versa, and so the first is a more complete account of my intentions. If you knew only that I intended to eat a hearty breakfast if I was hungry, you would not know that I believe I will be hungry, which is actually the case. But you might figure this out if you knew I intend to eat a hearty breakfast tomorrow.[20]

According to Davidson, if we know that he intends simply to eat breakfast, rather than to eat it if he's hungry, then we can infer that he expects to be hungry. What Davidson doesn't mention is that we might draw a different inference—namely, that he intends to eat breakfast whether he's hungry or not. For all we know, Davidson could be one of those health enthusiasts who force themselves to eat three square meals a day no matter what. But the intention of eating no matter what is not the intention that Davidson professes to have. He implies, on the contrary, that he has no intention of eating if he isn't hungry. But his intention is nevertheless unqualified, because he assumes that he will be hungry—which is what he expects us to infer.

The real moral of Davidson's story, then, is that there are two different ways of intending without qualification. An agent can flatly intend to do something either because he intends to do it under any condition or because he intends to do it under particular conditions that he believes will obtain.[21] Davidson's unqualified intention of eating breakfast can arise from either of two underlying states—an intention of eating whether or not he's hungry; or an intention of eating if he's hungry, together with the belief that he will be.

---

[19] For a slightly different though compatible explanation, see Anscombe, *Intention*, 92–93.

[20] "Intending," 100.

[21] See Michael Bratman, "Simple Intention," *Philosophical Studies* 36 (1979): 246: "Ordinary language distinguishes between conditions which are cited in the content of a conditional intention and those conditions whose expectation serves as a background against which one's intentions are held. Though these latter conditions are not cited in the content of one's intention, they constitute circumstances of the intended action whose expectation qualifies one's intention."

Because an unqualified intention can arise in two different ways, the implications of qualifying the statement of an intention are doubled. For as Davidson points out, stating a qualified intention is imprecise if one could have stated the same intention unqualified. The result is that if someone says "I intend to eat breakfast if I'm hungry" and purports to be speaking precisely, then he implies that he isn't in a position to form an unqualified intention of eating breakfast. As we have seen, he would have been in a position to form the unqualified intention either if he had intended to eat no matter what or if, in addition to intending to eat if he was hungry, he assumed that he would be hungry. Hence someone who says "I intend to eat if I'm hungry" implies, not only that he doesn't intend to eat unless he's hungry, but also that he isn't assuming that he will be.

We can now see that Davidson was mistaken to say that if intention entails belief, then the statement "I intend to do it if I can" says no more or less than "I intend to do it." As we have just seen, the qualified statement implies, not only that one doesn't intend to do the thing unless one can, but also that one isn't assuming that one can do it. The former implication may be trivial, if intention entails belief, but the latter is not. Conversely, the unqualified statement "I intend to do it" implies that one either intends to do the thing even if one can't or is assuming that one can. And although the former implication is absurd, if intention entails belief, the latter is not.

Davidson was equally mistaken when he said that if precision required an agent to mention one condition that he considered necessary to the intended outcome, then it would require him to mention all such conditions. What precision requires is that the agent mention only those conditions which meet two criteria—namely, that he considers them necessary to the intended outcome and that he isn't confident of their being satisfied. Hence precision may well require Davidson to say "I intend to make ten copies if this paper isn't too thick" but not ". . . if I'm not struck by lightning" and so on. For Davidson may assume that he won't be struck by lightning, while suspecting that the paper is indeed too thick.

I therefore reject Davidson's reasons against qualifying his statement of intention.[22] The point of saying "I intend to make ten copies if I

---

[22] Davidson offers one further reason, which I find equally unconvincing. He argues that the intention "I'll do it if I can" is not genuinely conditional, as is the intention "I'll leave the picnic if it starts to rain" ("Intending," 94). (The same point is made by McCann in "Rationality and the Range of Intention," 197.) True enough, the relation between antecedent and consequent in "I'll do it if I can" is different from that in "I'll leave if it rains." But all that this contrast can prove is that intentions can be conditional in

can" would not be to rule out the notion that he intends to make the copies even if he can't, which would be absurd whether or not intention entailed belief, but rather would be to express uncertainty about whether he can make the copies, which is precisely what prevents him (so he claims) from believing categorically that he will. The doubts that lead Davidson to qualify his statement of belief should therefore lead him to qualify his statement of intention, and so I stand by my contention that Davidson believes precisely what he intends.[23]

Does Intention Consist in Belief?

Thus far I have answered objections to the thesis that intention entails belief, a thesis that I share with Grice and Harman, among others. I part company with Grice, and perhaps with Harman, too, in stating the stronger thesis that intending to do something not only entails believing that one will do it but actually consists in that belief.[24] The stronger thesis has also been disputed, by Davidson and others.[25]

---

more than one way. We place conditions on some intentions in order to make them consistent with conditional desires—that is, desires to act only under certain conditions. We place conditions on other intentions in order to make them consistent with our beliefs about the conditions under which they can be fulfilled. The fact that the resulting intentions are conditional in different ways doesn't entail that some of them aren't genuinely conditional.

[23] I believe that the same arguments would prevail against a counterexample offered by Bratman in "Two Faces of Intention," 384–85.

[24] Harman seems to endorse this thesis in "Practical Reasoning," although he adds that intentions differ from mere beliefs in that they issue from practical rather than theoretical reasoning (448ff.). Some have interpreted this qualification as showing that Harman rejects the identification of intentions with beliefs (e.g., McCann, "Rationality and the Range of Intention," 191). Whatever his position in "Practical Reasoning," Harman does reject the identification of intentions with beliefs in his recent book, *Change in View*.

John Austin sometimes says that a future-directed intention consists solely in the belief that one is going to act. See, e.g., *Lectures on Jurisprudence*, 437: "Such being the forms of language, it is somewhat difficult to admit, at first hearing, 'that a present *intention* to do a future act is nothing but a present *belief* that we shall do an act in future.' But that nothing but this really passes in the mind any man may convince himself by examining the state of his mind when he intends a future act." On the preceding page, however, Austin says that a future-directed intention comprises not only the belief that one is going to act but the desire to act as well.

In *Thought and Action*, Hampshire says, "My intention to do something is a settled belief about my future action" (123). This remark is so offhand, however, that I hesitate to list Hampshire as a proponent of intention-belief identity.

[25] In this section I shall discuss the objections of Davidson, Bratman, and Brand. Objections raised by Grice have already been quoted in note 11 of chapter 2, and discussed in the accompanying text. Objections raised by Harman are discussed in the text accompanying note 46. Of the objections raised by K. W. Rankin, one has been discussed in

Davidson's argument.   Davidson's argument against identifying intention with belief is that "reasons for intending to do something are
in general quite different from reasons for believing one will do it":

> Here is why I intend to reef the main: I see a squall coming, I want
> to prevent the boat from capsizing, and I believe that reefing the
> main will prevent the boat from capsizing. I would put my reasons
> for intending to reef the main this way: a squall is coming, it
> would be a shame to capsize the boat, and reefing the main will
> prevent the boat from capsizing. But these reasons for intending
> to reef the main in themselves give me no reason to believe I will
> reef the main. Given additional assumptions, for example, that the
> approach of a squall is a reason to believe I believe a squall is
> coming, and that the shamefulness of capsizing the boat may be a
> reason to believe I want to prevent the boat from capsizing; and
> given that I have these beliefs and desires, it may be reasonable to
> suppose I intend to reef the main, and will in fact do so. So there
> may be a loose connection between reasons of the two kinds, but
> they are not at all identical (individual reasons may be the same,
> but a smallest natural set of reasons that supports the intention to
> act cannot be a set that supports the belief that the act will take
> place).[26]

note 20 of chapter 2; others will be discussed in this chapter's notes 47, 48, and 50. I
shall not devote any space in the text to the objections raised by Castañeda in chapter 6
of *Thinking and Doing.* Let me address them briefly here.
   Castañeda's major objections are all variants of the following. Suppose (to use one of
Castañeda's examples) that Martin intends to sell the house that he will inherit tomorrow. In that case, Martin must believe that he will inherit a house tomorrow. And if we
regard Martin's attitude toward selling the house, like his attitude toward inheriting it,
as a belief, then we must regard him as having the same attitude toward both the sale
and the inheritance. Yet whereas Martin intends to sell the house, he doesn't intend to
inherit it. (Castañeda makes similar remarks about conditional and disjunctive intentions.)
   My answer to this and similar objections is that they fail to recognize the full content
of the belief constituting an intention. The difference between Martin's attitude toward
selling the house and his attitude toward inheriting it is this: he believes that his selling
the house, but not his inheriting it, will be partly due to this very belief. Castañeda comes
close to considering this possibility (163) but he dismisses it as "circular."
   Castañeda also raises some objections having to do with the "logic" of intentions.
Since I deny that there is any such logic, I rule out such objections from the outset. (See
chapter 3, 108.)
   Finally, some discussions of the thesis that intention consists in belief contain objections that are obviously inapplicable to my version of the thesis. See Pears, "Intentions
as Judgements," and Meiland, *Nature of Intention,* chapter 9.
   [26] "Intending," 95.

I find this argument difficult to interpret, because it never explicitly describes the alleged difference between reasons for intending and reasons for believing. I think that Davidson must have something like the following in mind.[27] On the one hand, Davidson assumes that sufficient reason for believing "I'm going to reef the main" must consist in convincing prior evidence of its truth. And he rightly thinks that reasons for intending "I'm going to reef the main" cannot consist in prior evidence of its truth, since the whole point of having an intention with that content is to *make* it true. That is, the point of Davidson's intending to reef the main is to bring about his reefing the main, and so evidence showing that he is already going to reef the main would tend, not to favor the intention, but to prove it superfluous. Davidson therefore concludes that any set of reasons sufficient to support the belief would be sufficient to preempt the intention, while any set of reasons that didn't preempt the intention wouldn't support the belief. (This, I assume, is what Davidson means when he says, "[A] smallest natural set of reasons that supports the intention to act cannot be a set that supports the belief.")

On the other hand, Davidson thinks that reasons for intending to reef the main must include some desire or other "pro-attitude" whose fulfillment would be promoted by his reefing the main. And he seems to assume that wanting something that would be promoted by his reefing the main is no reason for believing that he will in fact reef the main. Davidson concedes that the fact of his having such a desire may, together with other facts about his psychological state, provide reason for the belief in question. But the desire itself is a state with an optative or evaluative content, such as "Let the boat not capsize!" or, as Davidson puts it, "It would be a shame to capsize the boat." And because such contents do not reflect on the truth of "I'm going to reef the main"—or of any other proposition, for that matter—Davidson assumes that they cannot provide reason for believing it.

A reply to Davidson's argument. I think that Davidson has correctly identified the difference between reasons for intending something and reasons for believing it in the ordinary way; but the belief with which I have identified intention is not an ordinary belief. It is an extraordinary belief, because it is consciously self-fulfilling, and one of the ex-

[27] In interpreting this argument I have been aided by a letter from Professor Davidson himself, for which I am most grateful. I should note, however, that my interpretation attributes to Davidson a more complicated argument than his letter avows. Roughly, I credit Davidson with a two-pronged argument, whereas Davidson's letter acknowledges only the latter prong. I believe that the text of "Intending" implicitly contains the former.

traordinary features of such a belief is precisely that the reasons for it
are more like reasons for intending than reasons for believing.

On the one hand, a self-fulfilling belief is one for which there can be
no convincing prior evidence and hence no sufficient reason, in the
sense that Davidson seems to have in mind. As I have already argued
and shall argue again, a self-fulfilling belief is not dictated by prior
evidence, since the evidence preceding such a belief shows only that it
or one of several other, incompatible beliefs will come true, depending
on which one is formed.[28] This evidence cannot dictate the adoption
of any particular belief, since the evidence shows that one would be
equally correct to adopt any of the alternatives.[29] Hence the reasons
for forming a self-fulfilling belief cannot be of the sort that would
preempt the corresponding intention.

On the other hand, forming a self-fulfilling belief is a means of making it true, and so any desire whose fulfillment would be promoted by
making it true provides a reason for forming it. Thus, a desire to prevent the boat from capsizing does provide reason for Davidson to form
the self-fulfilling belief that he'll reef the main, since forming that belief
is means of getting himself to reef the main, which will prevent the boat
from capsizing.

Thus, the reasons for forming a self-fulfilling belief cannot include
compelling evidence of its truth but can include a desire whose fulfillment would be promoted by its coming true. Reasons for intending
and reasons for believing are therefore exactly alike in the case of self-
fulfilling belief.

Bratman's argument.   Michael Bratman has improved on Davidson's
argument against identifying intentions with beliefs, by considering
what these attitudes provide reasons for, rather than what provides
reasons for them.[30] Bratman argues that intention cannot consist in
belief because the intention of doing something, unlike the belief that
one will do it, gives one reason to adopt some means of doing it. To
cite Bratman's example, intending to meet someone uptown gives one
a reason for taking the uptown bus, whereas believing in the same uptown rendezvous gives one no reason for taking steps to bring it about.

I am not yet in a position to answer Bratman's argument in detail,

---

[28] For my arguments on this point, see chapter 2, 58–64, and chapter 5, 149–58.

[29] This is true even if Davidson has convincing evidence about which action he is going
to expect. I have argued this point briefly in note 13 of chapter 2. I shall argue it at length
in chapter 5.

[30] "Intention and Means-End Reasoning," 252–56. Harman offers a similar objection
in "Willing and Intending," 375–76.

for two reasons. First, I have not yet discussed intentions of the sort that Bratman has in mind—long-range intentions whose fulfillment requires the adoption of subordinate means. Second, I have not yet presented my theory of reasons for acting. I can nevertheless foreshadow my answer to Bratman's argument, by reiterating that I have shown how expecting an action can constitute an intermediate step in a process of reasoning that concludes with the action's performance. If reasons for acting are something like considerations that would lead to action by a process of practical reasoning, then expecting to act can indeed be a reason for acting. I shall spell out this answer to Bratman in chapters 7 and 8.

Brand's argument. Myles Brand has argued that beliefs cannot attain the degree of complexity that is required in intentions. According to Brand, an intention "involves two distinct, though complementary representations":

> One is a prospective representation of the course of action and the other is a detailed pattern of representations for specific bodily movements. The first concerns the agent's plan for action and remains relatively stable throughout the activity; the second is the basis for feedback and correction during the course of the plan, and thus changes as the plan proceeds. . . . [T]he folk psychological notion of belief is not an attitude that can support contents of this complexity. Thus the cognitive component of intention is something other than belief.[31]

To begin with, I don't understand why Brand assumes that an agent's intention to perform an action must include a "basis" for monitoring and correcting his performance of the action as it unfolds. I am inclined to say that the basis for such in-flight guidance is the agent's know-how or skill—that is, his ability to perform the intended action. To be sure, an agent isn't entitled to intend to do something unless he knows how.[32] But his intention of performing the action needn't incorporate everything he knows about how to perform it.

More importantly, I disagree with Brand about the degree of complexity that beliefs can attain. I have already discussed instances of belief whose content, as understood by the unsophisticated observer,

[31] *Intending and Acting,* 153–54. See also Brand's "Intending and Believing," in *Agent, Language, and the Structure of the World,* ed. Tomberlin, 171–93.
[32] Of course, he needn't know how to do something in order to intend on doing it *later,* since he can intend on acquiring the requisite know-how in the interim. But in this chapter I have confined the discussion to immediate intentions.

is dizzyingly complex. I therefore see no reason to assume that beliefs cannot incorporate the kinds of complexity that Brand attributes to intentions. Brand has probably mistaken the very real limits on the complexity of what we can intelligibly say—and hence on the complexity of what we can intelligibly say that people believe—for limits on the complexity of belief itself. The fact that we have trouble stating something that we believe someone to believe doesn't entail that we have trouble believing him to believe it—as my earlier examples illustrate.[33]

Can Toddlers Intend?

Several colleagues who have heard my account of intentions have raised a further objection, as follows.[34] According to my account, intentions consist in beliefs of a sort that are available only to agents who have the appropriate desires for self-awareness and self-understanding. Agents who lack these desires will also lack any tendency to fulfill their reflective expectations. These agents will not be in a position to form reflective expectations as a means to their fulfillment, and so they will not be in a position to form intentions, as I conceive them. The objection is that my theory would therefore place intentions beyond the capacity of agents who are in fact capable of them, such as young children.

The logic of this objection is correct. I gladly concede that agents who lack the requisite desires must also lack the capacity for intentions, according to my theory. Where I demur is at the suggestion that my theory is therefore at odds with the facts, because there are agents who are capable of forming intentions without the desires in question. In particular, I doubt whether young children are such agents.

On the one hand, whether young children are capable of intentions is, to my mind, an open question. Of course, toddlers—and perhaps even infants—are capable of having goals and hence of acting with intentions, in one sense of the word. But I am using the word in a different sense, which denotes the state of being decided upon a course of action. And my own experience with children under the age of two leads me to wonder whether they can truly intend actions in this sense.

---

[33] Brand also argues that occurrent beliefs, which are the candidates for the cognitive component of intention, are accessible to consciousness and unchanging, whereas the guidance component of intention is not. I deny that beliefs must be either accessible or stable. For a relevant discussion of the ways in which beliefs change with the passage of time, see chapter 8, 216–21.

[34] Here I am grateful to Michael Bratman, among others. Gilbert Harman answers a similar objection to his theory of intention in "Practical Reasoning," 441 n.5.

On the other hand, there remains the question when children develop the desires for self-awareness and self-understanding. One would be wrong to assume that these desires require a fully articulated concept of the self, a concept of the sort that emerges only after the age of three. Surely, even infants have the desire to make sense of their world, and their world is at first composed mainly of themselves. As they gain control of their limbs, they must gradually discover their ability to make their world go intelligibly and predictably. They are then on the way to agency, as I conceive it, even before they have distinguished themselves from their surroundings.

I therefore see no reason to regard young children as obvious counterexamples to the theory that intentions require desires for self-knowledge. My guess is that the capacity for intentions and the requisite desires develop hand-in-hand during the first three years of life.

Can We Believe What We Like?

Another possible objection to my account of intention is that it overestimates a person's voluntary control over what he believes. When I identified intentions with reflective expectations, I argued that an agent can direct his expectations, like his intentions, toward any action he likes.[35] Yet some philosophers have claimed that beliefs cannot be formed at will.[36]

The conceptual argument. The most common argument against the possibility of believing at will is that mental states formed at will would fail to meet one of the conditions necessary for qualifying as a belief. Here is how Bernard Williams puts it:

> If I could acquire a belief at will, I could acquire it whether it was true or not; moreover I would know that I could acquire it whether it was true or not. If in full consciousness I could will to acquire a 'belief' irrespective of its truth, it is unclear that before the event I could seriously think of it as a belief, i.e. as something purporting to represent reality. At the very least, there must be a restriction on what is the case after the event; since I could not then, in full consciousness, regard this as a belief of mine, i.e. something I take to be true, and also know that I acquired it at

---

[35] Within limits, of course. These limits were spelled out in chapter 2, 57.

[36] See Williams, "Deciding to Believe," which I shall presently quote in the text. See also David Wiggins, "Freedom, Knowledge, Belief and Causality," in *Knowledge and Necessity*, ed. G.N.A. Vesey (London, 1970), 132–54; Hampshire, *Freedom of the Individual*, 86–87; Elster, *Ulysses and the Sirens*, 47–54, 105–6; and O'Shaughnessy, *The Will*, 1: 21ff.

will. With regard to no belief could I know—or, if all this is to be done in full consciousness, even suspect—that I had acquired it at will. But if I can acquire beliefs at will, I must know that I am able to do this; and could I know that I was capable of this feat, if with regard to every feat of this kind which I had performed I necessarily had to believe that it had not taken place?[37]

The gist of Williams's argument is this. According to Williams, if a person ever thought that he had come to believe something at will, then he would have to think that he believed it irrespective of its truth. But if he thought that he believed it irrespective of its truth, then he wouldn't really believe it, after all, since any attitude that isn't regarded by its subject as reflecting the truth isn't a belief. Hence the person's attitude wouldn't qualify as a belief if he thought that he had formed it at will. In order to form a belief at will, he would have to think that he hadn't done so. And Williams suggests that a person couldn't really have the ability to form beliefs at will if, in order to exercise that ability, he would have to remain ignorant of having exercised it.

I have my doubts about the last step in this argument.[38] But I am more interested in rebutting the first premise, which says that a person cannot regard his beliefs as representing the truth if he regards them as formed at will. This premise is obviously false in the case of beliefs that represent themselves as self-fulfilling.[39] For if a person thinks of his beliefs as self-fulfilling, then he will see that aligning them with his wishes won't entail taking them out of alignment with the truth, for the simple reason that the truth will take care of aligning itself with them. He can therefore think of himself both as believing what he likes and as believing only what's true, because what's true depends on what he believes.

Of course, the dependence between truth and belief in this case doesn't run in the direction that Williams has in mind. What Williams has in mind, when he says that beliefs formed at will would have to be formed irrespective of their truth, is that they could not be formed *because* they were true. He's right, of course, but he's forgetting that such beliefs could be true because they were formed—in which case, their

[37] "Deciding to Believe," 148.
[38] For a critique of this step, as well as other aspects of the argument, see Barbara Winters, "Believing at Will," *Journal of Philosophy* 76 (1979): 243–56.
[39] Elster notes this exception: "The causal efficacy of a belief for a given end can never provide grounds or reasons for *adopting* that belief, with the possible exception of self-fulfilling beliefs" (*Ulysses and the Sirens*, 48).

formation wouldn't be irrespective of their truth, after all. Whether a person thinks that he believes something because it's true or that it will come true because he believes it, his belief can still "purport to represent reality" and can therefore qualify as a full-fledged belief.[40]

The psychological argument. One might suggest that although beliefs could in principle respect both the truth and the subject's wishes, they simply don't respect his wishes in practice. Maybe the cognitive mechanisms that form beliefs just aren't hooked up, so to speak, to the conative mechanisms that transmit the force of desires. Maybe beliefs are somehow shielded from any force but that of the evidence.

This suggestion would also be obviously false. For if our beliefs were somehow insulated from our desires about what to believe, then there would be no such thing as wishful thinking—which there most certainly is. None of the philosophers writing about whether we can believe things at will has thought to question the fact that we often form the beliefs whose truth we most desire and that we form them because we want them to be true. The only question has been whether such wishful thinking could ever be elevated from a subliminal tendency of belief-formation to a deliberate policy. And the only obstacle that has been seen to stand in the way of deliberate wishful thinking is not that it would be wishful but that it would be deliberate. That is, the supposed obstacle to deliberate wishful thinking is that it would require acknowledging that one's beliefs constituted wishful thinking; which would be tantamount to acknowledging that they bore no connection to the truth; which would be tantamount, in turn, to abandoning them altogether.

I have shown that this obstacle is absent in the case of self-fulfilling beliefs. Because self-fulfilling beliefs cause their own truth, instead of being caused by it, their connection to the truth isn't threatened by the fact that they are caused by the subject's wishes. They remain reliably connected to the truth even if they are determined by what the subject wants to believe, and so they afford an opportunity for deliberate wishful thinking.

[40] The same mistake appears in Hampshire's argument, *Freedom of the Individual,* 86–87: "He who believes cannot at the same time suppose his belief to be misplaced and misguided. He cannot regard it as something that he happens to have, or as a fact about himself which he may deplore, but must accept. . . . The subject may in retrospect acknowledge that his beliefs were formed, or changed, by factors other than evidences of truth. But he cannot form them, or change them, except under the impression, whether illusory or not, that the evidences of truth require the change." Here Hampshire mistakenly equates regarding one's beliefs as *true* with regarding them as *formed in response to their truth.*

Having shown that wishful thinking could become deliberate in the case of self-fulfilling beliefs, I simply refuse to entertain the objection that wishful thinking is impossible in any case. Of course it isn't impossible. I do it all the time.

To those who still doubt whether they can adopt self-fulfilling beliefs at will, I commend the following passage from Anscombe's *Intention*: "People sometimes say that one can get one's arm to move by an act of will but not a matchbox; but if they mean 'Will a matchbox to move and it won't', the answer is 'If I will my arm to move in that way, it won't', and if they mean 'I can move my arm but not the matchbox' the answer is that I can move the matchbox—nothing easier."[41] I suspect that those who doubt their ability to adopt self-fulfilling beliefs at will are imagining how little they would accomplish by an inner act of willing themselves to believe. But they would accomplish just as little with an inner act of willing their arms to move. The fact remains that they can move their arms (or a matchbox) at will. Similarly, they can believe at will—nothing easier.

Self-supporting desires.   A more remote objection to the claim that one can jump to self-fulfilling conclusions might occur to readers of Stephen Schiffer's essay "A Paradox of Desire."[42] In that essay, Schiffer describes self-supporting desires of a kind that closely resemble self-fulfilling beliefs. The resemblance is so close, in fact, that if self-fulfilling beliefs are responsive to the will, then Schiffer's brand of desires should be, too. Since the idea of choosing to desire may seem just as implausible as that of choosing to believe, Schiffer's article may seem to indicate further unacceptable consequences of my argument.

A self-supporting desire, as described by Schiffer, is a desire whose object is the pleasure, or the relief from discomfort, that would result from satisfying this very desire in a particular way. Schiffer describes thirst, for example, as a desire for its own quenching—that is, a desire for the combined relief and pleasure that would result from appeasing this very desire with a drink.

Such a desire would indeed be odd. For according to Schiffer, one wouldn't be thirsty if one didn't want to quench one's thirst; yet how could one want to quench one's thirst if one wasn't already thirsty? Odd as this desire would be, however, it would be no odder than self-justifying beliefs. For according to my theory, one wouldn't be about

[41] P. 52.
[42] *American Philosophical Quarterly* 13 (1976): 195–203.

to act if one didn't expect to; yet how could one expect to act if one wasn't already about to?

The answer in the case of self-fulfilling beliefs, I have argued, is that one can simply adopt the expectation of acting, even before one is about to act, precisely because one will be about to act as soon as one expects to. But then a comparable answer should be available in the case of self-supporting desires. That is, one should be able to adopt the desire for an object even before its attainment seems desirable, precisely because its attainment will seem desirable as soon as one desires it. If one can adopt the belief "I'm going to act in order to bear out this very belief," then one should also be able to adopt the desire "Let me drink in order to satisfy this very desire." Why, then, can't one choose to be thirsty?

My answer to this question is, on the one hand, that thirst doesn't really fit Schiffer's description of a self-supporting desire and, on the other hand, that there are desires that do fit Schiffer's description and that can indeed be adopted at will. Hence truly self-supporting desires, far from refuting my thesis, actually confirm it.

The reason why thirst isn't a self-supporting desire is that the discomfort one wants to relieve when one desires a drink is not the discomfort of that very desire; indeed, it's not the discomfort of a desire at all. Rather, it's the discomfort of dehydration, a physical state that precedes and causes one's desire to drink. Thirst (like other appetites) is not merely a desire but a desire produced by, and referring to, a physical need. The associated pleasures and discomforts are due to the need, not to the desire.[43] The reason why one cannot choose to be thirsty is simply that one can't choose to be dehydrated or to suffer the discomforts characteristic of dehydration; and so the impossibility of choosing to be thirsty has no bearing on the possibility of choosing to have desires that would be truly self-supporting.

That one can indeed choose to have some desires is convincingly illustrated, I think, by an example of Gilbert Harman's.[44] Harman points out that when one is watching a game between two teams in which one has no antecedent interest, one can simply choose a side and adopt a desire for that side to win. I agree with Harman that such a desire can be adopted at will. I would simply add that the reason why it can be adopted at will is that it is a self-supporting desire in the sense defined by Schiffer. When one has adopted the desire for a particular

[43] For a similar critique of Schiffer, see Richard E. Grandy and Stephen L. Darwall, "On Schiffer's Desires," *The Southern Journal of Philosophy* 17 (1979): 193–98.
[44] "Practical Reasoning," 459.

team to win, one wants them to win because their victory would be gratifying, and their victory would be gratifying just because one wants them to win. In short, one wants their victory as a means of gratifying this very desire. And what enables one to adopt this desire at will is that having the desire makes its object desirable in precisely that respect in which one then desires it.[45] Hence self-supporting desires, like self-fulfilling beliefs, can be adopted at will.

False counterexamples. Now, I do not deny that particular people may find themselves incapable of mustering particular beliefs even though those beliefs would be self-fulfilling. Such people have psychological blocks against the beliefs in question—possibly because they know that the beliefs would be self-fulfilling and they have psychological blocks against promoting their fulfillment. In any case, their experience doesn't support a psychological generalization to the effect that no beliefs can be formed at will; all it supports is the narrower conclusion that some people have trouble forming some beliefs.

These cases, though incapable of refuting my thesis, are at least genuine exceptions to it. Unfortunately, other cases are likely to be mistaken for exceptions to my thesis even though they are not.

Consider the case of an insomniac who correctly believes that he'll lie awake and that he'll do so precisely because he believes so.[46] The

---

[45] Here I am disagreeing, by the way, with Harman's characterization of the adopted desire. Harman says that the adopted desire is an intrinsic desire, in that one doesn't want the team to win for the sake of any ulterior benefits that will accrue from their victory; I say that one wants the team to win for the sake of the gratification that their victory will afford this very desire. My guess is that Harman has mistakenly inferred, from the fact that the adopted desire isn't *motivated* by a *prior* expectation of benefits, to the conclusion that it isn't supported by any such expectation. The desire is in fact supported by an expectation of benefits, but it's supported by an expectation that couldn't have preceded the desire and hence couldn't have motivated it. One's expectation of gaining from the team's victory is dependent upon one's wanting them to win, since the gain that one expects is the gratification of that desire. And because the desire is necessary for the expectation of gain, it couldn't have been preceded or motivated by that expectation. As soon as one wants the team to win, however, one does expect to gain from their victory—and wants them to win because of that expected gain. My diagnosis of Harman's mistake, in short, is that he has confused the grounds and the occasion of a desire in much the same way that Anscombe confuses the grounds and the occasion of a belief.

[46] This case is discussed, for slightly different reasons, by Harman in "Practical Reasoning," 448; and "Willing and Intending," 375. Harman presents the case as a counterexample to the thesis that intentions consist in beliefs. But the version of this thesis that Harman considers is different from mine and is therefore subject to different counterexamples. The version that Harman considers says merely that intentions are self-consciously self-fulfilling beliefs, and this claim is indeed refuted by the case of the in-

insomniac would seem to be in a position to have either one of two self-fulfilling beliefs, since he lies awake because he believes that he will, and might not lie awake if he believed that he wouldn't. Yet he cannot simply choose to believe that he won't lie awake; if he could, he wouldn't have insomnia. What's more, the reason why he can't just choose to believe that he won't lie awake would seem to be that it isn't true. This case therefore seems to show that a person may be unable to form a belief that isn't already true, even though it would be true if he formed it.

I believe that this case and others like it show nothing of the kind, because they aren't actually cases of potentially self-fulfilling beliefs. Although the insomniac's believing that he won't fall asleep does ensure that he won't, his believing that he would fall asleep would not ensure that he would. Hence the insomniac is not in a position to form the latter belief with any confidence of thereby making it true, and so he's not in a position to form that belief at all.

The reason is that the insomniac's problem involves more than his beliefs. It involves, above all, his fear of not sleeping; it also involves the thought of not sleeping, quite independently of the associated belief. The insomniac's fear of not sleeping may be aroused long before he forms a belief on the subject: his fear is aroused as soon as the very thought of sleeplessness crosses his mind. (Similarly, one's fear of flying is aroused by the thought of a crash, whether or not one actually believes that a crash will occur.) When a fear is aroused, of course, it causes symptoms of anxiety, and symptoms of anxiety are precisely what prevent an insomniac from sleeping. In order to fall asleep, then, the insomniac must avoid the anxiety that would be provoked by thoughts of insomnia. Indeed, he must stop thinking about sleep altogether, since the thought of sleep reminds him of insomnia, which arouses his fear of insomnia, which causes symptoms of anxiety, which keep him awake.

Now, avoiding a thought is notoriously difficult, since the forbidden thought is brought to mind by any conscious effort to avoid it. As soon as the insomniac says to himself, "I have to avoid thinking about

---

somniac, since his belief that he won't sleep is self-consciously self-fulfilling and yet doesn't amount to an intention of not sleeping.

But the insomniac's belief isn't adopted out of the insomniac's desire for its fulfillment, nor does it represent itself as such; and so it doesn't qualify as a counterexample to my account of intentions. I have therefore redeployed this case to a front where it has a better chance of damaging my theory.

For some interesting comments on the phenomenology of insomnia, see Jon Elster, *Sour Grapes: Studies in the Subversion of Rationality* (Cambridge, 1983), 45–46.

sleep," he has already failed. To be sure, his task becomes even more difficult if he believes that he won't sleep. For he wants to sleep, and any desire tends to turn the desirer's thoughts to the desired object, especially if he is unsure of attaining it. If the insomniac were confident of sleeping, his desire to sleep would be placated, its object having been secured, and he might then have a better chance of laying his thoughts of sleep to rest. But if he doubts whether he'll sleep, his desire to sleep will continually remind him of its object, still to be attained. The insomniac's belief that he won't sleep is therefore self-fulfilling.

Yet the opposite belief wouldn't necessarily be self-fulfilling. For even if the insomniac believed that he would sleep, he wouldn't necessarily be able to avoid thinking of sleep and thereby arousing his fear of sleeplessness. An expectation of sleeping would eliminate one potential source of anxiety-provoking thoughts but not all sources of such thoughts, and so it wouldn't ensure that he would sleep. Hence the insomniac knows that he wouldn't necessarily sleep even if he believed so, and this knowledge is what prevents him from believing so.

Indeed, the very conditions that would prevent confidence of sleeping from lulling the insomniac to sleep would already have come about if he entertained the idea of adopting such confidence as a soporific. That is, if the insomniac asked himself, "Wouldn't I now be able to sleep if I adopted the belief that I can?" the answer would already be no, since entertaining this question would have raised the issue of sleep, thus arousing his fear of not sleeping, and so on. In order for the insomniac to be lulled to sleep by the belief that he would sleep, the belief would have to be unconscious, so that it didn't bring the unsettling issue of sleep to mind. And how could the insomniac adopt an unconscious belief at will?

Thus, the insomniac never really faces the possibility of adopting a self-fulfilling belief that he will sleep. Believing that he'd sleep might indeed improve his chances of sleeping. But if he consciously considered this possibility, he would thereby eliminate it. The insomniac's case therefore proves nothing about cases in which an agent faces the possibility of adopting a genuinely self-fulfilling belief.

The case of self-doubt. The insomniac's case isn't the only apparent counterexample to my claim that one can form self-fulfilling beliefs at will. There are many similar cases, each with its own psychological peculiarities. Consider the case of ordinary schoolchildren, whose academic ability tends to appear as high or as low as they think it is, but who cannot simply choose to believe that they are able students. I imagine that the psychological mechanism here is less sensitive to stray thoughts and more directly geared to beliefs than the mechanism that causes insomnia. That is, a child who believes in himself will probably vindicate that belief even if thoughts of failure cross his mind. I therefore cannot claim that what prevents a child from simply choosing a positive self-appraisal is the suspicion that the positive effects of such an appraisal would be cancelled by unnerving thoughts.[47]

Even so, this case doesn't refute the claim that self-fulfilling beliefs can be formed at will. All it shows, I suspect, is that schoolchildren do not know or fully understand that their self-appraisals are self-fulfilling. They think of themselves as immutably bright or dull—depending on which label was hung on them by their first teacher. Or they think that academic success is due less to self-confidence than to the teacher's whim. If they truly grasped the extent to which they can be as bright as they think, then to the same extent they would be able to think they were as bright as they wanted.[48]

Note that this is precisely the view we take of self-depreciation in people who are sophisticated enough to understand its effects. If an intelligent adult continually undermines his own projects by belittling himself, we begin to suspect either that he despairs of self-encouragement as destined to be foiled by anxiety-provoking thoughts, or that he has a mental block against believing in himself, or that he simply

---

[47] An intermediate case is Rankin's "self-faith-healer," who attempts to achieve a recovery from illness through the salutary effects of his own expectation of recovering ("Non-Causal Self-Fulfillment of Intention," 283ff.). Rankin points out that the self-faith-healer's success depends on his degree of confidence, whereas confidence plays no part in the effectiveness of intentions. The reason why confidence plays a part in the self-faith-healer's success, I suspect, is that his health is affected only slightly by each occurrent thought. If he once contemplates the possibility of a relapse, that thought won't directly cause a relapse in the way that a single thought of sleeplessness can cause sleeplessness; yet each thought of a relapse will take an incremental toll on his health. Hence the self-faith-healer wouldn't be entitled to a wavering expectation of recovery, since a lack of confidence would allow too many unhealthy thoughts to cross his mind, but he is entitled to a confident expectation, which keeps his unhealthy thoughts to a minimum.

As for Rankin's claim that intentions aren't sensitive to confidence, I think that it is refuted by Rankin's own example. For if a patient is sufficiently convinced of his power to heal himself with positive thinking, then he is likely to say that he can simply *decide* to recover (or that his pessimistic fellow patients are simply deciding to remain ill). And if he's right about his powers of self-healing, then he'll be right about being able to decide. Thus, the concept of intention is indeed used in contexts where confidence is thought to make a difference.

[48] I regard this case as similar, in its essentials, to Rankin's self-faith-healer, discussed in the preceding note, who "has acquired insight into the self-fulfillment of his anticipation." Rankin argues that the self-faith-healer must learn to form the requisite anticipation *despite* his insight, since such insight would ordinarily undermine the anticipation. I would argue, to the contrary, that what undermines most attempts at self-faith-healing is a failure of insight. That is, the patient cannot muster a belief in his recovery because he doesn't fully appreciate the power of that belief to cure him.

wants to fail. We may even take his predictions of failure as unwitting expressions of an intention to fail. That is, we may take these predictions to be motivated by his desire for their fulfillment, and to be justified by their tendency to fulfill themselves.

BORDERLINE CASES

Of course, a person who is said to will his own failures, in this sense, doesn't consciously think that he has adopted his negative self-appraisals as means to their own fulfillment: he doesn't think that he is choosing to disable himself by depreciating his abilities. His attitude therefore doesn't have all of the features by which I identified intentions. How, then, can we say that the self-depreciating agent intends to fail?

The Logical Status of My Theory

The answer, I think, is that we don't regulate our attributions of intention by any test of necessary and sufficient conditions. 'Intention' is a concept of commonsense psychology—a rough and ready concept that, like common sense itself, wouldn't be sufficiently ready if it weren't so rough. I see no reason to expect the phenomenon of intention to have clearly defined edges, and I follow Aristotle in aspiring to achieve no more clarity than my subject matter permits.[49]

I have therefore refrained from presenting a formal analysis of intention. All that I have presented is an argument for identifying intentions with reflective predictions, on the grounds of their sharing several significant features. I have not claimed that an attitude's having exactly those features is a necessary and sufficient condition for its being an intention. I suspect, in fact, that there are many borderline cases—defective intentions, near-intentions, pseudo-intentions—all consisting of reflective predictions that bear an imperfect similarity to the classic specimen. Whether these borderline cases really are intentions strikes me as a question without a determinate answer: they are and they aren't, and whether we call them intentions will depend on our interests at the time.

The Cases

Let me take a moment to examine some cases of defective intention more closely. Recall that I identified intentions with reflective predictions because these attitudes share three features. The first was that both attitudes represent a forthcoming action and tend to bring about

[49] *Nicomachean Ethics*, 1094b.

the action that they represent. Second, both the intention of doing something and the expectation of doing it are formed, not at the dictation of prior evidence that one will do it, but rather out of a desire to get oneself to do it. And third, both intentions and reflective predictions represent themselves as having the first two features. I have summed up all three features by saying that reflective predictions, like intentions, are self-fulfilling mental representations that are adopted out of a desire for their fulfillment and that represent themselves as such.

The will to fail.   Now, the will to fail is an attitude that has the first two features without the third: it is a self-fulfilling representation that causes its own fulfillment and is caused by a desire for its fulfillment but doesn't depict itself as such.[50] It differs from other intentions, then, in that it doesn't contain the agent's awareness of its having an intention's characteristic causes and effects, and so it can be called an unconscious intention. Note, however, that the reason why this intention can be called unconscious is that the agent is unconscious of its being an intention, not that he's unconscious of it altogether. In order for an agent to intend to fail, he must not only expect to fail but also be aware of his expectation. For if he were unaware of expecting to fail, then his expectation wouldn't interact with his desire for self-awareness in such a way as to bring about its own fulfillment,[51] and so it wouldn't qualify as an intention at all. Thus, an agent's ignorance of his intentions cannot extend as far as ignorance of the expectations in which they consist. The most he can fail to know about his intentions is that they are intentions.[52]

Just as unconscious intentions are means to their own fulfillment without purporting to be, so other intentions purport to be means to their fulfillment but aren't. Such intentions are also defective.

Ineffective intentions.   Suppose, for example, that someone thinks he wants to alleviate the suffering of famine victims in Ethiopia, and therefore comes to believe that, moved by this desire and his awareness

[50] Rankin claims, "No agent can be blind to the distinction between his intention and non-self-fulfilling types of anticipation" ("Non-Causal Self-Fulfillment of Intention," 283). If Rankin means to imply that an agent cannot mistake an intention for a non-self-fulfilling belief, then he is, to my way of thinking, simply wrong. The will to fail is an example of such an unrecognized intention.

[51] Remember that if an agent's expectation of acting is unconscious, then he will not regard the expected action as one in the performance of which he would know what he was doing. Consequently, he will not be inclined to perform it. See chapter 2, 50.

[52] If 'intention' means "goal," of course, then an agent can be unaware of his intentions under any description at all.

of it, he will hereby reinforce those predispositions to the point where he'll send a check to Oxfam. His belief may be untrue. Perhaps he is one of those selfish people who want to have the satisfaction of being generous without incurring the costs. His belief that he wants to alleviate the suffering of famine victims may therefore be nothing but a comfortable delusion, and his belief that he'll send money to charity may be nothing but a means of keeping this delusion alive. In that case, the latter belief isn't motivated, as it purports to be, by a desire to perform the action it represents. And without the help of such a desire, it is unlikely to fulfill its promise of bringing the action about. The agent will therefore find, to his surprise and embarrassment, that no matter how often he resolves to write a check to Oxfam, something else always diverts him, and he never gets around to writing it.

Did this agent ever truly intend to write that check? Well, yes and no. We could say that he never intended to write it, or we could say that he intended to write it but lacked the strength to carry through. Surely he *meant* to, in the sense that he had formed an attitude whose *meaning*, or content, was that he was thereby prompting himself to write the check. And yet he was never *intent* upon writing the check, since he didn't truly want to. Whether we say that he intended to write the check will therefore depend on where we draw the boundary of intention in that region between what someone is intent upon and what he means. Sometimes the word 'intention' refers only to effective intentions—attitudes that actually prompt the agent to perform or at least to attempt the intended action. A person doesn't really intend to do something, in this sense of the word, unless he thereby manages to get himself at least to try. At other times, 'intention' refers to attitudes with the characteristic content of intentions, whether or not they have the characteristic effects. In this latter sense of the term, though not in the former, an intention can be ineffective.

Intending to act out of habit.   Another kind of defective intention can be found in the habitual expectations that keep an agent abreast of his habitual actions. As I explained in chapter 2, an agent may have repeated a routine so often that at the completion of each step he habitually anticipates the next one, and he may consequently acquire the habit that when he begins an habitual routine, he drops his guard against acting unexpectedly.

The example I used in chapter 2 was my own routine of washing and undressing before bed. Whenever I initiate this routine, I habitually suspend my efforts to make sure that I have my next action in mind before I act, since I can rely instead on my habitual expectations to keep me abreast of what I'm doing. Those expectations still help to make me do what I expect, since any expected action is still especially attractive to me. But because I would probably act by force of habit alone even if the corresponding expectations failed to arise, their adoption isn't necessary as a means to their fulfillment. And in any case, I form these expectations by habit rather than out of a desire to get them fulfilled.

The ensuing expectations are therefore somewhat self-fulfilling, but they aren't adopted as a means to their fulfillment. And I'm aware of their anomalous status. Because I drop my guard against unexpected actions at times like this, I would now have been about to brush my teeth by force of habit even if the force of another habit hadn't led me to expect to—and I know it. Hence I know that I needn't adopt the expectation of brushing in order to get myself to brush. Yet by force of habit, I do expect that I'll now brush my teeth by force of habit, and I thereby make myself all the more likely to brush my teeth—and I know that, too. Hence my habitual expectation, though not adopted as a means of making it true, does reinforce its own truth, and that's how I regard it.

Habitual actions are thus preceded by pseudo-intentions. I sort of intend to brush my teeth, but that intention just occurs to me by habit and probably isn't necessary for my performing the intended action. It isn't an expectation that I form in order to get myself to act accordingly; it's an expectation that partly helps me to act accordingly, but mostly comes along for the ride.

Similar intentions accompany other kinds of habitual action, such as the exercise of a skill. My ability to drive an automobile, for instance, consists in a repertoire of habitual bodily responses to various cues. I habitually take my foot off the accelerator when I see the next traffic light turn red; I habitually shift up when I hear the engine begin to whine; I habitually actuate the turn-signal when I see my turn approaching; and so on. These physical habits are accompanied by the corresponding cognitive habits—habits of responding to the aforementioned cues with expectations of doing whatever I habitually do in response to the same cues. Consequently, the actions that I take in the driver's seat are accompanied and abetted by reflective expectations that are mildly self-fulfilling but not adopted as means to their fulfillment. And that's why I can be said to drive knowingly and willingly but not deliberately.

I think that my analysis of such defective intentions, like my analyses of the others, is true to experience. That is, when we act out of habit, we don't feel that we're actively deciding what to do, but we do feel that our actions are accompanied by a half-hearted intention. I thus regard the defective cases as confirming rather than undermining my account.[53]

CONCLUDING REMARKS

Before closing the present discussion of intentions, I'd like to tie up two loose ends.

The Content of Reflective Predictions

First, I'd like to return to a topic that caused some difficulty in the preceding chapter: the content of an agent's reflective predictions. The difficulty is that these predictions must represent themselves for what they are, on pain of invalidating the agent's self-inquiry. In particular, they must represent that they are self-fulfilling and that they have been adopted by the agent out of a desire for their fulfillment. And predictions that explicitly represent themselves in this way turn out to be convoluted indeed.

However, I have now developed greater resources for describing an agent's reflective predictions, and I can put these resources at the disposal of the predictions themselves, so to speak, for the purposes of their self-description. I have argued that being a self-fulfilling representation adopted out of a desire for its fulfillment is characteristic of an intention to act. I therefore suggest that an agent's reflective predictions can describe themselves appropriately by describing themselves as intentions.

Suppose that an agent forms the belief "I'll do this because I hereby intend to." He will then have formed an expectation of acting that correctly characterizes itself as cause of the expected action and as effect of the agent's desire to bring that action about—all by characterizing itself as an intention. His expectation will therefore meet the requirements for self-description that I laid down in chapter 3. The agent can achieve the same result simply by forming the belief "This is a successful intention of doing it," provided that by "successful intention" he means an intention that will succeed in bringing about the

[53] For arguments against saying that habitual actions are intended, see J. A. Passmore, "Intentions." For opposing arguments, see John J. Jenkins, "Motive and Intention," *Philosophical Quarterly* 15 (1965): 155–64. Passmore's fellow symposiast, P. L. Heath, takes an intermediate position, similar to mine (148).

William James also took an intermediate position on the question. He said that in habitual action, "the will, if any will be present, limits itself to a *permission*" (*Principles of Psychology*, 1: 118. See also 2: 523).

intended action. The agent's belief in the success of his intention will amount to the belief that the action will occur, and this belief in the action's occurrence will satisfy the requirements for self-description by characterizing itself as an intention.

Thus, an agent can intend an action by believing that he thereby successfully intends it. Of course, his believing that his intention is successful doesn't necessarily make it so: it ensures that his belief has the content of an intention but not necessarily the effects. Nevertheless, an agent does enjoy a measure of incorrigibility about his own intentions. For if he forms the belief that he is thereby forming a successful intention of doing something, then he is necessarily forming an intention of doing it, though perhaps not a successful one.[54]

Two Kinds of Immediate Intention

Finally, I'd like to point out that my theory provides for two different kinds of immediate intention, corresponding to the two kinds of reflective prediction by which an agent secures self-awareness. As I explained in the preceding chapter, an agent can secure an awareness of what he does, first, by anticipating what he will do next and, second, by recognizing when he is just about to do it. Both kinds of prediction can be means to their own fulfillment, and so they can both constitute immediate intentions—the one, an intention to do something *next*, and the other, an intention to do it *now*.

Recall, however, that the latter prediction can be dispensed with if the agent is paying attention to himself. So long as he knows what his next action will be, he can ensure that he'll have a concurrent awareness of what he's doing, simply by ensuring that he'll notice when the action begins. Consequently, an agent often dispenses with the intention that consists in an expectation of acting straightaway. Once he has formed a self-fulfilling expectation (and hence an intention) about what to do next, he can allow himself to do it whenever he is moved to, without forming the further self-fulfilling expectation (or intention) of doing it *now*. Provided that he can rely on his motives to make him

---

[54] When I say that an agent is incorrigible about his intentions, I do not mean that if an agent has an intention, then he necessarily knows that he has it. Some of the defective intentions discussed above, such as the intention to fail, can be held unwittingly. All that I am claiming here is that if an agent believes that he has an intention, then in one sense of the word, he does, and so his belief cannot be entirely false.

For a stronger claim, see Brice Noel Fleming, "On Intention," *Philosophical Review* 73 (1964): 315: "[T]o intend to do *x* is itself to know that you intend to do *x*: intending is itself awareness of intending." See also Ludwig Wittgenstein, *Philosophical Investigations*, trans. G.E.M. Anscombe (Oxford, 1967), 247; and Hampshire, *Thought and Action*, 123. For a contrasting view, see Passmore, "Intention," 134–38.

do what he expects (intends), he can leave the precise timing up to them.

No wonder, then, that we often act without an awareness of having goaded ourselves into action. William James illustrates this phenomenon with the example of getting out of bed: "If I may generalize from my own experience," he writes, "we more often than not get up without any struggle or decision at all. We suddenly find that we *have* got up."[55] Of course, when James says that we rise without a decision, he can't mean to imply that we are initially undecided about whether to rise at all: we aren't entertaining the possibility of staying in bed for another twenty-four hours. We already intend to rise sooner or later, and the only question is when. This is the question that we preempt by rising without a decision. We rise, not without intending to rise, but without having decided to do so *now*.[56]

My account of this phenomenon is quite different from James's. He attributes the onset of action to "a fortunate lapse of consciousness." I would say quite the reverse. We dispense with the intention of rising *now* because, lying there in the quiet of our room, we're bound to notice when we stir; and as soon as we notice ourselves stirring, we'll know that we're getting up, since that's what we already intend, and hence expect, to do next.[57] Having settled on getting up as our next move, we can lie there and let ourselves get up whenever the spirit moves us.

[55] *Principles of Psychology*, 2: 524.

[56] Here I am in disagreement with Wilfrid Sellars and Myles Brand, who think that the proximate cause of every action is the intention of acting *now*. (See Sellars, "Action and Events," *Nous* 7 [1973]: 195; and Brand, *Intending and Acting*, 35ff.)

[57] Thus, I would say not "we suddenly find that we *have* got up" but "we suddenly find that we *are* getting up."

FIVE

FREEDOM

If a creature can act from motives and form empirical theories, then it can have intentions, too. That was the upshot of the last two chapters. There I tried to show that the capacity for intentions emerges when the capacity for motives and the capacity for theories work together. And the latter two capacities work together, I argued, when particular motives are present—motives for the creature to theorize about its own actions. Those motives will induce the creature, not only to seek hypotheses that are true of its actions, but also to perform actions that are true to its hypotheses. In particular, then, those motives will incline the creature to do whatever it has predicted, and so the creature will be able to get itself to do things by predicting that it will do them. The resulting predictions, if properly self-describing, will constitute intentions to act.

I have said that intentions, so characterized, are the states that characteristically close or foreclose deliberation by settling the practical issue that was or would have been deliberated. They are states of being decided. Now, the range of possibilities within which an agent can decide, the range of issues that are for him to settle, is the range within which he is ordinarily conceived as exercising freedom, if he has any freedom to exercise. Although willing, in the traditional sense of the term, is not the same as deciding, the agent's freedom to decide is, I believe, what the term 'free will' usually denotes. The faculty of making decisions is the faculty whose freedom is at issue in the discussion of free will, and so it can be called the will for the purposes of discussing freedom—though not, perhaps, for other purposes. Having offered a theory of this faculty, I shall now examine the extent to which it is free.

THE PROBLEMS OF FREEDOM

I think that there are two equally important reasons why we seek an alternative to determinism as an account of how our actions come about. One reason is phenomenological: we just feel free. Determinism seems incompatible, in the first instance, with what it's like to be an agent. Our other reason for seeking an alternative to determinism is conceptual. We fear that if determinism is true, then we shall have to do without an entire class of concepts, including not only 'moral responsibility' and 'desert' but also 'decision', 'deliberation', and perhaps even 'action' itself.

The conceptual reason for worrying about determinism has tended to command more attention from philosophers than the phenomenological one, and the moral concepts of responsibility and desert have tended to command more attention than nonmoral concepts such as decision or action. The conflict between determinism and moral responsibility has taken the title role, so to speak, as The Problem of Free Will, whereas it is in fact only one among an ensemble of problems.

I think that the nonmoral action concepts and the phenomenology of action deserve attention in their own right. My view is that explaining what it's like to be an agent, and how it's possible to make a decision, are just as interesting as finding room in the world for punishment and blame. And even those who disagree with me on this score should consider that the problem of moral responsibility probably owes its survival to these other, related problems.

What I mean here is that the problem of moral responsibility survives only because we cling to moral concepts that have proven difficult to reconcile with determinism; and I think that we cling to those concepts partly because facing decisions and feeling free have convinced us that determinism will have to give way somewhere in any case. Our practical lives continually seem to bear witness against determinism, by presenting us with instances in which the concepts 'decision' and 'choice' clearly apply and in which we feel free. If these phenomena hadn't seemed to spell eventual defeat for determinism, we might long ago have come to terms with it, by adopting one of the conceptual reforms that compatibilists have been advocating for centuries. Our worries about the moral concepts might then have disappeared. One reason why compatibilist conceptions of responsibility and desert have not gained general acceptance, I believe, is that the continual necessity of making decisions, and the attendant feeling of freedom, embolden us to stand our conceptual ground.[1]

I therefore think that even those philosophers whose primary interest is in the problem of moral responsibility should also take an interest

[1] Philosophers who explicitly cite the phenomenology of action as grounds for holding out against determinism include C. A. Campbell, *On Selfhood and Goodhood* (London, 1957), 158–79; Richard Taylor, *Metaphysics* (Englewood Cliffs, N.J., 1983), 23–50; and to a lesser extent, Roderick Chisholm, "Human Freedom and the Self," in *Free Will*, ed. Gary Watson (Oxford, 1982), 31–32.

in the problems posed by the nonmoral action concepts and the phenomenology of action. They should want to know whether the decisions we make and the freedom we feel actually justify us in holding out against determinism; they should want to know whether these phenomena really indicate that we are, in the relevant sense, free.

What I hope to show is that these phenomena do not in fact justify us in resisting determinism, because they are compatible with it. Even if determinism is true, I shall argue, it needn't preclude us from making decisions or feeling free. Although I shall say almost nothing directly about the concepts of responsibility and desert, my arguments will bear indirectly on those concepts, by undermining one of our motives for refusing to redefine them along compatibilist lines. I suspect that my arguments will also suggest new possibilities for compatibilist conceptions of responsibility and desert, but I shall not explore those possibilities in detail.[2]

EPISTEMIC FREEDOM

Let me begin with the feeling of freedom and postpone the concept of decision until the end of this section.

Two Ways of Feeling Free

The freedom that we feel can be described from two perspectives, one looking outward, or forward, and the other looking inward, or back. When we survey our future conduct, it looks open, unsettled, long on possibilities and short on certainties. When we reflect on our motives for acting, we feel that they cannot make us decide to act. Both views support us in the conviction that we are free.

My theory of intention accounts for both of these experiences. It explains why our future looks open and why our motives don't feel overpowering. The theory vindicates these appearances: it says that the future feels open because it really is and that our motives feel uncompelling because they really are. But the theory is also compatibilist, in that it portrays our future as open in a sense that's compatible with its being predetermined, and our motives as uncompelling in a sense that's compatible with their being causally effective. Thus, the theory upholds our feeling of freedom while undermining the assumption that the feeling is evidence against determinism.

Of course, to say that our future is both predetermined and open, or that our motives are both effective and uncompelling, sounds flatly

---

[2] These possibilities are briefly canvassed at the end of chapter 6.

self-contradictory. But no contradiction is involved. The reason is that the predicates in these statements are ambiguous, having both epistemic and metaphysical senses. What we are feeling, in feeling free, is an epistemic freedom that we can possess without being free in the metaphysical sense. We are correct to take this feeling as a perception of freedom, but if we take it as a perception of freedom from determinism, we are mistaken.

I shall now outline how my compatibilism applies to the feeling of freedom as it is experienced from each of the two perspectives defined above.

The openness of the future. Whenever we face a decision, we feel that some aspect of our future is up to us. This feeling is naturally interpreted as a perception of indeterminacy in our future; how much indeterminacy is a delicate question. One might think that our sense of deciding an aspect of the future intimates that there is no antecedent fact as to how that aspect will turn out. Alternatively, one might think that our sense of deciding an aspect of the future doesn't indicate that there is no fact about it but only that any such fact isn't causally determined by the present state of the world. Under either interpretation, the experience is taken to suggest a denial of determinism, the first denial being considerably stronger than the second.

My theory of intention shows that both interpretations are wrong. Our sense of an open future is an intimation of genuine indeterminacy, but it shouldn't be interpreted as suggesting that determinism is false. For there are two senses in which the future might be undetermined. On the one hand, there may be no particular way that the future is going to turn out—or, at least, no way that's necessitated, under the laws of nature, by the present state of the world. In that case, the future would be metaphysically or causally open. On the other hand, there may be no particular way that we must describe the future as turning out, in order to describe it correctly—or, at least, no way that's necessitated, under the laws of nature, by a correct description of the present state of the world. In that case, the future would be, as I put it, epistemically open.

So formulated, these two kinds of indeterminacy seem inextricably linked. We naturally assume that if there is a way that the future will turn out, then that's the way we must describe it as turning out, in order to give a true description of it; and we assume that if the present will determine the future, under the laws of nature, then a true description of the present will determine, under the same laws, how we must describe the future in order to describe it correctly.

I shall argue that these assumptions are false. For even if there is already something that we're going to do next, we would be correct in expecting ourselves to do something else, insofar as our alternative expectation would amount to an effective intention to perform the alternative action. The most common reason why we're predetermined to do something is that we're predetermined to intend it, by means of a self-fulfilling expectation. Hence the fact that we're predetermined to do it does not entail that we would be wrong to expect otherwise, since if we did expect otherwise, we would thereby intend otherwise and consequently do otherwise. Even if there is a particular action that we're going to perform, there isn't a particular action that we must expect in order to have a true expectation.

I believe that this indeterminacy—the absence of a particular action that we must expect ourselves to perform—is the openness that we feel as we approach a decision about what to do. As we consider our next action, the question of what we're going to do remains open, in the sense that no particular answer is forced upon us as exclusively correct. What's remarkable is that the question of what we're going to do remains open in this fashion even if what we're going to do—the action itself—does not. That is, even if there is an action that we're going to perform, the fact remains that expecting to perform it isn't the only way of correctly answering the question of what we're going to do; for if we answered the question differently, by expecting to perform a different action, we'd perform that action instead, thus rendering our alternative answer correct. Hence the truth of determinism needn't deprive us of our feeling that the future is open. How we should conceive of the future remains genuinely open, even if the future itself is fixed.

Obviously, this explanation for the openness of the future depends on arguments made in chapter 2 about the agent's license to form expectations contrary to the evidence.[3] I am going to repeat and expand those arguments below, but first let me introduce my phenomenology of freedom from the inward-looking perspective.

Freedom from our motives. The other perspective from which we appear to be free is the perspective of introspection. When we reflect on our motives for potential actions, we feel that their causal force has no coercive hold over us. Although various motives are pressing us to do various things, our choice among those actions does not seem to be determined by motivational pressures. We don't feel forced by our motives to decide upon one action or another; in particular, we don't feel

---

[3] Pp. 58–64.

forced to decide upon whichever action is favored by the motives that are strongest.

Here again, my theory of intention shows that we describe our experience of freedom ambiguously. There are two different ways in which our motives might constrain our decisions, and hence two different ways in which our decisions can be unconstrained.

The reason why there are two different ways in which our motives might constrain our decisions is that the state of being decided—that is, an intention—consists in a self-fulfilling expectation of acting, and our motives might impinge on such an expectation in two different ways. On the one hand, because an intention consists in an expectation of acting, it might be subject to evidence about how we'll act. On the other hand, because an intention is an expectation that we may form as we like, it might be subject to our preferences about what to expect.[4] Hence an intention could potentially be constrained by the availability of grounds for it, on the one hand, and motives for it, on the other. And both the grounds for expecting an action and our motives for expecting it are supplied by our motives for acting. That is, our motives for performing an action constitute not only the evidence that the action is to be expected of us but also our inclination to expect it. Our motives therefore have both a causal and an evidentiary bearing on our reflective expectations, and so there are two different forces that a free decision might elude.

According to my account, our decisions do elude some of the evidentiary force of our motives, because prior evidence cannot dictate the expectations that will constitute our being decided upon one course of action or another. We make a decision by forming an intention, and in forming an intention we are making a behavioral prediction that isn't fully constrained by the motivational evidence. Our motives indicate which action we're going to perform next, and yet we aren't obliged, epistemically speaking, to predict the action they indicate. For they indicate which action we'll perform next only by virtue of indicating which action we'll intend, and if we predicted some alternative action to be our next, we would thereby intend it, thus making our alternative prediction come true. Thus, even though our motives foreshadow what we'll do next, we would be correct in telling an alternative story.

Here, too, my account of epistemic freedom depends on the arguments that I gave in chapter 2 about an agent's freedom from the evidence foreshadowing his actions. Before elaborating on the concept of epistemic freedom, then, let me return to those arguments.

---

[4] Within limits, of course. I discussed these limits in chapter 2, 57.

Freedom from the Evidence

As I explained in chapter 2, an agent's desire to know what he's doing, as soon as he's doing it, restrains him from doing anything until he anticipates what he'll do next, whereas once he anticipates doing something next, the same desire becomes an additional motive for doing what he has anticipated and against doing anything else.[5]

Self-fulfilling expectations (again).   One result is that before the agent anticipates his next action, his overriding motive is an inhibition against acting. Another result is that his remaining motives do not necessarily tend, on balance, in the same direction as the motives that he will have when the inhibition is lifted. That is, what the agent would now be most inclined to do, if he weren't disinclined to do anything, is not necessarily what he will be most inclined to do when he loses that disinclination. He will lose his disinclination to act only when he anticipates some action, whereupon he will gain an additional motive for the anticipated action and against any others. Hence some of the motives that the agent will have when he's finally ready to act have not yet added their weight to the motivational balance. Those motives won't weigh in until the agent anticipates what he's going to do.

When the agent does anticipate what he's going to do next, the motives he thereby adds to the balance will tip it toward the anticipated action. Consequently, even if the agent would currently be most inclined to do one thing, were he inclined to do anything, there are ordinarily several other things that he would be equally correct in expecting to do. The agent needn't expect his forthcoming action to be the one that is currently favored by greater motives than any of the alternatives, because the weight of his motives for that action would be diminished, and the weight of his motives for an alternative action increased, if he expected the latter action. Expecting himself to do something other than what he would currently be most inclined to do may make him more inclined to do the other thing instead. The agent is therefore in a position to expect as his next action, from among the actions of which he's capable, any action whose motives would become the greatest if he expected it to be his next. In order to know

[5] To be precise, the desire restrains him from doing anything until he *believes* that he anticipates doing something, and then it becomes an additional motive for doing what he *believes* that he anticipates. But as I explained in chapter 2, an agent's believing that he anticipates an action is tantamount to his anticipating the action—at least for my purposes. And since an unconscious anticipation of acting cannot constitute an intention, as I explained in chapter 4, 137, I confine my attention to conscious anticipation.

which actions these are, the agent must have a rough idea of what he's capable of doing and what he has moderately strong motives for doing next. But he will usually be aware of several such actions, each of which he would perform next if he expected to.

Among these actions, the agent may expect whichever one he prefers—that is, whichever action he most wants to expect.[6] And he can have various motives for and against expecting a particular action. One motive for expecting an action is the desire that he perform it, since the agent knows that he'll be prompted to perform whichever action he expects.[7] Another motive for expecting an action is the desire for self-understanding, which encourages the agent to expect, and thereby prompt himself to perform, whichever action he consciously believes that he most wants himself to perform, since that action strikes him as the one that he would understand prompting and hence understand performing.

These motives will determine which action the agent expects and, consequently, which action he performs. Yet they will not determine his expectation in the usual way, by presenting him with evidence that compels him to expect one action rather than another. Rather, these motives will determine which action the agent expects by determining which action he'd like to expect, given that he feels entitled to expect whichever action he likes.

The evidence.   Because these motives will thus determine which action the agent performs, their presence constitutes compelling evidence for expecting him to perform one action rather than another. But this evidence still cannot compel the agent himself; for if the agent were to contravene this evidence, he would thereby refute it. The only grounds on which to predict the agent's next action, as he prepares to predict it, is evidence about which action he is going to predict. But the agent himself cannot be compelled to predict an action on the grounds that he's going to predict it. For if he doesn't predict it, he will thereby prove that he wasn't going to, after all—and hence that he needn't have, in the first place.

The evidence about an agent's forthcoming action is compelling only to an outside observer. It's compelling to the observer because it indicates that the action is going to be predicted and consequently per-

[6] For the sake of brevity, I shall sometimes omit the words 'next' and 'forthcoming' from references to the action whose performance is expected. I hope that the reader will keep in mind that the only expectations being discussed here are immediate expectations of acting. Long-range expectations are discussed in chapter 8.

[7] For a definition of the word 'prompt' in this context, see note 25 of chapter 2.

formed by the agent whether or not the observer expects so, and hence that the observer had better expect so, on pain of error. But the evidence indicates something different to the agent. To him it indicates— not that the action will be performed whether or not he expects so— but rather that it will be performed because he's about to expect so. Thus, it doesn't indicate that he had better expect that action, on pain of error. Quite the reverse: it indicates that if he doesn't expect that action, it won't occur—and hence that he is immune from error. The evidence therefore compels the outside observer but not the agent.

One might think that the evidence, as I have described it, would compel the agent, before he ever expected an action, to form a second-order expectation about which action he was going to expect—whereupon he'd be compelled to go ahead and expect that action, on the grounds that he'd be likely to fulfill the projected expectation. But this account of the agent's situation would be wrong.

Suppose that the agent confronted the evidence while his next action was pending—that is, while he was ready to do something but had not yet decided what to do. In that case, the agent's second-order premise that he would expect a particular action couldn't compel him to expect that action; for if he expected a different action, he would thereby refute the premise—and, in any case, his alternative expectation would prompt him to act differently, thus securing its own truth.

Prior knowledge. Of course, we can imagine the agent gaining access to the relevant evidence well in advance, at a time when an alternative expectation would neither refute the evidence nor lead to an alternative action, because the time of the projected action had not yet arrived. In that case, he would indeed be compelled to expect the action that the evidence indicated he would later expect and hence perform. Indeed, the agent could then be said to know what he was going to do.

Nevertheless, the agent would still be correct in changing his expectation at the last minute, when the time for acting finally arrived. For if he then expected a different action, he would act differently. The agent could at most be temporarily bound by the evidence, and he would eventually win free of it, as soon as his next action was near enough to be influenced by his expectation.

One might think that an agent could never rightly be said to know that he is going to do one thing if he would subsequently be correct in changing his mind and expecting to do another thing instead. But this description of the agent's position is not really inconsistent; it only sounds inconsistent, because it is easily misconstrued as implying that the agent could correctly change his mind, so as to expect the second action, and *still have known* that he was going to perform the first. In reality, if the agent changed his mind and expected to perform the second action, then he would indeed perform it, and so his prior expectation of performing the first action would have been false and could hardly have qualified as knowledge. If his prior expectation does qualify as knowledge, the reason must be that he isn't going to change his mind, but the fact that he isn't going to change his mind doesn't entail that he would be wrong in doing so.

Thus, if a person knows that he's going to do something, then it must be the case that when the time comes, he will still expect to do it. But the reason why he will still expect to do it is not that he will be required to expect so by his prior knowledge that he was going to do it. Quite the reverse: the reason is that if he didn't still expect the action, then he wouldn't perform it, and therefore wouldn't really have known that he was going to, in the first place. In short, his prior knowledge of what he's going to do doesn't forbid him to change his mind but rather depends on his being destined not to change it. The agent would be correct in recanting what he currently knows, but if he was going to recant it, then he wouldn't currently know it.

There are two potential sources of confusion here. First, my claim that the agent's recanting what he knows would result in his not having known it seems to imply that the agent has the magical power of influencing the past. All it actually implies, however, is that the agent has the power of influencing the epistemic status of his past beliefs—a power that requires no magic. If the agent expects an action, then he will always have expected it, no matter how he changes his mind later on. Yet his later changes of mind, by affecting how he acts, will affect whether his earlier expectation of acting was true and hence whether it constituted knowledge.

A second source of confusion is the surprising potential for contradictions between what someone correctly believes and what would be correct for him to believe. Ordinarily, if someone is correct in believing something, then he wouldn't be correct in believing the opposite. His having knowledge about some matter therefore entails that he would be wrong to change his mind about it. In the case of self-fulfilling beliefs, however, truth can attach to actual and counterfactual beliefs that are mutually contradictory, since a person can be correct in believing something even though he would be equally correct to believe the reverse. The surprising result is that his knowing something doesn't entail that he would be wrong to think otherwise.

If the agent's knowing that he'll do something doesn't entail that he'd be wrong to think otherwise, why doesn't he think otherwise? The answer is that if he doesn't think otherwise, the reason must be that he doesn't want to. What makes him continue to expect the same action that he knows he'll perform is—not that he'd be wrong to stop expecting it (he wouldn't be)—but rather that he wants himself to perform the action and knows that the way to get himself to perform it is by expecting to.

Incomplete evidence. The foregoing arguments all rely on the assumption that the agent is confronted by all of the evidence about his future action, and that he fully appreciates its evidentiary force. This complete evidence cannot require the agent to draw a particular conclusion about what he'll do—or, at least, not a conclusion that he can be required to keep until the end. Oddly enough, however, the agent can be required to draw a conclusion, and indeed the right conclusion, by incomplete evidence. The result is that the less evidence an agent has, the more compelling it is.

A good example of what I mean by incomplete evidence is that prop of philosophical fiction, a book of life.[8] The fiction is this. We are invited to imagine that we find a book bearing our name on the cover and a complete chronicle of our lives within. The book contains an entry describing our behavior at every minute of every day from birth to death. As we read the entries for times past, we find, to our amazement, that the book is both exhaustive and unerring. Everything we've ever done is accurately recorded. We turn to the entry for the present moment and find that it, too, is correct, since it says that at this moment we are reading and marvelling at the book itself. Finally, the book's entries for future times are continually borne out as life goes on.

The philosophical moral of the story is supposed to be that once we have verified the book's reliability on enough occasions, we have good grounds for believing its reports about times to come. It presents us with compelling evidence about what we'll be doing at every moment from now on.

I accept this moral, but I add that the evidence presented by the book of life is compelling only because it is incomplete. It is therefore like many kinds of evidence whose initial authority is undermined by further information.

The book of life is incomplete because it doesn't tell us the causal antecedents of the behavior that it chronicles so prophetically. It de-

---

[8] For the classic discussion of books of life, see Goldman, *Theory of Human Action*, chapter 6.

scribes what we do at every moment, without revealing what causes us to do it. Yet unless the book is the product of a miracle, it must have been written by someone who was able to peer down the relevant chains of causes to where they would terminate in our behavior. Thus, when our anonymous biographer chose not to mention the causes of our behavior, he chose to keep us in the dark about how he could predict that behavior so reliably. The evidence provided by the book therefore has a gap right at its center. All the book shows is that someone, a person who had more information than we have, was a reliable authority on our future. How he earned that authority, how he knew what he seems to have known, remains a mystery.

Now suppose that the author of our book of life had divulged his secrets. In that case, his book would have described the chains of causes leading up to each of our actions. And on many of those chains, a proximate cause of the action would have been our expectation of performing it. The book would therefore have revealed that our immediate expectations of acting are self-fulfilling, it would thereby have revealed that we could expect whichever action we liked, and so it would have betrayed its own lack of authority over our expectations. It would have said to us, in effect, "You're going to do such-and-such, because you're going to believe that you're going to do it." And this statement would have worn on its face the implication that we didn't have to believe it. By bidding us to believe a proposition on the grounds that we were going to believe it, the statement would have shown us how to eliminate any grounds for believing the proposition, simply by refusing to believe it. Of course, if the author was infallible, as the fiction assumes, then we would indeed have believed the assertion, but we would have believed it because we wanted to, not because we had no correct alternative.

In short, the more the author told us about how he knew what we were going to do, the less we'd be obliged to believe him. On first glance, this result isn't at all paradoxical. Often we find that rationality at first requires us to believe an informant who has proved reliable in the past but then requires us to disregard him once we have examined his credentials more closely. In such cases, we say that the informant's evidence initially seemed compelling—and indeed was compelling, in the absence of other evidence—but that in the light of full information it wasn't really compelling at all. This is precisely what I want to say about the author of the book of life. What's odd about this author's case is that the information that should undermine his authority in our eyes is precisely the information that should establish his authority in the eyes of others.

The nurse's book of life.   One can better appreciate why books of life would have no authority over self-fulfilling beliefs by considering what authority they would have over self-fulfilling utterances. An example of a self-fulfilling utterance is the assertion made by the doctor in Anscombe's hospital story—the doctor who says to a patient in the presence of a nurse, "Nurse will take you to the operating theater." Consider the following variation on that story.

As the doctor is browsing in the hospital library one day, he finds the nurse's book of life and decides to test the book's reliability. He spends the next few months surreptitiously trailing the nurse around the hospital, comparing the nurse's actual behavior against that predicted in the book. The book passes every test.

One day the doctor enters a patient's room for a routine examination and finds himself face to face with the nurse whom he has been studying from a distance for all these months. During a lull in the subsequent conversation, the doctor extracts the nurse's book of life from his pocket in order to see what happens next. Flipping to the entry for the present date and time, he reads this: "Takes patient to operating theater." The doctor hasn't bothered to consider for himself what the nurse might do next: all he knows is that the book is always right. He thinks, "The operating theater, is it? Well, then, I'd better tell the patient"—whereupon he reports his discovery by saying, "Nurse will take you to the operating theater." The nurse, who knows nothing about books of life, interprets the doctor's utterance as a command and immediately complies.

In this version of the story, the doctor's prediction is dictated by the evidence available to him. In the absence of any other information, the book's proven reliability forbids him to gainsay the next entry. His information indicates that if he wants to speak the truth about the nurse's actions, he had better go by the book.

Yet the doctor's prediction is dictated by his evidence in this case only because that evidence is incomplete. In particular, the evidence dictating the doctor's prediction doesn't include information about his own role in causing the events predicted. The doctor therefore becomes the unwitting collaborator of the nurse's anonymous biographer, in somewhat the same way that Jocasta and Laius, the parents of Oedipus, became unwitting collaborators of fate when they reacted to the prophecy about their infant son by taking steps that eventually ensured the prophecy's fulfillment. The difference, of course, is that Oedipus' fate would have been fulfilled no matter what—or so the myth asks us to believe—whereas the biographer's prediction about the nurse would not have been fulfilled without the doctor's collaboration. And the doctor feels compelled by the biographer's prediction only because he doesn't realize that without his collaboration it won't be fulfilled.[9]

For consider another version of the story, in which the nurse's biographer has recorded, not just the nurse's future actions, but also the chains of causes leading up to them—the chains down which the author must have peered in order to foresee the actions, in the first place. In this version, the doctor finds a more informative entry for the present date and time. He reads, "Hears the doctor say, 'Nurse will take you to the operating theater,' and is prompted to comply." Reading this entry, the doctor realizes that the nurse will take the patient to the operating theater because he's going to say so. Does he now say to himself, "I'd better tell the patient"? Does he feel that in order to warn the patient of impending events, he must echo the prediction written in the book? Surely not. He realizes that unless and until he repeats the book's prediction, it won't be fulfilled—and so he doesn't have to repeat it. He also realizes that he can utter alternative predictions without fear of a mistake.

Of course, even in this version of the story, the doctor says, "Nurse will take you to the operating theater." If he didn't, the book of life would contain an error, whereas the story presupposes that the book is infallible. But when the doctor says "Nurse will take you to the operating theater" in this version of the story, he says it because he wants the nurse to take the patient to the operating theater, or for some such reason, and not because he thinks that he had better repeat what's in the book in order to warn the patient of impending events.

Indeed, the nurse's superhuman biographer must have realized that if he was going to reveal the causal inferences behind his entries in the book, then he couldn't write an entry whose truth depended on the doctor's thinking that he had better repeat it for the patient's information. The reason is that the doctor would never think this about an entry if it was explicitly based on the premise that he was going to think so. After all, the doctor wouldn't think that such an entry was worth repeating for the patient's information if he didn't think that its stated premise was true; but he wouldn't think that the premise was true unless he thought that the entry was worth repeating for the patient's

---

[9] Note that in this version of the story, the biographer's prediction must have been based on his knowledge that the doctor would find the prediction compelling and consequently report it to the others, thereby unwittingly securing its truth. Evidently, then, the biographer could have written many other entries for the relevant date and time, in the knowledge that the doctor would feel compelled to report whatever was written and that the nurse would be prompted to comply. Hence the biographer himself wasn't compelled by prior evidence. But that's another story.

information. If the nurse's book of life said to him, in effect, "The following prediction is true because you are going to find it worth repeating for the patient's information," he would read the prediction and rightly think, "Why should I repeat that? If I thought that the author had some *other* grounds for his prediction, I might think that it was true and hence worth repeating to the patient. But if his only grounds for the prediction was that I would find it worth repeating to the patient, then I don't."[10] The author must therefore have realized that in order to make a true prediction for which he could record his causal inferences, he would have to make a prediction that did not rely on the doctor's feeling compelled to repeat it.

What the author could rely on, and must have known he could rely on, was that if he alerted the doctor to his potential influence over the nurse, then the doctor would feel free, even in the face of a reliable prediction, to say what he wanted about the nurse's next action. Hence the author must have realized that so long as he made sure to write his entry in such a way as to reveal the doctor's potential influence, he could figure out what else to write simply by figuring out which action the doctor would want the nurse to perform. In recording his causal inferences, the author must therefore have written, "Doctor wants nurse to take patient to the operating theater and therefore chooses to say, 'Nurse will take you to the operating theater' . . ." and so on. Reading this, the doctor thinks—not "I'd better tell the patient"—but rather "That *is* what I want to say. How clever of him!" And then he proceeds to say what he wants, and to say it only because he wants to.

So it is with an agent's prediction of his next action. The agent's knowing what he will do entails that he'll still expect to do it when the time arrives, just as the book's infallibility entails that the doctor will repeat its prediction about the nurse. But the reason why the agent will still expect to act when the time arrives is not that his prior knowledge shows that he would be wrong to expect otherwise, any more than the

---

[10] Once again, the doctor might feel that the prediction was worth repeating if the evidence offered for it was incomplete. Suppose the doctor began to suspect that the nurse's biographer must have possessed not only infallible foresight about his subject but also hypnotic power over his readers. If the doctor then read "You are going to repeat, 'Nurse will take you to the operating theater,' " he might regard it as conveying a threat that the author was capable of carrying out. The doctor might then say to himself, "He's going to compel me to say that the nurse will take the patient to the operating theater. But if I say that, the nurse will do it. I'd better warn the patient." The doctor would thereupon blurt out, "Nurse will take you to the operating theater"—realizing too late that he had just been tricked into fulfilling the author's threat. Of course, if the author had recorded the psychological processes by which he expected to trick the doctor, the doctor would never have fallen for the trick.

doctor repeats the book's prediction because it shows that he would be wrong to say otherwise. The doctor repeats the book's prediction because he wants to, and the agent expects his action because he wants to, both being free from epistemic compulsion.

Intentions.   The beliefs whose epistemology I have outlined here are the mental states that I identify with immediate intentions to act. Substituting the word 'intention' for 'expectation' in the foregoing story eliminates much of the attendant mystery. For instance, the possibility of *expecting* whatever one wants seems less odd when it's redescribed as the possibility of *intending* whatever one wants. And although there is something odd about the idea of predicting an action on the grounds that the agent will *expect* it, there is nothing odd about the idea of predicting an action on the grounds that the agent will *intend* it. Thus, many of the claims that I have made about reflective expectations become more intelligible in light of the fact that they are really about intentions.

I am now trying to demonstrate, conversely, that many of the claims that are ordinarily made about intentions are more intelligible in light of the fact that they are really about reflective expectations. In particular, I am saying, the fact that intentions consist in reflective expectations helps to explain much of what is ordinarily said about freedom of the will. For in forming intentions, an agent is forming self-fulfilling expectations about what he'll do next, and in forming such expectations, he cannot be constrained by the evidence of his motives or by the fixedness of his future. As the agent considers the question of what he is going to do next, he sees that there is no exclusively correct answer, no answer dictated to him by the state of his motives. Insofar as there is no particular action that he must expect, his future looks open, and insofar as his expectation cannot be dictated by the motivational evidence, his intention is free of a potential motivational constraint. Therein lies the epistemic freedom of his will.

The Limits of Epistemic Freedom

So defined, free will has various limitations, physical and psychological. To begin with, we wouldn't be correct in expecting an action if some external obstacle or physiological deficit would prevent us from performing it. Our epistemic freedom is therefore limited by our physical powers.

Furthermore, we have no latitude in what we'd be correct to expect unless our competing motives are more or less evenly matched. As I have explained in previous chapters, we wouldn't be correct in predicting an action other than the one favored by the current balance of our motives unless our prediction would be sufficient to shift the motivational balance in favor of the action predicted. And if the current balance of our motives were too lopsided, a reflective prediction might be insufficient to shift it. In that case, we wouldn't be correct in predicting any action other than the one whose motives were currently strongest, and so we would lack free will.[11]

What's more, even when we would be correct in making some predictions at odds with the motivational evidence, the range of potentially correct predictions is limited. There are always many actions—innumerably many, in fact—that we wouldn't perform next even if we predicted them, and these we wouldn't be correct in predicting. Our freedom is limited to the actions whose motives are already strong enough that they would prevail if reinforced by our prediction.

I believe that these limits are precisely the limits that we ordinarily feel in exercising our will. For we are sometimes impelled to do something by motives so strong that we couldn't will or do otherwise, and we are never so free that we can will or do just anything. We must therefore conceive of the will as lying under such limits, no matter how we conceive it.

(Having outlined these limits, here and elsewhere, I shall not feel obliged to repeat them at every turn. In subsequent sections I shall assume that the only actions in question are those which fall within the relevant limits.)

Epistemic vs. Metaphysical Freedom

Although our epistemic freedom explains and vindicates our feeling of being free, it does not entail any metaphysical form of freedom. To say that our intentions, considered as predictions, are independent of our motives, considered as evidence, is not to say that our intentions are causally independent of our motives. According to my theory, we invent our next action without being restricted to what our motives foreshadow, but we don't invent anything unless we have adequate mo-

[11] In this case, we would lack not only the capacity to predict, and hence intend, any action *other* than the one favored by our strongest motives but also the capacity to intend the latter action. For we would inevitably perform that action no matter what we predicted, and so our prediction of performing it wouldn't be self-fulfilling in the appropriate sense. And a prediction that wasn't appropriately self-fulfilling wouldn't qualify as a full-blooded intention, according to my theory. Thus, we cannot form an intention, as I define it, unless we could form alternative intentions. Another way of putting the same point is to say that there is no such thing as a will that isn't free. (See Baier, "Act and Intent," 657: "We cannot intend the things we cannot prevent, such as digesting or breathing. . . .")

tives for inventing it. Insofar as we are entitled to predict whatever we want, we are liberated from the motivational evidence, but insofar as we don't predict anything unless we want to, we are still the slaves of our motives.

Similarly, to say that there's no one action that's correct for us to expect is not to say that there's no one action that we're going to perform. Our future conduct is open in the sense that we are entitled to conceive of it as we like. But we are entitled to conceive of our future conduct as we like only because that conduct will be determined by our conception of it, and since our conception of our conduct is determined, in turn, by how we'd like to conceive of it, the conduct itself is fully determined.

In short, the freedom that I have characterized is not metaphysical freedom. Metaphysical openness and contracausal freedom are no part of my theory. According to my account, there is something that we are going to do, and it's whatever we most want to do. In this respect, our actions are fully determined, and they're determined by our motives for acting.

Unfortunately, we may be tempted to express our feeling of epistemic freedom in words that can be interpreted metaphysically. We may say, for instance, that we can form intentions contrary to our strongest motives. This statement is true so long as it means that, no matter what our strongest motives indicate that we shall intend and consequently do next, we would be correct in expecting, and thereby intending, to do something else. But the same statement may be taken to mean that our intentions or actions can somehow buck the causal force of our strongest motives. In the latter, metaphysical interpretation, the statement is simply false.

The confusion between these two interpretations is something like the confusion to which Hume attributed the very concept of a causal connection. Hume believed that we think of two events as causally connected insofar as we feel constrained to infer the occurrence of one event from that of the other. The concept of causal necessity, according to Hume, is simply the feeling of inferential constraint mistakenly projected onto the event inferred, and the concept of freedom from causality is a similar projection of our freedom from inferential constraint.[12]

My theory attributes our belief in contracausal freedom to a similar confusion. An intention is a behavioral prediction that needn't be de-

---

[12] For this view about the concept of freedom, see, e.g., *A Treatise of Human Nature*, 408.

rived from our motives in their capacity as evidence. But our forming an intention is an event, and this event is caused by our motives in their capacity as dispositions. Unfortunately, the inferential slack between motives as evidence and intentions as beliefs is mistaken for causal slack between the corresponding dispositions and events.[13] Thus is the epistemic freedom of our wills mistakenly projected onto the world as metaphysical freedom.

The Significance of Epistemic Freedom

One might suspect that I have overstated our epistemic freedom, given my admission that we are not metaphysically free. Although we may indeed believe what we like about our forthcoming action, the reason might seem to be not that we're entitled to contravene the evidence but that we're predetermined not to contravene it. After all, if the evidence indicates that we're bound to do something next because our desires will make us expect to, then our desires will make us expect precisely what the evidence indicates that we're bound to do. Perhaps, then, the reason why we may believe what we want about our next action is that our wants can be relied upon to induce a belief that's in line with the prior evidence.

But no. To say that we may believe what we want because it is bound to be congruent with the prior evidence is to suggest that congruence with that evidence is a desideratum for us—which it isn't. The idea of relying on our desires to keep us in line with the prior evidence misrepresents our situation, in which conformity to such evidence is of no concern to us, because in departing from it we would necessarily refute it. Of course, our departing from the evidence may be causally impossible, but it would be epistemically permissible. And precisely because it would be epistemically permissible, its impossibility is unimportant.

Still, epistemic freedom may seem worthless without its metaphysical counterpart. If we don't have metaphysical freedom, then our right to contravene the motivational evidence is a right that we haven't the power to exercise. Although we're entitled to expect an action other than the one indicated by the evidence, our motives predetermine that we're not going to form that alternative expectation. What good is an epistemic license that we are predetermined not to invoke?

---

[13] This confusion is somewhat different from the one that Hume describes. First, Hume says that we confuse our ability not to believe in an event with the possibility that it won't occur, whereas I say that we mistake our license not to form a belief with the possibility that we won't form it. Second, Hume regards the inferential freedom involved as purely psychological: it's a gap in the force of habit. I regard it as having a logical dimension: it's a gap in the force of evidence.

Well, to say that we lack the metaphysical freedom to contravene the evidence is not to say that we never rely on our epistemic license to do so. We rely on our license to contravene the evidence whenever we let our desires determine our beliefs. We believe what we want about our next action, and we do so precisely because the evidence has no authority over us. To be sure, we end up believing just what the evidence would have dictated if it had authority; but we believe what we believe because we want to, not because the evidence would have dictated it. Thus, our stance toward the resulting belief—which constitutes our intention—is radically altered by our epistemic freedom, even if the content of that belief is not.

The Feeling of Freedom Explained

In order to illustrate how epistemic freedom accounts for the feeling of being free, let me introduce another story about a self-fulfilling prediction. My story is this. You go to a restaurant for lunch. The waiter gives you time to peruse the menu and then asks, "What will you have?" You reply, "I'll have a club sandwich." The end.

I take it to be uncontroversial that your utterance in this case expresses your decision about what to have for lunch. I propose, somewhat more controversially, that your utterance is also a self-fulfilling assertion. Just as the doctor asserted "Nurse will take you to the operating theater" in such a way as to bring about the patient's being taken there, so you assert "I'll have a club sandwich" in such a way as to bring about your having a club sandwich. You say that you'll have a club sandwich on the assumption that if you say so, then a club sandwich is what you'll get and consequently what you'll have.

Some may object that your utterance in my story is a request or a command rather than an assertion, but this interpretation strikes me as inaccurate. If you said, "I'll have a club sandwich," and the waiter replied, "We're all out of turkey," then a natural thing for you to say would be, "Then I guess I won't have a club sandwich"—which goes to show that you would regard your utterance as having misfired because of being false. (If you had started off with "Please bring me a club sandwich," the waiter's reply would not similarly lead you to say, "Then please don't bring me one.") I therefore feel safe in saying that your utterance purports to be true and, to that extent at least, qualifies as an assertion.

Now suppose that you were carrying a copy of your book of life, which you had tested and authenticated in the usual way. When the waiter asked, "What will you have for lunch?" would you feel the need to consult the book before giving an answer that purported to be true?

If you had already read that you were going to have a club sandwich, would you feel compelled to say so, on pain of speaking falsely? Would you be afraid to say "I'll have a chef's salad," lest your answer misfire? Certainly not. The reason, as I hope is now clear, is that you are epistemically free in relation to your reply. When the question is what you will have for lunch, you are entitled to say whatever you like, because you'll have whatever you say.

For the same reason, conclusive motivational evidence about what you were going to select from the menu would also fail to make you feel constrained in your reply. A host of psychologists armed with unassailable evidence that your desire for a club sandwich was going to prevail, and hence that you were going to order a club sandwich, could not persuade you that you would be wrong to say "I'll have a chef's salad." For as before, if you said "I'll have a chef's salad," you'd be right. Of course, if the psychologists knew their business, then you would indeed say "I'll have a club sandwich," as they predicted, but you'd say so only because you wanted to, not because their evidence proved that you'd be wrong to say otherwise.

Now, I contend that confronting the waiter's question makes you feel that your future is open and that your choices are not dictated by your motives. You feel your future to be open in respect to what you'll have for lunch because you feel that there isn't one, predetermined thing that you must say you are going to have, in order to speak the truth; and you feel that your motives don't dictate your choice of what to have because they don't dictate what you must say you'll have, in order to speak the truth. What I have shown is that these feelings are veridical even if there is something that you are predetermined to have and even if you are so predetermined by your motives. You feel free to decide what you'll have for lunch because there is, in your mouth, no unique true answer to the question "What will you have?" Yet as I have shown, your feeling is compatible with the fact that there is a unique truth of the matter.

I do not claim, of course, that you are aware of the compatibility between your epistemic freedom and determinism. On the contrary, you mistake your feeling of freedom for evidence that determinism is false. Your awareness that there is no unique true answer for you to give in response to the waiter's question makes you feel that what you are going to have for lunch is still open. And your awareness that your motives cannot dictate how you should answer the waiter's question makes you feel that your motives don't determine your reply. But in feeling that your luncheon selection is open, or that it isn't determined by your motives, you are mistaking epistemic for causal freedom. *All that's open is, not what you are going to have for lunch, but rather what you would be correct in saying you are going to have. All that your motives fail to determine is, not what you say to the waiter, but rather what you would be correct in saying.* You mistake your license to say any one of various things about what you'll have for the possibility that you'll order and have any one of various things.

My theory of intention places all of your decisions on a par with your utterance in this story. Just as you say "I'll have a club sandwich" with the understanding that you'll have one only because you're hereby saying so, and that you're saying so out of a desire to make it so; similarly, you believe "I'll do this next" with the understanding that you'll do it because you hereby expect so, and that you expect so out of a desire to make it so. And just as you feel that your luncheon selection is undetermined, because there is no one thing that you must say you'll have, in order to speak correctly; similarly, you feel that your action is undetermined, because there is no one thing that you must expect to do, in order to expect correctly. What you are feeling here, I have argued, is a genuine freedom of the epistemic variety: you really are entitled to believe any one of several things about what you'll do, irrespective of the motivational evidence. But insofar as you take yourself to be feeling metaphysical freedom, you are mistaken, since there is a single thing that your motives predetermine you to do.

Does Epistemic Freedom Entail Metaphysical Freedom?

Some philosophers have attempted to bridge the gap between epistemic and metaphysical freedom by showing that the existence of the one entails the existence of the other.[14]

[14] Those who make this attempt include Carl Ginet, "Can the Will Be Caused?" *Philosophical Review* 71 (1962): 49–55; and Richard Taylor, "Deliberation and Foreknowledge," *American Philosophical Quarterly* 1 (1964): 73–80. Related arguments appear in: Hampshire and Hart, "Decision, Intention and Certainty"; Hampshire, *Thought and Action*; Hampshire, *Freedom of the Individual*; and D. M. MacKay, "On the Logical Indeterminacy of a Free Choice," *Mind* 69 (1960): 31–40. For comments on these works, see J. W. Roxbee Cox, "Can I Know Beforehand What I am Going to Decide?" *Philosophical Review* 72 (1963): 88–92; Pears, "Predicting and Deciding"; John Canfield, "Knowing about Future Decisions," *Analysis* 22 (1962): 127–29; Andrew Oldenquist, "Causes, Predictions and Decisions," *Analysis* 24 (1964): 55–58; David P. Gauthier, "How Decisions Are Caused," *Journal of Philosophy* 64 (1967): 147–51, and "How Decisions are Caused (But Not Predicted)," *Journal of Philosophy* 65 (1968): 170–71, with John O'Connor, "How Decisions Are Predicted," *Journal of Philosophy* 64 (1967): 429–30; Goldman, *Theory of Human Action*, chapter 6; Davis, *Theory of Action*, 73–77; and Roy A. Sorensen, "Uncaused Decisions and Pre-Decisional Blindspots," *Philosophical Studies* 45 (1984): 51–56. See also Perry, "Prediction, Explanation and Freedom."

Their argument, in its clearest form, goes something like this.[15] A person cannot predict an action immediately before he decides whether to perform it, since his foreknowledge would imply that the issue to be decided was moot, thus preempting his decision. If a person's decisions were caused, however, there would be grounds on which he could predict them, and if he could predict the decisions, then he could also predict the resulting actions. But as we have just seen, a person cannot predict actions that he is to decide. Hence his decisions must not be caused.

Unfortunately, the most that this argument can show is that in order for a set of conditions to be sufficient to cause a decision, they must be sufficient to prevent the decider from knowing about them.[16] If the causes of a decision kept themselves hidden from the decider, they would prevent him from acquiring the foreknowledge that would preempt his decision, and then they could succeed in causing him to make it. Hence the fact that decisions cannot be foreknown doesn't entail that they can't be caused.

However, I do not wish to avail myself of this objection, since I don't believe that the conditions causing a decision hide themselves from the decider. The conditions causing a decision, I believe, are the decider's motives, which he discovers in his reflective reasoning—the very reasoning that leads to his decision, according to my account. Thus, if I want to reject the present argument from epistemic to metaphysical freedom, I shall have to find some other objection to it.

My objection is that the argument neglects the possibility of epistemic freedom. The argument assumes that an agent's knowing in advance that he is going to do something preempts his decision to do it, by closing the question whether he's going to. But I have shown that an agent's prior knowledge does not close that question, from his perspective, any more than your knowing what you'll have for lunch closes the question "What will you have?" as posed to you by the waiter. Even if you know that you'll have a club sandwich, you'd be correct in telling the waiter that you'd have a chef's salad; similarly,

[15] Here I am using Ginet's argument, as clarified by Sorensen. See Ginet, "Can the Will Be Caused," p. 51: "For a person to claim that he knows what he will decide to do, hence, what he will at least try to do, and then to begin the process of making up his mind what he will do—trying to persuade himself one way or another by offering himself reasons for and against the various alternatives—would surely be a procedure of which we could make no sense. Either his undertaking to make a decision belies his prior claim to knowledge, or his prior claim makes a farce of his undertaking to make a decision."

[16] Sorensen offers a somewhat similar objection.

the agent would be correct in expecting to do something other than what he knows that he's going do. Hence these questions remain open, in the sense that there are several incompatible answers each of which would be equally correct. Your knowledge of what you'll have for lunch cannot dictate what you should tell the waiter that you'll have, and an agent's knowledge of what he'll do next cannot dictate what he should think he'll do.[17] Thus, prior knowledge of your actions cannot preempt your decisions.

The Concept of Decision

Now, I believe that the argument I have just undercut, by appealing to epistemic freedom, is our only reason for thinking that the truth of determinism would rule out the possibility of decisionmaking. That is, we think that we wouldn't be able to make decisions in a deterministic world only because we think that there would be just one correct answer to the question "What am I going to do?" and hence that there would be nothing for us to decide. Our answer to the question—"I'll do this"—wouldn't qualify as a decision, we fear, because it would have been the only true answer available, given that our action was predetermined. When we faced the question "What am I going to do?" we would actually, though perhaps unwittingly, be in the position of discovering rather than inventing the answer, because the answer would already be fixed. Or so we are inclined to think.

I have now shown that these thoughts are erroneous. Even in a deterministic world, we are not in the position of having to discover the answer to the question "What am I going to do?"; for there is not, from our perspective, a uniquely true answer. Any answer that we give will have been one of several incompatible answers each of which would have been equally true, and so we shall give it because we want to, not because we have no correct alternative. We are therefore in the position of inventing our answer—which is, I think, the position of making a decision.

I conclude, then, that the truth of determinism would not rule out

---

[17] Compare my argument with Gauthier's in "How Decisions Are Caused" and "How Decisions Are Caused (But Not Predicted)." Like me, Gauthier hypothesizes that an agent's awareness of the causes influencing his decision has a causal influence of its own. But from this hypothesis Gauthier infers that an agent can never take account of all the influences on any particular decision, since each accounting of influences brings into existence a new influence, which requires a new accounting. What Gauthier is overlooking, I think, is that any particular accounting of influences can take itself into account, thus stemming the threatened regress. Hence epistemic freedom is not to be found in the agent's ignorance.

the possibility of our making decisions or that of our feeling free. For even if determinism were true, we would still have our epistemic freedom.

EXISTENTIAL FREEDOM

Thus far, I have argued that our feeling of being free and making decisions is veridical, though not in a sense that entails a metaphysical form of freedom. We believe in metaphysical freedom, I have claimed, only because we misdescribe our real freedom, which is epistemic. I turn now to another mistake that can lead us to believe in metaphysical freedom. This mistake is not a mischaracterization of a freedom that we really have; it's just a mischaracterization of ourselves and, in particular, of the division between our cognitive and conative natures.

The Feeling of Radical Freedom

Sometimes, in a moment of decision, we attempt to stand back from ourselves and review our motives for taking various courses of action. We immediately see that the motives under review are not forcing us to do anything. Here we stand, reviewing them; there they lie, patiently awaiting our review. Clearly, they aren't about to interrupt our reflections and carry us off by surprise.

The reason, of course, is that we want to know and to understand whatever we're doing, and these two desires are restraining our other motives from making us do anything until we have finished reflecting on what we'll do. In reality, then, we are doing just what our predominant motives favor—our predominant motives, at the moment, being intellectual desires that favor our doing nothing until we have access to a description and an explanation of what we'll do. But these intellectual desires are motives that belong to us as reflective observers, and we removed such motives from the picture when we pretended to stand back, as observers, from the selves whom we observed. In withdrawing to our vantage of detachment, we carried our intellectual motives along with us, so to speak; when we turned to look back upon ourselves, those motives were no longer within our field of view. The remaining motives—the ones that we left behind—seem to favor our doing something and yet to fall short of making us do it. Our motives therefore strike us as oddly ineffectual.

To believe that our motives really are so ineffectual would be to take our own pretense of detachment too seriously. It would be to believe that when we stand back from ourselves, our personalities truly fission, yielding a pure intellect and a complete motivational system, one passively contemplating the other. In fact, our observing selves aren't pure, passive intellects. They have desires, too—the intellectual desires that move us to reflect—and these desires are continually interfering with the motives being observed. Our current inaction is fully determined by all of our motives, taken together. But it is not thus determined by that subset of our motives which we can look upon with detachment. The motives that we can look upon with detachment don't include the ones that are directing our gaze, and these are the motives that are currently restraining us.

Our false sense of detachment engenders a further mistake when we consider intending to do something other than what we would currently prefer to do. What we'd currently prefer to do, were we to do anything, is only one of several things that we would do if we intended to. The reason is that if we intended to do something else, we would consequently prefer to do that thing instead, because our intellectual desires, which now favor our doing nothing, would then favor our doing whatever we intended. But these intellectual desires are precisely the ones that we tend to overlook in our reflections, because they are the motives behind the reflections themselves. Having overlooked these desires, we think that the remaining motives—the motives that determine which action we'd prefer—are the only motives we have. And then the possibility of prompting a different action simply by intending it looks like the possibility of thwarting all of our motives with an act of pure intellect.

Thus, by disregarding the desires that move us to fulfill our intentions, we come to think that any intention contravening our current preference would have a force of its own in virtue of which it could stem the tide of all our motives combined; whereas in fact, we have motives in virtue of which the tide would turn by itself in response to such an intention. We pretend to be a dispassionate intellect whose edicts can hold back all of our passions, whereas we are merely a system of passions in which some—the intellectual ones—can hold back the others.

Finally, our pretense of detachment distorts our perception of how our intentions originate. When we review our motives for forming various intentions, we find, as before, that these motives aren't forcing us to intend anything. Surely (we imagine) if our motives could determine our intentions, they would do so by themselves and at their own time, whether or not we were aware of them. And yet we almost never find intentions thrust upon us by unidentified motives; what we find, instead, are motives that seem to await our supervision before moving us to intend. Our formation of an intention is finally occasioned, not by some overwhelming urge, but rather by our cool and conscious assessment of which intention we most want to form. This assessment, and the control that it exerts over our motives, seem to arise from our detached, observing selves. Once again, the dispassionate intellect seems to rule the passions.

But again, what's happening is that an intellectual passion—our desire to understand what we're doing—first restrains us from intending some action that we think we wouldn't understand and then encourages us to intend an action that we think we would. This desire doesn't appear in an arm's-length survey of our motives, precisely because, being the motive behind that very survey, it doesn't lie at an arm's length in front of it. But it is a motive nonetheless, and when its force is acknowledged, our motives must be acknowledged as fully determining our intentions.

Thus, a feeling of radical freedom—a feeling that we can defy the force of all our motives combined—is the result of a failure to engage in genuine self-inquiry, as I described it in chapter 3. There, you may recall, I claimed that the norms of inquiry permit us to influence our conduct even while we theorize about it, provided that our theorizing takes proper account of its own influence. I have now shown that if we misrepresent the motivational influence of our self-inquiry, an illusory sense of freedom can result. That sense of freedom results, in particular, when we recognize that our reflections often reinforce or suppress the motives on which we're reflecting, and yet deny that they do so by means of other motives—namely, our motives for reflecting. By denying that the influence of our reflections is due to the force of the motives behind them, we can pretend to be a dispassionate intellect controlling our passions, the unmoved mover of the practical realm.

The Feeling of Radical Constraint

A similar failure can have precisely the opposite result. By completely denying the influence of our own reflections, we can pretend to be reflecting on a self-contained, deterministic system. When we predict our behavior, for instance, we can pretend to be extrapolating from preexisting psychological causes to their inevitable behavioral effects. We can then point to the fulfillment of our prediction as proof that our behavior really was predetermined by the conditions from which we predicted it. In reality, of course, our reflective prediction is fulfilled not because it correctly projects the outcome of antecedent conditions but because the prediction itself prompts us to fulfill it. By denying the behavioral influence of our reflective prediction, however, we can portray our behavior as determined by forces that are outside of our reflecting selves, and so we can pretend that our future course of action is revealed to us as an inexorable fact.

This latter misrepresentation of self-inquiry is tantamount to a disavowal of our intentions.[18] To pretend that we are drawing a conclusion from prior evidence of its truth, rather than jumping to a conclusion in order to make it true, is to pretend that we are forming an ordinary prediction rather than an intention.[19] Hence when we deny the effects of our reflective predictions, we deny that we are intending the actions we predict.

Misrepresenting self-inquiry can thus lead us either to exaggerate our freedom or to underestimate it. On the one hand, we can acknowledge that our reflections influence our conduct, while denying that their influence is due to our intellectual motives. We shall then think that all of our motives combined are insufficient to determine our conduct without the help of our intentions, which we shall not regard as implicated in the workings of motivation. On the other hand, we can deny the behavioral influence of our reflections altogether; and then we shall think that our motives determine our conduct so effectively that we have no will at all.

I therefore conclude that the feeling of radical freedom is similar in origin to its opposite, the feeling of radical constraint. They originate in correlative misrepresentations of reflective inquiry.

Who Is in Bad Faith?

Another way of putting the same conclusion is to say that the existentialist's doctrine of free will is similar in origin to the attitude that it condemns under the phrase "bad faith."[20]

According to Sartre, an agent is in bad faith when he supposes his actions to be determined by his nature and then chooses his actions in accordance with his supposed nature, as if he could thereby prove that it determines them. Such an agent is guilty of bad faith, in Sartre's eyes, because he attributes his actions to psychological causes. I find such an agent in bad faith, too, but on different grounds. In my opinion, such an agent is in bad faith because he attributes his actions to psychological causes that are prior to, and independent of, that very attribution.[21] He expects that his nature will determine him to perform var-

---

[18] One case of a disavowed intention is the will to fail, which I discussed in chapter 4, 136–37.

[19] I discuss the distinction between predictions and intentions in chapter 3, 98–99.

[20] *Being and Nothingness*, 47–70.

[21] David Pears makes a similar point in discussing Sartre's notion of self-deception

ious actions whether or not he expects so, and he consequently thinks that in determining his action, his nature preempts any exertion of his will. In fact, the agent's expectations of acting are what finally determine him to act, and far from preempting his will, they constitute it, because they are his intentions. The agent is in bad faith, then, not because he disavows his radical freedom—he doesn't have any to disavow—but rather because he disavows the effects of his own reflective reasoning, effects that are essential to his capacity for intentions.

Meanwhile, I would say that Sartre's doctrine of radical freedom is the result of a similar exercise in bad faith. Consider, for example, Sartre's claim that radical freedom is revealed to him in his experience of vertigo. He imagines himself standing at a precipice and then says, "At the very moment when I apprehend my being as *horror* of the precipice, I am conscious of that horror as *not determinant* in relation to my possible conduct."[22] In other words, as soon as he reflects on his motive for recoiling from the precipice, he recognizes that it isn't sufficient to prevent him from throwing himself over the precipice instead. In Sartre's eyes, this recognition conveys only part of a larger truth: "*nothing* prevents me from precipitating myself into the abyss."[23]

Let me say at the outset that I thoroughly agree with Sartre's diagnosis of his vertigo as a fear not of falling but of jumping—indeed, as the fear that *this very fear* of jumping might be insufficient to prevent him from doing just that. I disagree with Sartre only about the grounds for this fear. In my view, Sartre is afraid that his fear of jumping might fail to restrain him because he realizes that he would jump, despite his fear, if he intended to. What's more, this realization arouses thoughts that are disturbingly similar to the feared intention. For if he formed the intention of jumping, it would consist in the self-fulfilling belief that he was going to jump. Sartre doesn't form that belief, but he does form the related belief that he would jump if he intended to, and he thereby pictures himself jumping. This mental image, though not an intention, is too close for comfort. Sartre's fantasy of how he *might* jump is disturbingly similar to the belief that he *will* jump, which would constitute an intention of jumping. In short, the realization that he would jump if he intended to arouses the fear that this very representation of jumping might already embody the fatal intention; hence the familiar sense of tottering on the edge.

According to Sartre, however, he is afraid of jumping because he

---

(*Motivated Irrationality*, 34). I have already quoted Pears's point (in note 4 of chapter 3), although I there omitted the references to Sartre.

[22] *Being and Nothingness*, 31.

[23] *Being and Nothingness*, 32.

realizes that all of his motives combined are incapable of preventing him: "*nothing* prevents me from precipitating myself into the abyss." Sartre regards vertigo as a revelation of his metaphysical freedom, which consists in the causal insufficiency of his motives.

But in regarding his motives as causally insufficient, I would argue, Sartre is guilty of bad faith. He is pretending to reflect on his motives from afar and hence seeing only the motives that can be seen from afar, which never include his motives for reflecting. Sartre is right in thinking that the motives he can see from afar are insufficient to determine his behavior, but he is wrong about the reason: the reason is simply that the motives he can see from afar aren't all of his motives. Because they don't include his motives for reflecting, they don't include the motives by which his reflections suppress and reinforce the motives that he can see. Sartre mistakes the motives in view for all of his motives, and so he thinks that all of his motives, taken together, can be suppressed or reinforced by his unmotivated intellect. Therein lies the bad faith of existentialism.

SIX

AUTONOMY

I closed the preceding chapter with a description of two ways in which we can misrepresent our reflective reasoning. On the one hand, we can predict our own actions as if they were predetermined independently of our predictions, in which case we shall be denying that our predictions actually constitute intentions to act. On the other hand, we can deny that our intentions, as embodied in those predictions, take effect by appealing to our intellectual desires, in which case we shall think that all of our desires can be tamed by a glance from the impassive eye of our mind. Because both views are mistaken, and in similar ways, I called both of them forms of bad faith.

SELF-GOVERNANCE

Now suppose that we steer a middle course, avoiding both forms of bad faith. In that case, we shall not pretend to predict our actions entirely on the basis of preexisting psychological causes: we shall acknowledge that the actions we predict will be caused, in part, by our predicting them and that our predictions therefore constitute intentions. Yet when the conscious belief that we prefer an action leads us to intend it, or when the intention leads us to perform it, we shall not pretend that our intellect is thereby operating outside the web of motivational causality: we shall acknowledge that an assessment of our motives yields an intention, and an intention yields an action, partly by the force of intellectual motives that incline us to intend what we'll understand and to do what we intend.

The Will as a Desire-Driven Faculty of Practical Reason

I suggest that we shall then have characterized the will, not as a locus of metaphysical freedom, but as a locus of autonomy. The will, so characterized, is a locus of autonomy, I say, in the sense that it contains motives by which it can restrain, redirect, and reinforce our other motives for acting, in accordance with our own conception of those motives.

The suggestion that the will contains any motives at all sounds odd, I admit. But I believe it to be true.

Consider, to begin with, what the will consists in.[1] According to my account of intentions, our faculty of forming intentions is a composite of intellectual and motivational components. We can form intentions only because we have the cognitive capacity to identify and explain human actions, in general, and the desires to identify and explain our own actions, in particular. Without the capacity to know and understand what someone is doing, we couldn't make behavioral predictions; without the desires to know and understand what we're doing, we wouldn't be moved to carry out such predictions made about ourselves, and so we would have no grounds for making the predictions that constitute intentions.[2] Our capacity for intentions requires not only the mind of a commonsense psychologist but also the motives for using it reflectively. Those motives, being essential to our capacity for intentions, can justly be regarded as integral to the will.

Indeed, these motives are integral not only to the will but also to our capacity for practical reasoning. For if we didn't want to know and understand what we're doing, we wouldn't follow our peculiar procedure for attaining self-awareness and self-understanding—the only procedure, I have argued, that deserves to be called both reasoning and practical. The desire to know what we're doing is what makes us try to anticipate what we'll do and then to do whatever we anticipate. To that end, it leads us to secure a knowledge of our motives, to form intentions that our motives will enable us to fulfill, and then, of course, to fulfill the intentions we've formed, since they consist in expectations that will then constitute knowledge of what we're doing. Our desire to understand what we're doing is what makes us try to understand what we'll do and then to do what we'll understand. To that end, it leads us to secure a knowledge of our motives, to form intentions that we can understand in light of those motives, and then to fulfill those intentions, since that is the most understandable thing for us to do. Together, then, the desires to know and understand what we're doing

[1] Let me repeat here what I said at the beginning of the previous chapter about the term 'will'. I do not pretend that the faculty of forming intentions is what philosophers have traditionally identified as the will. However, I do think that it's the faculty whose freedom is at issue in discussions of free will. I therefore take the liberty of calling it the will—meaning, roughly, that which freedom-of-will would make free.

[2] One might wonder why I include the desire for self-understanding here. After all, our primary motive for fulfilling our reflective predictions is the desire for self-awareness, not self-understanding. Recall, however, that these two motives are mutually reinforcing. (See chapter 2, 73–76.)

move us to form a conception of our motives, to conform our intentions to that conception, and to conform our actions to those intentions. In so doing, they yield nothing less than practical reasoning.

These considerations somewhat mitigate the strangeness of my suggestion that motives are integral to the will. You might have balked when I said that the will contains two specific motives. But at the word 'motives', you probably imagined desires of the sort whose content can vary among autonomous agents, as tastes and interests vary. I would then have sounded to you as if I was making the absurd suggestion that any creature who lacked some purely contingent tastes or interests would therefore be devoid of a will. In fact, the motives that I had in mind are not contingent—at least, not to autonomous agents. They are simply the motives that are necessary for the exercise of practical reasoning, and there is nothing strange about the suggestion that the exercise of practical reasoning is necessary for autonomy or for the possession of a will, since this is no more than a philosophical commonplace.

Of course, the philosopher who is best known for locating our autonomy in our exercise of practical reason did not characterize that reasoning as motivated by desires. Kant regarded practical reasoning as a function of the dispassionate intellect and as the means by which such an intellect can master the passions. Here I gladly depart from the Kantian tradition. In fact, my theory can be regarded as a naturalistic revision of that tradition—as an explanation of how the will could be a locus of autonomy while belonging to a faculty of practical reasoning that was driven by desires.

The Autonomy of the Will

Let me now complete that explanation, by showing how the will, as I conceive it, makes us autonomous.

I regard the will as making us autonomous in an etymologically precise sense of the word: that is, it makes us self-governing. Here again, I am offering a naturalistic version of Kant, who defined the will like this: "Everything in nature works in accordance with laws. Only a rational being has the power to act *in accordance with his idea* of laws—that is, in accordance with principles—and only so has he a *will*. Since *reason* is required in order to derive actions from laws, the will is nothing but practical reason."[3] The conventional interpretation of this passage assumes that it equivocates on the word 'law'. That is, the first sentence is interpreted as referring to causal laws, of the sort that pro-

---

[3] *Groundwork of the Metaphysic of Morals*, trans. H. J. Paton (New York, 1964), 80.

vide explanations, and the second sentence is interpreted as referring
to normative laws, of the sort that provide prescriptions.[4] But suppose
that the word 'law' in this passage referred to causal laws throughout.[5]
The passage would then define the will as the capacity to act in accordance with one's idea of the causal laws governing one's actions. I
doubt whether this interpretation would be faithful to Kant's conception of autonomy; I offer it only in order to convey my own conception. For I believe that we are autonomous insofar as our actions are
determined by our idea of what determines them.

To be sure, our actions are fully determined by our motives: we do
whatever we most want to do. Nevertheless, what we most want to do
depends, in part, on the intellectual desires that belong to our faculty
of practical reason. Those desires incline us to refrain from doing anything until we are aware of having formed a conception of our motives
and our forthcoming actions, and then they incline us to fulfill that
reflective conception. They therefore introduce an additional link into
the causal chain between our motives and our actions, a link consisting
in our own conception of that very causal chain. They incorporate, as
part of the workings behind our conduct, our conception of those very
workings. Consequently, we are a self-governing mechanism—a mechanism that is governed, in part, by its own conception of how it is
governed. The will, if you like, is a faculty for writing part of our own
constitution, in the form of a theory of how we are constituted.

SELF-CONTROL

The measure of autonomy that I have provided for may seem scant
indeed. Even if our intentions and actions are partly determined by our
conception of our motives, the fact remains that insofar as that conception is accurate, it will make little difference. Our self-conception
guides our intentions and actions because we have a motive that favors
the intentions and actions that strike us as intelligible. Yet the intentions and actions that strike us as intelligible are the ones that we conceive to be favored by our strongest motives. And if we're right about
what our strongest motives favor, we shall thereby acquire an additional motive in favor of precisely those intentions and actions which
were already our favorites anyway. Apparently, then, our self-concep-

[4] See, e.g., H. J. Paton, *The Categorical Imperative: A Study in Kant's Moral Philosophy* (Philadelphia, 1971), 81–82.
[5] Rüdiger Bittner informs me that this second, less orthodox interpretation of Kant
has been advocated by Konrad Cramer, "Hypothetische Imperative?" in *Rehabilitierung
der praktischen Philosophie*, ed. M. Riedel (Freiburg, 1972), vol. 1.

tion may intervene between our motives and actions only to redouble the causal forces that our motives would have exerted by themselves.

I shall now argue that this appearance is not entirely correct. My theory of the will shows, I believe, how even an accurate self-conception can alter the balance of our motives. Briefly, the reason why an accurate self-conception can alter the balance of our motives is that if we conceive of that balance as changing, it will change to fit our conception, so that our conception of it will still be accurate. We can be moved to induce such changes in our motives by so-called second-order desires—desires to have different preferences from the ones we currently have.

Wanting to Change Our Wants

There are important differences, in my opinion, between desires to change one's desires and desires to change one's preferences. Consider first desires to change one's desires.

Sometimes I wish that I had a stronger desire to solve philosophical problems and a weaker desire for professional advancement as a philosopher. At other times I wish that I was less interested in solving philosophical problems and more interested in mowing the lawn or getting a good night's sleep.

Unfortunately, I cannot just want whatever I want to: desires aren't things that can be donned or doffed at will.[6] I can of course undertake a program of self-reform, but such a program will require indirect measures, whose influence will be gradual at best. I can attempt to cultivate an interest in lawn work, for example, by trying to conjure up pleasant thoughts in association with that of pushing a lawnmower, but the desired motive will be long in developing and may never be especially hardy.

Note, however, that I don't usually want new or different desires for their own sake; I usually want them for the sake of one or more of their manifestations. That is, I may wish that my desire for professional advancement were weaker so that I could maintain my composure in philosophical debate or feel more resigned to my rejection slips from *The Philosophical Review*. Alternatively, I may wish that my philosophical curiosity were weaker so that my philosophical thoughts would abate and let me get some sleep.

If what I want from a desire is one of its involuntary manifestations,

[6] Here I overgeneralize. As I argued in chapter 4, 130–32, some desires can indeed be formed at will—namely, desires for their own satisfaction. However, such desires are of limited utility. For present purposes, I shall assume that the desires I want to have are intrinsic desires, which cannot be adopted at will.

nothing but the desire itself will do. Given that I have to mow the lawn, for instance, I may wish that I could tackle the chore with zest rather than my usual reluctance. What I want in this instance is not just a motive to impel me through my task but a motive that will imbue my performance of the task with a particular feeling or tone. I want a desire that will enable me not only to do the work but also to enjoy it. And enjoying my work is not something that the appropriate desire would move me to do intentionally; rather, it would be an involuntary psychological byproduct of the desire. In such cases, my only hope is to develop the desire whose involuntary manifestations I seek. If I want to enjoy working on my lawn, I had better develop a desire to work on it.

By contrast, the motivational force that a desire contributes toward the performance of an intentional action is somewhat easier to simulate or replace. On those Sunday afternoons when I'm considering whether to mow the lawn or to work on this book, I find that my desire to do one is weaker than my desire to do the other, and yet I don't find that my decision is straightforwardly dictated by the relative strengths of these desires or by my perception thereof. Even if I cannot muster a stronger interest in lawn work per se, I can at least muster another motive, equivalent to it in force, favoring a decision to mow the lawn, and so mowing the lawn remains a live option for me.

Another way of describing my flexibility in such a case is to say that even when I cannot change my desires, I can often change my preferences. The word 'preference' refers, not necessarily to any particular desire, but to the predominance of all the desires favoring one action over all the desires favoring another. A preference for mowing the lawn need not involve a desire to do lawn work per se; all it requires is my having some motives for mowing that are jointly stronger than the sum of my motives for any alternative action. And if what I really want is the contribution that a particular desire would make toward a preference for mowing the lawn, then I may be able to make do with some other desire that would favor mowing to the same degree.

My claim, then, is that even though we may not be able to adopt or discard a specific desire, we can effect an equivalent change in the balance of our motives and hence adopt or discard specific preferences. But how?

Getting Antecedent Desires to Team Up

One way in which we feel that we can change a preference is by enlisting one existing desire in support of another. For instance, I feel that I can reinforce what little intrinsic interest I have in mowing the lawn with my desire for the good opinion of my neighbors.

To say that *I* can reinforce one desire with another sounds odd, of course. After all, if I want my neighbors to think well of me, then that desire—together with the knowledge that my neighbors judge a man by his lawn—would seem by its very existence to reinforce my intrinsic interest in mowing the lawn. One might expect these motives to join forces all by themselves, leaving nothing for me to do by way of enlisting one in support of the other. If such were the case, then my total inclination to mow the lawn would already be as great as it could ever be, given my current desires, and I wouldn't be able to increase it without acquiring entirely new ones.

But remember that my motives influence me twice—once as they are, and once as I perceive them to be.[7] Even though my intrinsic interest in mowing the lawn is reinforced by other motives, I may not realize that it is, and so I may underestimate my motives for mowing the lawn. If I then think that I prefer to work on my book instead, I will regard working on my book as more intelligible—in which case my motives for working on the book will be reinforced by my desire for self-understanding, and I may indeed prefer to work on it, after all. Conversely, by uncovering additional motives for mowing the lawn, I can bolster my perception of motives for lawn work, and if I can thereby come to see myself as preferring lawn work, then my desire for self-understanding will reinforce my motives for it, with the result that I may come to prefer it.

In that case, of course, I won't really be adding one prior motive for lawn work to another. But I will be adding the perception of one prior motive to my perception of another, and the resulting perception, of motives that are stronger than previously perceived, will lead my desire for self-understanding to favor lawn work, thus causing the sum of my motives for lawn work to be greater than it previously was. I will be discovering an unknown motive that has always reinforced the motive I already knew, but I will thereby cause my desire for self-understanding to reinforce both motives, and I may therefore feel, understandably though mistakenly, that I am reinforcing the known prior motive with the strength of the newly discovered one—and hence enlisting one prior motive in support of the other.

As I have already explained, however, this process cannot alter my

---

[7] If you like, read the word 'perceive' here as meaning "knowingly believe." Remember that what influences me is, not which motives I know about, but which motives I *think* I know about. (See 35–36.) I shall henceforth feel free to gloss over this distinction whenever it would make no difference.

antecedent preferences unless it somehow goes awry—that is, unless I fail to uncover some of my motives. For if I discover all of my motives for various actions, then I shall regard myself as preferring whichever one is actually favored by the balance of my antecedent motives, and my desire for self-understanding will then do no more than second my antecedent preference.

What I have promised to show is how our preferences can be altered by an accurate self-conception. And, as I have said, this demonstration will invoke our second-order desires.

Deciding What to Prefer

Suppose that I initially prefer working on my book to mowing the lawn. But suppose that I have a second-order desire for my preference to be the reverse—that I want myself to prefer mowing the lawn. In that case, I can simply decide to have the preference I want.[8]

A decision to prefer mowing the lawn would consist, of course, in the formation of an intention, and an intention to prefer mowing the lawn would consist in a self-fulfilling belief that I so prefer, self-consciously adopted out of a desire for its fulfillment. The question is how such a belief is possible.

The possibility of deciding to prefer. Well, if I consciously believe that I prefer to mow the lawn instead of working on my book, then I will regard mowing the lawn as the more intelligible thing to do. And if I regard mowing the lawn as more intelligible, then my desire for self-understanding will favor my mowing the lawn. Of course, the prior balance of my motives may be so lopsided that the addition of another motive for mowing the lawn wouldn't reverse it. If so, I would still prefer working on my book to mowing the lawn, even if I believed the opposite, and then such a belief wouldn't be self-fulfilling—in which case I'm not entitled to form it.

But the prior advantage that my philosophical motives enjoy over my horticultural motives may be sufficiently slim to be reversed by the defection of a single motive from one side to the other. In that case, I can simply change my mind about what I prefer. Although I currently believe that I prefer to work on my book, I can adopt the conscious

---

[8] The main claim of this section resembles that of Charles Taylor in "Responsibility for Self" and "What is Human Agency?" It is also closely related to claims made by Harry Frankfurt in "Freedom of the Will and the Concept of a Person," *Journal of Philosophy* 68 (1971): 5–20. See also Jonathan Glover, "Self-Creation," *Proceedings of the British Academy* 69 (1983): 445–71.

belief that I prefer to mow the lawn.[9] For I shall then come to regard mowing rather than writing as the most intelligible thing to do, my desire for self-understanding will be transformed from a motive for writing into a motive for mowing, and the balance of my motives will consequently shift. I shall end up with the preference that I believe in.[10]

In short, because I want to do whatever makes sense to me, I can jump to the conclusion that I prefer to do something, since doing it will then make sense to me, and I shall therefore prefer to do it. If my conclusion represents itself accurately, as a self-fulfilling belief adopted out of a desire for its fulfillment, then it will constitute a full-blooded intention. And as I explained in chapter 4,[11] it can represent itself in this way simply by representing itself as an effective intention—in this case, as an effective intention to have a particular preference. I can thus decide to have the preference I prefer.

The constraints on deciding to prefer. This argument may seem to imply that preferences are so ephemeral as to be unreal. One's ability to prefer anything may seem to entail that one really prefers nothing. How can a person seriously be said to have a preference if it is in fact so changeable?

The answer is that the foregoing argument places perfectly sensible constraints on the instability of preferences. To begin with, I have ex-

---

[9] Insofar as this belief is based on the appropriate evidence, it will of necessity be conscious, since the evidence that's appropriate for supporting this belief is precisely the fact that I've formed it. Another way of putting this point is that the belief is bound to be conscious insofar as it amounts to an intention, since an intention is a belief that represents itself.

[10] The complete motivational story here is somewhat more complicated than the one I tell in the text. What enlists my desire for self-understanding in favor of mowing the lawn is not the belief that I prefer to mow the lawn but the belief that I correctly believe so. If I'm unaware of believing that I prefer to mow the lawn, or if I suspect that this belief is mistaken, then I won't necessarily think of mowing the lawn as a course of action that I'm prepared to explain. What makes me think that I'm prepared to explain mowing the lawn, and hence what enlists my desire for self-understanding in favor of lawn work, is the belief that I know myself to prefer it.

Since this is the belief that makes lawn work seem intelligible, and hence attractive, it's the belief that I must adopt in order to induce a preference for lawn work. I must therefore adopt the belief "I correctly believe that I prefer mowing the lawn." Of course, this belief already contains the fact that I prefer mowing the lawn, since it says that I'm correct to believe in that fact. In referring to my belief that I prefer mowing the lawn, then, it can simply refer to itself: "I hereby correctly believe that I prefer mowing the lawn." It then becomes a conscious belief that I prefer mowing the lawn—which is what I have been calling it in the text. (For an introduction to the issues discussed here see chapter 1, 35–36.)

[11] Pp. 140–41.

plained that if a preference is too strong to be reversed by the defection of a single motive, then it may in fact be irreversible. Furthermore, I have said that even if a preference is weak enough to be changed, a person must decide to change it, and his decision will itself have to be motivated. To say that a person can prefer what he most wants to prefer is not to say that he can prefer just anything, whether he wants to or not. He must want to prefer something before he'll be moved to decide upon preferring it.

Let me point out, moreover, that a person is unlikely to change a preference unless he not only has a predominant desire to change it but is also aware of that desire. Keep in mind that one's decision to prefer an action causes one to prefer the action by enabling one to understand performing it. Yet if someone understood that he was going to perform an action because he was hereby deciding to prefer it, but didn't know why he was deciding to prefer it, then he wouldn't really understand why he was going to perform it, after all. And if an inexplicable decision to prefer an action wouldn't really enable him to explain performing the action, then the decision wouldn't in fact cause him to prefer the action—in which case he wouldn't be in a position to make that decision, in the first place.

Let me run that one by you again. An agent's belief that he prefers a particular action is capable of inducing that preference only if it renders the action intelligible in his eyes and thereby gives him an additional motive for it. But if the belief portrayed him as preferring the action only because of having adopted this very belief, and if he didn't understand why he had adopted the belief, in the first place, then it wouldn't lend intelligibility to the resulting action in any case. The action would seem, at best, the potential result of a mysteriously self-induced preference, and being consequently somewhat mysterious itself, it would not be what the agent preferred, after all. That is, if the agent didn't know why he had adopted the purportedly self-fulfilling belief that he preferred the action, then the belief wouldn't succeed in fulfilling itself, since it wouldn't make the action seem intelligible and hence wouldn't induce him to prefer it. Thus, the agent can induce a preference by believing in it only if he knows of sufficient motives for doing so.

The end of decisions to prefer.   The necessity of believing oneself to prefer a preference, before inducing the latter preference by believing in it, may seem to bring one to the brink of an infinite regress. Wouldn't one's second-order preferences be subject to alteration, in turn, by what one believed about *them*? Those beliefs would then have to be understood in light of third-order preferences, which would also be belief-induced, and so on.

The problem is this. The agent chooses a particular first-order preference by adopting the self-fulfilling belief that he has it, but he isn't moved to adopt such a belief, or even entitled to adopt it, unless he has a belief about which second-order preference is moving him to adopt it. Yet that belief about his second-order preference is also self-fulfilling and would therefore seem to require the agent to understand why he has adopted *it* instead of some equally self-fulfilling alternative. That understanding would seem to require a belief about a third-order preference, which would also be self-fulfilling. And so on, one might think, without end.

Well, such an infinite regress is possible in principle but, of course, impossible in reality. And the reason why it is impossible is that the agent cannot have infinitely many orders of distinct preferences or infinitely many distinct beliefs about them. He may have one preference while preferring to have another, but he is then likely to be content with his second-order preference, and with his being content with it, and so on. Here the phrase 'and so on' doesn't describe an infinite series of attitudes, each constituting contentment with the last; rather, it expresses a single attitude in which the agent waives, at a stroke, all higher orders of discontent. The agent has second thoughts about his initial preference, but his third thought, so to speak, is "Let *that* be the end of the matter," an attitude that, by implication, quantifies over all possible higher-order thoughts and renounces them en bloc.

Another way of imagining how the agent stops the potential regress of attitudes is to think of his highest-order attitude as self-referential. That is, the agent may feel a contentment that includes itself within its own scope, an attitude of being content not only with the previous attitude in the series—say, his second-order preference—but also with this very contentment. No further attitude is needed in order for the agent to be content with this attitude, and so no regress need ensue.

In either case, the agent needn't have an infinite series of preferences, each ratifying its predecessor. He may prefer a particular action and be content with that preference (and let that be the end of the matter), or he may prefer inducing a different preference and be content with *that* preference (and let *that* be the end of the matter), and so on—but not *ad infinitum*. And as soon as he is content with a preference, he will be content with the belief that he has it, since that belief reinforces the preference believed in. He will therefore be content not to form any alternative belief, which would induce an alternative preference. Then he can understand the resulting action as ultimately due to a preference that was induced by a belief that was, in turn, due to a preference . . . that he was content to ratify by believing in it.[12]

Deciding by default.   Often one is content with a preference without even knowing what it is; indeed, the level at which such blind contentment sets in is often the first.

Of course, if an agent thinks that he is unaware of his first-order preference—if there isn't a particular action that he knowingly believes himself to prefer—then he will prefer to do nothing (other than looking for something that he'd rather do), since there is nothing (else) that he thinks he is prepared to understand doing.[13] And he is unlikely to be content with this particular, paralyzing preference. Nevertheless, he may be content to have whichever alternative preference he would already have if he weren't thus inhibited by his reflective ignorance. That is, he may be content to prefer whichever one of the available actions he would now prefer if he weren't averse to all of them because of not knowing which one he prefers. In that case, he may simply examine his motives for the available actions, figure out which ones are strongest, and form the conscious belief that they constitute his preference— whereupon they will, in fact, constitute his preference, since his belief to that effect will have reinforced them and removed his inhibition against acting.

In this situation, the agent may feel that he hasn't decided what to prefer but rather discovered a preexistent preference, and in a sense his feeling will be justified. After all, he doesn't begin with the desire to have a particular preference and then attempt to induce that preference by forming the belief that he has it. Rather, he begins with the evidence of his prior motives for various actions, and he then believes himself to prefer that action for which his prior motives are strongest.

Nevertheless, the resulting belief closely resembles an intention. The agent would have continued preferring to take no action at all if he hadn't formed some belief about which action he preferred, and he would have come to prefer a different action if he had formed a different belief about his preference. His belief is therefore only one of several potentially self-fulfilling alternatives, and it will represent itself as such, if the agent is frank with himself about it.

I therefore regard the belief in question as a defective instance of

[12] The phenomenon that I am discussing here is like the one discussed by Harry Frankfurt in "Freedom of the Will and the Concept of a Person," 16–17. There Frankfurt says that a person's identification with one of his lower-order preferences sometimes " 're-sounds' throughout the potentially endless array of higher orders."

[13] See chapter 1, 34–35.

intention, like the other defective instances that I discussed in chapter 4.[14] I would call it a decision reached by default. It's a belief that the agent has chosen to read off of his motivational state even though he would have been justified in forming an alternative belief on his own initiative. Because his actual belief has thus been read off of his antecedent state rather than adopted out of a desire for its fulfillment, it is defective as a case of intention. But because the agent chose to read his antecedent state when he could have believed in (and thereby induced) a different one, his belief still counts as his decision. Thus, even when an agent constitutes his preference out of his antecedently strongest motives, he is deciding to have that preference, albeit by default.

The motives for deciding to prefer.   Note, finally, that a person's motives for deciding on a preference need not include a desire to have that preference per se. Indeed, a person's motives for deciding on a preference sometimes derive entirely from his desire for self-understanding. For he may find, on some occasion, that none of the actions available to him would make much sense in light of his current preferences. His desire to understand his action then gives him a motive to adopt different preferences, which would render some available action understandable, so that he can then perform an action that he understands in light of his preferences.

   Thus, for example, if I discover that both my lawnmower and my word processor are broken, I may be prevented from pursuing either of the activities for which I have significant motives, and I may temporarily find myself at a loss for an alternative that I want to pursue. That is, I may not feel like doing any of the things that are currently available to me—including idly sulking over having nothing to do. In that case, I shall want to muster up an interest in some available activity, so that there is some activity that makes sense for me to pursue. I shall rummage among the remaining options, seeking one that I can successfully decide to prefer. And by deciding to prefer that option, I shall give some intelligible shape to my afternoon.

Two Kinds of Self-Control

The foregoing considerations reveal that our knowledge of our own preferences is often practical knowledge, and that it is ineluctably practical.[15] When we examine our moderate preferences, we cannot hon-

[14] Pp. 136–40.

[15] The notion of practical knowledge about one's preferences is probably akin to what Kierkegaard had in mind when he spoke of knowing oneself by "choosing oneself": "The ethical individual knows himself, but this knowledge is not a mere contemplation

estly regard ourselves as discovering preferences that are antecedently fixed. In representing these preferences, we are either altering them or, at the very least, ratifying them, since even representing them as they are amounts to foregoing an opportunity to alter them. Our representation thus causes the preferences that it represents, if only to the minimal extent of causing them to persist, and unless we deceive ourselves, it will represent itself as doing so. It therefore qualifies as practical knowledge.

The phenomenological consequence is that we find ourselves unable to reflect on most of our preferences with complete detachment. Even as we examine these preferences, we are engaged in their formation or maintenance, and so we remain fully implicated in that which we are examining. We do not have the option of entering the forum of introspection as mere observers: as soon as we enter, we influence much of what we see.

Some of what we observe introspectively is beyond our influence, however, as I have already explained. If a preference is so strong that a shift in our desire for self-understanding wouldn't reverse it, then we must represent it as it already is, since a different representation wouldn't bring about a different preference. Such irreversible preferences can and indeed must be viewed with detachment, since they are impervious to the influence that we exert as observers.

Now, the expression 'self-control' is usually reserved for our mastery over preferences that we cannot simply decide to change. Only when preferences resist our attempts to will their reversal are we obliged to adopt a deliberate strategy for attaining mastery over them. Hence the part of ourselves that we control, when we attain self-control, is a part over which we are unusually impotent and from which we are therefore unusually detached. Self-control is thus, in a sense, less than full control over something that is less than fully ourselves.

One way of defining autonomy, I think—an alternative to the Kantian definition—is to describe it as that to which self-control is second-best. Autonomy is the unavoidable control that we exert over those parts of ourselves that we cannot disown. It's our relation to those aspects of our personality and behavior which we cannot view with detachment, precisely because viewing them inevitably entails becoming implicated in creating or perpetuating them.

. . . , it is a reflection upon himself which itself is an action, and therefore I have deliberately preferred to use the expression "choose oneself" instead of know oneself. . . . [T]his knowledge is in the highest degree fruitful, and from it proceeds the true individual." (*Either/Or*, trans. Walter Lowrie [Princeton, N.J., 1946], 2: 216).

MORAL RESPONSIBILITY

My concern in this chapter and the preceding one has not been to solve the problem of moral responsibility, but I have in the end managed to locate applications for the slogans that have traditionally been used to discuss that problem. Philosophers have traditionally argued that no one could merit praise or blame for doing or preferring anything unless he could have decided to do or to prefer otherwise, and hence that moral judgment presupposes a freedom consisting of genuine alternative possibilities. I have located alternative possibilities in the epistemic perspective of the agent. Someone who does something or prefers something could have decided to do or to prefer otherwise, I have argued, in the sense that such a decision would have consisted in a belief to which he was epistemically entitled.

The question of course remains whether my sense of the phrase 'could have decided otherwise' has anything to do with the presuppositions of moral judgment. Can a mere epistemic license make someone a fit object for moral praise and blame, reward and punishment, resentment and forgiveness? Or do the alternative possibilities that I have located fail to satisfy the requirements of moral responsibility?

I am not going to answer this question, because I think that an answer would require a detailed account of moral judgment, and such an account is beyond the scope of this book, not to mention my philosophical grasp. Were I to seek an account of moral judgment, however, I would grope in various directions that are suggested by the arguments of this chapter. Let me conclude the chapter, then, by gesturing in those directions.

To begin with, let me point out that the range of alternative actions and preferences on which the agent could have decided, according to my theory, is the range of actions and preferences that would have ensued if he had believed in them; which is the range within which he is governed by his self-conception; which, in turn, is the range of his autonomy, in my sense of the term. In order to answer the question of moral responsibility, then, I would want to consider whether autonomy, as I define it, might satisfy the presuppositions of the moral attitudes. That is, might a creature's being governed by a self-conception make him an appropriate object of praise and blame?

I have various hunches about the prospects for an affirmative answer to this question. For instance, I suspect that we can blame a creature insofar as we regard it as capable of blaming itself, and that the capacity to blame oneself has something to do with being governed by a self-conception. But since I have no detailed account of blame, I can make no further progress in this direction.

A slightly different approach would be to consider whether my definition of autonomy might yield a corollary or two about personhood or personal identity, and hence about personal responsibility—that is, about how actions can be attributed to persons. Surely, a theory of autonomy should tell us something about personal identity, since autonomy is self-governance, and one's identity is one's self. My theory says that to be autonomous, or governed by one's self, is to be governed by one's self-conception, and so my theory suggests that a person's self-conception defines or even embodies his self, or his personal identity. Perhaps, then, a person creates his own identity when he creates a governing self-conception, and perhaps that self-conception is the locus of responsibility and the object of our moral attitudes. I have no idea whether this account of personal identity will yield any interesting consequences, and I am rather doubtful whether it would resolve the problem of moral responsibility. All the same, I offer it as a proposal for future research.

SEVEN

REASONS FOR ACTING

I turn now to a different but closely related question: whether an agent's reasons for acting are the causes of his action. The question whether reasons are causes is related to the question of autonomy because acting for reasons would seem to require autonomy, whereas acting under the constraint of causes would seem to preclude it.

The Problem of Reasons and Causes

When we explain why someone did something, we often cite the reasons for which he did it. The question is whether explaining an action in terms of the agent's reasons is the same as giving a causal explanation.

On the one hand, the reasons cited in such explanations often include the desires and beliefs that motivated the action, and our commonsense notion of motivation seems to be straightforwardly causal. That is, when we say that a desire or belief moved someone to act, we think of those motives as exerting a force, of which the action was a result, or we think of the motives as dispositions, of which the action was a consummation.

On the other hand, to cite reasons for an action is also to give a justification for it, to present it as the right or rational thing to do, and to cite the agent's reasons is to give the justification that he would have given or that he actually gave to himself. Considered in this light, the force that reasons exert toward action is prescriptive or normative. The problem is that the normative force of reasons can seem to be incompatible with the force of causality.

I think that the apparent incompatibility here is partly real and partly illusory. What's real is that the normative force of reasons would indeed be incompatible with their causing actions in particular ways, and these happen to be precisely the ways in which reasons have been thought by many philosophers to cause actions. But I shall argue that the normative force of reasons is not incompatible with their causing actions in other ways, which my theory of practical reasoning describes.[1]

[1] My theory of reasons has a structure similar to that of Stephen Toulmin's in "Rea-

Requirements for a Theory of Reasons

Let me begin my argument with three presuppositions that I think any theory of reasons must satisfy. These presuppositions are purposely vague, because they contain terms that different theories of reasons will explicate differently. The point is simply that any theory of reasons must explicate these terms in such a way that the presuppositions containing them come out true.

The first presupposition is that reasons for acting recommend the action for which they are reasons. This presupposition is just another way of phrasing the point that reasons have normative force. How reasons recommend an action is a question for each theory of reasons to answer in its own way. My first presupposition merely says that any adequate theory of reasons must have an answer to this question.

Of course, the only things that can recommend anything, literally speaking, are people and the statements that people make. Since reasons obviously aren't people, my first presupposition might be taken to imply that reasons must be statements.[2] I am inclined to be more broad-minded, however. All I mean when I say that reasons recommend actions is that they have some meaning or significance that is favorable to actions, and I use 'meaning' and 'significance' figuratively here, so as to encompass features not only of statements but also of events or states of affairs.

How could events or states of affairs have the meaning of recommendations? Once again, the answer is to be provided by particular theories of reasons—in this case, by any theory that defines reasons as consisting in events or states of affairs. Let me just sketch how two such theories might go. One theory would be that some events or states are such that asserting their occurrence or existence is tantamount to recommending an action. For example, to assert that an action would be pleasant might already be to recommend it, in which case the state of affairs consisting in the action's being pleasant could also be said to recommend the action. Another theory would be that some events or states of affairs are such as to entail that an action is prescribed by a norm of rationality. For instance, there might be a norm instructing us to pursue pleasure, in which case an action's being pleasant could be said to recommend the action by bringing it within the scope of that norm. According to the former theory, the normative meaning of an

---

sons and Causes," in *Explanation in the Behavioural Sciences*, ed. Robert Borger and Frank Cioffi (Cambridge, 1969), 1–26.

  [2] Stephen L. Darwall makes this requirement in *Impartial Reason* (Ithaca, N.Y., 1983), 33, when he says that reasons must be *dicta*.

event or state of affairs is just the meaning of its description; according to the latter theory, the normative meaning of an event or state of affairs is that which it entails—namely, the proposition that some action is prescribed by a particular norm of rationality. I don't believe either of these theories, but I do concede that they satisfy my first presupposition about reasons, by showing how reasons recommend actions.

My second presupposition is that when an agent acts for a reason, real or imagined, he is influenced in the appropriate way by the reason's recommendation. Here the phrase 'the appropriate way' refers to whichever way of being influenced is appropriate to the way in which reasons recommend. A recommendation is something designed or suited to exert an influence, and an agent acts for a reason when he undergoes the kind of influence that the reason is suited to exert in its recommending capacity. Insofar as different theories offer different accounts of how reasons recommend, they will have to offer different accounts of the influence that those recommendations are meant to have, and so they will yield different accounts of what happens when an agent acts for a reason.

My third and final presupposition is that the influence appropriate to a recommendation, of any kind, must involve the agent's grasp of its meaning. In this respect, a recommendation is like a command. The utterance "Jump!" can cause a person to jump either because he understands it and obeys or because it startles him; but in the latter case, it does not have the influence appropriate to a command, since its influence isn't mediated by the person's understanding of what is said.[3] Similarly, the influence appropriate to a recommendation must be mediated by the agent's grasp of the recommendation's meaning.

Suppose that I hear a Frenchman say, "Ma tête me démange," and I respond by saying, "Then you ought to scratch it." He might understand what I've said and comply, or he might be monolingual and attempt to signify his incomprehension by scratching his head. In the latter case, of course, he still acts in accordance with my recommendation, but he isn't guided by it in its capacity *as* a recommendation, and so he wouldn't be said to act *on* my recommendation, however well his action happens to accord with it. In the former case, he acts not only in accordance with my recommendation but also on it.

---

[3] This example is adapted from Anscombe, *Intention*, 33. See two similar examples in Elster's *Sour Grapes*, 53–54: "The other day my eight year old son was instructing me to laugh. . . . I found the instruction ridiculous and laughable; in fact I laughed at it, and thus he achieved the result desired, but non-standardly. Similarly one might conceive a person commanding one to admire him, and one might in fact admire him for the colossal effrontery of saying this."

My assumption is that to act for a reason is to act on the recommendation that the reason embodies and hence to be influenced by an understanding of the reason's recommending significance. Here again, my talk of significance and understanding is deliberately vague. If reasons are propositions or statements, then they will have meaning that can be grasped in the literal sense of the phrase. But if reasons are events or states of affairs, then they may have meaning in only a figurative sense—for example, in the sense that their descriptions have meaning or in the sense that they entail propositions about the applicability of norms. In the latter case, to grasp the recommending significance of reasons will be to grasp either their descriptions or their implications rather than the reasons themselves.

To repeat, I am trying to remain neutral, for the moment, on the questions of what reasons are and how they recommend. The point of my discussion is that the answers to these questions, whatever the answers may be, must entail that to act for a reason is to be influenced by one's grasp of a recommendation.

How Reasons Can and Cannot Cause Actions

I see no point in denying that being influenced by one's grasp of a recommendation might be a causal process. Maybe the meaning of a proposition or state of affairs can cause one to understand it, and maybe understanding a recommendation can cause one to act. Such a picture of how reasons exert their influence is not obviously wrong. I therefore refuse to rule out the possibility that reasons cause actions. If reasons do cause actions, however, they must do so by way of one's understanding their recommending significance, and this requirement rules out particular causal processes. Most significantly, it rules out the process posited by the causal theory that currently prevails in the philosophy of action.

The prevailing causal theory is that of Donald Davidson.[4] According to Davidson, reasons for acting consist in beliefs and desires, or (more generally) beliefs and "pro attitudes," and an agent acts for reasons when his action is motivated by the beliefs and desires that constitute reasons for him to perform it. The problem here is that beliefs and desires do not move an agent by way of anything that might be called his grasp of their recommending significance.

Part of the problem may be that beliefs and desires can move an agent even though he is completely unaware of them and would deny having them. Davidson's theory therefore has the puzzling conse-

---

[4] See "Actions, Reasons, and Causes," in *Essays on Actions and Events*, 3–19.

quence that an agent can act for reasons of which he remains unaware.[5]

Yet the problem with Davidson's theory runs deeper than this. For suppose that being influenced by reasons can be a fully subconscious process that doesn't require the agent's awareness of the reasons involved. Even so, a problem remains. The process of being influenced by reasons, whether conscious or subconscious, must proceed by way of something that can be called the agent's grasping the significance of those reasons, consciously or subconsciously. But the process of motivation simply doesn't require the agent to understand, at any level, the significance of the attitudes that move him. Simply to have a desire or "pro attitude" toward a type of action is already to have an inclination toward performing actions believed to be of that type. This inclination is an essential feature or an immediate consequence of the desire, and it requires nothing that might be called a grasp of the desire's significance as a reason or recommendation. The agent needn't understand a description of the desire—not even subconsciously—nor does he have to understand the desire as entailing anything, such as the applicability of norms. All he needs is to *have* the desire, and he's already inclined to act.[6] The motivational force of his desire is thus independent of his grasping any normative significance that the desire may have. Consequently, it is not the sort of force that a reason would exert.

There is a temptation to dissolve this problem by saying that reasons for acting consist in the contents of desires and beliefs, rather than in

---

[5] Similar points have been raised in connection with the subject of psychoanalytic explanation, which invariably implies that the agent is unaware of his operative motives. See Peter Alexander, "Rational Behaviour and Psychoanalytic Explanation," *Mind* 71 (1962): 326–41, and Harvey Mullane, "Psychoanalytic Explanation and Rationality," *Journal of Philosophy* 68 (1971): 413–26. The positions of Alexander and Mullane are criticized by Theodore Mischel, "Concerning Rational Behaviour and Psychoanalytic Explanation," *Mind* 74 (1965): 71–78; and Robert Audi, "Psychoanalytic Explanation and the Concept of Rational Action," *Monist* 56 (1972): 444–64. Unfortunately, the discussion is largely undermined by the assumption that *acting for a reason* is the same thing as *acting rationally*. I would say that a person can act rationally while acting for no reason at all.

Others who support the view that one must be aware of a reason in order to act *for* it include: D. E. Milligan, "Reasons as Explanations," *Mind* 83 (1974): 180–93; Don Locke, "Reasons, Wants, and Causes," *American Philosophical Quarterly* 11 (1974): 169–79; Kurt Baier, "The Social Source of Reason," *Proceedings of the American Philosophical Association* 51 (1978): 707–33; Darwall, *Impartial Reason*, 29, 205; and Robert Audi, "Acting for Reasons," *Philosophical Review* 95 (1986): 511–46.

[6] See N.J.H. Dent's excellent descriptions of the phenomenological difference between normative force and motivational force in chapter 4 of *The Moral Psychology of the Virtues* (Cambridge, 1984).

the attitudes themselves, and that the attitudes constitute one's grasp of those contents and hence one's grasp of reasons. According to this view, the reason for taking steps to promote an outcome is not one's desire for the outcome but rather *that the outcome is desirable*—something that's reflected or registered in one's desire. Being moved by one's desire can then be viewed as being influenced by one's grasp of a reason for acting.

The problem with this view is that it requires an unduly cognitive model of desire. In order for a desire to count as one's grasp of a reason for acting, it must be something like a perception of desirability. Yet one sometimes just wants things without in any sense perceiving them as desirable.[7] One can just want a book to be aligned with the edge of one's desk without seeing anything desirable about that state of affairs. One can just want to know what a companion is thinking, or to shake a fortunate person's hand, while regarding these accomplishments as having no intrinsic or instrumental worth.[8] Yet such desires, which do not involve any perception of desirability, are regarded as introducing reasons for acting into one's situation. If one just wants to know what's on someone's mind, then one has a reason for asking, even if one isn't committed to the proposition that the knowledge in question is somehow desirable.

I therefore think that Davidson is not merely being careless when he identifies reasons with desires rather than with the desirability of their objects. Desiring something is ordinarily regarded as a reason for pursuing it, not as a recognition or appreciation of something else that qualifies as a reason. Yet if the desire itself is to serve as the agent's reason for an action, then it must influence him through his cognizance of it as recommending the action, and so it must influence him in some way other than by straightforwardly motivating his action or his proximate motives for it. In short, it must influence him not just as a motive but also as a reason, by way of his understanding.

[7] Here I am disagreeing with Anscombe's claim that objects must be desired under some "desirability characterization" (*Intention*, 70ff.). Anscombe illustrates her claim by saying that a person cannot just want a pin, or a saucer of mud, without finding something desirable about it. These illustrations strike me as proving, not that a person cannot just want things, but that pins and saucers of mud are the wrong sorts of things. That only some things can be desired does not entail that a person can only desire things about which he finds something desirable.

[8] Of course, there is a sense of the word 'desirable' that means no more than "desired." In this sense, whatever a person desires is ipso facto desirable to him. But his desire for the thing is not a perception of the thing's desirability, in this sense of the word, since it is not a perception of the thing's being desired by him.

Competing Forces

The upshot of the foregoing discussion of Davidson is that the normative force of an agent's motives cannot be identical with their motivational force. Yet the distinctness of normative and motivational force entails that the one is in danger of being preempted by the other. For if an agent's desires and beliefs are sufficient to cause his action in their capacity as motives, then there would seem to be no room for them to exert any independent influence in their capacity as reasons. What point would there be in their recommending an action to the agent if they were going to cause him to perform it whether he grasped their recommendation or not?

Some philosophers are therefore tempted to think that the possibility of acting for reasons requires that motivational causation be less than totally effective. They think that the sum of an agent's motives must be insufficient to make him act, if the states in which they consist are to exert any rational influence on him.

In my opinion, this thought is only partly right. True enough, the motivational efficacy of particular desires and beliefs must be less than total if those same attitudes are to have any effect as reasons. But to deny the efficacy of particular motives is not to deny the efficacy of motivation altogether. The possibility remains that when an agent understands the significance of his desires and beliefs as reasons for acting, his understanding causes action motivationally, by combining with yet further desires.

Suppose that reasons for acting made recommendations of a kind with which any rational agent would want to comply once he grasped their significance. A rational agent would then be influenced by his grasp of a reason's significance, since once he understood the reason, he would want to comply. The desires and beliefs that constituted reasons for him to act could therefore exert an influence by way of his understanding them as reasons, and this influence would be distinct from their motivating force, which they would exert whether or not they were so understood. Yet their influence as reasons wouldn't be independent of the agent's motives, since it would operate motivationally—that is, via the agent's grasp of their normative significance and his desire to comply with recommendations of that kind. His behavior could therefore be fully determined by the sum of his motives and yet influenced by reasons as well, since his susceptibility to reasons would be among the determining motives. The efficacy of his motives would include rather than preclude his being influenced by reasons for acting.

The problem of reasons and causes is thus dissolved by the possibility of motives that mediate the force of reasons. Only by neglecting this possibility do we induce ourselves to perceive a problem. Sometimes, when we know of ordinary beliefs and desires that have served as both motives and reasons for an agent, we imagine that they were his only motives for acting as he did. We then have to wonder: If they were causally sufficient in their capacity as motives, how could they have served as reasons, too? What we're forgetting is that when an agent has acted on reasons consisting in desires and beliefs, he has usually been moved not only by those attitudes but by other motives as well—namely, his understanding of those attitudes as recommending action, and his desire to act in accordance with such recommendations. What was causally sufficient to determine his behavior was his full complement of motives, which included not only the ones constituting his reasons but also the ones mediating their normative force. Hence his motives, far from preempting the force of his reasons, actually transmitted that force.

Note, finally, that the motive mediating the force of reasons need not be a desire to act in accordance with reasons or recommendations per se. Reasons may turn out to consist in a specifiable kind of fact about the actions they recommend, and rational agents may turn out to have a desire to perform whichever actions are implicated in such facts. The question, then, is what kind of facts constitute reasons for acting and why rational agents would want to act in accordance with them.

Proposal for a Theory of Reasons

I believe that the foregoing chapters suggest an answer to this question. Notice that our perception of a problem about reasons and causes arises from mistakes similar to those discussed in chapter 5 as giving rise to our perception of radical freedom. In both cases, we are led to think that the causal efficacy of our motives would be incompatible with our being governed by our intellect, and what leads us to thinks this, in both cases, is our failure to take account of our intellectual motives. There the neglected motives were our desires to know and to understand what we're doing; here it's the desire to perform actions implicated in facts that constitute reasons. I now want to suggest that these motives are in fact numerically identical and that our mistakes in reference to them are one and the same mistake. In short, I want to convert my earlier theory of practical reasoning into a theory of reasons for acting.

A THEORY OF REASONS FOR ACTING

The way to convert a theory of practical reasoning into a theory of reasons for acting is this. Assume that reasons for acting are the propositions contained in, or the states of affairs represented by, the premises of practical reasoning; and assume that the action for which they are reasons is that action performing which, or intending which, is the practical conclusion appropriate to those premises.

The Problem of Normativity

Before I perform this conversion on my theory of practical reasoning, I should note that it will force me to start rectifying the current one-sidedness of that theory. As I explained in chapter 3, my theory of practical reasoning has its origin in considerations about the nature of agency. Thus far, my only defense for the claim that reflective reasoning is practical reasoning has been to show how reflection underlies the distinctive features of human action. I have not yet shown how reflection constitutes the agent's calculation of the best thing to do; and so there is a major function of practical reasoning that I have not yet shown it to play.

I am now going to define reasons for an action as things whose representation in the premises of reflective reasoning would lead to the action as a conclusion. But I have just stipulated, at the beginning of this chapter, that reasons for acting must recommend the action for which they are reasons. In order to define reasons as being represented in the premises of reflective reasoning, then, I ought to show how the things represented in those premises recommend the action that follows as a conclusion. I ought to show that the premises of reflective theoretical reasoning have not only factual content but normative content as well. I ought to show, in short, that reflective reasoning is really reasoning about what to do—which is precisely what I haven't yet shown.

One of my goals for this chapter, then, is to begin filling this gap in my theory of practical reasoning. I shall try to explain how the things represented in the premises of reflective theoretical reasoning can be understood as recommending an action, and hence how reflective theoretical reasoning itself can be understood as having not just a practical terminus but also a practical topic. I shall not be able to finish the explanation within the confines of the present chapter, but I shall at least make a start.

A Definition of Reasons for Acting

The reasoning that qualifies as practical, in my view, is the reasoning by which we attain self-awareness and self-understanding. What makes this reasoning practical is that it incorporates intentions and actions as the penultimate and ultimate steps in its procedure for yielding reflective knowledge. It incorporates actions because its procedure involves, not only adopting various beliefs that describe or explain our behavior, but also behaving so as to satisfy those explanations and descriptions. It incorporates intentions because intentions consist in reflective beliefs that we adopt in order to prompt ourselves to satisfy those beliefs as well as associated explanations.

I thus characterize practical reasoning by the peculiar way in which its concluding steps clinch the agent's self-knowledge. The question is what light this characterization sheds on reasons for acting if we assume that such reasons are represented in the premises of practical reasoning.

Well, propositions qualify as premises for some procedure of reasoning if believing them would put one in a position to draw a conclusion in accordance with that procedure. Premises for practical reasoning must therefore be such that believing them would put one in a position to draw a conclusion by practical reasoning. And drawing a conclusion by practical reasoning, according to my theory, is performing an action or forming an intention that increases one's self-knowledge by satisfying, or prompting one to satisfy, some reflective description or explanation. My theory thus implies that the premises of practical reasoning are propositions of which the following is true: that a person's believing them would put him in a position to increase his self-knowledge by acting, or forming an intention to act, so as to satisfy some reflective description or explanation.

Having identified the premises of practical reasoning, I can now identify reasons for an action. The reasons for an action are things represented in premises from which intending or performing the action would follow as a conclusion in accordance with practical reasoning. And intending or performing an action follows as a practical conclusion, I have said, if it would enhance the agent's self-knowledge by satisfying some self-conception. *Thus, reasons for an action are those things belief in which, on the agent's part, would put him in a position to enhance his self-knowledge, in this distinctively practical way, by intending or performing that action.*

Examples of Reasons for Acting

What qualifies as a reason for acting under this definition? Let me start with the most familiar example.

Motives as reasons. Among the reasons for an action, according to my definition, is the fact that one has motives for it. The fact that one has motives for an action is a potential explanation for one's performing the action, and believing this fact would put one in a position to increase one's self-understanding by satisfying the reflective explanation contained in that very belief. Hence the fact that one has motives for an action could be represented in premises that would lead to the action as a practical conclusion.

Consider a smoker who wants to avoid getting cancer and believes that smoking causes it. This agent has motives for quitting tobacco, and if he were aware of those motives, he would be in a position to understand what he was doing by quitting tobacco. Quitting is therefore the practical conclusion that would follow from the premises that he wants to avoid cancer and believes that smoking causes it. The facts represented in these premises therefore jointly qualify as reasons for him to quit.

In ordinary discourse, of course, we would say that reasons for the smoker to quit include his belief that smoking causes cancer—the belief itself, that is, rather than the fact that he has it. We would also say that the fact believed in, the fact that smoking causes cancer, is reason for him to quit, though we wouldn't say that this fact, the belief in it, and the fact of the agent's having this belief constitute three independent reasons for quitting. Rather, we would regard them as three different embodiments of one and the same reason.

According to my theory of reasons, the agent's having the belief that smoking causes cancer is the fundamental embodiment of the reason at issue, since it is what's represented in the premise to which quitting would be a fitting conclusion. But my theory can afford to be tolerant of the alternative embodiments of this reason. The premise to which the smoker's quitting would be a fitting conclusion can just as accurately be said to represent the agent's belief that smoking causes cancer as to represent the agent's having that belief. Hence my account is more or less indifferent between the agent's belief and the fact that he has it. Similarly, the agent's premise that he believes smoking to cause cancer can also be regarded as representing the fact that smoking causes cancer, since one often represents a fact to oneself by representing oneself as believing it, just as one often states a fact to others by stating that one believes it. Just as the statement "I believe your roast is burning" is a way of telling someone that his roast is burning, so the thought "I believe that smoking causes cancer" is a way of thinking that smoking causes cancer. Indeed, to believe in the fact that smoking causes cancer by believing that one believes in it is just to believe in it consciously rather than unconsciously—a conscious belief being simply a belief that involves an awareness of itself. Hence the fact that smoking causes cancer qualifies as a reason for quitting because a conscious belief in it would constitute a premise from which quitting would follow as a practical conclusion.[9]

Intentions as reasons.   Another proposition that counts as a reason, according to my definition, is the proposition contained in an intention to act. An intention to act, I have argued, consists in a self-fulfilling belief that we shall act at the prompting of this very belief. If, at the prompting of this belief, we do what the belief represents itself as prompting us to do, then the belief will provide us with an awareness of what we are doing, as well as a partial explanation of our doing it. And the reason why we are prompted to act by the belief is that we can thereby take advantage of the potential knowledge that it contains. Hence the belief constituting an intention puts us in a position to increase our self-knowledge by satisfying that very belief. The content of this belief therefore qualifies as a reason for acting, according to my definition.

What is the content of the belief constituting an intention? As I explained in chapter 4,[10] the content of an intention to act can be formulated most clearly as "This is a successful intention to act." What qualifies as a reason for acting, then, is the fact that one has a successful intention to act—this being the content of the belief that would give the agent self-knowledge, if he satisfied it by acting.[11]

Classifying an intention to act as a reason for acting accords with

[9] Are false beliefs reasons for acting? Yes, they are. But their falsity is a reason for abandoning them and hence also a reason against acting on them in their capacity as reasons.

For an opposing view on the relation between the various embodiments of a reason for acting, see Joseph Raz, *Practical Reason and Norms* (London, 1975), 16–20.

[10] See 140–41.

[11] I have now provided part of the answer to Michael Bratman's argument against identifying intentions with beliefs (see chapter 4, 124–25). Bratman argues ("Intention and Means-End Reasoning") that intentions cannot be beliefs because intending to act is a reason for acting, whereas believing that one will act is not. I have now shown how the beliefs that constitute intentions can provide reasons for acting.

common sense about reasons.[12] For we often charge people with irrationality if they fail to follow through on their intentions. Indeed, we think that deciding upon a course of action can alter the balance of reasons in its favor. If a person has equally strong reasons for each of two incompatible actions, then we assume that he must choose arbitrarily; that is, he must decide upon one action without having any particular reason for deciding upon it instead of the other. But once the agent has decided upon one of the available actions, we do not think that which action he performs is still arbitrary. Having decided upon one action, he would no longer be just as rational to perform the other: rationality favors following through on his decision. Thus, an intention can tip the balance of reasons in favor of an action that was previously no more highly recommended than the alternatives.[13]

But here is a problem. If someone forms an intention and fails to carry it out, then his intention wasn't successful; and if his intention wasn't successful, then according to my definition, it provided no reason for acting, after all. Consequently, a person's failure to act as he intended shouldn't occasion a charge of irrationality, since it proves that he didn't have a reason for acting, in the first place.

The solution to this problem lies in the realization that even an unsuccessful intention purports to be successful. An unsuccessful intention, according to my theory, is an expectation of acting that represents itself as self-fulfilling but isn't. And the way an expectation represents itself as self-fulfilling, I have argued, is by representing itself as a successful intention. Thus, an agent who fails to carry out an intention must nevertheless have regarded it as successful; otherwise, it wouldn't have qualified as an intention at all. As far as he knew, then, he had a reason for acting, and his failure to act on his intention was a failure to act on reasons, as they must have appeared to him. The charge of irrationality therefore sticks.

This account of the reason embodied in an immediate intention still has the consequence that if the intention turns out to be ineffective, then the agent didn't actually have a reason for carrying it out. But this

---

[12] It also accords with the views of Joseph Raz, "Reasons for Action, Decisions and Norms," *Mind* 84 (1975): 481–99, and *Practical Reason and Norms*; Aune, *Reason and Action*, 122; Michael H. Robins, *Promising, Intending, and Moral Autonomy* (Cambridge, 1984), chapter 2; and Bratman, "Intention and Means-End Reasoning."

[13] There is one important difference between intentions and other reasons for acting, but I am not yet in a position to explain it. Roughly, the difference is that an intention, though exerting a normative force in favor of the intended action, does not tend to indicate that the action would be a good thing to do. I shall discuss this distinction at length in chapter 11.

consequence is tolerable. For if an immediate intention proves ineffective, then there will be a sense in which the agent didn't really or fully intend to act, after all. And an agent doesn't in fact have any intention-based reason to do something that he never really or fully intended to do.

Habits as reasons.   My theory of reasons departs from the philosophical tradition—though not, I think, from common sense—in expanding the category of reasons for acting so as to include habits. For if one knows that one has a habit of doing something, then one has a potential explanation for doing it, and so by doing the thing, one can take advantage of the potential self-understanding contained in one's knowledge of the habit. By my definition, then, having the habit of doing something qualifies as a reason for doing it.

Some will balk at this result, but I find it congruent with our ordinary discourse about reasons. If you asked me why I had Cheerios for breakfast this morning, I would reply, "Because I always have Cheerios for breakfast"—meaning that I'm in the habit of having them. And I would be giving you not just the cause but also the reason for my choice. I ate my Cheerios on the grounds, and not just under the impetus, of my habit. If you asked me why I was wearing blue jeans to class, I would say, "I'm a casual dresser," thereby indicating my sartorial habits as grounds for my choice of trousers. I often choose particular items of clothing because they will manifest my way of dressing, which is largely a matter of habit. If you asked me why I set my alarm for 6:00 A.M., I would say, "I'm an early riser," since my sleeping habits are my primary reason for setting the alarm as I do.

Of course, all of the habits cited here are enmeshed in a system of other dispositions, including my tastes, traits of character, and desires. I tend to cultivate or maintain those habits which are consonant with my desires and to eradicate or suppress the habits that clash with them. Some philosophers will therefore want to claim that whenever I cite habits as my reasons for acting, I must actually be alluding to the associated desires, because desires are the only dispositions qualified to serve as reasons. Citing my habit of dressing casually as my reason for wearing blue jeans, they'll say, is just an imprecise or indirect way of citing the desires that led me to form and keep that habit in the first place, such as my desire to present a youthful appearance, my desire for bodily comfort, or my desire to defy authority. These have to be my real reasons for wearing jeans, according to the traditional conception of reasons.

Now, I do not wish to deny that such desires are potential reasons for me to wear jeans; nor do I wish to deny that they are my actual reasons for having the habit of wearing jeans. But I do deny, most emphatically, that they are my actual reasons for wearing jeans on any particular day or for buying any particular pair of jeans. Each morning as I take a pair of jeans out of the closet and leave behind the grey flannel trousers, I do so for a reason. That is, I act partly under the influence of a consideration that recommends blue denim over grey flannel. And the consideration influencing me is not that I want to present a youthful appearance or promote my bodily comfort or defy authority. Such thoughts are the farthest thing from my mind. The operative consideration on any particular morning is something like this: "Today is Tuesday; I'm going to work; when I go to work, I wear jeans." If you were to leap out from behind the hangers, proferring my grey flannel trousers, I would reply, "I don't wear those to work," and I would thereby rationalize my choice by invoking a habit. Of course, if you then asked why I don't wear grey flannel trousers to work, I'd have to reflect on my reasons for being in the habit of wearing jeans, and we might then have a profitable discussion about the desires recommending various habits of dress. But in that case we would be discussing just that—reasons for having various habits—which is not the same as discussing my reason for wearing blue jeans today. My reason for wearing jeans today is that jeans are what I habitually wear to work.

Similarly, my reason for buying a pair of jeans, when I'm shopping for trousers, is usually that jeans are what I wear. I do not treat each trip to the men's store as an occasion for reconsidering my habits of dress. As I browse through the racks of clothing, I do not actively exercise my tastes, evaluating each style afresh for its appearance and utility. Even when I am buying a new brand or size or color, I look for what would fit my habits of dress. The question on my mind is not "Do I like this pair?" but "Is this the sort of thing that I wear?" An affirmative answer to the latter question is almost always my reason for buying a particular item. My reason, then, is a habit rather than a desire.

Another possible objection to classifying habits as reasons for acting is that undesirable habits are never regarded as having the force of reasons. My reply is that in this respect the thesis that desires are reasons fares no better. Unwanted desires are no more credited with the force of reasons than unwanted habits. What's more, my theory can explain why both habits and desires lose the status of reasons when they are unwanted. The explanation is that insofar as their motivating force is opposed by the agent's desire to suppress them, they lose their capacity to account for his behavior and hence their value for reflective reasoning. (I shall elaborate on this kind of argument in the next two chapters.)

Finally, let me point out that the issue of habit is somewhat clouded by our use of the term. I suspect that when a habit comes to the agent's attention and is accepted as a reason for acting, it comes to be called a custom or part of the agent's way of life rather than a habit. The term 'habit' tends to be reserved for those habits which operate subconsciously, without being recognized in practical reasoning. In order to respect this usage, I should probably have said that my reason for wearing jeans this morning was that it's my custom to do so. But the term 'custom' here would simply have meant a habit that had influenced me in its capacity as a reason.

The Normative Force of Reasons

Those philosophers who believe that reasons for acting must be based on desires will always be able to concoct desire-based reasons for any occasion on which an ordinary speaker would cite habits as his reasons. The question is not whether ordinary discourse can be replaced or reinterpreted in this fashion; the question is why we should replace or reinterpret it. What do desires have that habits don't have, when it comes to recommending actions, that would require our refusing to take ordinary habit-based justifications at face value? True enough, desires move us to act; but then, so do habits. And in any case, the motivational force of desires cannot be their recommending force. What is their recommending force, then? To my knowledge, proponents of the traditional conception of reasons have no answer to this question, except perhaps to say that desires recommend actions because they are reasons for acting—which is a viciously circular answer, since desires need recommending force in order to qualify as reasons in the first place. After saying that desires qualify as reasons because they recommend action, one cannot turn around and say that they recommend action because they're reasons for acting.

I have an answer to the question how desires recommend actions, and it's an answer according to which habits recommend actions as well. That my answer thereby enables us to preserve rather than replace the habit-based justifications that arise in ordinary discourse is, to my mind, a virtue rather than a flaw.

The normative force of reasons for acting, as I conceive them, is their capacity to make actions attractive to us in a particular way. Reasons for an action, I have said, are propositions or states of affairs belief in which would put us in a position to increase our self-knowledge by intending or performing the action. They are things whose representation in our beliefs would put us in a position to arrive at the action, or the decision to perform it, as our practical conclusion. Now, our awareness of being in that position makes the action or intention attractive to our desires for self-awareness and self-understanding. Reasons are therefore such that our awareness of knowing them makes intending or performing the action attractive to our reflective intellectual desires. I now say that the capacity of reasons to make an action attractive in this way is what constitutes their normative force. That is, if propositions are reasons for an action, then they recommend that action to us in the sense that our awareness of knowing them would make the action, or the decision to perform it, desirable to us; and as I have said, it would make the action or decision desirable by making it seem like a potential concluding step toward the self-knowledge and self-understanding that we desire.

Why do I speak of our awareness of knowing reasons rather than simply our knowledge of the reasons? The answer is that, as I explained in chapters 1 and 2, our desires for self-knowledge interact only indirectly with our self-knowledge, by interacting with our beliefs about it.[14] These desires incline us toward an action only insofar as we believe that, in performing it, we would know and understand what we were doing. Thus, we aren't moved to act simply by being in a position to enjoy self-knowledge if we do; we're moved only by our awareness that we are in such a position, together with our desire to take advantage of it. And since our knowledge of reasons is what puts us in that position, they move us only if we're aware of knowing them.

This result brings my theory into conformity with my requirements for a theory of reasons. I stipulated, remember, that acting for a reason must involve being influenced by one's grasp of the reason's normative significance. Well, to be aware that knowing something has put one in a position to enhance one's self-knowledge by acting—that, I contend, is one and the same as to grasp the significance of the thing in its capacity as a reason. One's having particular motives, for instance, qualifies as a reason for acting, I have said, insofar as knowing it would put one in a position to enhance one's self-knowledge by acting. One's awareness of being placed in that position by knowing about one's motives therefore amounts to an understanding of their normative significance.

Replies to Objections

Here I may seem to have misunderstood what normative force is supposed to be. Surely, one might think, the normative force of reasons

[14] See 35–36, 50.

cannot consist in their appeal to anything so narrow or so ephemeral as particular desires. A person's being subject to reasons—his being a creature to whom they address their recommendations—shouldn't be made to depend on his having specific tastes or interests. Of course, a person's tastes and interests may determine whether something is a reason for him to act; but if something *is* a reason for him to act, then the normative force of that reason would seem to be independent of any further psychological contingencies. We would say, for instance, that seeing a train pull out of the station isn't a reason for running unless one wants to catch the train, but we wouldn't say that if it is a reason for running, it may still fail to recommend running unless one has some additional inclination.

Normativity and the will.   Keep in mind, however, that the desires for self-understanding and self-knowledge aren't any ordinary inclinations: they are necessary constituents of the will and of our faculty of practical reason. The fact that they are necessary to the faculty of practical reason, and to the will, should reconcile us to the notion that they are necessary to the normative force of reasons as well. To be sure, whether reasons for an action have the power of recommending that action to us cannot depend on whether we have some purely contingent tastes or interests, but it can depend on whether we have a capacity for practical reasoning or on whether we have a will. There is nothing odd about saying that a creature incapable of practical reasoning or devoid of a will is a creature to whom reasons cannot prescribe or recommend. Hence there should be nothing odd about saying that the normative force of reasons depends on particular desires, if those desires are necessary to the will and to the faculty of practical reason.

One might still object that the force exerted by reasons, as I define them, isn't really the force of a genuinely rational recommendation. Most philosophers conceive of reasons as recommending an action to an agent by indicating that it's categorically the best one for him to perform,[15] whereas I conceive of reasons as recommending an action by indicating that it's the best for a very specific purpose—namely, the pursuit of self-knowledge.[16] Of course, indicating that an action is best for the pursuit of self-knowledge is a way of recommending it to those who care about self-knowledge. But such is the broadest and most general recommendation of which reasons are capable, according to my

[15] Perhaps the clearest statement of this conception is in Kurt Baier, *The Moral Point of View* (Ithaca, N.Y., 1958).

[16] Here I use the word 'indicate' to allow for prima facie reasons, which don't prove conclusively that an action is the best but merely provide indications to that effect.

theory: it is the recommendation that they provide simply by virtue of being reasons. One might have expected the recommendations provided by reasons as such to be far less particular.

My response, once again, is that the particularity of rational recommendations, as I conceive them, is only fitting, given my conception of agency. For I conceive of agency itself as being constituted by a particular purpose, the very purpose to which I have subordinated the force of reasons—the pursuit of self-knowledge. To say that reasons recommend an action to someone only insofar as he cares about self-knowledge is, in my book, to say that they recommend it to him only insofar as he is an agent. What's wrong with that?

My conception of normative force will seem odd only to those who persist in conceiving of agency as a universal capacity for pursuits, in itself neutral among them. If one thinks that being an agent is just being capable of pursuing desired outcomes, in general, then one will think that the recommending force of reasons as such—the recommendations that they make simply by virtue of being reasons—must transcend the pursuit of any particular outcome. But to me being an agent is not a neutral capacity for pursuit; it's a substantive commitment to a particular, second-order pursuit, that of knowing about one's own pursuits. And how could the recommendations provided by reasons as such transcend the commitments that are intrinsic to agency?

Normativity and evaluation.   Finally, one might turn my response on its head, by calling it a *reductio* of my conception of agency. A conception of agency cannot be correct, one might argue, if it requires the recommendations provided by reasons as such to be subordinated to a particular pursuit. One might insist that an adequate conception of agency must show the agent to be a creature for whom there can be rational recommendations that are worthy of the name—that is, reasons for acting that, as such, recommend an action by showing it to be categorically the best.

I shall not give a full answer to this objection here. The entire topic will be central to part 4, below, where I discuss the relation between rationality and value. Here I can give only an outline of my answer.

My answer to this last objection will be that we do not in practice recognize recommendations more general than those addressed to our interest in self-knowledge. We do, I think, have a notion of categorical value as something that renders objects desirable irrespective of our particular interests. But value of this sort is something to which we have no direct access; indeed, we have no conception of what it would be like. In our attempt to detect it, then, we must adopt a test that we are capable of applying in practice. And our test of the best action is just an action's appeal to the interests that make us agents.

One argument for this admittedly unusual claim is a simple fact of ordinary language. The fact is that we freely profess to recognize what's best by means of its intelligibility. When we're trying to discover the best thing to do, we look for what would make the most sense to do, and when we find what would make the most sense, we take ourselves to have discovered what's best. One might think, of course, that I have here reversed the logical order between our judgments of what's best and our judgments of what makes most sense. One might think, in other words, that an action seems to make sense only if and because it seems best, instead of seeming best because it seems to make sense. What I shall argue in part 4 is that this conception of the priority between intelligibility and value is wrong and that mine is right—at least, that is, for value as we measure it in practice.

To repeat, I do not deny that we have the concept of perfectly colorless value, pure value, value consisting in an appealingness that appeals to no specific interest. I simply deny that any such value guides us in practice. What guides us in practice, I claim, is a test of such value, a test that consists in an action's appeal to the intellectual interests that constitute us as agents.

If this account of value is correct, then reasons for an action, as I define them, do indicate that the action is the best—at least, by our test—since reasons for an action, as I define them, are facts in light of which the action would make sense. Whether this account of value is correct, however, is a question that must be postponed until part 4.

The Relation between Reasons and Causes

Let me return briefly to the supposed incompatibility between the force that beliefs and desires exert as motives and their force as reasons. At the outset of this chapter, I sketched a strategy for resolving the incompatibility. I would now like to show how my theory of reasons for acting implements that strategy.

Reasons and Intention

Let me begin by pointing out and resolving a similar problem in the case of intentions. The problem here is that the effectiveness of an intention, like that of a motive, would seem to preempt the force of any reason embodied in that intention. How can having a successful intention be a reason for acting, as I claim, when a successful intention is, by definition, one that will produce the action anyway?[17]

The answer is that an intention's success is not only compatible with the force of the associated reason but is actually a manifestation of that force. A successful intention consists in a belief that prompts us to perform the intended action, and this belief prompts us to perform the action precisely because it makes the action attractive as a means of realizing the potential self-knowledge inherent in the belief itself. Now, a belief's capacity to make an action attractive as a means of realizing potential self-knowledge, I have claimed, constitutes normative force belonging to the proposition believed in. And the content of the belief constituting an effective intention is just this: that it constitutes a successful intention. Hence a successful intention consists in a belief that prompts us to act by exerting the normative force of the fact that it constitutes a successful intention.

What makes an intention effective, in short, is the normative force of the fact that it's an intention—which is the force that the intention exerts in its capacity as a reason for acting. Hence our intentions get us to act only because we are susceptible to their force as reasons. The causal efficacy of intentions, far from being incompatible with their normative force, is identical with it.

Reasons and Motives

So, too, the efficacy of our motives usually includes rather than precludes their normative force. To be sure, the normative force of the reasons that consist in particular desires and beliefs is distinct from the motivational force of those same attitudes, but it isn't distinct from motivational force altogether. The normative force of the reasons that consist in desires and beliefs is their capacity, by being represented in our conscious self-conception, to elicit the force of other motives—that is, of our motives for acting in accordance with that conception. Hence when our conduct is determined by all of our motives combined, it is being determined, in part, by our response to the normative force of reasons.

To ask whether the combined forces of all our motives can be deflected by reasons for acting, or baffled by the lack of them, is to betray a fundamental misunderstanding. By the time that the forces of all our motives have been combined, the influence of reasons or of their absence has already registered. To repeat, our motives include the desires

---

[17] One philosopher who addresses this apparent problem is Robins, *Promising, Intending, and Moral Autonomy*, chapter 2.

for self-knowledge and self-understanding, and these desires are what restrain us from acting until we find reasons, and then convey the force of the reasons we find. Hence the normative force of reasons doesn't compete with the total of motivational forces; rather, it is imparted to some of our motives, thus altering the total.

Even though we shall inevitably do whatever we have the strongest motives for doing, the question what we have reason for doing isn't moot, since what we have the strongest motives for doing will depend, in part, on whether we discover any reasons for acting and, if so, what force their discovery imparts to the desires constituting our faculty of practical reason. When we fear that the efficacy of our motives would preempt the normative force of reasons, we are in the grip of a false image. That image, once again, is that reasons for acting exert a distinct, extramotivational force that competes with the force of all our motives combined.

The same image is what makes us feel that our motives are in fact inefficacious. When we are brought up short by the absence of reasons or swayed by their presence—either of which happens, in fact, only because some of our motives are opposed or reinforced by others—the image of reasons as competing with our motives makes us feel as if all of our motives together have been thwarted or deflected. We therefore feel that our motives are insufficient to determine our actions.

Indeed, the image of reasons as exerting an extramotivational force in competition with our motives corresponds to the image of practical reason as a dispassionate faculty in competition with the passions. And I have already explained, in the preceding chapter, how the latter image induces the appearance of inefficacy in our motives. As we survey our motives, I said, we pretend to be doing so from a distance and hence from a standpoint that is motive-free. Our survey thus omits those desires which motivate the survey itself—and which not only motivate the survey but also interfere with the motives being surveyed. These desires decisively repress the rest of our motives until we have a conscious conception of our motives, and then they reinforce the rest of our motives in accordance with that conception. Yet because we disregard these desires, we seem to see our motives repressed and reinforced by the presence or absence of the conception alone—and hence by pure practical thought. All of our motives combined then appear to be overpowered by the unaided intellect, and so they appear inefficacious.

This earlier explanation of their apparent inefficacy is equivalent to the present explanation. According to my account, to disregard the desires through which our self-conception can alter the balance of our motives is the same as to disregard the desires in virtue of which reasons have normative force. In both cases—which are really the same case, twice described—we view the intellect as master of the passions because we disavow the intellectual passions through which it exerts its influence.

Now, About that Walk of Yours . . .

Seven chapters have gone by, and you're still standing on Fifth Avenue, wondering why you came this far, wondering where to go from here. Well, at least you brought along something to read.

What you're reading can't help you out of your predicament, of course. Philosophy books never can. But like most philosophy books, this one can offer a potential way of redescribing your predicament. It offers a hypothetical model of agency as a system of intellectual desires and reflective beliefs. In the terms of that model, your predicament would be described as follows.

- In walking up Fifth Avenue without knowing why, you temporarily lost not only your self-awareness but also your autonomy; for you were no longer governed by your conception of what was governing you.
- In refusing to go on without knowing of a motive for going on, you were refusing to act without a reason.
- In trying to figure out what would make sense for you to do next, you were engaged in ordinary practical reasoning—reasoning whose terminus would be an action and whose topic was the best thing to do.

Now go home.

PART THREE

AGENCY EXTENDED

EIGHT

INTO THE FUTURE

The agent whom I have described thus far is woefully myopic. He can appreciate reasons for acting, but only those reasons which bear upon his next step and consist in its immediate psychological precursors; he can form immediate intentions, but no long-range plans; and his self-knowledge rarely extends beyond his impending action or beneath its superficial causes.

Extending this agent's horizons is the purpose of the next two chapters. How can practical reasoning produce decisions that reach farther into the future and that rest on a deeper rationale? How can an agent exercise autonomy not just in moving his limbs but also in shaping his life? These are the questions to which I now turn. In this chapter I shall attempt to expand the scope of my hypothetical agent's intentions, by showing how this agent could form long-range intentions of the sort that are ordinarily called plans. In the following chapter I shall attempt to deepen the agent's appreciation of reasons for acting.

LONG-RANGE PLANS

In chapters 3 and 4, I described an agent's intentions as self-fulfilling expectations of acting that are adopted out of the agent's desire for their fulfillment, rather than dictated by the evidence, and that represent themselves as such. An agent's expectations of acting fit this description, I argued, because his desire to know what he's doing moves him to do nothing until there is something that he expects to do, whereupon the same desire moves him to do whatever he expects.

Yet this strategy for self-awareness relies on the immediacy of the agent's expectations. The agent wants concurrent knowledge of his actions: he wants to know about them as he performs them. And expecting to perform an action in the distant future won't assure the agent of knowing about it as he performs it, since he might forget about it in the meantime. The expectation of an action doesn't promise to yield knowledge concurrent with the action's performance unless the action is expected to be performed before it can be forgotten. What's more, even if a long-range expectation promised to yield knowledge concurrent with the expected action, that promise couldn't motivate the action at a distance: in order to motivate the action, it would have to be present shortly before the action was to occur. Hence the arguments of chapters 3 and 4 show only that expecting an action can prompt[1] one to perform it if the expectation closely precedes the action and represents it as closely following. Such an expectation constitutes an immediate intention.

The question therefore arises whether my theory of intentions can be expanded so as to account for long-range plans. Can such plans, like their shortsighted counterparts, consist in self-fulfilling expectations self-consciously adopted out of a desire for their fulfillment?

The answer will depend on whether the agent's long-range expectations of acting can initiate a series of events that will lead him to act in the long run, just as his immediate expectations of acting lead him to act immediately. If his expecting now to do something later can somehow lead to his doing it later, then he'll be in a position to adopt self-fulfilling long-range expectations out of a desire for their fulfillment rather than at the dictation of prior evidence; and if the resulting expectations represent themselves accurately, they will constitute full-fledged intentions.

But how could an agent's present expectations lead to action in the further future?

How Expectations Get Updated

One possibility is that present expectations of acting in the future could lead to future expectations of acting presently—which, in turn, would lead to the expected action. After all, a person's believing now that something is far in the future can lead to his later believing that it's imminent,[2] and believing that an action of his is imminent can lead him to perform it.

Suppose that I now expect to receive an important telephone call at noon tomorrow. At 11:59 tomorrow I shall probably expect to receive the call momentarily. The latter expectation will result from the former by an inference of a familiar sort, by which I update my temporal frame of reference.[3] Even if I can already name the date and hour at

---

[1] For an explanation of how I use the word 'prompt' in this context, see note 25 of chapter 2.

[2] See Wilfrid Sellars, *Science and Metaphysics: Variations on Kantian Themes* (London, 1968), 179: "That one's 'place' in time is constantly and systematically changing is an essential feature of our conceptual framework, one which is reflected in and, indeed, constituted by, a systematic change in the content of thought with respect to tense, temporal connectives and the like."

[3] If today I believe "I'll get a call tomorrow," and tomorrow I believe "I'll get a call

which the call is going to arrive, I shall also need to estimate the distance between that time and the present. For in order to ensure that I'll be within reach of the phone when the call arrives, I must know how much time is left before its arrival. Knowing that the call will arrive at noon on June 27th will do me no good if tonight, unaware that June 27th is tomorrow, I board a boat for Jamaica, or if at 11:59 tomorrow, unaware that noon is about to strike, I step into the shower. Hence whether or not my expectation specifies the absolute date and hour of the call, it is likely to specify the interval between now and then, and the latter specification must be periodically updated as the interval closes.[4]

Expecting an event to occur in the further future can thus lead me to update that expectation from time to time until it becomes, at the last moment, the expectation that the event will occur momentarily. Perhaps, then, expecting to perform an action in the further future would lead me to update *that* expectation until it became an expectation of performing the action next—an expectation that would prompt me to act accordingly, as we saw in earlier chapters.[5]

---

today," then do I have one belief or two? These beliefs are one and the same in the sense that their content can be represented by the same tenseless proposition. But they are two different beliefs in the sense that, regarded as psychological states, they have very different behavioral effects. For technical purposes, I ought to adopt a consistent policy for individuating them.

Since my purposes aren't technical, however, I am going to do without a consistent policy. I shall say that tomorrow's expectation is the result of my *retaining* and *updating* today's. And I shall thereby equivocate on the word 'expectation', since what gets retained is the tenseless propositional content, which—being tenseless—doesn't get updated, whereas what gets updated is the temporal perspective, of which nothing is retained.

[4] Note that I update my expectation only periodically. At 11:59 tomorrow I may still find myself thinking of the call as hours away. Then I'll look at my watch, remember that the call is due at noon, and say, "Why, no: it's due any minute." My surprise will indicate that I have neglected to update my expectation until just then.

[5] See Sellars, *Science and Metaphysics*, 179:

The simplest connection of an intention with a volition is illustrated by the example of Smith, who has formed the intention of raising his hand in ten minutes. He *thinks*
   I shall raise my hand in ten minutes
and, if we suppose that the intention continues as an occurrent, rather than lapsing into dispositional status, which, however, would leave the example untouched in relevant respects, and if we suppose that nothing leads him to consider an alternative course of action, we may picture him as thinking
   I shall raise my hand in ten minutes
   .
   .
   .

Well, suppose that I expect to place a call at noon tomorrow rather than receive one. Will my present expectation be similarly updated until, at 11:59 tomorrow, it yields the expectation that I'm just about to place the call? It may. Say I've been kidnapped, and my captors tell me that at noon tomorrow they will force me to call my bank manager. In that case, I shall expect to call my bank manager at noon tomorrow, and I shall probably update my expectation until, at 11:59 tomorrow, I expect that I'll be forced to place the call momentarily.

However, this particular expectation of acting won't qualify as an intention, since it won't be and won't purport to be self-fulfilling or adopted out of a desire for its fulfillment. I shall expect, quite correctly, that I'll be forced to call the bank manager whether or not I expect to, and so my expectation will correctly represent itself as dictated by the evidence—which is incompatible with its being an intention.

But suppose that what I expected was that I would be prompted to place a call at noon not by kidnappers but by an 11:59 update of this very expectation. In that case, my expectation would at least purport to have the features of an intention. That is, it would represent itself as bringing about the expected action by leading to a future expectation that would in turn prompt me to act; and it would represent itself as self-fulfilling rather than dictated by the evidence, since it would suggest that if I hadn't hereby expected to act, then there would have been no expectation to be updated, no update to prompt the action, and hence no action to be expected.

Note, furthermore, that if I retained this expectation to the end and updated it at the last minute, the result could be an immediate intention of acting. If my original expectation was "I'll be prompted to call at noon by a last-minute update of this expectation," then updating it at the last minute would yield "I'll be prompted to call momentarily by this expectation"—"this expectation" being the updated way of denoting what was previously denoted by "a last-minute update." The resulting expectation, "I'll be prompted to call momentarily by this expectation," could constitute an immediate intention of calling. Hence my long-range expectation, if retained and updated, could mature into an immediate intention—which is just what a long-range plan ought to do.

I shall raise my hand in six minutes
.
.
I shall raise my hand *now*
the last of which, . . . becomes a raising of his hand.

Of course, even if such a long-range expectation were retained and updated, its final update might fail to prompt the expected action. Although the final update would represent the action as imminent and thereby cause my desire for self-awareness to favor it, the resulting sum of motives in favor of the action might still be inadequate. The expected action would ensue only if the other motives favoring it were strong enough to prevail when thus reinforced by my desire for self-awareness. Even if a present expectation would be retained and updated, then, I couldn't expect its final update to prompt an action for which I didn't already expect to have motives that would be within one reinforcement of prevailing.[6]

Still, a tendency to retain and update those long-range expectations which purported to be intentions would greatly ease the task of predicting my actions. Without such a tendency, I couldn't predict an action unless I had already ascertained that my motives for it were definitely going to prevail; with such a tendency, I could predict an action as soon as I had ascertained that my motives for it would be moderately close to prevailing. Instead of having to pinpoint which action was going to emerge as my favorite, I could simply identify which actions were likely to be in the running. Among the latter actions, I could predict whichever I liked, since any action that would otherwise be in the running would be propelled into the lead by the final update of my prediction. Thus, if I already expected to have some motives at noon for placing a call, and if I now preferred that those motives prevail, then I could expect that a last-minute update of this very expectation would shift the balance in their favor, enabling them to make me place the call.

The only remaining question is whether I actually have the tendency in question, a tendency to retain and update the relevant sort of expectation, whose content is that of an intention. I do tend to retain and update ordinary expectations of ordinary events; would I do the same with an expectation that purported to be a means to its own fulfillment? If not, the expectation wouldn't be self-fulfilling, as it purported to be, since it would not in fact lead to an updated expectation capable of prompting the expected action. And if the present expectation

---

[6] When I say that I "could" expect something, I mean that I would be entitled to expect it and consequently able to expect it. I am thus assuming that I would know what I was entitled to expect, and that I would be able to expect anything, and only things, that I was aware of being entitled to expect. These assumptions constitute an idealization, of course, but they are harmless in the present context. Some of them will be made more explicit shortly.

wouldn't be self-fulfilling, I wouldn't be entitled to adopt it in the first place.

Why Self-fulfilling Expectations Wouldn't Get Updated

Unfortunately, such an expectation would not tend to be retained and updated, precisely because of purporting to be a means to its own fulfillment. Ordinarily I retain and update my expectation of an event because I am reminded about the event and find that I have good reason for continuing to expect it from my new temporal perspective. And I usually find that I have good reason for continuing to expect an event so long as the passage of time hasn't revealed anything that impeaches my original reasons for expecting it. Unless I find new evidence to the contrary, I assume that I originally expected the event for good reasons and that those reasons also justify continuing to expect the event from my present standpoint.

However, if my original expectation purported to have been adopted as a means to its own fulfillment, rather than to have been dictated by the evidence, then I would never have any more reason for updating it than for discarding it altogether. For in that case, my original reasons for expecting a future action would include the assumption that I would continue expecting it to the last minute, when my expectation, updated for the last time, would prompt me to act. Consequently, if I stopped expecting the action before the last minute, I would invalidate one of my original reasons for expecting it, and so I would justify my having discarded the expectation. I could discard my present expectation at any time, on the grounds that I was thereby eliminating the source of the future expectation that would have made it come true.

In short, updates of my expectation would never be dictated by the evidence: each successive update would have to be willingly adopted out of a desire for its fulfillment, like the initial expectation itself. If I initially chose to expect an action on the grounds that I would continue to expect it from subsequent perspectives, then nothing would require me to expect the action from subsequent perspectives if I didn't want to. For if I refused to continue expecting the action, I would thereby eliminate the grounds for expecting it, thus justifying my refusal. In order to expect that I would continue expecting the action to the last minute, I would have to expect that I would continue wanting to expect it.

On what grounds could I expect myself to continue wanting to expect a future action? Well, if I knew that I had a lasting preference for myself to perform the action (and lasting conscious knowledge of that preference), then I could expect myself to continue trying to ensure that I would perform the action, by continuing to expect it. If I knew that from now until 11:59 tomorrow, placing a telephone call would be what I knowingly preferred for myself to be doing at noon, then I could expect that I would choose to continue expecting to place the call—until 11:59, when my expectation, suitably updated, would prompt me to place it.

Yet if I knew that at 11:59 I would knowingly prefer to place the call, I could already expect that I would then—at the last minute— adopt a self-fulfilling expectation of placing it, whether or not I had previously expected to. That is, I could anticipate that I would form an immediate intention of placing the call even if I would not thereby be reaffirming a previous, long-range intention. My present, long-range expectation would therefore seem to contribute nothing toward its own fulfillment; it would seem destined to be fulfilled whether or not I formed it; and so it would seem to be dictated by the evidence, contrary to its self-description.

Here's a dilemma. A long-range expectation couldn't claim to bring about its own fulfillment via future updates of itself, because such a claim would be undermined in one of two ways. Such an expectation would either have no assurance of being updated at all or, if it did, whatever ensured its being updated would have ensured its being fulfilled whether or not it had been formed in the first place.

How Plans Get Updated

But suppose that I do have some attitude or other that amounts to an independent and stable inclination to retain and update the relevant expectations of acting—namely, those which purport to have been adopted out of a desire for their fulfillment rather than at the dictation of prior evidence. And suppose that I'm aware of this inclination to retain such expectations. Never mind what might give me that inclination: we'll get to that later. For the moment, just suppose that I have it—that I'm consciously inclined to go on expecting any action of mine that I already expect, provided that I originally expected it on the grounds of my having adopted that very expectation.

In that case, I can choose to form long-range expectations of acting that aren't dictated by the evidence and that will be, and not just purport to be, self-fulfilling. For instance, I can choose to expect that (because of the inclination just postulated) I'll retain this very expectation until an update of it can prompt me to place a telephone call at noon tomorrow; and I can choose to expect this even if I don't have antecedent reason to expect that from now until noon tomorrow I'll consciously prefer for myself to place the call. So long as I have antecedent reason to believe that I'll have some motives for getting myself to place the call, I can expect that I'll get myself to place it, by retaining and updating this expectation. For even if my future motives for getting myself to place the call would not have been sufficient to make me *form* the expectation of placing it, they may well be sufficient to ensure that I *retain* such an expectation *if I already have one and if it's of a sort that I'm already inclined to retain.* I can therefore expect that those motives which I was already going to have for expecting to call, as a means of getting myself to call, will now be reinforced because of doxastic inertia—that is, because of my inclination to retain the expectation of calling that I shall already have, because I am hereby forming it in advance.[7]

In sum, I can expect that by forming the present expectation of placing a call, I am shifting the balance in favor of whatever motives I was already going to have for expecting to place the call. I can therefore regard my forming the present expectation as instrumental in ensuring that I'll have the future expectation that will make it come true.

To repeat, I have yet to explain what would incline me to retain my long-range plans. All I have explained thus far is how such an inclination would entitle me to form long-range plans. More precisely, I have said that I would be entitled to form such plans if I had both a stable inclination to retain them and evidence of having that inclination, so that I had grounds for expecting to act because of having retained this very expectation.

How Plans Rely on Evidence

In the model that I am constructing, plans rely on prior evidence. Prior evidence doesn't dictate what an agent should plan: within limits, he may plan whatever he likes. But the limits on what he is entitled to plan, like those on what he can immediately intend, are indeed fixed by prior evidence.

I have already mentioned two kinds of evidence that an agent needs, in my model, in order to form a valid long-range plan. First and most important is evidence of a tendency to retain the plans he forms. Without this evidence, the agent could expect himself to perform a planned action only if he could have expected himself to perform that action

---

[7] What's more, if I already think that my tendency to retain this expectation will reinforce my other motives for expecting to call, then I can also expect to think so at the time; so I can expect that I shall regard retaining my expectation as an intelligible thing to do, thereby further reinforcing my inclination to retain my expectation of calling.

anyway, even if he hadn't planned it.[8] He would therefore have to regard his plan as making no difference in his future conduct—in which case it wouldn't really be a plan at all. Secondly, an agent can usually plan to do only those things for which he can already expect to have some motives. For if he cannot expect to have motives for the planned action, he cannot expect that his inclination to retain plans will be sufficient to make him retain this one, and he cannot expect that this plan, if retained, would be sufficient to make him act.

Here is a third kind of evidence that's essential for a valid plan. In order to plan an action, an agent must have reason to believe that he will remember about it in time—that is, in time to update his plan into an immediate intention that can prompt him to act. For example, my expectation of placing a call at noon tomorrow would rely not only on my retaining this expectation but also on my transforming it shortly before noon into an expectation of placing the call next—an expectation of the sort that could prompt me to pick up the phone. Now, even if at 11:59 I still expected to place the call at noon, I wouldn't expect to place it next unless I realized that the time at which I expected to do so was imminent. Consequently, I cannot expect to prompt an action with a last-minute update of this expectation unless I have grounds for expecting to notice when the time at which I expect to do so has arrived. In other words, prior evidence limits me to those plans whose expected time of execution I can expect to recognize in time to execute them.

When I say that long-range plans rest on evidence, I am once again setting myself in opposition to those philosophers who have claimed that a person's intentions give him reflective knowledge that requires no evidence at all. Stuart Hampshire, a proponent of this view, concedes that such knowledge can be undermined by evidence. He acknowledges, for instance, that if an agent has regularly failed to carry out his plans in the past, then he has reason to doubt the validity of his current plans. But Hampshire still insists that the knowledge embodied in valid plans requires no evidential support.[9]

I see no reason to posit such an asymmetry in an agent's knowledge of his future. Nor, I think, is this asymmetry compatible with common sense. On the contrary, commonsense psychology takes note of the evidence on which valid plans rely.

---

[8] As I have already explained in note 6, I am using the phrase 'could expect' to mean "would be entitled and therefore able to expect." The phrase thus incorporates the assumptions that the agent knows what he's entitled to expect and that his expectations are appropriately constrained by that knowledge.

[9] See *Freedom of the Individual*, 54ff.

Common sense recognizes, for instance, that an agent is not justified in forming a plan unless he has reason to believe that he'll have sufficient motives for retaining and executing it. When a convict announces to his parole board that he plans to go straight, for instance, they will suspect him of lying, either to them or to himself, unless he has somehow altered his personality or his circumstances so as to assure himself of having some motives that support it. We discount a child's plan of becoming a fireman when he grows up because we think that between now and then he'll lose his desire to have a job that calls for a red hat.

Common sense also recognizes that an agent is not justified in planning to do something unless he can expect himself to realize when the time for doing it has arrived. We therefore try to plan actions for times at which we can expect to be reminded of them, and we develop habits that provide us with grounds for expecting future reminders—habits such as regularly consulting an appointment book or reviewing a mental checklist before leaving the house.

Most importantly, commonsense psychology recognizes that one must have a record of retaining plans in order to be justified in forming them. The tendency to retain plans is variously called constancy, persistence, determination, perseverance, reliability, resoluteness, tenacity. And in the eyes of common sense, a person's record of constancy (as I shall call it) determines how ambitious he is entitled to be in his plans. Someone who has faithfully stuck to his plans in the past is thought to be in a position to count on himself for the future, whereas someone who has repeatedly abandoned plans may be regarded as no longer in a position to make plans at all—at least, not without deceiving himself about his tendency to retain them. We thus acknowledge that valid plans rely on prior evidence of the planner's constancy.[10]

This is not to say that an agent must consider the necessary evidence before placing confidence in a plan. Someone with a long-standing record of constancy can take that trait for granted: he need not review the evidence of his constancy every time he plans to act. Such evidence recedes into the background of the agent's self-inquiry. He relies on it tacitly, habitually—just as he continually relies, for example, on evidence for the veracity of his eyes and ears. Yet such evidence is relegated to the background precisely because it is so often indispensable.

---

[10] See Fleming, "On Intention," 317: "[A] man can for years intend to go to Europe, and never do anything about actually going. Or we can intend to write letters that never get written or even begun. These are intentions, all right, although I think the more we realize that such an intention is never going to be carried out, the less right we have to call it an intention."

The evidence that gets noticed is the evidence that isn't in continual use.

What Constancy Consists In

I think that common sense even recognizes that our need for evidence to support the plans that we make today gives us a further motive for retaining the plans we made yesterday. Consider this example. One year a friend of mine spent the month of September shuttling between law school and a graduate program in literature, changing her mind from week to week about which course of study she was going to pursue. She eventually had to stop changing her mind, and not just because the deans were losing patience with her. She had to stop changing her mind because she was in danger of losing faith in herself. Had she gone on adopting and discarding plans, she would have lost all grounds on which to plan a career with any confidence. In order to redeem her record of sticking to such plans, she had to make some plan and stick to it. As her vacillation continued, she and I knew intuitively that the fear of losing her self-confidence would soon loom larger than her interest in either course of study, eventually becoming her overriding motive to stop vacillating.

Why an agent wants grounds on which to plan. What this example suggests is that an agent wants to have grounds for believing in his plans, so that he can make plans that are credible. Why does an agent want grounds on which to make credible plans? The reason, I suggest, is that he wants the ability to ascertain how he's going to act in the future. An agent who lacks grounds on which to plan cannot forecast his behavior except by forecasting future psychological states whose relation to his present state is hopelessly complex. What he will do tomorrow morning, or fifteen minutes from now, depends on what he'll prefer to do at the time, and what he'll prefer at that time doesn't depend in any perspicuous way on his present state of mind. Reflective forecasts are therefore difficult. But if an agent has grounds on which to plan, then he can easily forecast his behavior, since he can rely on his forecasts to be self-fulfilling. Of course, the agent still cannot forecast an action unless he can foresee having some motives for it and no overwhelming motives against it. Nevertheless, he can forecast an action without having to ascertain on independent grounds that his motives for that action will be stronger than their opposition, since by forecasting the action, he can ensure that they will be. He therefore has grounds not just for projecting his future conduct from his present state of mind but for projecting it from the state of mind consisting in that very projection.

Having grounds on which to plan thus enables an agent to regard himself as predictable in a sense that doesn't threaten his autonomy. Ordinarily, calling someone predictable means that the evidence of his past behavior dictates a prediction of similar behavior in the future. Evidence that made an agent regard himself as predictable in this sense would hardly be desirable, since it would portray his future behavior as predetermined independently of his will. But the evidence that supports planning doesn't render the agent predictable by dictating a particular prediction about him; on the contrary, it renders him predictable by entitling him to predict whichever behavior he likes. Such evidence supports the agent's self-predictions by indicating that his behavior will be governed partly by his predictions about it. Thus, it renders him predictable precisely by indicating that he is autonomous.[11]

How the desire for grounds on which to plan provides grounds on which to plan.   The desire for grounds on which to predict one's conduct, by forming plans, is a motive for retaining the plans that one has already made. This desire can therefore constitute a stable inclination to retain one's plans, and so it can provide the very thing it seeks—namely, grounds on which to predict one's conduct, by forming plans.

Consider an agent who wants to have grounds on which to plan. He will want grounds on which to believe that he will retain his plans. The best grounds for this belief would consist in evidence that he has a stable inclination to retain his plans, and the best evidence of this inclination would consist in a perfect record of plans made and retained. The agent's desire for grounds on which to make new plans will therefore be a motive for retaining the old ones, in order to compile a record of retaining plans. And insofar as the agent will always want grounds on which to make plans, that desire will give him a stable inclination to retain them—the very inclination that it makes him want evidence of having.[12]

Here, then, is my account of the inclination to retain and update

---

[11] See my discussion of autonomy in chapter 6, 175–76.

[12] Jon Elster describes a somewhat similar situation, in which an agent is moved to do something by the desire to disprove the unwelcome conclusion that he'll never do it: "The odds that you will perform some unpleasant task now rather than postpone it for the future are increased if you tell yourself that your reasons for postponing it will be equally strong when the future time arrives. A present failure will predict future failure, so that the consequences of the choice become more fateful than if you look at the immediate sequel only" (*Ulysses and the Sirens*, 43–44).

long-range plans—the inclination that I earlier called essential to the capacity for planning but whose precise nature I left temporarily mysterious. This inclination, which I call constancy, consists in the desire for grounds on which to make plans, which is the desire for evidence of having precisely this inclination.

Why this procedure is legitimate. Something fishy seems to be going on here, I'll admit. After all, an agent doesn't want to have just any grounds for believing that he has a stable inclination to retain his plans, since he doesn't want to hold this belief if it's false. What he wants is to have grounds that arise from the belief's being true—that is, from his really having a stable inclination to retain his plans. Consequently, he wants himself to act as if he has such an inclination only if—and only because—he really has one, and not otherwise. Yet retaining his plans simply in order to give himself grounds for believing that he's inclined to retain them would seem like a pretense, like an effort to fool himself into believing in an inclination that really isn't there. How, then, could the desire for grounds on which to plan move the agent to retain his plans without implicating him in self-deception?

Here is how. True enough, the agent's desire for grounds on which to plan makes him want to retain his plans only if he thinks that he will thereby be manifesting a genuine inclination to do so. But consider how this desire will move him when he considers the question whether the desire itself constitutes such an inclination. The agent may think that his desire for grounds on which to plan doesn't constitute a stable inclination to retain his plans; in that case, the desire will not make him want that he retain his plans if in doing so he would be manifesting that desire. But conversely, the agent might think that his desire for grounds on which to plan does constitute a stable inclination to retain his plans, and in that case, the desire will make him want to retain his plans even if he would thereby be manifesting that desire. Thus, if the agent thinks that his desire for grounds on which to plan is a motive for retaining plans, then it will make him want to retain his plans even in light of the fact that it's what's making him want to. The upshot is that this desire will be a motive for retaining plans if the agent thinks it is, and so he can think it is if he wants. And of course, he wants to think it is, since he wants to have grounds on which to plan.

In general, there need be no deception going on when an agent does something out of a desire to prove that he has motives for doing it. The reason why the taint of deception clings to such behavior is that it is easily confused with behavior of a kind that does involve deception. Sometimes an agent wants to prove that he has not just some motive for doing a thing but a particular motive, a different motive from his desire to prove it. One example would be an agent I discussed in chapter 4, the agent who wants to prove that he has benevolent motives for contributing to charity.[13] If that agent does contribute to charity out of a desire to prove his benevolence, then he is of course guilty of deception, since his contribution isn't motivated by benevolence at all. But the case of this phony philanthropist is different from that of an agent who wants grounds on which to plan. All the latter agent wants to prove is that he has some motive—any motive—for retaining his plans, including perhaps this very desire. If this desire moves him to retain his plans, then it is a motive for retaining them—which is all that he's trying to prove. Hence no deception occurs.

How the same desire motivates execution of plans.   For similar reasons, the desire for grounds on which to make plans is also a motive for carrying them out. I have already explained that in order to form a credible plan, an agent must be able to expect, not just that his plan will be retained to the last minute and then updated, but also that he will have motives for performing the planned action—motives that, when reinforced by the last-minute update of his plan, will be sufficient to make him act. Now, if the agent had a standing motive for performing whichever actions he had planned, he could always expect to have the requisite motive, and if he was already expecting other motives for a planned action, he could expect them to receive yet further reinforcement from his motive for doing whatever he's planned. In either case, he would have better grounds on which to plan. The desire for grounds on which to plan therefore makes the agent want to prove that he has a standing motive for doing whatever he has planned. And as before, he can prove this by doing what he has planned out of his desire to prove it.

The habit of constancy.   My claim that an agent retains and fulfills his plans at the instance of a desire is an idealization. Like the desire for immediate self-awareness, the desire for grounds on which to plan is, in time, reinforced by a habit. As an agent repeatedly fulfills expectations in the form of plans, he gets into the habit of fulfilling them. Each memory of having thus expected an action then becomes a cue, to which compliance is an habitual response. And insofar as this habit gives the agent further grounds on which to plan, his desire for such grounds encourages him to maintain it.

Thus, when an agent fulfills a plan, as when he fulfills an immediate

[13] See 137–38.

intention, he is usually acting out of a desire that's reinforced by a habit that's sustained by that very desire.[14] Hence my description of plan-fulfillment, which refers only to the desire, makes the agent sound more purposeful in his pursuit of self-knowledge than he really is. I regard this discrepancy, once again, as a harmless idealization.

How Firm Resolutions Are Formed

Let me suggest one final complication in the workings of the desire for grounds on which to make plans. This complication explains, I think, how we can make plans with an especially high degree of resolve, thereby holding a more secure rein over our future conduct.[15]

Although we want to have grounds for planning in general, we don't care equally about grounds for all plans. We know that there will always be some actions whose future performance we especially want to be able to count on, and we especially want to have grounds for planning those actions. We therefore have an unusually strong desire to prove that we tend to retain and fulfill plans of a particular kind—namely, plans whose fulfillment we have an unusually strong desire to count on. Hence if we remember that we especially wanted to count on performing an action that we've planned, then we shall especially want to retain and fulfill our plan of performing it, since we especially want to prove that we tend to retain and fulfill plans of that kind. The result is that—in this respect, at least—we have better grounds for making those plans whose fulfillment is of special concern to us.

I think that the difference between firmly resolving to do something and simply planning it is this. When we firmly resolve to do something, we tell ourselves, as we plan to do it, how very much we want to have grounds for believing that we shall fulfill this plan. We thereby dispatch a message, through the conduit of memory, to our future selves: "This is an action that I very much wanted to count on myself to perform." Our future selves will then have an especially strong motive for retaining and fulfilling this plan, since it is of a kind that we shall especially want to prove that we tend to retain and fulfill. We therefore have correspondingly better grounds for counting on ourselves to do whatever we firmly resolve to do.

How Plans Get Filled In

Thus far I have spoken only of plans that commit the agent to a specific action at a specific time. I have yet to discuss more general plans of

---

[14] For the corresponding point about immediate intentions, see chapter 2, 72.

[15] I cannot imagine why Myles Brand denies that intentions can differ in strength (*Intending and Acting*, 125).

action, plans from which many of the specifics have been omitted. The latter sort of plans differ from the former, I think, but only in requiring more extensive updates.

Suppose that I plan to learn Chinese. Learning Chinese is not something that I'll just get up and do at some future moment. Rather, I'll learn Chinese by doing many other things over the course of months or years—by reading books, attending classes, listening to tapes, and so on. And yet my plan need not specify what I'll do in order to learn Chinese: I can leave the details to be filled in later. For the moment, I can plan simply to learn Chinese.

The question is how such a plan can be a self-fulfilling expectation. How can the expectation of learning Chinese prompt me to read a book, attend a class, or switch on a tape recorder? And how can I expect to learn Chinese if I don't know how I'll do it?

The answer, I think, begins with the fact that my plan to learn Chinese must represent itself as incomplete. My attitude toward learning Chinese differs in this respect from my attitude toward specific actions that I plan to perform. When I plan to wave at my son if he's looking out the window as I arrive home, or to scream the next time I hear someone say "Y'know," my plan represents me as performing the specified action at a stroke, without intermediate steps. What I plan is that when I see my son, I'll just wave, or that the next time I hear someone say "Y'know," I'll just scream. But since I know that learning Chinese isn't something that I can just do, my plan of learning Chinese must represent its object somewhat differently. The content of that plan is not simply that I'll learn Chinese but that I'll take steps toward learning Chinese, that I'll do what's necessary to learn Chinese, or something that would similarly indicate the need for intermediate steps, as yet unspecified.

The precise content of my plan will depend on how urgent a plan it is. If I want to give Chinese priority over all my other projects, then my plan may be to do whatever is most conducive to my learning Chinese as soon as possible. Conversely, my plan may be merely to take some actions, some day, that will eventually result in my learning Chinese. Usually my plans fall somewhere between these extremes. I may plan, for instance, to do whatever is necessary in order for me to learn Chinese in the next two years, provided that my other activities aren't unduly disrupted.

Let me reiterate here that the content of an agent's intention, though identified in indirect discourse, is not something that he says, even to himself. I may never have said to myself any more than "I'd like to learn Chinese." But if someone suggests that I quit my job and move to Hong Kong, I'm likely to say, "That's not what I had in mind."

Obviously, then, what I had in mind is not the same as what I articulated in thought.

Suppose, then, that I plan to do what's necessary in order for me to learn Chinese in the next two years, barring undue disruption of my other activities. My plan then consists in an expectation that requires future updates to bring it into line, not only with new temporal perspectives, but also with new epistemic perspectives—new perspectives on what's necessary for my purpose of learning Chinese. That is, my plan consists in the expectation that successive updates of this very expectation will prompt me to do whatever is necessary for that purpose, and I will have to update this expectation whenever I learn that a particular step is necessary.

For instance, I may realize that unless I take a minute now to read about the foreign language courses offered this semester, I'll miss registration, and that if I don't register for a course this semester, I probably won't succeed in learning Chinese in the next two years without unduly disrupting my other activities. Given my knowledge that I would have to read the catalog now in order to accomplish my original purpose, I shall feel compelled either to expect that I'll read the catalog or to give up expecting that I'll do everything necessary to that purpose. And since the latter expectation constitutes a plan, my desire for grounds on which to plan makes me want to retain it. The same desire therefore makes me want to expect that I'll read the course catalog. That is, if I want to retain the expectation that I'll do everything necessary to my purpose, and if that expectation would become untenable, in light of my current knowledge, unless I also expected to read the catalog, then I shall also want to expect that I'll read the catalog.[16]

Of course, although I want to retain my expectation of learning Chinese, I don't want to retain it even if it's false, nor do I want to expect that I'll read the catalog unless I really will. Fortunately, however, I can make both expectations true simply by having them; for if I want, I can expect that I shall read the catalog at the prompting of this very expectation, just as I can expect that future updates of *this* expectation will prompt me to do whatever else is necessary to my learning Chinese.

Indeed, these two expectations, taken together, constitute an intermediate update of my original, long-range expectation. The original expectation was that future updates of that very expectation would prompt me to do whatever was necessary to my learning Chinese in

[16] Here, as elsewhere, my argument coincides with that of Gilbert Harman's "Practical Reasoning." Harman regards the elaboration of plans as a means of maintaining "explanatory coherence" in one's view of the future.

two otherwise undisrupted years. I can now update that expectation by expecting that this very update will prompt me to read the course catalog and that future updates will prompt me to do whatever else is necessary to my original purpose. Whereas the original plan consisted in the general intention of taking all steps necessary to my purpose, this updated version consists in the immediate intention of taking one particular step considered to be necessary, together with the general intention of taking all such steps in the future.

My plan can thus get updated not only when I notice that the time of action is approaching but also when I recognize specific actions as satisfying the terms of the plan. As before, the process relies on my inclination to go on expecting what I already expected, but from a new perspective.

Sometimes I may seem to have the option of retaining my original expectation without incorporating new information. For instance, if all that I expected was that I'd eventually do something about learning Chinese, then no matter how often I recognized an action as conducive to my learning Chinese, I could always decline to expect that I would take it, while continuing to expect that I'd eventually do something of the sort. Why, then, would I ever bother to update my expectation? And if I had no inclination to update it, what grounds would I have for forming it?

The answer is that if I expected to learn Chinese because of having chosen to expect so, I would want to retain that expectation, and in order to retain the expectation I would need stronger grounds than the logical possibility that it was true. I'd need evidence in favor of its truth—evidence for believing that I really was going to do something about learning Chinese. Yet as I continually declined opportunities to learn Chinese, I would be amassing evidence to the contrary. The longer I refused to do anything about learning Chinese, the weaker my grounds would become for believing that I ever would. Pretty soon, I'd have to do something about my plan or lose confidence in it. And since I want grounds for making such plans, I would want to prove that I had motives for retaining and fulfilling them. I would therefore want at least to fill in my plan so as to make it more likely to prompt some action. Thus, even the vaguest plans tend to be updated.[17]

What Motivates Plan-Formation

A long-range plan predetermines and predicts the planner's future intentions and actions. When an agent forms the intention of doing

[17] See the quotation from Elster in note 12.

something in the further future, he causes himself to go on intending to do it until that intention causes him to do it, and his intention consists in a corresponding prediction—a prediction that he will hereby be caused to go on predicting the action until that prediction causes him to perform it. Accordingly, an agent can have various motives for planning a particular course of action.[18] On the one hand, he may want to predetermine that he will later intend to take the action or that he will eventually take it; on the other hand, he may simply want to predict what his future intentions or actions will be.

Thus, in my earlier example, I may plan to call someone at noon tomorrow simply because I want myself to do so. Perhaps tomorrow is the person's birthday, I expect him to be home at noon, and I regard a telephone call as the most appropriate way of conveying my best wishes. In that case, I shall plan the call out of a desire to ensure that I place it.

However, my motive to plan the call may instead be a desire to know whether I'm going to place it. Perhaps I would be just as happy to send flowers but would have to order them before the florist closes tonight. In that case, I'll want to know before tonight whether I'm going to call the person tomorrow, so that I can ascertain whether I need to visit the florist today. I may therefore plan to call, not because I particularly want to call, but because I want to know whether I shall.[19] (And then, of course, I shall be moved to retain, update, and fulfill my plan by my desire to have grounds for making such predictions on other occasions.)

Similarly, I can be moved to plan by a desire either to predetermine or to predict my future intentions. Suppose I plan that if I'm ever awakened during the night by the sound of intruders downstairs, I'll immediately dial 911. One of my motives for forming this plan is likely to be a desire to ensure that I'll dial 911 if awakened by intruders. But I may have another motive—namely, a desire to ensure that if I'm awakened by intruders, I won't waste any time figuring out what to do. By planning what I'll do in those circumstances, I can ensure that when the circumstances arise, I'll already have a plan, a ready-made intention that will save me the trouble of deliberating at the time. One of

[18] For a more extensive discussion of this issue, see Bratman, "Taking Plans Seriously," and "Castañeda's Theory," 159ff.

[19] The idea that one sometimes forms a plan in order to ascertain rather than influence one's future conduct is endorsed not only by Bratman (as cited in the previous note), but also by Pears, "Predicting and Deciding," 197: "[P]eople do sometimes decide to do A with the primary purpose of achieving certainty that they will in fact do A. . . ."

my motives for planning, then, can be a desire to bring about a future intention.

My motives for planning to dial 911 if awakened by intruders may also include a desire to know my intentions in advance. Perhaps my block association is holding a meeting tonight about neighborhood security, and I expect to be asked to state and justify my emergency plans. In that case, I may want to know what my plans will be, so that I can begin to prepare my reply. The desire to know my future intentions can thus be a motive for forming them now.

Finally, my motives for forming a plan usually include the desire for self-understanding. For I don't want to make plans without knowing why, and I therefore hesitate to plan until I'm aware of knowing some motives for planning, whereupon I'm all the more inclined toward whichever plans I find motives for. Indeed, I'm inclined to form those plans that I'm aware of knowing the strongest motives for forming— those being the plans whose formation I can best understand. Long-range plans thus issue from reflective reasoning similar to that which yields immediate intentions to act.

The difference is that the reasoning behind an immediate intention takes account of the agent's present motives twice: once as grounds on which to explain his forming the intention, and again as grounds for the expectation of acting that constitutes the intention itself. By contrast, the reasoning behind a long-range plan takes the agent's present motives only as grounds on which to explain his forming a plan, and his future motives as grounds for the constituent expectation. That is, in order to understand his plan, the agent must know of present motives for forming it, but in order to form the plan, he must know of future motives for fulfilling it, since the plan consists in an expectation of its own fulfillment.

LONG-RANGE DELIBERATION

Note that the foregoing theory of long-range plans is a natural companion to my theory of immediate intentions. My theory of immediate intentions said that if an agent has a desire for a concurrent awareness of what he's doing, then he has grounds on which to form self-fulfilling expectations of what he'll do next, since his desire will move him to do whatever he expects—that being the thing that he would know about doing, if he did it. My theory of long-range plans says that if an agent has a desire for the capacity to predict his future conduct, then he has grounds on which to form self-fulfilling expectations of what he'll do in the future, since his desire will move him to retain, to update, and ultimately to fulfill those expectations—that being the way to assure himself of grounds for predicting his conduct. In both theories, a desire for self-knowledge moves the agent in such a way that he fulfills his own reflective expectations; in both theories, the agent's having the relevant desire enables him to form reflective expectations on the grounds that he'll be moved so as to fulfill them; and in both theories, the resulting expectations constitute intentions of acting.[20]

When the one theory is added to the other, I think, the scope of an agent's will seems to expand in proportion to his desires for reflective knowledge. If the agent wants only a concurrent awareness of his actions, then he can form only immediate intentions of acting; if he also wants the ability to predict his future actions, then he can also form long-range plans.[21]

Here, then, is a potential solution to the problem with which I introduced this chapter. That problem, you may recall, was that the agent whom I described in previous chapters has such narrow horizons. What my theory of long-range plans now suggests is that this agent's horizons are narrow because his intellectual desires are narrow. Perhaps if that agent wanted a broader and deeper view of his conduct, then he would attain not only greater self-knowledge but a broader and deeper measure of autonomy as well.

I shall devote the remainder of the present chapter, and most of chapter 8, to exploring this possibility. I shall first consider how a de-

[20] There is one notable difference between my theories of immediate and long-range intentions. The difference lies in the desires posited by these theories. My theory of immediate intentions posits a desire to know what one is doing, whereas my theory of long-range plans posits a desire for the ability to ascertain what one will do. The latter desire is not simply a future-tense version of the former. If the desire to know what one is doing were transposed into the future tense, it would become the desire to know what one will do, whereas the desire posited by my theory of planning is a desire for the ability to ascertain what one will do—that is, not for a full-blown knowledge of one's future actions but merely for the ability to attain it.

This asymmetry is in keeping with the facts, I think. Surely, we don't want to be burdened with a thorough knowledge of what we'll be doing at every future moment. Rather, various parts of the future interest us at various times, and we want the ability to ascertain, at any present time, what we'll be doing in those parts of the future which happen to interest us at present. But the present moment will always be of interest to us, simply by virtue of being present, and so we want to have a fully realized knowledge, at any moment, of what we're doing at that moment. Thus, we want to know what we're doing, but we want only the ability to ascertain what we're going to do.

[21] Note that one cannot have the capacity for plans if one doesn't have the capacity for immediate intentions. The capacity to form plans relies not only on a tendency to retain them but also on a tendency to fulfill them. And the tendency to fulfill plans consists partly in the tendency to fulfill the immediate intentions in which their last-minute updates will consist.

sire for the ability to predict one's conduct would affect one's practical reasoning. I shall then consider the effects of a desire for a deeper self-understanding.

Plans as Reasons for Acting

I have already explained how an agent's desire for the ability to predict his future conduct moves him to retain, update, and fulfill his long-range plans. Let me now explain how this process can be viewed as an expansion of the agent's practical reasoning.

Two kinds of practical reasoning. There are actually two ways in which this process could exemplify practical reasoning, in my sense of the phrase. On the one hand, an agent might maintain and execute his plans partly because he's aware of knowing his motives for doing so and therefore finds it an intelligible thing to do. An agent may know that he wants grounds on which to make reflective predictions, and in light of that desire, maintaining and executing his plans may strike him as understandable. He may then be moved to maintain and execute a plan, not only by his desire for grounds on which to predict his conduct, but also by his desire for self-understanding. In that case, his behavior will exemplify practical reasoning of the sort that I described in chapter 3—the reasoning that yields concurrent self-awareness and self-understanding partly by means of practical steps.

On the other hand, retaining, updating, and fulfilling a plan can be regarded as steps in a distinct mode of practical reasoning. After all, these are steps by which the agent secures evidence on which to predict what he's going to do. Marshalling the evidence on which to make predictions is a kind of reasoning in its own right, whether or not it is done as a step in some other kind of reasoning—that is, as a practical step toward concurrent self-understanding. My theory of long-range plans suggests that the marshalling of evidence for reflective predictions is a form of reasoning that has practical steps of its own.

One learns how to predict the behavior of other organisms by discerning the patterns they follow, but one learns how to predict one's own behavior both by discerning patterns followed and by following the right patterns. One doesn't just sift for evidence of behavioral dispositions on which to base one's predictions; one also tries to evince those dispositions on which predictions can most easily be based—in particular, the disposition to retain, update, and fulfill one's own predictions. Just as an agent attains self-understanding partly by doing what he understands, just as he attains self-awareness partly by doing what he's aware of, so, too, he obtains support for predicting his conduct by doing what will support his predictions. Hence, the reasoning by which an agent learns to predict his future conduct has a practical phase and qualifies as a mode of practical reasoning.

When an agent maintains or executes a plan partly for the sake of concurrent self-understanding, he is actually engaged in two kinds of practical reasoning at once. That is, he is taking a step toward self-understanding by taking a step toward the capacity for self-prediction (that being the understandable thing for him to do), and he is taking a step toward the capacity for self-prediction by maintaining and fulfilling his plans (that being the way to obtain grounds on which to plan).

Two kinds of reason. Another way of putting the same point is this. The agent's desire for the capacity to predict his conduct is a reason for him to take his having a plan as a reason for maintaining and executing that plan. Hence in maintaining and executing his plan, the agent can be acting on two different sorts of reason at once.

After all, each distinct mode of practical reasoning defines a distinct class of reasons for acting. According to my theory of reasons, the reasons for an action are propositions that could serve as premises from which practical reasoning would yield the action as a conclusion. Hence for each way in which practical conclusions can follow from their premises, there is a way in which actions can be supported by reasons. In previous chapters I traced two different paths between reasons and actions. The fact that one has motives for an action qualifies as a reason for performing it, I said, because one's believing this fact would provide a potential understanding of the action, thereby making the action a practical step toward self-understanding. The fact that one has an immediate intention qualifies as a reason because one's belief in this fact—the very belief that constitutes the intention—provides a potential awareness of the action, thereby making the action a practical step toward self-awareness.

I have now traced a third path from propositions to practical conclusions. For as I have pointed out, the belief that one has a plan puts one in a position to increase one's self-knowledge by satisfying a particular reflective description, which says that one tends to maintain and execute plans. Satisfying this description increases one's self-knowledge because it provides evidence on which one can form further plans and hence further predictions of one's future conduct. The fact that one has a plan can thus be regarded as a premise from which the maintenance and execution of the plan follow as conclusions, in accordance with that mode of reasoning by which one acquires the capacity for self-prediction. This fact therefore qualifies as a reason for acting.

In its capacity as a reason for acting, a plan has normative or recommending force: its recommending force, like that of the reasons examined earlier, is its capacity to make an action attractive to a desire
that's integral to the will. The desire in this case is the desire for
grounds on which to predict one's future conduct, a desire essential to
that department of the will which forms long-range plans. As we have
just seen, a creature that didn't want the ability to predict its conduct
wouldn't be in a position to form long-range plans, precisely because
it wouldn't be inclined to maintain and execute them. Thus, the normative force of plans is mediated by a desire constitutive of the will,
the desire that constitutes one's ability to make plans.

The content of plans.   Like immediate intentions, plans can be formulated so as to assert their own success as plans. A successful plan is
a prediction whose future updates actually prompt the action that it
predicts they will. Consequently, to believe that one herein has a successful plan of doing something is to predict that future updates of this
very belief will actually prompt one to do it, as one is hereby predicting—which is to have a belief with the content of a plan.

Future Desires as Reasons for Acting

Maintaining and executing plans are not the only practical steps in the
reasoning by which one learns to predict one's conduct. Such reasoning can also entail providing for the satisfaction of future desires. Here
is an example illustrating how consideration of one's future desires can
enter into this mode of practical reasoning.

Imagine that on a visit to a local gallery you are smitten by a work
of sculpture, a piece so unusual, so seductive, that you feel compelled
to make it yours. Unfortunately, the price is only slightly lower than
the current balance in your checking account. If you bought the sculpture, you would certainly run out of money before the end of the
month.

Now, your desire to avoid the discomforts of insolvency may outweigh your partiality to the sculpture. But suppose that it doesn't. The
sculpture beckons to you here and now, whereas the discomforts of
insolvency are no more than distant shadows. For the moment, you are
under the spell of Art and indifferent to next week's groceries. You feel
the urge to reach for your checkbook. What reason could you have for
resisting?

Well, ask yourself which discomforts, exactly, insolvency would
cause. Oddly enough, you cannot say; for you don't know how you
would choose among the undesirable options that would suddenly

confront you if you went broke. You might forgo eating until payday, or ask your brother-in-law for a loan, or pawn the sculpture, or try your hand at petty crime. But you can foresee being strongly averse to each of these options, and so you cannot foresee which one you would take. By emptying your bank account today, you would be letting yourself in for a conflict of desires in the future, a conflict whose outcome would be hard to predict.

Nor would you be in a position to clarify your future course by planning it. No matter what plan you formed, you would be able to foresee having strong motives against carrying it out. Hence you couldn't form a plan with any confidence—which means that you wouldn't be entitled to form a plan at all.

To be sure, your motives against carrying out a plan would be matched by motives against each of the alternatives, but you couldn't rely on the latter motives to make you carry out your plan, since repulsion is a far less predictable force than attraction. Suppose that you planned to borrow money from your brother-in-law in order to tide you over until payday. You already know all the motives that would later deter you from popping the question—a dislike of losing face, a fear of being refused, mortification at the thought of having to explain your predicament. No doubt, these motives would deter you until you began to feel some countervailing pressure, but once you were under pressure, your behavior would become increasingly erratic. You might dial your brother-in-law's number only to panic at the sound of his voice and give some frivolous pretext for the call. Who knows what you might then resort to in your desperation?

Now, the problem of predicting your choice among unpalatable alternatives is precisely what would be impressed upon you by the voice of prudence as it counselled against buying the statue. When you reached for your checkbook, the voice of prudence would say something like "What are you going to do next week, when you run out of money?" This would of course be a rhetorical question, designed to make you reconsider purchasing the statue. It would make you reconsider partly because it would make you realize how much you currently want to avoid all of the actions that would be your only options after the purchase. The question would thus direct your attention to current reasons against purchasing the statue—that is, to current motives in light of which your purchasing the statue wouldn't make sense.

But the question would also direct you toward another mode of practical reasoning. It would demand your plan for dealing with the consequences of the proposed purchase; it would thereby be demanding a reflective prediction; and by demanding a reflective prediction, it would be pointing out that the proposed purchase would impede your ability to make one. The question "What are you going to do next week?" would implicitly suggest the answer "See? You can't predict." And by thus pointing out that the purchase would impede your ability to make a prediction, the question would reveal that purchase to be a step away from the capacity for self-prediction, and hence a failure in practical reasoning.

Here, then, is one sense in which your future motives can count as reasons for being prudent. The future motives that would make your response to insolvency so unpredictable are reasons for you to avoid insolvency because in light of those motives, avoiding insolvency is necessary for your capacity to predict your conduct. The representation of those motives would therefore constitute premises from which the avoidance of insolvency would follow as a conclusion, in accordance with that reasoning by which you attain the capacity for self-prediction.

There is more to say about the rationality of being prudent, I believe, but I am not in a position to say it here. I shall therefore postpone a fuller exposition of the topic until chapter 11. For the moment, I shall turn to another way in which the reflective agent's autonomy might be expanded by an expansion of his intellectual desires.

NINE

BELOW THE SURFACE

Suppose that an agent wasn't content with a knowledge of his proximate motives for acting: suppose that he wanted to know why he has those motives. How would this desire for deeper self-understanding affect his practical reasoning?

DEEPER SELF-UNDERSTANDING

The desire in question could take two forms.[1] A person may want to understand the motives on which he acts, or he may want to understand all of the motives he has, including the ones that aren't manifested in his actions. I am inclined to believe that the ordinary person has both of these desires together. That is, he has some interest in understanding all of his motives and a special interest in understanding those motives on which he happens to act. The latter desire is the one whose motivational consequences I shall examine.

This desire, like the other intellectual desires that I have discussed, moves a person to take practical as well as cognitive steps. In addition to seeking explanations for the motives on which he acts, a person can also seek to act on motives that he can explain. In the latter case, he will be attempting to increase his self-knowledge by acting so as to satisfy a reflective explanation, an explanation that provides a potential understanding not only of his action but also of his motives for it. He will therefore be engaged in practical reasoning.

Now, a person's motives comprise both desires and beliefs, but I shall discuss only his efforts to understand his desires. My reason is not that a person's understanding of his beliefs is an uninteresting or unfruitful topic; on the contrary, it is entirely too interesting and too fruitful. I think that a person's efforts to understand his beliefs would make a suitable topic for an entire book, but a different book from the one I'm writing here. A thesis of the present book is that we can transform a rudimentary model of human motivation into a sophisticated model of autonomous agency merely by positing desires for reflective

[1] It has more than two possible forms, of course, but I shall ignore many of them by assuming that this desire is similar to the one discussed in chapter 1, 27–30.

knowledge. A different but related thesis would be that by positing similar motives, we can transform a rudimentary model of computational states into a sophisticated model of cognition.[2] The way to establish the latter thesis would be to discuss a person's efforts to understand his own beliefs—or rather, his efforts to attain some purely computational analog of that self-understanding.[3] Such a discussion would require a book unto itself, and so for the purposes of this book, I shall discuss only the explanation of desires.

How Desires Are Explained

Commonsense psychology usually explains desires in one of four ways. Some desires are explained as having been motivated by other desires, together with the appropriate beliefs. Some desires are explained as arising from emotions. Some desires are explained as the products of conditioning. And some desires are explained in terms of the subject's personality or traits of character.

Ulterior motives. Motivated desires are a familiar component in the commonsense model of motivation. According to that model, the desire for one state of affairs will motivate a desire for another state of affairs if the latter state is believed to be a means to the former. The motivated desire endures only for the duration of the motivating desire and is proportionate in strength to that desire as well as to the subject's degree of confidence in the efficacy of the means in question. Of course, not all desires can be explained in terms of motives, since a person's motives cannot recede in an infinite series. There must be unmotivated motivators, so to speak, which get explained in some other way—perhaps in terms of the person's character, conditioning, or emotions.

Emotions. Sometimes a desire is explained as the result of the subject's emotions or moods. The explanation of someone's wanting to hurt another person may be that he's angry with him; the explanation of someone's wanting to withdraw from human company may be that he's grieving; the explanation of someone's wanting to burst into song may be that he's jubilant. I shall not attempt an analysis of emotions

---

[2] I believe that this suggestion bears some resemblance to theses currently under discussion in the field of artificial intelligence. See, e.g., Douglas R. Hofstadter's "Can Inspiration Be Mechanized?" *Scientific American* 247 (1982): 18–34.

[3] To talk about efforts to *understand* one's *beliefs* would be to beg the question, by referring to cognitive states of the very sort that one was promising to explain in terms of those efforts. If I knew how to avoid begging this question, I would be writing that book instead of this one.

themselves: my interest is in their familiar role in explaining a person's desires and hence, in some cases, his motives for acting.

Conditioning. The term 'conditioning' refers to the psychological process by which a person's experiences implant or eradicate desires.[4] The most familiar form of conditioning takes place when a person acquires a desire for something, or an aversion to something, by experiencing pleasure or pain in association with the thing or with the thought of it. This is perhaps the only form of conditioning that is cited by commonsense explanations, but it is cited frequently. For we often explain why a person wants something, or is averse to something, by pointing out that he has had pleasant or unpleasant experiences with it in the past.

Traits of character. Finally, we sometimes explain a person's desires or emotions in terms of his character or personality. Here I shall use the terms 'character' and 'personality' in their most general and nontechnical senses. When I speak of someone's character, for instance, I shall not necessarily be referring to his moral fiber: I shall be using a broader sense of the word, which encompasses the person's nonmoral traits as well. My sense of the word is akin to the sense that we use when we praise a novelist's attention to character as opposed to plot, or when we call someone an interesting character. In this sense, the term denotes a broad category of lasting dispositions by which a person's motives and behavior can sometimes be explained.

I am not going to offer an exhaustive analysis of traits of character, either. As in the case of emotions, all that interests me about traits of character is that they can sometimes account for the desires on which a person acts. In that capacity, I think, traits of character can be regarded as dispositions to have prevailing desires and emotions of particular sorts.[5] Thus, a fastidious person is disposed to have desires for neatness in his person and possessions, and consequently to go about straightening pictures or picking lint; an adventurous person is disposed to have desires for excitingly risky activities and consequently to favor mountaineering over chess, or aviation over dentistry; a morose person is disposed to feel melancholy and consequently to mope about; and so on.

---

[4] For a philosophical discussion of this topic, see R. B. Brandt, *A Theory of the Good and the Right* (Oxford, 1979), chapter 5.

[5] Perhaps some traits of character are dispositions *not* to have desires of particular sorts. If so, then understanding a desire may entail seeing it to be compatible with one's negative dispositions. I shall henceforth disregard this complication.

Note that these dispositions entail particular kinds of desires, not just particular kinds of preferences. A person is not necessarily fastidious just because he often has stronger motives for tidying up than for alternative activities: such a preference may manifest self-consciousness or conformism instead of fastidiousness. Similarly, a person who usually prefers risky pastimes may be either adventurous or suicidal, depending on which desires his preference reflects. And a person who is moved to complain and sulk may be either morose or malcontent, depending on which emotion produces his motives for such behavior. What makes a person fastidious is not just that he often prefers to tidy up but also that this preference reflects a particular kind of desire—namely, desires for tidiness per se. What makes a person adventurous is not just a preference for risky pastimes but a preference based on desires for the attendant thrills rather than the possible ill consequences. And what makes a person morose is that his motives for sulking and complaining arise from depression rather than jealousy.

By the same token, tending to have particular desires or emotions doesn't in itself constitute a trait of character if those attitudes don't tend to govern the subject's behavior.[6] Someone who usually wants his person and possessions to be neat isn't fastidious if other desires always prevent him from grooming or housekeeping; someone who always feels averse to exertion needn't accuse himself of laziness unless he actually shirks exertion as well; and someone who often feels sad isn't for that reason morose if he manages to hide his feelings.

Thus, traits of character are dispositions to have desires and emotions that are of particular kinds and that are capable of prevailing against the motivational opposition. Let me make two further remarks about these dispositions.

The first remark is that although a trait gives rise to desires, it doesn't motivate them as an ulterior desire would.[7] To be adventurous

---

[6] When I speak of an emotion as governing someone's behavior, in this context, I mean that it gives rise to desires that do so. Thus, anger governs a person's behavior when it makes him want to strike someone and that desire moves him to swing his fist.

I do not mean to deny that emotions have direct behavioral consequences, which are brought about without the intermediation of desires. Grief can directly cause weeping, for instance, and embarrassment can directly cause blushing. But insofar as these behaviors are directly caused by emotion, they are involuntary and do not qualify as actions. (When weeping is an action, I suspect, it is caused not solely by emotion but at least partly by desire—say, by the desire to have a good cry. I doubt whether blushing can ever be an action.) In this book I am interested in emotions only as the causes of action and hence only as causing behavior through the intermediation of desires.

[7] Here I am disagreeing with Richard Brandt, who analyzes traits of character as desires and aversions ("Traits of Character: a Conceptual Analysis," *American Philosoph-*

is not to have a standing desire to experience lots of thrills—that is, a desire for an overarching end to which particular adventures would be desired as means. The adventurous person is drawn to each adventure in its own right, and his adventurousness is simply a disposition to conceive prevailing desires for particular adventures as such. Similarly, laziness is not a standing desire to live a life of ease; it's a disposition to become averse to particular exertions, each in its own right. Such traits account for particular desires, not because they motivate those desires, but simply because they are dispositions to have desires of particular sorts.

Finally, I would suggest that there are more recognizable traits of character than we can name. For we can often recognize several of a person's desires or emotions as bearing an affinity to one another and hence as manifesting a disposition to have desires and emotions of a particular sort, even though we have no name for the sort involved.[8] Understanding the person's motives for acting may then amount to no more than seeing that they "go together" in some unspecified way.

Acting on Understandable Desires

If someone wants to understand the desires behind his actions, as well as the actions themselves, then he has a motive for taking actions that meet two criteria. In order to understand his actions, he will want to take those actions for which he seems to have the strongest motives. In order to understand the desires behind his actions, he will want to take actions whose motives comprise desires that he understands. And in order to understand both the actions and their motivating desires, he will want to take actions that meet both criteria at once.[9]

The desire for more than a superficial self-understanding will therefore restrain an agent from taking any action until he is aware of

---

ical Quarterly 7 [1970]: 23–27). Of course, the word "aversion" is ambiguous, in that it can denote either a particular attitude of aversion to something or a tendency to have such attitudes toward things of a particular kind. The word "desire" lacks this ambiguity; perhaps for this reason, Brandt tends to use the word 'need' instead. The problem is that Brandt persists in referring to needs and aversions as *motives*, whereas they are in fact *dispositions to have motives*.

[8] Alternatively, there may be a name associated with the disposition, but it may not name a trait of character. It may, for example, name a well-known person, real or fictional, who exemplifies the disposition.

[9] In previous chapters, I have distinguished between an intention and the resulting action. Here I gloss over this distinction for the sake of simplicity. When I speak of 'taking action', I mean forming and executing an intention. When I speak of taking an action that one understands, I mean forming an intelligible intention that leads one to perform an intelligible action.

knowing, not only what he has the strongest motives for doing, but also the explanations for some of those motives. But suppose the agent finds that his strongest set of motives contains desires that he cannot explain. In that case, one might think, he won't be able to act so as to understand both his action and the desires behind it. If he takes the action that would make sense, by doing what he seems to prefer, then he will end up acting on desires that seem unintelligible; yet in order to act on intelligible desires, he would have to act, unaccountably, on less than his strongest motives. How, then, will he manage to understand both his action and his operative desires?

The answer is that the set of motives that initially seems strongest to the agent is not the only set that he can justifiably regard as his strongest. As we saw in chapter 6,[10] an agent usually has several different sets of motives, each of which would become his strongest if it was reinforced by the agent's desire for self-understanding; and among these motives, the agent can simply decide which set is to predominate. For if he consciously believes that a particular action is the one for which his motives are the strongest, then that action will strike him as intelligible, and his motives for it—now reinforced by his desire for self-understanding—will become the strongest, if they weren't already. The agent can therefore adopt a conscious belief that he prefers any one of the actions for which he has motives that are within one reinforcement of predominating. This self-fulfilling belief, self-consciously adopted as a means to its fulfillment, will constitute an intention.[11]

Now, if the agent wants to act on a set of motives that can be seen as predominant and as containing intelligible desires, then he will want there to be such a set, if there isn't one already. That is, he will want some intelligible desires to dominate the unintelligible ones, so that he can understand acting on desires that he understands. And if he wants a particular set of motives to predominate, then he may be in a position to decide that they will, by believing that they do. The agent can therefore decide that some intelligible desires, though previously dominated by other desires, shall henceforth constitute his preference. And he can thereby make it sensible for him to act on desires that make sense to him, so that he can understand both his action and his operative desires.

Of course, an agent may find more than one set of motives whose constituent desires he is aware of understanding, but even those desires

[10] Pp. 180–85.
[11] This belief is bound to be conscious insofar as it is based on the appropriate evidence, since the evidence appropriate for supporting it is the very fact that it has been formed.

will not be equal in the eyes of his self-inquiry. Some will be explicable to him only in terms of personality traits, emotions, or ulterior desires that are themselves somewhat puzzling to him, because they seem to be at odds with his remaining dispositions. Others will be explicable in terms of dispositions that seem to stem from his deepest aspirations or to harmonize with his character overall. Conferring predominance on either sort of desires would put the agent in the position of understanding his operative desires, but conferring predominance on the latter would lead to a deeper, more inclusive self-understanding.

Hence an agent's desire for more than a superficial understanding of his actions may move him not just to perform the action that best expresses his preference (as he perceives it) but also to constitute that preference out of the desires that best express his goals, his emotions, his past experience, and his character (as he conceives them). He will thus ensure that he can do what makes the most sense by acting on the desires that make the most sense, and so he will attain the greatest self-understanding.

The irrationality of acting on whims. The most familiar example of this phenomenon, I think, is the suppression of whims. The essence of a whim, after all, is that it seems to come out of the blue, not out of one's prior experience or underlying dispositions.[12] Any desire that one can regard as arising from some ulterior desire or conditioned by prior experience or rooted in one's character doesn't count as a whim. Whims are desires that one cannot explain.

Obviously, the desire to understand one's operative desires is itself a motive for making a whim inoperative, by refusing it the status of a preference and consequently refusing to act on it. Suppressing a whim can therefore be a practical step in the reasoning by which one attains self-understanding.

No wonder, then, that we often regard whimsical actions as irrational, even though they are, in a sense, what the agent most wants to do. Suppose that you wake up one morning with an unaccountable urge to affect a Cockney accent. If you then claim that you have good reason for dropping your h's and greeting your friends as "Guv'nah," we are likely to disagree. We think that some desires, no matter how faint, deserve to be taken seriously as reasons for acting, while others

[12] Of course, a whim may be explicable in one sense, since whimsicality can itself be a trait of character, consisting in a proneness to inexplicable desires. Nevertheless, whimsicality can at most account for the fact that one has desires that one cannot explain; if it accounted for which such desires one had, then they wouldn't be inexplicable, after all—in which case they wouldn't be whims, and it wouldn't be whimsicality.

deserve to be discounted, no matter how strong. And among the latter
we tend to include the desires that have no recognizable basis in the
agent's history, ultimate aims, emotions, or lasting tastes.

Our grounds for discounting such desires as reasons for acting, I
think, is that their normative force is largely blunted. The desire to do
something counts as a reason for doing it only because in light of that
desire, doing the thing becomes a step toward self-understanding. But
if the desire itself baffles one's efforts to understand it, then acting on
that desire may become, on balance, a step away from self-understanding, and the normative force of that desire—its power to make the action attractive to one's intellectual desires—may then be undermined.

Thus, although you feel the urge to speak Cockney, the way to maximize your self-understanding may be to decide that you would prefer
to speak normally instead, lest the only sensible course be to manifest
an unintelligible desire. If so, your speaking Cockney on a whim would
seem to betray a failure in your procedure for attaining self-understanding and hence a failure of practical reasoning. Therein lies the
irrationality of whimsical behavior.

Countervailing reasons.   To be sure, one may have a reason for suc-
cumbing to whims—namely, a desire to let some whimsy into one's
life, a desire for spontaneity. In light of this desire, elevating a whim to
a preference and then acting on it may yield greater self-understanding
than suppressing it. And if one's desire for spontaneity is itself intelligible—say, because it results from an acknowledged emotion such as
boredom or from a known trait such as humorousness—then whimsical behavior is almost certain to maximize self-understanding.

Conversely, one may have reason for resisting desires that one understands, since one may be averse to the desires themselves or to their
potential manifestations. If a person knows that he is lazy, for example, he will understand the lassitude that he feels at the start of any
project; but if he also knows that he wants a project to succeed, or that
he wants in general to be more energetic, then he may also understand
refusing to let his lassitude prevail. Once again, if his motives for coun-
teracting his laziness are themselves intelligible to him, then he will
stand to gain even greater self-understanding from deciding and acting
on an alternative preference.

Note, here, that our terms for many traits of character connote approval or disapproval and thereby express the very attitudes that make
it understandable for one to indulge or to suppress the trait in question.
If a person approves of his disposition to shrink from vigorous activity,
then he is unlikely to think of it as laziness: he may think that he's

placid or easygoing, perhaps, but not lazy. To think of oneself as lazy is to disapprove, and if a person disapproves of his aversion to activity, then he has the sort of attitude in light of which it wouldn't make sense for him to confer predominance on that aversion.

Hence being lazy, as such, doesn't count as a reason for loafing—although being placid or easygoing does, according to my theory of reasons. That is, in light of one's self-ascribed placidity (and the approval expressed by that ascription), preferring to avoid vigorous activity and consequently avoiding it may be the way to maximize one's self-understanding. If so, one's placidity is indeed a reason for one to act accordingly. But in light of the disapproval expressed by a self-ascription of laziness, the way to maximize self-understanding may be to constitute one's preference differently.

Traits as reasons for acting. Here my theory of reasons for acting departs abruptly from the philosophical tradition. Reasons for acting have traditionally been thought to include desires and beliefs but not traits of character. In this respect, however, I consider my theory more faithful to common sense. For in ordinary discourse, traits of character do count as reasons for acting—at least, among speakers whose common sense has not been tainted by utilitarian theories of decision-making.

Suppose that I do you a favor, and when asked why I'm doing it, I answer, "Because I'm a nice guy." This reply conveys, above all, negative information, to the effect that I'm not acting on any selfish motive or reason. But it also conveys positive information—namely, that I'm performing the favor out of my characteristic benevolence. And in this respect, I am identifying not just the cause of my action but also the reason for it. When I say that I'm doing you a favor because I'm a nice guy, I don't mean simply that my good nature causes me to do it; I mean that I conceive of the favor as a manifestation of my good nature, and I'm performing it partly because it makes sense to me, so conceived.

I thus identify my good nature as the rationale for my action. That is, I identify it as the aspect of my self-image under which I comprehend the action and by which I am thus led to perform it. I'm doing you a favor not just *as a result of* my being good natured but also *in light of* my being so, because it makes sense for me to act like the good-natured person I am.

Similarly, if you request a favor of me and I ask why I should do it, you may reply, "Because you're a nice guy." Here again, negative information is the most salient, since you are conceding that I have no selfish reason for complying. But as before, positive information is also conveyed, and this information is about a reason in favor of my compliance. In referring to my good nature, you are giving me a rationale for doing you a favor—that is, a conception under which my doing the favor would make sense. You are recommending the requested favor by suggesting that I perform it in order to be the nice guy that I am.

Consider different examples. If you ask me why I spoke so bluntly to a mutual friend, I may reply, "Because I'm a frank person." Alternatively, you may advise me to be blunt, by saying, "It wouldn't be like you to equivocate." Here again, a trait of my character provides a context in which the action can be understood, rationalizing the action and thereby recommending it. Similarly, I may rationalize my behavior at a party by pointing out that I'm gregarious or shy, and I may cite my tenaciousness as grounds for pursuing an argument. In each case, the trait of character recommends action by rendering it intelligible— by showing it to make sense.

Of course, those philosophers who believe that all reasons must be based on desires can always reinterpret character-based justifications as alluding to the desires in which the relevant traits of character would be expressed. Frankness, for example, is a disposition to have desires to speak particular pieces of one's mind, and citing a person's frankness as a reason for speaking his mind can always be interpreted as an indirect way of citing his desire to speak the particular piece in question. I do not deny that ordinary discourse can be reinterpreted in this fashion; I merely point out that my theory can hardly be faulted for not forcing us into such a reinterpretation. The ability to take character-based justifications at face value is a merit of my theory, not a drawback.

Emotions as reasons for acting.   My theory also accounts for our commonsense practice of citing emotions as reasons for acting. We think that outrage not only causes but also justifies protest, that grief justifies acts of mourning, and that joy justifies acts of celebration. As before, utilitarian theories of decisionmaking must reinterpret these thoughts as referring indirectly to the desires that spring from the emotions mentioned. Thus, a joyous person's reason for celebrating is said to be his desire to celebrate, not the joy that gives rise to that desire, and a grieving person's reason for avoiding lively company is said to be his desire to withdraw rather than the grief underlying that desire. Once again, I consider it a merit of my theory that it can preserve and explain ordinary discourse about such cases.[13]

---

[13] I think that my theory also suggests a way of understanding the rationality of emo-

Autonomy over Traits of Character

Consider the following three claims that I have recently made. First, I have said that a trait of character consists in a tendency to have prevailing desires or emotions of a particular kind. Second, I have said that if a person doesn't want particular desires to prevail, then he can simply decide that they won't (provided that their predominance over his other desires is not already so strong as to be irreversible). Third, I have said that there are some trait-names, such as 'laziness', that necessarily express disapproval of the trait named.[14]

These three claims imply, I believe, that no one should ever have to think of himself as lazy. One wouldn't think of oneself as lazy rather than easygoing unless one disliked being lazy; but being lazy consists in a tendency to have prevailing desires to avoid work; and if one disliked having these prevailing desires, one could simply decide that they weren't going to prevail—in which case one wouldn't be lazy, after all. Thus, if a person had the attitude expressed by a charge of laziness, he could easily render himself innocent of the charge. Similarly, one wouldn't think of oneself as morose rather than serious and sensitive unless one disliked the trait; but being morose consists in a tendency to have prevailing desires that arise from melancholy; and if one disliked that tendency, one could simply decide that one's melancholy desires wouldn't prevail—in which case one wouldn't be morose.

Bad faith about traits of character.[15]   Here again, I think, my theory accords with common sense. For when we hear someone call himself lazy (or morose, or dishonest, or the like), we immediately suspect him of insincerity. We feel like saying to him, "Well, if you really meant that you were *lazy*, you would change."[16]

To be sure, there are cases in which we do not assume a person's critique of his own character to be insincere, but these are cases in which—as my theory would predict—the traits in question are assumed to involve desires too strong to be suppressed by countervailing intentions. A person may tend to have desires of a particular sort in strengths sufficient to prevail against his attempts at deciding to prefer

---

tions themselves. I suspect that rational emotions are the ones that make sense in light of a person's beliefs, desires, and other features. However, this book is not the place to develop a theory of the emotions.

[14] Here I am disregarding ironic uses of these words. A person may call himself lazy not to express sincere self-depreciation but to mock the disapproval that others might feel. In this ironic usage, the word does not express the speaker's own disapproval.

[15] On the topic of this section, see Margaret Gilbert, "Vices and Self-Knowledge," *Journal of Philosophy* 68 (1971): 443–53; and Sartre, *Being and Nothingness*, 273ff.

[16] This point is made by Glover in "Self-Creation," 449.

otherwise. He then has a trait of character that cannot be willed away, and so his having the trait is perfectly consistent with his disliking it. Thus, someone may genuinely reproach himself as a coward, since his urge to flee from danger may tend to be so powerful that a decision to prefer standing fast would be ineffectual. That is, his motives for standing fast wouldn't dominate his urge to flee even if the former were reinforced by his desire for self-understanding, and so he wouldn't prefer to stand fast even if he decided to. Such a person remains a coward involuntarily, despite the self-reproach that his use of the term conveys.

Still, there are willing cowards in the world, and common sense recognizes their existence. These are people who could prefer not to flee if they chose to have that preference but are content to prefer fleeing. The self-reproaches of such people must be dismissed as insincere.

Indeed, the self-reproaches of a coward are often construed, quite rightly, as expressing the very decision that impeaches their sincerity.[17] When someone calls himself a coward, we may suspect that he is even then opting for cowardice—that he is embracing his cowardice in the very utterance by which he pretends to condemn it. The reason for our suspicion is that ascribing a trait of character to oneself can constitute a decision to have it. The belief that one has a trait of character, remember, is the belief that one tends to have prevailing desires of a particular kind. This belief will help one to understand acting on desires of that kind, and so one's awareness of it will cause the motivational force of such desires to be bolstered by one's desire for self-understanding. The desires in question may then prevail precisely because one believes that they tend to—in which case one will have acquired a trait of character by believing that one has it. Thus, to believe that one is a coward is just to believe that one tends to have prevailing desires to flee from danger, and one's desires to flee from danger may tend to prevail precisely because this belief renders flight intelligible.

The belief that one is a coward will then constitute an intention—albeit a defective intention, similar to the intention to fail, which I discussed in an earlier chapter.[18] The intention here is defective because a person who believes that he's a coward doesn't believe that his cowardice is due to that very belief. His belief doesn't represent itself as adopted out of a desire for its fulfillment, and so it falls short of being

[17] Here, as before, my argument echoes that of Charles Taylor, in "Responsibility for Self," 281–99; and "What is Human Agency?" 103–35.
[18] Chapter 4, 136–37.

a classic intention. But it is indeed self-fulfilling, and it isn't dictated by the evidence. It therefore qualifies as an intention of some sort.

Self-deception about traits of character. Fortunately, the virtues are just as amenable to the will as the vices. Some virtues, of course, we cannot will into existence, because we aren't disposed to have the appropriate desires or because the desires that we are disposed to have are too weak to prevail even if reinforced by our desire for self-understanding. Other virtues, however, are ours for the choosing. We may be capable of deciding to be honest, by believing that we're honest— or, in other words, by believing that we tend to have prevailing aversions to acts of deception. For even if our motives for deceit have thus far tended to dominate our aversions to it, the aversions may now gain predominance precisely because our conscious belief in their predominance will make acts of deception unintelligible to us. Similarly, we may be in a position to believe—and hence decide—that we're kindhearted, even if our sympathy for others has heretofore yielded to callousness, since the belief that we're kindhearted will now render acts of sympathy intelligible to us, thereby enabling sympathy to prevail. We therefore have a measure of autonomy not only over our actions but also over our characters.

Note, however, that this autonomy is an invitation to self-deception. Because we can sometimes become virtuous by believing that we are, we may be tempted to believe that we're virtuous even when we cannot thereby become so. All that we need to do in order to deceive ourselves about our own virtue is to believe that we're virtuous while conniving at the ineffectiveness of that belief.

AN EXAMPLE OF DELIBERATION

I have now identified two different modes of practical reasoning. There is, on the one hand, the reasoning by which we attain self-understanding; this reasoning encompasses practical steps toward understanding not only our actions but also our operative desires. On the other hand, there is the reasoning by which we attain self-awareness; this reasoning encompasses our efforts to secure prior access to our future actions as well as a concurrent awareness of our present ones.

This bifurcation in the process that I have denominated practical reasoning is likely to puzzle the philosophical reader, who is accustomed to thinking of practical reason as unified. Yet I believe that practical reasoning, as conceived by common sense, does in fact bifurcate and that the philosophical notion of unity in practical reason is an un-

warranted idealization. How exactly common sense distinguishes between the two forks of practical reason is a question that I shall postpone until chapter 11. Roughly, my answer will be that one mode of
practical reasoning is that by which we decide what to do, and the
other is that by which we carry out our decisions. But the details of
this distinction cannot be made clear until I have discussed evaluative
reasoning, which is the main topic of chapter 10.

For the moment, then, I shall simply ask the reader to suspend judgment about my claim that practical reasoning is a two-track process.
For the remainder of this chapter, I want to examine what happens
when these two tracks diverge, pulling the agent in opposite directions.

A Conflict of Reasons

Suppose that you have always planned to become a Wall Street lawyer.
You initially formed this plan with the strongest resolve, you have periodically reaffirmed it, and you have accumulated subsidiary plans
about how to fulfill it, as well as independent plans that rely on its
fulfillment. After two years of law school, however, you find yourself
dreaming of the scholarly life, the life you would have lived if you had
gone to graduate school in English.

Now that you reflect upon your motives for an academic career, in
fact, you find that they better express your deepest values than your
motives for a career at law. What's more, your motives for becoming
a lawyer strike you as crass, whereas your yearnings for an academic
career strike you as manifesting loftier traits of character. You thus
have second-order preferences for suppressing some of these motives
while fostering others.

You have a problem. On the one hand, to persevere in law school
would be to take the course that suits you less—a course for which
your motives, though powerful, are also discordant with your underlying values and character. On the other hand, to enroll in graduate
school would be to overthrow years of planning. And how could you
plan to persevere toward a Ph.D. in English if you would thereby be
forsaking your plan of earning a J.D.? In short, the decision that would
enhance your reflective insight would cloud your reflective foresight,
and vice versa.

Further Considerations

Of course, if you expect to become increasingly disillusioned with your
legal studies, then you may have grounds to suspect that a renewed
resolution to complete them would sooner or later be abandoned. In
that case, the constancy that you'd display by reaffirming your current

plans might not justify much confidence in them anyway, and a change of plan, though evidence of inconstancy, might leave you with no less self-confidence. But if you have already vacillated in the past about your career, if you already have one or two false starts behind you, then yet another change of plans may threaten to undermine your self-confidence completely. Then your desire to have grounds for predicting your future conduct will take on a special urgency, which may make perseverance more understandable.

Then again, some of the preferences and character traits that are relevant to your dilemma may themselves be open to revision. Being a lawyer may be in keeping with your contentiousness. But are you necessarily and immutably contentious? Or is contentiousness one of those traits which you have actively confirmed in yourself by means of your self-description? You may come to realize that your itch for controversy, though always present, was for many years hidden by what you then conceived of as reticence. Only when the ethos of law school made contentiousness seem attractive did you gradually shed your reticence and bring your contentious impulses to the fore, by ratifying them under that name. Perhaps these same impulses could now be reconstituted as a scholar's thirst for the truth; or perhaps you still have it in you to be the bookworm you once were.

You may have desires for new preferences or traits of character in themselves—a growing distaste for your contentiousness, as I have suggested, or a nostalgic fondness for your former reticence. But even if you lack such intrinsic desires, you may still have a motive for altering your dispositions—namely, your desire for self-understanding. For suppose that your current state includes dispositions that both favor and oppose either of the careers available to you. You may then have trouble ascertaining which career would make sense. One way to solve your problem would of course be to scrutinize yourself more closely, refining your estimates of the conflicting dispositions. But another solution would be to resolve the conflicts by adopting preferences and traits that are less equivocal. In order to see your way clear to one career or the other, you can try to adopt dispositions that clear the way to it. And the prospect of achieving a state in light of which some choice would be clearly understandable will naturally be attractive to your desire for self-understanding.

Indeed, the desire for self-understanding is a motive for seeking the psychological state that would yield the best overall self-understanding when conjoined with the appropriate choice of career. You can choose among alternative personalities, some suited to law and others to literature, but not all of these personalities would be equally suited to their respective careers or to your underlying impulses. You must therefore try on different self-images, together with the careers that would suit them, in order to see which combination would yield the most perspicuous whole. And the desire for self-understanding will favor your adopting the optimal combination of dispositions and choices.[19] Hence the question before you is not simply which career would make better sense in light of the person who you currently are but also which personality you might now embrace in order to make better sense of a career.

Resolving the Conflict

How do you resolve this welter of considerations into a coherent case for one career or the other?

To begin with, you will have to compare the strength of conflicting reasons within each mode of practical reasoning. Some facts may be more relevant than others to the intelligibility of various decisions or to the impact that various decisions would have on your grounds for self-prediction. For instance, your becoming a lawyer might gain more intelligibility from your political ambition than your becoming a professor would gain from your partiality to tweeds. If so, your political ambition, in its capacity as a reason for staying in law school, outweighs your partiality to tweeds, in its capacity as a reason for quitting.

But you must also compare reasons that appeal to different modes of practical reasoning. Suppose, on the one hand, that studying law was already your third try at learning a profession. That fact would make dropping out of law school especially damaging to your capacity for self-prediction, and it would therefore count as a strong reason against dropping out. On the other hand, suppose that, in your heart, you hold truth in higher esteem than justice. That fact would make a change of career highly intelligible and would therefore count as a strong reason for change. One of these reasons is a consideration of reflective foresight; the other, of reflective insight. Even if you can rate each reason in relation to others of its kind, the question remains whether reasons of different kinds, if rated similarly, are to carry similar weight.

The answer to this question is that every reason exerts a determinate normative force on you, by appealing either to your desire for reflective foresight or to your desire for reflective insight. The relative strengths

[19] Unless this desire seems like an adequate motive for adopting new traits and preferences, of course, you wouldn't be able to understand adopting them—and so it wouldn't favor your doing so. Hence the personalities that this desire would move you to adopt are restricted to the ones that it seems like an adequate motive for adopting.

of these intellectual desires, and the relative latitude that you have in satisfying them, will determine which kind of reason tends to weigh more heavily with you.

Now, I am inclined to think that your need for concurrent self-understanding and self-awareness is always more urgent than your need for predictability. All that you want by way of predictability is the capacity to ascertain features of your future conduct as they come into question.[20] And even if you take a step that obscures your view of the future, you may still be able to restore that view before any future-tense question arises. Hence a temporary loss of predictability may turn out to be harmless. But questions about your present action are ever present, and they always demand immediate answers, since you want to know and understand what you're doing even as you're doing it. To be baffled or surprised by one of your actions is therefore to suffer an intrinsically undesirable interruption in the stream of self-knowledge. You can of course recover from such an interruption, by scrutinizing your action in retrospect and by ensuring that subsequent actions are better known and understood; but you cannot erase the interruption itself, which already offends your desire for concurrent self-knowledge. Considerations of concurrent self-knowledge therefore tend to take precedence over those of predictability.

What's more, the greater urgency in your need for concurrent self-knowledge is a reason for giving precedence to the corresponding reasons. That is, choosing the course that keeps you in touch with your present conduct, over the course that would make your future conduct predictable, is itself an intelligible course to take, given that you'll have an opportunity to recover your predictability before it's needed.

The Shape of Deliberation

Although reasons for acting, as I define them, can thus be balanced against one another, the balancing of reasons is not, to my mind, the primary task in deliberation. As my account of the foregoing example shows, I do not picture deliberation as an effective decision procedure—as a straightforward matter of toting up the pluses and minuses of determinate options.

In my experience, the work of deliberation is largely descriptive, not quantitative. When we deliberate, we mostly experiment with various descriptions of the alternatives, of their attractions, of ourselves, and of our futures, seeking that combination of action, motive, character, and plan which would make our lives most amenable to explanation

[20] See chapter 8, note 20.

and prediction. Usually a decision emerges as soon as we have found the most satisfying description of our selves and circumstances: rarely do pros and cons remain to be computed. Once we know how to describe the options, and how to describe ourselves, we usually know what to do.[21]

Philosophers have traditionally ignored the descriptive phase of deliberation, on the assumption that the agent and his circumstances are fully constituted even before they have been described. They assume that describing our selves and our options is a trivial matter of stating preexistent facts. The interesting question is thought to arise only after our dispositions and our alternatives have been fully characterized. For only then can we ask how an agent *like this* should choose among options *like these*.

But to imagine a fully characterized agent choosing among fully characterized options is to misconceive the conditions of deliberation. Our options are as variable as the intentions that we could effectively form; our characters are as variable as the self-images that we could effectively endorse; *and we can never be sure of having exhausted the possibilities, since we can always try to invent new self-fulfilling conceptions of ourselves and our options.* Hence the deliberative question is not just how an agent like us should choose among options like ours but first what we and our options should be like. We have to invent our predicament before we can resolve it, and most of the work gets done in the invention, not the resolution. Deliberation is a creative and open-ended endeavor. It is the process by which we rewrite our lives, and its principles are those of lucid composition.

Here, as before, I find William James to be the most perceptive observer of how we reason. In *The Principles of Psychology*, James writes:

> When [a man] debates, Shall I commit this crime? choose that profession? accept that office, or marry this fortune?—his choice really lies between one of several equally possible future Characters. ... [I]n these critical ethical moments, what consciously *seems* to be in question is the complexion of the character itself. The problem with the man is less what act he shall now choose to do, than what being he shall now resolve to become.[22]

[21] Similar points are made by S. Hampshire, "Fallacies in Moral Philosophy," *Mind* 58 (1949): 466–82; and David Wiggins, "Deliberation and Practical Reason," *Proceedings of the Aristotelian Society* 76 (1975): 29–51. Both Hampshire and Wiggins refer to Aristotle's interest in the importance of perception (*aisthesis*) for practical reasoning.
[22] I: 288.

And again:

> It may be said in general that a great part of every deliberation
> consists in the turning over of all the possible modes of *conceiving*
> the doing or not doing of the act in point. The moment we hit
> upon a conception which lets us apply some principle of action
> which is a fixed and stable part of our Ego, our state of doubt is
> at an end. . . . *In action as in reasoning, then, the great thing is the*
> *quest of the right conception.* The concrete dilemmas do not come
> to us with labels gummed upon their backs.[23]

I only wish that James had remembered, in writing the latter passage,
what he had already said in the former, to the effect that deliberation
shapes the "Ego" as well as the act. Then he might have said, as I do,
that we deliberate by reviewing possible descriptions not only of the
available actions but also of ourselves.

[23] 2: 531–32.

PART FOUR

RATIONALITY AND VALUE

TEN

EVALUATIVE REASONING

Before I proceed with this chapter, I'd like to greet those who have turned here directly from the Contents page with the idea of getting straight to the good stuff. Naturally, I'm grateful for your attention, if only for two chapters. But I must warn you that these two chapters will make little sense to you if you haven't read the preceding ten, and that they will in any case be sketchy and speculative. They do not lay out a full theory of value and morals, as you might have inferred from their titles. Rather, they describe a possible theory, without developing it in detail, their primary purpose being to fill a gap in the theory of agency that I have developed thus far. I believe in the theory that I outline in these chapters, but I have no illusion of being able to elaborate it fully within the scope of this book.

THE MISSING CONNECTION

Philosophers have approached the subject of practical reasoning from two different directions. Some ask what mode of reasoning would give rise to the features characteristic of rational agents, such as free will or autonomy. This is the question that I have been asking in the preceding chapters, although I have added self-knowledge to the traditional list of features to be explained. Other philosophers approach practical reasoning from a different direction, by asking what procedures an agent should follow for ascertaining the best thing to do. This question I have yet to address.

The latter question has dominated recent discussions of practical reasoning, even among philosophers who call themselves or are called followers of Kant. I would have thought that following Kant on this subject entailed studying practical reason in its capacity as the necessary condition of autonomy rather than as a method for optimizing choices. Since I have taken the former approach, I must seem to be out of step even with those who share my historical sympathies.

Whichever approach one takes, I believe, one should try to effect a meeting with the opposite approach. That is, any theory of practical reasoning as the basis of agency should explain how that reasoning identifies the best thing to do, while any theory of how to ascertain the best thing to do should explain what the recommended procedure contributes toward making us agents. I shall not comment here on the efforts, or lack of effort, on the part of others to forge this connection from the latter direction; I shall simply do my best to forge it from the former.

In forging this connection, I shall be fulfilling a promise made in chapter 7, during my discussion of reasons for acting. There I defined reasons for acting as considerations in light of which intending or performing an action would enhance one's self-knowledge by satisfying some reflective conception, and I claimed that reasons, so defined, can be said to recommend an action by making it attractive to the intellectual desires constitutive of the will. But I conceded that I was not yet in a position to say that reasons, as I define them, recommend an action by indicating that it's the best thing to do, and I promised that I would eventually locate such evaluative force in the reasons that I had defined. Now, to locate evaluative force in reasons for acting, as I define them, is to locate it in the premises of reflective practical reasoning, since I have defined reasons in such a way that they correspond to the contents of those premises. Hence showing practical reasoning to be evaluative and showing reasons for acting to be evaluative are, for me, one and the same task.

For the purposes of this task, I shall avail myself of a simplifying assumption that is frequently made without apology by those philosophers who approach practical reasoning from the opposite direction. This assumption is that evaluative reasoning consists entirely of consequentialist evaluation, which first evaluates which ends are worth desiring and then evaluates actions as worth performing insofar as they promote our desired ends. In reality, I think, our evaluative reasoning is not entirely or purely consequentialist, but since many other philosophers assume that it is, I feel free to borrow their assumption temporarily, for the sake of simplicity. I shall discard the assumption in the next chapter, where I'll discuss instances of nonconsequentialist evaluation.

CONSEQUENTIALIST EVALUATION

When I speak of consequentialist evaluation, I am not referring to instrumental reasoning about the most effective means to an end. How to achieve an end is a technological question, which can be answered by empirical inquiry into the likely effects of various actions. The evaluative question is which action one ought to perform, and in consequentialist reasoning, this question is interpreted as asking which action has the greatest value, or is most worth performing. An action's causal powers may be evidence of its value, of course, but they aren't the same thing as its value. Which action will accomplish what is one question; which action is most worth performing is quite another.

Consequentialist reasoning answers the latter question in two stages. The first stage is to ascertain what's worth desiring; the second stage is to ascertain what's worth doing in light of what one desires. Accordingly, any theory of consequentialist reasoning must offer two explanations. It must explain what can possibly count as evidence that an end is worth desiring, and it must explain how an action's conduciveness to desired ends can count as evidence that the action is worth performing. I shall attempt both explanations, in reverse order.

The Test of Value in Actions

My first explanation, then, will show how an action's conduciveness to what we want counts as evidence for the action's value. How does an action's power to promote our ends indicate that it would be a good thing to do?

I have already explained, in chapter 7, how an action's perceived conduciveness to something that we desire counts as a reason for the action, according to my conception of reasons. (My explanation, you may recall, was that the action's perceived conduciveness to what we desire makes the action intelligible to us, thereby commending it to the motives that constitute our rational will and hence qualifying as a reason for it.) What I haven't yet explained is how this reason indicates that the action in question has value or is a good thing to do. I might be tempted to say that it indicates the action to be good by virtue of being a reason for it, on the principle that the best action is the one for which there are the best reasons. But this explanation would be viciously circular. For I have already said that reasons for an action qualify as reasons for it by virtue of recommending it, and so I am not entitled to say that they recommend the action by virtue of being reasons for it. My explanation is rather that when we reflect on an action's perceived conduciveness to what we desire, the action makes sense to us, and *what makes sense* is our test of a good thing to do.

Here I am propounding a new description of reflective practical reasoning. Until now I have said that when consequentialist reasons make an action intelligible to us, they render it attractive to the intellectual desires constitutive of the will. I am now saying that when such reasons make an action intelligible, they show it to meet our test for a good thing to do. How these two descriptions fit together is not clear at the moment, I know, but I hope that it will become clear shortly.

My new description of reflective practical reasoning involves a claim about our method of evaluating actions. This claim rests on a feature of ordinary language, interpreted as evidence of a corresponding feature in ordinary thought. When we evaluate actions, we tend to use the phrases 'what's best' and 'what makes most sense' interchangeably. I am claiming that we do so because when it comes to actions, what makes the most sense is our test of what's best. We proceed on the assumption that the way to ascertain the best thing to do is to figure out what makes the most sense for us to do, and that once we have figured out what makes the most sense, we have all the evidence that can be had about what's best.

I do not mean to imply that when we recommend an action by saying that it would make the most sense, we consciously understand ourselves to be speaking about the action's intelligibility. The phrase 'what makes most sense' is often used without descriptive intent, as a vague term of approval. But the fact that a phrase is used without descriptive intent doesn't preclude the suspicion that it's an accurate description: sometimes our choice of words is more apt than we consciously intend. The reason why we don't think of the phrase 'what makes most sense' as a description, I suspect, is simply that we don't usually think about our practices of evaluation. We judge an action by its intelligibility much as we judge a person's intelligence by his bearing—that is, without being fully conscious of what test we're applying. Nevertheless, our evaluative practices have probably determined, subliminally or historically, which phrases are imbued with evaluative force, and can therefore explain why we use one idiom rather than another in expressing our evaluations. Saying that an action makes sense, like calling someone a jerk, betrays more than we realize about our processes of thought.

Note also that to call intelligibility our test of value in actions is not the same as to say that we value intelligibility. I believe that we do value intelligibility in actions, of course, but at present I am saying something rather different. I am saying that we treat an action's intelligibility as indicative of its categorical value: we proceed on the assumption that an action makes sense only if and because it's a good thing to do.

An Analogy: The Test of Truth

My point will become clearer, I think, if I compare it with the corresponding point about theoretical reasoning. Ordinary theoretical reasoning is our usual method for arriving at true beliefs, and we imagine that a belief is true insofar as it corresponds to reality. But reflection on how we actually theorize reveals that we do not vet our beliefs by direct inspection of their truth, so conceived. The parts of reality to which most of our beliefs purport to correspond cannot be directly compared with our beliefs, and so whether our beliefs correspond to them cannot be ascertained immediately. What we actually do in theoretical reasoning is to develop a body of belief that is simple, stable, coherent, and capable of yielding explanations and predictions of our experiences, which we assume to have been caused by the realities believed in. Our test for true beliefs, then, is that they're intellectually satisfying beliefs—intellectual satisfaction being proportionate to simplicity, stability, coherence, explanatory and predictive power, and the like.

I am currently making an analogous claim about the evaluation of actions. My claim is that we evaluate actions not by direct inspection of their value but by an indirect test—indeed, by a test whose content is quite similar to our test of true belief. Just as what passes for true belief is intellectually satisfying belief, so what passes for a good action is the intellectually satisfying action. I have simply translated this claim into the vernacular by referring to intellectually satisfying action as that which "makes sense."

The Problem of Skepticism

Of course, the realization that we regulate our beliefs by an indirect test of truth raises skeptical questions. We have to ask whether we have any reason for taking the intellectual satisfactions afforded by a set of beliefs as an index of their correspondence to reality. Thus far in the history of philosophy, no convincing answer has appeared. Because we have no access to the truth of most beliefs independently of their intellectual satisfactions, we cannot tell whether those satisfactions are significantly correlated with truth. We are therefore left to conclude that, for all we know, intellectual satisfactions may be a bad test of truth; but for better or worse, they remain our test.

Why do they remain our test of truth? The suspicion arises that our test of truth is a post facto rationalization—or an unduly rationalistic description—of the processes that we cannot help but follow in forming our beliefs. That is, we adopt the intellectually satisfying beliefs because we cannot do otherwise: our minds just work that way. To believe the elegant and powerful theory is our cognitive nature. Nevertheless, to believe a theory is to believe it *true*, and so such things as elegance and explanatory power emerge as our test of truth.[1] They're not our test of truth in the sense that we chose them from among alternative tests on the grounds of their superiority as indicators of what matches reality. Rather, they're our test of truth in the sense that we cannot help but be guided by them in adopting our beliefs, and to adopt beliefs just is to adopt them as true.

Our evaluation of actions has a similar structure, according to my account. I say that doing what makes sense is part of our nature as agents. In choosing among actions, we cannot help but be guided by their intelligibility. But we then choose an action *as* the best thing to do, and so intelligibility emerges as our test of the best action, not because it has won our adherence as the most reliable indicator of value in actions, but because it's the feature by which we naturally and necessarily select actions as best.

Here, then, is how my two descriptions of reflective practical reasoning fit together. Saying that intelligibility makes an action attractive to the desires constitutive of the will is like saying that a theory's elegance and explanatory power make it attractive to our cognitive faculties. Saying that intelligibility is our test of what's best is like saying that elegance and explanatory power are our test of what's true. In either case, the latter remarks are simply redescriptions of the psychological mechanisms described in the former.

Practical Skepticism

Many moral philosophers refuse to expose practical reasoning to the kind of radical skepticism that besets theoretical reasoning. They tend to express this refusal in one of two ways. Some deny that practical reasoning applies mundane tests of the sort that might fail to indicate what's truly optimal. These philosophers include the intuitionists, who say that we can have a direct apprehension of value in the world and hence that we have some hope of arriving at the action that's really and objectively the best. Other philosophers deny that our evaluative language denotes anything over and above the justifiability of actions by our standards or by some idealized version thereof. They define 'best' as meaning "ideally justifiable" or "ideally rational," thereby raising the hope that our practices of justification will bring us to what's best, or at least into its vicinity.

This latter strategy is somewhat like the pragmatist strategy of defining 'true' to mean "rationally acceptable," and I am therefore puzzled

---

[1] Some philosophers would dispute the claim that adopting a theory entails accepting it as true. See Bas van Fraassen, *The Scientific Image* (Oxford, 1980).

when its adherents call themselves moral realists. In any case, I am not willing to join in redefining evaluative language. I think that we have a concept of the best action as that which really ought to be done, just as we have a concept of the true as that which really ought to be believed. And I think that we have as little notion of how our actual standards of action steer us in the direction of the good as we have of how our actual standards of belief steer us in the direction of the true. We think of the best action as being really the best—a privileged path that stretches out before us, beckoning us on, like a yellow brick road. Yet our practical reasoning applies a particular test for identifying the best action, and we are hard pressed to say how an action's passing that test correlates with its being really the best.

I shall address the problem of practical skepticism at the end of this chapter. First, however, I need to complete my account of consequentialist evaluation.

Thus far, I have explained how we take an action's perceived conduciveness to desired ends as indicating that the action is a good thing to do. My explanation is that the action's perceived conduciveness to desired ends indicates that the action would make sense, thus indicating that it passes our test of value in actions. What remains for me to explain is how we evaluate potential objects of desire—how we figure out what's worth desiring—which is the first stage of consequentialist reasoning. I therefore turn to an account of our reasoning about ends.

Reasoning about Ends

Until now I have assumed that desires are beyond the influence of deliberation. The reason is that I have regarded deliberation as running its course on a single occasion, and so I have regarded it as arriving at only those conclusions which can be reached straightaway. Since desires cannot be adopted or altered on the spot, I have assumed that they are not among the conclusions that deliberation can reach.[2]

Nevertheless, a person can cultivate new desires indirectly, through various kinds of self-conditioning.[3] And having new desires would of course entitle a person to apply new reflective descriptions and explanations, which might in turn provide enhanced self-knowledge. With

[2] Keep in mind here that desires are not the same as preferences. A preference is a state of having stronger motives for one course than for any of the alternatives; hence agents with very different desires can have the same preferences. Unlike most desires, preferences can be formed at will, as I argued in chapter 6, 180–85.

[3] For a review of the psychological literature on this subject, see Brandt, *Theory of the Good and the Right*, chapter 5.

enough persistence, then, a person might eventually gain in self-knowledge by cultivating new desires. Cultivating these desires wouldn't be as straightforward as a single step of practical reasoning: it would be more like a long-term project. But this project would still be recognizable as self-inquiry of a kind akin to practical reasoning, since it would aim at producing dispositions that enhanced the agent's self-knowledge by virtue of the descriptions and explanations that they entitled him to apply.

What kinds of desires would emerge from this continuing project of self-inquiry? What other dispositions might the project yield? Answers to these questions will reveal whether my theory of practical reasoning successfully reconstructs our practices of consequentialist evaluation.

Long-Term Self-Inquiry

Let me begin with some general remarks about the motives and the method of long-term self-inquiry.

The motives. An agent wouldn't pursue the project that I have in mind unless he were more farsighted in his intellectual desires than I have previously assumed. Until now I have posited only the desires necessary to motivate actions that would increase the agent's self-knowledge immediately, by virtue of the descriptions or explanations that the actions would warrant in themselves. To be sure, these have included actions by which an agent secures evidence for predicting his future conduct; but what lies in the future, in this case, is the conduct to be predicted, not the evidence for predicting it. The agent's grounds for predicting his conduct arise immediately, as soon as he takes an action satisfying the appropriate description. This step, and others like it, would require only that the agent care about the state of his self-knowledge from one moment to the next.

In cultivating new desires, however, the agent would be seeking to satisfy descriptions that he couldn't satisfy in a single step. He would therefore need motives not just for pursuing immediate self-knowledge but also for investing in his epistemic future. Steps taken today would not produce new desires, or the resulting enhancements in self-knowledge, for months or years, and so the agent would take no steps today unless he cared about being abreast of his conduct, or being entitled to venture predictions, at a later date.

For the purposes of this chapter, then, I shall assume that an agent cares about having reflective knowledge both now and in the further future. Like my other assumptions about intellectual desires, this one will yield a hypothetical model of some aspect of agency, a model showing what that aspect of agency might consist in. The aspect being modelled at present is our evaluative reasoning about what is worth desiring.

Now, if an agent cares about his future self-knowledge, then he will be moved to compile a lasting self-conception that is likely to serve his future needs for reflective description and explanation. He will not be content with continually identifying his motives at the last minute, as they become relevant to his next decision. Rather, he will want to prepare for future decisions, by learning in advance what motives he always has and what motives he is likely to have in various foreseeable circumstances. A standing conception of what he tends to want in typical situations will tell him, whenever those situations arise, which intentions he would fulfill and which ones would make sense for him to form. He will then be able to form effective and understandable intentions, so that he'll know and understand what he's doing—all without having to take a fresh reading of his motivational state.

Surely, we have a standing self-conception of this kind, and it is partly responsible for the ease with which we find actions whose performance we can anticipate and understand. We needn't continually check and compare our motives for various courses of action, because we know of some things that we always want, of other things that we regularly want, and of yet other things that never interest us. Knowing ourselves in this way, we rarely need to ask ourselves what we most desire.

Such knowledge derives from a standing conception of ourselves that is continually being modified and extended in the light of experience. Like the other elements of reflective knowledge, this conception is not merely a reflection of static facts; for in addition to refining our self-conception to fit our desires, we can gradually reform our desires to fit a particular conception. And we can thereby arrive at that self-conception which yields the greatest overall reflective knowledge.

The self-conception.   But how could one self-conception yield greater knowledge than another, given that we wouldn't adopt either one unless it already fit? Adopting a conception of our desires cannot immediately cause it to come true. We must therefore postpone adopting such a conception until it is already true, and so we are never in a position of wanting to make a conception of our desires true simply because we have already adopted it. Yet what other cognitive grounds could we have for preferring to satisfy a particular self-conception?

My answer to this question, in rough outline, is this. When the possibility of holding and satisfying one conception of ourselves is com-

pared with the possibility of holding and satisfying another conception, there can be no difference in terms of knowing the truth about
ourselves, since in either case our self-conception would, by hypothesis, be true. But there can still be a difference in terms of our self-understanding, since one self-conception may be more perspicuous, more
coherent, or more elegant than the other and may therefore offer a
better understanding of its object than the other conception, even
though the two would be equally true of their respective objects. To
have the whole truth about some phenomenon is not necessarily to
comprehend that phenomenon, to grasp it, to "get" it, as one might
say. Consequently, even if being and conceiving of ourselves as one
kind of person wouldn't involve knowing more reflective truths than
being and conceiving of ourselves as another kind of person, it might
still involve more success at grasping or comprehending or "getting"
the sort of person involved. We can therefore prefer to hold and satisfy
some self-conceptions rather than others on the grounds that they
would afford us a better understanding than the others of the person
we'd be if we satisfied them.

This explanation of our preference among potential self-conceptions
depends on a notion of understanding as distinct from knowing the
truth.[4] What is this notion of understanding? In order to answer that
question, I shall digress briefly and informally into the philosophy of
science. I suggest that the self-conception by which an agent understands himself amounts to a theory—an unscientific theory, to be sure,
but one that shares much, in structure and function, with its scientific
counterparts. And because an agent's self-conception is a theory, I
shall argue, his preference among possible self-conceptions as potential
vehicles of self-understanding is governed by the same principles as
preferences among alternative theories of any phenomenon.

A reflective theory.   Crediting every agent with a theory about himself
may seem extravagant. Many people would be pleasantly surprised to
hear that they theorize about themselves, just as Molière's bourgeois
gentleman is surprised to hear that he speaks in prose. Some might
even decline the compliment. Their self-image, they might say, is just
common sense, and common sense is innocent of theory.

True enough, common sense is not what we would ordinarily call
theoretical, since it isn't especially abstract, systematic, or speculative.

---

[4] The notion of understanding as a distinct cognitive goal has been discussed in the
literature on explanation. See, e.g., Michael Friedman, "Explanation and Scientific Understanding," *Journal of Philosophy* 71 (1974): 5–19.

It isn't a theory in the sense of being divorced from practice, as music theory is from performance, or legal theory is from litigation. Unlike the theories of gravity, relativity, and evolution, common sense wasn't formulated by a particular person or revealed in a particular text. And unlike game theory or quantum theory, it isn't organized into axioms and proofs.[5]

Yet a person's commonsense self-conception does the same jobs as a theory: it enables him to predict and explain his behavior. And it uses the same tools as a scientific theory—namely, hypotheses based on experience. Of course, commonsense hypotheses are neither as precise nor as accurate as the scientific hypotheses known as laws. Though crude and inarticulate, however, commonsense hypotheses can still enable an agent to predict and explain what he does.

If an agent's self-understanding is embodied in a theory about himself, then what counts as a better self-understanding ought to be formulable in terms of the criteria for a better theory. Hence the philosophy of theory-choice ought to illuminate an agent's preferences among potential self-conceptions. I shall therefore offer a brief and informal outline of some criteria that apply to the choice of theories.

The theory of theory-choice. An ideal theory would satisfy criteria such as the following. It would be *general*; that is, it would enable us to predict and explain as many events as possible. It would be *precise*; that is, it would enable us to predict and explain events in terms that distinguish them from alternative possibilities. It would be *accurate*; that is, events would tend to confirm rather than confute its assertions. And it would be *simple*; that is, its premises would be concise, and the explanations and predictions that it yielded would be straightforward.

This list of criteria is incomplete, and it raises a host of philosophical problems, none of which I intend to address. For my purposes, the concepts of generality, precision, accuracy, and simplicity can remain vague and problematic. I shall leave them ill-defined, in the confidence that any adequate definition would still have them stand for some of the foremost desiderata of theoretical reasoning.

Note that these desiderata pull the theorist in different directions.

---

[5] For a discussion of the differences between science and common sense, see K. V. Wilkes, *Physicalism* (New York, 1978), chapter 3; Brand, *Intending and Acting*, 160–65; Stephen P. Stich, *From Folk Psychology to Cognitive Science: The Case against Belief* (Cambridge, Mass., 1983); and Adam Morton, *Frames of Mind* (Oxford, 1980). For a discussion of further similarities, see Paul M. Churchland, *Scientific Realism and the Plasticity of Mind* (New York, 1979), chapter 4, and "Eliminative Materialism and the Propositional Attitudes," *Journal of Philosophy* 74 (1981): 67–90.

He can sum up all events accurately and simply by saying, "Things happen." But then he makes his theory general, accurate, and simple only by making it imprecise, since he hasn't specified what happens. He can generalize more precisely by saying, "Acceleration is equal to force divided by mass," but he thereby sacrifices generality, since his statement now covers only a fraction of what occurs. He can then add further generalizations of equal precision, in order to cover more events. But each addition to his theory is also a complication, a debit on the side of simplicity. And of course, if he tries to account for everything in a few precise statements, those statements are bound to be confuted.

An ideal theory must therefore embody a compromise among competing ideals. It isn't the best of all possible theories on any one dimension—not the most general, not the most precise, nor the simplest or most accurate. Rather, on each dimension it is better than those alternatives which can compete with it on the others. It's more general than those theories which are comparable in simplicity, accuracy, and precision; more precise than those theories which are comparable in accuracy, simplicity, and precision; and so on.[6] The theorist is like a shopper who wants, not the highest possible quality or the lowest possible price, but the best combination of quality and price—the best value for his money. Like the shopper, the theorist seeks a best combination of several mutually limiting virtues.

Comparisons of intelligibility.   Now, some of the things that we theorize about drive a harder bargain, so to speak, than others. They won't yield to any simple or general characterization, say, except at a high price in accuracy and precision. They thus present us with steeper trade-offs among our theoretic ideals, and so we say that they are harder to understand. Other subjects of inquiry, by comparison, practically give themselves away. We can characterize them more simply and generally without giving up as much precision or accuracy, and so we find them more intelligible.

For instance, you probably find the workings of your bicycle easier

[6] My reason for speaking, rather vaguely, about theories that are "comparable to" the ideal theory in various respects is that I wish to remain neutral on the question whether the criteria of theory-choice bear equal weight. If generality, simplicity, and the rest are of equal importance, then the ideal theory will be more general than those which are *equally* simple, accurate, and precise; more precise than those which are *equally* accurate, simple, and general; and so on. But if one criterion bears more weight than the others, then a theory that excels on that criterion may be preferred even to those which somewhat surpass it on other criteria.

to explain and predict than those of your car. The car has a profusion of parts and is governed by myriad principles—mechanical, chemical, and electrical—that make it harder to understand. Your conception of it is correspondingly incomplete, approximate, unwieldy, or vague. The bicycle can be comprehended more generally, more precisely, more simply, and more accurately all at once.

Similarly, the apparent motions of the stars are easier to predict and explain than those of the clouds. The former are regular and correspond straightforwardly to the revolutions and rotations of the earth; the latter are a complex function of air speed, temperature, pressure, humidity, geography, and pollution, among other variables. The one phenomenon is therefore easier to grasp than the other.

In short, some phenomena are intrinsically more intelligible than others.[7] They are more intelligible in the sense that they can be better understood, and they can be better understood in the sense that a complete, true theory of them embodies more of the virtues that we seek in a theory.

Of course, some will object that truth is the primary virtue that we seek in a theory and hence that if we have equally true theories of two phenomena, then we understand them equally well. To this my reply is that features such as generality and simplicity are widely recognized as independent theoretic virtues and can therefore be used, as I am using them, to construct a conception of understanding as more than merely knowing the truth. After all, I am considering whether we can have any cognitive grounds for distinguishing among self-conceptions that would be equally true, since they would be adopted only after we had come to satisfy them. Surely, a choice among equally true theories is a juncture at which other theoretic virtues can come into play. My point is that a virtue such as simplicity is just the sort of feature that would enable one theory to convey a better understanding of its object

---

[7] Here I am using the word 'intrinsic' in a relative and perhaps misleading sense. I do not mean to deny that the intelligibility of a phenomenon is relative to our vocabulary or conceptual scheme. Perhaps there are vocabularies or conceptual schemes that would make the movements of the clouds more intelligible than those of the stars. Perhaps, then, I shouldn't say that the intelligibility of these phenomena is intrinsic.

For the purposes of the following discussion, however, the possibility of alternative conceptual schemes is irrelevant. I assume that an agent will use the concepts and terms of commonsense psychology as he finds it. He is not seeking to introduce innovations into the existing psychological vocabulary; rather, he is trying to use that vocabulary in describing himself. And once a vocabulary is fixed, some phenomena will be easier to characterize than others—and hence more intelligible in a sense that is independent of how much is known about them.

than another even if the two were equally true of their respective objects.

A review of intellectual motives.   The importance of theoretic ideals other than truth, in the present context, is guaranteed by the nature of the intellectual motives at work. Keep in mind that our desire for self-understanding is the desire to understand—not the actions of a particular person, who we happen to be—but rather the actions of whichever person we are.[8] If what we wanted was to understand the behavior of a particular personality, then we wouldn't want a better grasp of that personality than could be had by knowing the truth about it. But since what we want is to understand the behavior of whichever personality we have, we can indeed aspire to a better grasp of ourselves than can be had by knowing what is currently the truth. For we can aspire to making a different self-conception true.

Consider, by way of analogy, two desires that you might have for understanding your car. On the one hand, you might want to understand a particular vehicle, the one on which you currently rely for transportation; on the other hand, you might want it to be the case that you understand whichever vehicle you rely on. In the former case, you would be content with having a true theory of the car you currently drive; in the latter case, however, having a true theory of that car might still be less desirable to you than driving a different car for which you could have a true theory that was, for example, simpler. And your preference for the latter combination of car and theory would be based on cognitive grounds—namely, on the grounds that it would put you in the position of having a better understanding of your car. Wanting to understand your car can thus be a motive for finding a car that's easier to understand.

The latter desire is the one that's analogous to our desire for self-understanding. My claim is that wanting to understand ourselves is a motive for seeking selves that are more intelligible. And I have now spelled out what makes for greater intelligibility: susceptibility to a theory that better combines the theoretic virtues.

Intelligible personalities.   In previous chapters, I have argued that an agent is inclined toward actions that he is aware of already knowing how to explain, and I have described such actions as intelligible. Yet the actions that are intelligible to an agent in the sense that he knows how to explain them need not be especially intelligible in the sense that

---

[8] See chapter 1, 27–29.

I have now defined. Even if an agent knows all about his motives and can hence explain whatever he does, his conduct may still be relatively hard to grasp in that it resists an explanation that exemplifies all of the theoretic virtues to a high degree. The motivational forces at work may admit of no characterization that isn't either complicated, incomplete, inaccurate, or vague.

If the agent cares only about the self-knowledge that he can attain immediately, then taking the actions that he can already explain is the most that he can do. On such short notice, he cannot hope to make the operative motivational forces any easier to grasp. But if he wants to enhance his future prospects for self-knowledge, then he can try to refine his motivational makeup in such a way as to make his future conduct intrinsically intelligible. He can try to ensure that the explanations and predictions available to him in the future will better exemplify the theoretic virtues than the ones available now.

The long-term project of self-inquiry should therefore lead an agent, not just to seek the commonsense description that best captures the motives that he has, but also to cultivate motives that can be well captured in a commonsense description. Whenever his current personality requires steep trade-offs among his theoretic ideals, he can try to cultivate a different personality that is easier to deal with. The sort of person he eventually becomes—his underlying desires and overarching intentions—will bear witness to his intellectual ideals, since he will become that sort of person partly in order to warrant an ideal self-conception.

Before I describe the pursuit of intrinsic intelligibility in detail, I should point out that this pursuit constitutes only one trend or theme among many in an agent's long-term self-inquiry. It's what we ordinarily conceive of as the trend toward integration and consolidation of one's personality, a trend that's essential to rationality in the long run but is also tempered by countervailing trends toward variety and spontaneity. I shall discuss the latter trends in due course, but first I want to focus on the trend toward intelligibility.

Intrinsic Rationality

What kinds of desire, or other disposition, would make a person easy to comprehend?

The key to intrinsic intelligibility, I think, is regularity. Unless a person's desires follow some regular patterns, no simple self-conception will be able to sum them up accurately and precisely. The more orderly a person's motives, the better his chances of formulating concise generalizations that will yield informative explanations and predictions of his behavior in a wide range of circumstances.[9]

A source of order.   One kind of order that can always be found in a person's desires is their subordination to ulterior motives. A person can generalize informatively about his desires by specifying the things that he wants in themselves and then saying simply that he also wants the means to those things. By specifying only his intrinsic desires, he can attain a self-conception that is simple and yet contains the first premise for every potential desire-based explanation and prediction about his behavior. And he can always expand this condensed self-conception into a full roster of his desires simply by positing further desires for whatever he takes to be the means to the specified ends.

I shall therefore assume that an agent's standing self-conception contains information only about his intrinsic desires. The question then becomes which intrinsic desires would make for the most perspicuous and powerful self-conception.

A source of disorder.   One potential locus of disorder in a person's intrinsic desires is in their temporal aspect. Every desire has two connections in time. There is the time *at which* the desire exists and exerts its motivational force, and then there is the time *toward which* the desire looks—the time of the desired event or state of affairs.

Just imagine a person whose intrinsic desires followed no temporal pattern in either of these respects. At any one time he would want things to happen at various other times, in no particular pattern; and these wants would change from time to time, also in no particular pattern. The only lasting self-conception available to such a person would be a complete schedule of departures and arrivals, so to speak, detailing which desires he would have at each moment, toward each moment. No generalizations would be possible.

What would we say of someone whose desires were so miscellaneous and erratic? Surely, we'd say that he doesn't know what he wants. And this ordinary expression, which is perfectly innocent of philosophy, would reveal our thorough familiarity with the subtleties of self-in-

---

[9] This last statement is probably a tautology. For if you asked me what *orderly* motives are, I would have to say that they are ones that can be characterized simply without any loss of generality, accuracy, or precision.

Let me point out here that order, like simplicity, is relative to a vocabulary or conceptual scheme. But I am assuming that an agent already has a conceptual scheme—namely, the commonsense psychology of his place and time—and is seeking to understand himself, and to become understandable, in terms of that psychology.

quiry. When we say that a person doesn't know what he wants, we don't usually mean that he wants something but doesn't know it: we don't assume that some stable and potentially unifying desire is lurking in an unexamined corner of his heart. We usually mean quite the reverse, that there is no stable or unifying desire to be found in the person and hence that his desires need better governance, not closer scrutiny. "He doesn't know what he wants" tends to mean "He wants too many things all at once" or "He wants different things at different times"— in short, that the person's desires are in disarray. Why, then, do we phrase this remark in terms of the person's self-knowledge? The reason, I would suggest, is that we have a rudimentary grasp of the relation between self-understanding and motivational order. We see that orderly desires are the only desires that one can comprehend well and hence that disorderly desires result, above all, in reflective confusion.[10]

Reasons for avoiding disorder. Of course, disorderly desires would be undesirable for reasons other than their resistance to summarization. If a person's desires toward a particular time changed from moment to moment, he would never attain most of the things he desired for that time, since he would in the long run desire many mutually incompatible things. And when the target time arrived, he probably wouldn't be in a position to attain what he wanted *at* that time, since at previous times he would have wanted, and hence been moved to promote, various other, incompatible outcomes. Such mutually defeating motives would be undesirable, since a person usually has, in addition to his various first-order desires, a further, second-order desire to avoid the frustration of his first-order desires, whatever they may be. This latter desire is a reason against having desires that are likely to be frustrated or likely to motivate behavior that would tend to frustrate other desires.

Similar drawbacks would attach to desires that obeyed no pattern in respect to their target times. If a person wanted different and irregular outcomes for every day of the week, every week of the year, he wouldn't be able to pool the resources he amassed for fulfilling any of his desires, he wouldn't be able to benefit from regular practice at pro-

---

[10] See Stephen E. Toulmin, "Self-Knowledge and Knowledge of the 'Self'," in *The Self: Psychological and Philosophical Issues,* ed. Theodore Mischel (Totowa, N.J., 1977), 304: "If we describe someone as 'not knowing his own mind' . . . we are commonly remarking not on his incompetence as a self-observer but rather on his indecisiveness or vacillation." Toulmin's article touches on many of the themes that I have attempted to develop throughout this book, especially "the *interdependence* of self-understanding and self-command" (304).

moting particular outcomes, and he wouldn't be able to take advantage of such useful strategies as developing habits and routines conducive to his ends. Imagine, for example, what the task of shopping would be like for a person who never wanted to eat any dish twice. The desire to avoid frustration is a reason against having such desires, whose demands on one's resources and abilities are eventually bound to be frustrated.

Rationality without reasons. What interests me, however, is that practical reasoning would oppose disorderly desires in themselves, independently of any particular desire that may constitute a reason for avoiding them. Disorderly desires would be opposed by practical reasoning because they are inimical to self-understanding. No particular premises need to serve as a background against which disorderly desires impede self-understanding: they impede self-understanding in themselves, by requiring the agent to have a more unwieldy or less adequate self-conception and hence an inferior understanding of himself. Eliminating disorder in one's desires is therefore an independently valid move in the reasoning that I call practical.

The categories of what practical reasoning favors or opposes thus turn out to be broader than the categories of what there are reasons for or against. I think that we tend to use the terms 'rational' and 'irrational' for the former categories, and so I would state the present point by saying that things can be rational or irrational even in the absence of reasons for or against them. Having one's ends in chaos counts as irrational not because having chaotic ends runs afoul of some particular reasons but because it is in itself a state of irrationality.

I am not denying here that there are reasons against having chaotic ends; I am merely pointing out that the irrationality of having chaotic ends cannot be reduced without remainder to the existence of such reasons.[11] I therefore hesitate to judge the rationality of dispositions

[11] For another example, consider one's desire for self-understanding, one of the desires that motivates self-inquiry. On the one hand, this desire constitutes a reason for bringing one's motives to order. That is, reforming one's disorderly motives would make sense in light of one's desire for self-understanding; and so that desire could be represented in premises from which motivational reform would follow as a practical conclusion. On the other hand, reforming disorderly motives is conducive to self-understanding quite apart from its being an understandable thing to do in light of one's desire to understand oneself. Indeed, one's desire for self-understanding wouldn't render it understandable unless it were conducive to self-understanding in itself to begin with. Thus, the rationality of orderly desires doesn't depend on one's having this particular reason for cultivating them; on the contrary, one's having this reason for cultivating orderly desires depends on the rationality of such desires in themselves.

simply by weighing reasons for or against them. Some dispositions, or sets of dispositions, may be intrinsically rational or irrational in ways not reflected by the relevant reasons. This possibility is of particular relevance to the rationality of being moral, which I shall discuss in the next chapter. Most philosophers assume that the way to demonstrate the rationality of being moral is to offer reasons for being moral. But if being moral is a dispositional state, as I believe it to be, then being moral may be rational even though there is no particular reason for it.

The Rationality of Values in General

I have gotten ahead of myself. Before I consider the rationality of being moral, let me return to the temporal aspect of one's desires. How might one try to avoid confusion in one's schedule of motives?

The most obvious strategy, I think, is to increase the proportion of one's desires that can be described without temporal qualification of one sort or another. There are some desires for which one can avoid specifying the *time at which* one has them, for example, simply because one always has them. Because I always have the desire to live a long and fruitful life, I can include this desire in my standing self-conception without any reference to when it occurs. One can also avoid specifying the *time toward which* some desires look, because they look toward all times, their objects being permanent states of affairs or continually repeated outcomes. Thus, my standing self-conception can include a completely unqualified desire for world peace; for not only do I always want the world to be at peace, but I also want the world to be at peace always. Similarly, my self-conception can include a temporally unqualified desire to win at tennis, if I always want that I win whenever I play.

Naturally, a person cannot avoid having desires whose existence or object is confined to a limited time, nor would a person gain in self-understanding by arbitrarily cultivating just any desires whose existence or object happened to be timeless. What a person can do and benefit from doing, however, is to find timeless desires whose cultivation would be congenial to his other known interests, and hence intelligible. He can then foster those desires to the point where they frequently dominate his more transient and narrowly focused desires—a point where they would also yield predictions and explanations for much of his behavior. The more behavior he can subsume under these desires, the more explanatory and predictive power he can obtain from a very simple and stable self-conception. Self-inquiry therefore leads a person to identify outcomes that make sense for him to want *at all* times, or to want *for* all times, or both; and then it leads him to establish these desires at the head of his motives.

Values as stable, categorical desires. Among the resulting desires, the ones whose existence and object are both timeless would ordinarily be called the person's values, I believe. For when we talk about someone's values, we are generally thinking of stable and broadly focused desires that are fundamental to the person's conduct and self-conception. The objects of a person's values don't include the things that he wants only now and then, or only for particular periods, nor do they include things that he disavows or dislikes wanting. The objects of a person's values, I would say, are the things that he knowingly and willingly desires at all times, for all times.[12] And such desires would be among the products of self-inquiry.[13]

I am not saying that people actually form their values in the course of self-inquiry: most people just absorb the values of their elders and fellows.[14] My point is that strong values are dispositions that self-inquiry would produce if they weren't already present and that self-inquiry in any case reinforces. Hence having strong values is rational even if one doesn't owe them to self-inquiry. What's more, I think that people's values, though largely inherited or borrowed, are at least refined by measures of self-reform that serve the interests of self-understanding. Each person identifies with only some of the values that he has inherited or could borrow, and to identify with a value, I think, is just to cultivate it as a fitting component not only of one's self but also of one's self-image.

The rationality of having values is acknowledged by common sense, I believe, though not by those philosophical theories which equate ra-

[12] Of course, a person can value, say, good food without wanting to be eating at every moment. The point is that such a desire isn't temporally qualified; it's conditional. The desire for good food is the desire (always) to have good food whenever one eats.

[13] See Dent, *Moral Psychology of the Virtues*, 111: "Now it is, I think, barely conceivable that someone of adult years should not have 'taken stock' of the variety of concerns he has felt from time to time and with varying intensity and permanence. These concerns will establish first this, then that, as being for a time of cardinal or substantial importance to him in his life. But he will come to some sense of which of these things have a more enduring significance to him, a sense of their significance which will survive the occasional disappearance or overlaying of any passionally engendered sense of their importance. One could say that he will come to an appreciation of their value." On this and many other issues, I embrace Dent's description of the phenomena while differing with him on their explanation.

[14] How a person assimilates values from others is a question that I shall discuss in the next chapter.

tionality with the intelligent choice of means to whatever ends one happens to have. In the everyday world, we perceive a difference of rationality between agents who are equally adept at choosing means, the difference being precisely that some are applying those means to the sustained pursuit of lasting states of affairs, while others are taking a random walk from one ephemeral outcome to another. We regard the former agents' values as imbuing their lives with a rationale, and hence a kind of rationality, that is lacking from the lives of the latter. These agents understand what they're doing in the broadest possible way: they know what they're all about. And the reason is that they have fundamental values in light of which their conduct can be broadly understood.

Values as involving value judgments. Another way of drawing the distinction between a person's values and his mere desires has traditionally been to say that values have a cognitive as well as a motivational component. Values are unlike mere desires in that they involve the judgment that their object is good, valuable, or worth desiring.[15]

I endorse this way of drawing the distinction, although I have chosen to distinguish values first in terms of their intrinsic intelligibility. In the last part of this chapter, I shall try to show that these two ways of distinguishing between values and mere desires are coextensive. I shall argue that the intrinsically intelligible desires that I have identified with a person's values tend to be accompanied by judgments to the effect that their objects are good.

Before turning to the cognitive component of values, however, I want to lend further support to my claim that values can be conceived as intrinsically intelligible desires. I shall lend support to this claim by showing that the things we actually value are the things that long-term self-inquiry would lead us to desire.

The Rationality of Particular Values

One might wonder whether self-inquiry, as I have now defined it, would stop at motivational reforms as mild as the cultivation of values. One might suspect, for instance, that the most intelligible personality would actually be a personality driven by a single, unchanging desire. If you were literally a monomaniac, then your every move could be precisely and accurately explained in the simplest terms. There would

---

[15] This distinction is drawn by Gary Watson in "Free Agency," *Journal of Philosophy* 72 (1975): 205–20. I do not endorse everything that Watson says about the distinction. In particular, I do not agree with Watson that mere desires do not provide prima facie reasons for acting.

be no motivational conflicts, no subtle balance of forces, no unpredictable impulses—just the headlong pursuit of a single end. Why, then, shouldn't self-inquiry lead you to eradicate all but one desire?

Why monomania is and isn't irrational. I am inclined to answer this question in two different though compatible ways. On the one hand, I want to say that the monomaniacal personality is indeed the most rational, in some sense of the word—which just goes to show that too much rationality can be a bad thing. Sometimes when we call a person rational, we mean that his ultimate ends are simple and stable, or that he has a coherent plan of life. This familiar sense of the term 'rational' is among the ones that my account of long-term self-inquiry is designed to explicate; for I would contend that a simple and stable set of ends, or a coherent plan of life, is what results from the pursuit of intrinsic intelligibility. I concede that in this sense of the word a monomaniac would qualify as consummately rational. But then, I think that we can almost hear ourselves calling him consummately rational—that is, if we didn't prefer to say that he was all too rational, or rational to a fault.

On the other hand, I also want to say that becoming a monomaniac wouldn't be rational for you, since it would entail an unintelligible process of self-reform. After all, your future prospects for self-knowledge are not your only intellectual concern: you also want to know and understand what you're doing here and now. And eradicating all but one desire wouldn't be an intelligible thing for you to do, in light of all your other second-order attitudes about which desires to have. There are many desires that you positively want to keep for their own sakes. You also want, more generally, to maintain variety in your desires, since a life spent in the service of any single desire would be aesthetically unsatisfactory, as well as threatening to your autonomy. Finally and most generally, you have a motive for avoiding any reform that threatens to alter you too radically. Reform that would obliterate your current personality is contrary to your desire for self-preservation, a desire that urges the preservation not just of any self but of a particular self, the self you currently are.[16]

Given the strength of these conservative inclinations, revolutionizing yourself for the sake of future self-knowledge would undermine your present self-knowledge. To be sure, you might make far more sense to

---

[16] This conception of self-preservation is discussed by Phillip Bricker in "Prudence," *Journal of Philosophy* 77 (1980): 400.

yourself if you were a very different person, but trying to become such a person would make no sense in light of the person you are.[17]

What emerges, then, is that the long-term project of self-inquiry must negotiate between two different kinds of epistemic constraint. On the one hand, it must produce a more intelligible personality in the long run. On the other hand, it must proceed via discrete acts of self-conditioning each of which must stand the test of intelligibility here and now. You must not only fashion a more understandable self but also fashion it in an understandable way.

The necessity of proceeding by intelligible steps won't prevent you from undertaking a moderate program of self-reform. After all, you are interested in having an intrinsically intelligible personality, and that interest will account for some amount of psychic renovation. The point is merely that your desire for intelligibility will not be sufficient to explain demolishing your current personality and rebuilding from the ground up. The most intelligible program of self-reform is likely to rely on strategic, minor changes that yield disproportionately large epistemic gains. No such program will produce a monomaniac.

Still, our judgments of rationality are often divided along the lines of the two constraints that guide long-term self-inquiry. We think that a monomaniac is rational in a sense—that is, in a sense that recognizes intrinsic intelligibility as one intellectual goal, alongside the goal of understanding one's particular actions. But we also think that there is a sense in which a monomaniac is irrational. And the sense in which he's irrational is precisely this: he's more rational than particular, rational actions could ever have made him and hence more rational than anyone could rationally become.

Why prudence is rational. There is one timeless desire that almost any agent can make sense of cultivating—namely, the persisting desire

---

[17] You might think that you'd be better off, for the purposes of self-inquiry, if you didn't have any of your conservative inclinations. Without them you could rationally attempt any transformation that promised a more intelligible personality. Perhaps, then, self-inquiry should follow a two-stage procedure, in which you would first become less conservative and only then try to become radically different.

But no: many of the considerations that weigh against radical reform also weigh against mere liberalization. For instance, you not only prefer to maintain variety in your interests but also prefer to keep that preference. More importantly, you want to keep your desire for self-preservation; in fact, you want to keep it largely in order to preserve yourself. The desire for self-preservation is so deeply embedded in your personality that if you didn't have it, you would be a very different person. Hence the desire for self-preservation is self-preserving: it would oppose its own elimination. In light of your conservatism, then, doing away with your conservatism wouldn't make sense.

for his own persisting happiness. This desire is of course a motive for acting prudently; indeed, it can be regarded as identical with prudence, the disposition. The rationality of prudence can then be subsumed under the rationality of values. That is, if we suppose that prudence consists in wanting one's own happiness without any temporal qualification, then we can explain that it's rational because this sort of timeless desire, being conducive to self-understanding, is a typical outcome of self-inquiry.[18]

Why information-resistant desires are rational. An agent cannot have a standing self-image that will be of use for future reference unless his intrinsic desires are sufficiently robust to endure changes in his circumstances and perspective. Desires that are likely to disappear as he lives and learns aren't worth incorporating into his standing self-conception, since that conception is designed to provide him with self-understanding in the long run, which the desires in question will not survive. Actions motivated by unstable desires must therefore be explained ad hoc rather than in terms of the agent's standing reflective theory. And since ad hoc explanations complicate the agent's self-understanding, long-term self-inquiry opposes the unstable desires that occasion them.

Perhaps the least robust of intrinsic desires are the ones whose existence depends on the agent's present ignorance or disregard of information that already is or eventually will become available to him. Insofar as an agent wants things that he wouldn't want if only he knew things that he might learn, his desires are continually in danger of being overturned. Self-inquiry therefore favors desires whose survival is compatible with the growth of the agent's knowledge—desires that can bear the light.

Among desires that cannot bear the light, the most unstable are those which favor a course of action that would uncover the very information that's capable of withering them—like the desire for an outcome that the agent will no longer want as soon as he has experienced it. These desires are virtually self-destructive, and so they are especially detrimental to self-inquiry. They are also, not surprisingly, especially irrational in the eyes of common sense. Common sense condemns these desires on the grounds that they will lead the agent into disillusionment

---

[18] See chapter 8, 238–40, for a different explanation of why prudence is rational. I see no reason why there shouldn't be more than one explanation, especially since they deal with different conceptions of prudence. The explanation given in chapter 8 showed how future desires can provide present reasons for acting. The explanation given here is about the rationality of having a prudential motive.

and regret. I would say that these desires are intrinsically irrational because they are inherently unstable and hence an obstacle to the project of long-range self-inquiry.[19]

Some philosophers have made this particular case of irrationality the basis for a global theory of rational desire. They define rational desires as the ones that an agent would have, or would want himself to have, if only he knew everything.[20] I think these philosophers depart from common sense in two unfortunate respects.

First, common sense favors merely information-resistant desires without necessarily favoring a particular set of desires from among all the various sets that might be information resistant. An agent may be capable of cultivating many different sets of desires that would weather exposure to the facts. Some of these sets might include desires that the agent doesn't currently have and wouldn't acquire simply by exposing himself to information; some of them might exclude desires that the agent currently has and wouldn't lose simply by exposing himself to information.[21] Training in "est," for example, might instill ambitions in the agent that wouldn't be instilled by information alone but, once instilled, wouldn't be dispelled by information, either; daily meditation might banish desires that information would never have banished but is equally unable to reinstate. Having the former desires and lacking the latter would therefore be just as information-resistant a state as the reverse. But the philosophers I've cited define the reverse as the rational state, simply because it's the one that the agent could reach from his present state simply by learning more. In this respect, they put too fine a point on the commonsense requirement that desires be information resistant.

[19] Of course, insofar as an agent wants to avoid disillusionment and regret, he has a reason against having the desires in question. My point here is that the irrationality of desires that will lead to disillusionment and regret doesn't depend on, and cannot be reduced to, a desire to avoid those outcomes. They are irrational in themselves, being inimical to self-inquiry.

[20] This view has roots in Mill's *Utilitarianism*, but its first clear exposition (to my knowledge) appears in Sidgwick, *Methods of Ethics*, book 1, chapter 9. See also John Rawls, *A Theory of Justice* (Cambridge, Mass., 1971), 407ff.; Brandt, *Theory of the Good and the Right*; R.M. Hare, *Moral Thinking: Its Method, Levels and Point* (Oxford, 1981), 101–5, 214–18; Peter Railton, "Moral Realism," *The Philosophical Review* 95 (1986): 163–207, and "Facts and Values," *Philosophical Topics* 14 (1986): 5–31.

[21] I have directed this argument against Brandt's version of the theory, which defines the good in terms of the desires that the agent would have after exposure to the facts. Railton defines the good in terms of the desires that the agent's fully informed counterpart would want him to have. But this difference makes no difference for purposes of the present argument, which could easily be recast in Railton's terms.

The same philosophers then turn around and overgeneralize the commonsense requirement, by assuming that if resistance to some information is good, then resistance to all possible information must be best. They therefore define rational desires as those which the agent would have after assimilating all of the facts—more facts than he can ever assimilate in reality. According to my theory, however, rationality requires only that desires be resistant to information that the agent might actually acquire; indeed, the more likely he is to acquire a particular piece of information, given a particular desire, the stronger is the requirement that the desire be resistant to it. This version of the requirement matches our stronger commonsense strictures against desires that will lead to disillusionment. I therefore think that my theory of rational desire yields more plausible results.

Why masochism is irrational.   I think that my theory can also explain why masochism—the desire to suffer—is ordinarily considered irrational. But in order to discuss the rationality of masochism, I need to chart a second dimension of intrinsic intelligibility. For I regard the rationality of masochism as having to do with the synchronic coherence of desires rather than their diachronic regularity.

In my account of character traits, I suggested that we often recognize several of a person's desires as belonging together and hence as betraying a disposition toward desires of a recognizable kind, even if we have no name for the kind in question.[22] Conversely, we sometimes regard a person's desires as mutually incongruent, perhaps in equally ineffable ways. I now venture to suggest that the perceived coherence of a person's desires amounts to a kind of simplicity in our conception of them. That is, when the constituents of a personality seem to "go together," our conception of that personality is simpler by virtue of its perceived coherence, whereas our conception of a motley personality is correspondingly complicated by its perceived incoherence.

(Note, by the way, that I could have listed coherence as a theoretic virtue in its own right, on a par with simplicity, generality, and the others. My decision to treat coherence as a species of simplicity is not essential to what follows.)

Now, the clearest case of incoherence in a person's desires is the case of desires that directly conflict. When someone simultaneously likes and dislikes an object, or wants and fears an outcome, we say that he is of two minds, precisely because we have trouble fitting both atti-

---

[22] Chapter 9, 245.

tudes into a single, coherent conception of him. This expression, "being of two minds," illustrates how incoherence breeds complexity.

The reason why masochism is commonly viewed as irrational, I suggest, is that human nature is commonly viewed as inhospitable to it. Common sense acknowledges that some people do have masochistic impulses, but it treats those impulses as exceptions, excrescences—as necessarily at odds with the rest of human nature. We tend to think that masochists are people in whom a desire for pain opposes and sometimes overcomes the natural desire for pleasure; for we assume that no human being can be wholeheartedly, straightforwardly, and unambivalently masochistic.

I am not necessarily defending this bit of commonsense sociobiology. Rather, I am simply pointing to it as the premise behind a commonsense judgment of rationality. We tend to think that masochism is irrational for anyone—that there is no such creature as a rational masochist. I am suggesting that this judgment presupposes, or even subtly conveys, a generalization about human nature. When we say that masochism is invariably irrational, what we have in mind is that the desire to suffer invariably introduces conflict and incoherence into a personality and hence that eliminating this desire would invariably make the person more intelligible.

Our judgment about the rationality of masochism thus relies on an assumption about the personalities that are possible for creatures like us. We assume, of any human masochist, that he is actually of two minds about suffering, because no one can be a single-minded masochist. If there were a single-minded masochist, he might well be rational.[23]

Limits on Moral Philosophy

Note, however, that I cannot offer a general and incontestable proof that masochism is irrational. Whether this disposition and the others discussed above are rational or irrational for a particular person depends on how well they would fit in with his other dispositions, how much psychic dislocation their cultivation would cause—indeed, whether he could successfully cultivate them at all. My guess is that for most people a continuing interest in their own continuing happiness is a sensible disposition to cultivate, partly because it produces a personality that makes more sense overall; whereas a desire for pain produces

---

[23] Bentham expresses this commonsense view when he says, "The principle of asceticism never was, nor ever can be, consistently pursued by any living creature" (*An Introduction to the Principles of Morals and Legislation* [New York, 1948], 13).

a less intelligible personality. Still, I cannot prove that these or any other dispositions are categorically rational or irrational.

For this reason, there is no point in dreaming up hypothetical personalities that would be especially easy to comprehend. Self-inquiry, as I conceive it, is an empirical discipline that proceeds by trial and error. You start with the person you already are and the self-conception that you already have. Then you try out various adjustments—in yourself and your self-conception—always seeking, on the one hand, to increase your intrinsic intelligibility and, on the other, to do so by steps that are themselves intelligible. You don't always know in advance which changes of personality you can accomplish; you don't always know, before actively entertaining such changes, just how much sense they would make in light of your current motives; and you don't always know just how successful the resulting self-conception will be. You have to experiment.

I do not believe that moral philosophy can dictate the outcome of empirical self-inquiry, any more than the philosophy of science can dictate the outcome of scientific inquiry. The most we philosophers can do is to provide an enlightening commentary on the contest among rival theories as it is played out on the field of experience. I am therefore skeptical about the possibility of proving that rationality requires any particular ends or life-plans. What rationality requires is that we get on with the task of self-inquiry, whose future course is not for philosophy to dictate. In our philosophical moments, we must be content to survey the ends and plans that we have arrived at and to ask whether we have arrived at them, or would have arrived at them, through a process of inquiry consistent with our stated intellectual ideals.[24]

Summary

In this section I have tried to show that the search for intelligible desires is coextensive with what we would ordinarily call a search for values. I have argued that it favors desires that resemble values in being stable and categorical, and in having as their objects the things that we actually value, such as our own persisting happiness. The congruence of these results with those of our actual search for values provides some support for my contention that the search for values and the search for intelligible desires are one and the same. In the next chapter,

---

[24] Here I am in sympathy with a remark of Annette Baier's: "A moral compass to guide us . . . is not something we are likely to think up in an armchair, but something that will itself evolve by the testing of generations of people" ("Theory and Reflective Practices," in *Postures of the Mind: Essays on Mind and Morals* [Minneapolis, 1985], 224).

I shall attempt to offer more support of the same kind, by showing how long-term self-inquiry leads to those values which we ordinarily call moral. I shall devote the remainder of this chapter to the cognitive component of values—that is, to our judgments about what's good.

A Skeptical Theory of the Good

Thus far I have characterized values as desires. Yet as I have already noted, some philosophers distinguish values from desires on the grounds that values are not just conative but cognitive as well. Values involve value judgments, as mere desires do not.

Now, I think that the desires formed by long-term self-inquiry are likely to be accompanied by value judgments. Indeed, their rationality as desires is precisely what earns them this cognitive accompaniment. Here is why.

Instrumentalism about the Good

My arguments here have a structure that can be thought of as instru-mentalist. Instrumentalism about a body of discourse is the view that the discourse is systematically false and yet defensible on other than epistemic grounds. My theory of evaluative reasoning yields an instru-mentalist account of value judgments.

A thought experiment.   In order to see why, perform the following thought experiment. Take evaluative reasoning, as I describe it—the process of enhancing the intelligibility of our desires—and imagine re-placing each of the desires with a judgment to the effect that the de-sire's object is good. The search for a stable, coherent, and simple set of desires will then appear in the guise of a search for a stable, coher-ent, and simple set of judgments about what's good. Thus disguised, it will look much like theoretical reasoning about a real property of things. The reason is that the intellectual satisfactions we demand from desires are the same as the ones we demand from beliefs. When the desires involved in evaluative reasoning are replaced by value judg-ments, our demand for a robust and unified set of desires becomes the demand for a robust and unified theory, and the resulting reasoning mimics theoretical reasoning about a phenomenon called value. This phenomenon will seem real at the end of our reasoning precisely be-cause we will have come to identify it in judgments that are simple, stable, coherent—in short, in judgments that offer some of the intellec-tual satisfactions that we look for in a plausible description of reality.

I believe that the foregoing thought experiment correctly represents how we actually reason about the good. Evaluative reasoning is fundamentally a search for intelligible desires, but in the context of that search we tend to treat desires as interchangeable with judgments to the effect that their objects are good. The reason is that our search for intellectually satisfying desires has the same structure as a search for intellectually satisfying beliefs, and so we can switch back and forth between thinking about what to desire and thinking about what's good, with the assurance that a plausible set of judgments will correspond to a sensible set of desires, and vice versa. As our desires attain reflective rationality, the corresponding judgments attain a semblance of truth.

Here, then, is my explanation why the desires that I have called values tend to be accompanied by judgments to the effect that their objects are good. Values are the desires in which we have managed to attain the coherence and stability that corresponds to the structure of rational belief. They are therefore the desires that we can most comfortably match with plausible-looking beliefs about goodness, and so they are the desires whose objects we are most inclined to call good.

A theory fragment.   Now, when I say that the value judgments issuing from evaluative reasoning are intellectually satisfying, or have a semblance of truth, I do not mean that they constitute the best available theory about those aspects of the world with which evaluative reasoning deals. For I believe that evaluative reasoning doesn't actually deal with the states of affairs or properties posited in value judgments—that is, with things' being good. According to my theory, evaluative reasoning is really a process of developing a stable and coherent set of desires for the sake of self-understanding, and judgments of goodness attain the structure of a plausible theory only because they serve as surrogates for, and hence come to mirror the structure of, the desires under development.[25] I therefore think that the plausibility of value judgments has nothing to do with whether those judgments are true. The best explanation of why we think that things are good, I say, is not that things really are good but rather that we organize our desires in a way that can be mirrored in a plausible-looking set of value judgments. According to my theory, then, value judgments lack a crucial kind of explanatory power, in that they do not appear in the best explanation of how we form them. And a theory that doesn't figure in

[25] Why do I think that this is the best explanation of how we arrive at value judgments? Because it explains why we reach the particular judgments we do; because it explains our inclination to be skeptics about value (see below); and, above all, because it coheres with a theory that explains the phenomena of agency—intention, long-range planning, practical reasoning, autonomy, practical self-knowledge, and so on.

the best explanation of its own formation fails to cohere with the rest of our beliefs.[26]

Thus, when I say that value judgments can offer the intellectual satisfactions characteristic of a plausible theory, I do not mean that they can offer the best combination of those satisfactions. Value judgments constitute, at best, a fragment of a theory, possessing an intrinsic coherence of the kind that makes for plausibility but lacking an equally important kind of extrinsic coherence—that is, coherence with other plausible theories and, in particular, with our best theory of how the judgments themselves are formed.

The upshot of my account therefore seems to be that making value judgments is a big mistake. For if I am right about evaluative reasoning, then to accept value judgments is just to accept a theory that is fundamentally flawed. How can I hold a view that leads to such an intolerable consequence?

Skepticism about the Good

To begin with, let me acknowledge what is indeed a consequence of my view. I do believe that any theory describing things as good or bad

---

[26] Here I may seem to be entering a debate already in progress, between Gilbert Harman and Nicholas Sturgeon. (See Harman, *The Nature of Morality* [Oxford, 1977], chapters 1 and 2; Sturgeon, "Moral Explanations," in *Morality, Reason and Truth*, ed. David Copp and David Zimmerman [Totowa, N.J., 1985], 49–78; Harman, "Moral Explanations of Natural Facts—Can Moral Claims Be Tested against Moral Reality?" *Southern Journal of Philosophy* 24 [1986]: 57–68; Sturgeon, "Harman on Moral Explanations of Natural Facts," *Southern Journal of Philosophy* 24 [1986]: 69–78.)

In fact, however, I do not think that Harman's or Sturgeon's arguments have much bearing on mine. Harman does at times say that the truth of moral judgments is not the best explanation of why those judgments are made, but he never really says what the best explanation of moral judgments is, in his opinion. And at other times he expresses his claim differently, either as the claim that the truth of moral judgments cannot explain the making of the judgments at all, or as the claim that the truth of moral judgments cannot explain anything whatsoever. Sturgeon argues, in reply, that the truth of moral judgments can explain some things, including why those judgments are made.

But I haven't claimed that explaining value judgments in terms of their truth is obviously impossible or invalid or absurd. Unlike Harman, I have developed a detailed alternative explanation, and I have stated the grounds on which I believe it to be the best—namely, on the grounds of its belonging to a fruitful general theory of agency. All I share with Harman, then, is the fundamental assumption—unchallenged by Sturgeon—that if the best explanation of our making value judgments has nothing to do with their truth, then our faith in their truth should be shaken.

Furthermore, I am not trying to shake anyone's faith in the truth of value judgments. There are surely easier ways of converting people to moral skepticism than by converting them to my theory of agency first. All I am doing here is tracing the consequences of my theory for those who might consider adopting it. One consequence of my theory is that it tends to debunk value judgments, by explaining them without reference to their truth.

will ultimately be unsatisfactory and hence, to the best of our knowledge, false. Things aren't really good or bad—that is, not to the best of our knowledge.

Having acknowledged this much, however, I must add that the apparent falsity of value judgments doesn't entail that our accepting them is a mistake. We often accept theories that fail our test of truth, and we sometimes have good reason for doing so.

Consider, for example, the theory that characterizes evolution as an intelligent agent redesigning species in the interest of their survival. This theory is false, to the best of our knowledge. The best explanation for the evolution of species is that random, heritable variations in a population repeatedly pass through a screen of natural selection. Yet even after we learn the latter theory and perceive its superiority over the former, we go on speaking and thinking of species as having been intelligently designed. There must even be a sense in which we still believe the teleological theory of evolution, since we need to remind ourselves periodically that it's false. Perhaps the best way to put it is that we *make believe* that evolution is an intelligent designer, even though we don't seriously believe it.

Why do we pretend that a theory is true even after we recognize it as false? The reason is that even as we recognize the theory to be false, we see that it is a harmless and convenient proxy for the truth. Thinking of evolution as a bioengineer is easier than thinking of it as a mechanism of variation and selection, and it usually leads to conclusions that are all but true—that is, all but the teleology, which can easily be factored out whenever complete accuracy is required. The false theory is therefore retained for its instrumental value.

My view is that value judgments are believed in the same fashion. That is, we don't seriously believe that things are good or bad, but we make believe that they are, because the pretense is useful for long-term self-inquiry. What makes the pretense useful is that value judgments are convenient proxies for our desires in the procedure by which we pursue personal integration and self-understanding.

That we do not seriously believe things to have value is, of course, a controversial claim. And in fairness to myself, I should point out that I do not strictly need to make this claim, since I could always argue that anyone who does believe seriously in value should simply reform his thinking—not by putting value out of his thoughts, mind you, but rather by replacing his earnest value judgments with the corresponding make-believe. But I happen to think that we are already skeptics about value, at least in our reflective moments. In this respect, moral skepticism differs fundamentally from epistemological skepticism, which rarely enters the ordinary person's head. People who haven't studied philosophy do not usually think that the material world might not exist, but almost everyone is inclined to think, from time to time, that there is no accounting for tastes or that value is in the eye of the beholder.

Why are we naturally skeptical about value? One reason for our skepticism is the absence of intersubjectivity in the results of evaluative reasoning. Although each of us reasons as if we were reasoning about the occurrence of a real property in the world, we find ourselves repeatedly coming to different conclusions, and so we are tempted to concede that there is no such property.[27]

Another reason for our skepticism about value is that evaluative reasoning mimics theoretical reasoning only partially and imperfectly. In particular, evaluative hypotheses aren't tested in quite the same way as ordinary theoretical hypotheses. When we entertain the hypothesis that something is intrinsically good, we are in fact entertaining the possibility of adopting or cultivating an intrinsic desire for that thing. We therefore consider how the complexion of our personality would be altered by the desire in question and how easily and intelligibly we could effect the alteration. We ask, "What would I be like if I wanted this thing?", "How easily could I want it?", "Would that desire make sense for me?" And we try on the new desire partly by trying on the corresponding value judgment, asking ourselves, "What would I be like if I thought this thing was good?"

Now, trying on an hypothesis is a procedure that's common in ordinary theoretical reasoning: it's the procedure of tentatively adopting the hypothesis for the purpose of testing it. But in ordinary theorizing, the hypothesis, once tentatively adopted, is tested against the phenomena that it purports to describe or explain, phenomena conceived as already satisfying or not satisfying the hypothesis independently of whether we adopt it. In evaluative reasoning, by contrast, the hypothesis that something is good doesn't get tested against any phenomenon conceived as independently fixed. When we try on a desire, and the corresponding thought that a thing is good, we don't ask whether the thing answers these tentative feelings or thoughts, nor do we ask whether the feelings or thoughts are already present in us. We often know that even if we don't already desire or approve of the thing spontaneously, we can eventually learn to, and hence that it can come to

---

[27] As Peter Railton has pointed out to me, lack of intersubjectivity in value judgments is no grounds for skepticism about *relational* value—that is, value consisting in a thing's being *good for me*, or *good for you*, and so on. (See Railton's "Moral Realism," and "Facts and Values.")

seem just as desirable as we like. There is thus no antecedent feature of the object, or of our relation to it, against which our evaluative hypothesis gets tested. We have the power to fabricate all the confirmation that an evaluative hypothesis can ever obtain, simply by cultivating a desire or a liking for the object being evaluated. The only question we ask is how coherent a conception of the good we would have, and how intelligible a set of desires, if we molded ourselves into conformity with this hypothesis rather than another.

We are therefore aware that value is our invention rather than a discovery. Developing a theory of what's good is really a matter of inducing ourselves to see things *as* good. And yet when we induce ourselves to see things as good, we induce ourselves to see them as really and objectively good; for we insist on developing a robust and unified theory of value, which looks like a theory of something that's really and objectively there.

A Skeptical Justification of Value-Judgments

Instrumentalism says that we can be perfectly justified in thinking about the good as if it were real despite our awareness that it isn't. Our justification, according to my version of instrumentalism, is that the process of developing a plausible conception of what's good, though not a means of discovering truths, is a means of developing an intelligible set of desires, which is something we'd want whether or not anything was really good. The point of seeking a set of value judgments to believe is not that any such judgments are true; the point is that where there's a believable-looking set of value judgments, there's likely to be an intelligible set of desires, which is what we're really after. Treating value judgments as true is justified not by their actually being true but by the utility of treating them as such.

Instrumentalism about the good thus explains the psychological instability of evaluative skepticism. Our doubts about the existence of value never deter us from thinking about what's valuable. And the explanation is that our motive for thinking about what's valuable is quite independent of the assumption that anything really is. Our motive for thinking about what's valuable is our drive for a stable and coherent conception of ourselves—a drive that is an ineradicable element of our natures as agents, whether value exists or not.

A Skeptical Justification of Practical Reasoning

My views on how we reason about what to do are much the same as my views on how we reason about what to desire. That is, just as we try to figure out what would make the most sense for us to want, so we try to figure out what would make the most sense for us to do, given our desires. And just as we apply the label 'good' to the things that make sense for us to want, so we apply it to the things that make sense for us to do—intellectual satisfactions being our test of value in either case.

The point of applying this test, I believe, is not that intelligibility is a reliable index of real value as instantiated by objects or actions. Nothing is objectively worth desiring, I believe, and neither is anything objectively worth doing, not even in relation to our natures. There are no yellow brick roads, outside of Oz. Nevertheless, I do not think that our test of value in ends or actions requires there to be any such thing. The justification for trying to want or to do what makes most sense is not that we thereby arrive at ends or actions that are objectively correct; it's that we thereby make sense of ourselves, something that we'd want to do whether or not any action was correct.

Indeed, trying to make sense of ourselves is what constitutes us as agents in the first place. To stop seeking the action that makes the most sense would be to stop being an autonomous agent—to abandon the motives in virtue of which one can make decisions, choose preferences or traits of character, make plans. Of course, I am not in a position to say that being an agent is really and objectively a good thing. The most I can say in behalf of practical reasoning is that autonomous agents have no alternative, except to cease being autonomous agents.

ELEVEN

MORALITY

In chapter 10 I confined my attention to consequentialist reasoning, which concerns what's worth desiring and what's worth doing in light of our desires. I claimed that we figure out what's worth desiring by ascertaining what would make sense for us to desire, and that we figure out what's worth doing in light of our desires by ascertaining what would make sense, in light of our desires, for us to do.

I now want to broaden the scope of discussion from consequentialist reasoning to all practical reasoning, which, according to my theory, encompasses more than the pursuit of desired ends. What is the evaluative force of the nonconsequentialist considerations that enter into reflective practical reasoning?

NONEVALUATIVE REASONS

Note, to begin with, that evaluative reasoning, as I have defined it, is not perfectly coextensive with practical reasoning; nor are evaluative considerations perfectly coextensive with reasons for acting. Reflective practical reasoning encompasses not just our efforts to understand our conduct but also our efforts to maintain access to an awareness of what we're doing or are going to do; and reasons for acting include not only considerations in light of which an action would promote our self-understanding but also those in light of which an action would promote our access to self-awareness. The latter efforts and considerations, having nothing to do with our intelligibility, do not invoke the criteria of value that I have now defined.

I think that this discrepancy between the scope of practical reasoning and the scope of evaluative reasoning is (as the programmers say) a feature of my theory rather than a bug. For I think that requiring all practical reasoning or all reasons for acting to have evaluative force would be unrealistic. Practical reasoning has two phases—the phase in which we arrive at a decision and the phase in which we carry it out—and only the former phase is ordinarily evaluative. We evaluate potential actions in the course of deciding what to do; carrying out our decision is a further step of practical reasoning, but it's a step in which further evaluation is not often involved. The decision to act is an intermediate finding to which the action itself is the appropriate final conclusion, and in this sense the decision has a normative force recommending the action, but it doesn't necessarily recommend the action by indicating it to have any additional merits beyond those in response to which the decision itself was made. Hence the normative force of a decision is not evaluative.

The Procedural Claim of Plans

This distinction is clearest, I think, in the case of long-range plans that require subsidiary planning.[1] On the one hand, a plan is a premise that rules out various alternative courses of action by constraining our subsequent reasoning to the evaluation of potential ways of fulfilling the plan. On the other hand, a plan doesn't necessarily constrain our subsequent evaluative reasoning by indicating that actions in fulfillment of the plan would be better than any alternatives. The mere fact that one has planned to see a film rather than a concert, for instance, needn't indicate that seeing the film would be better. The film and the concert might have been equally eligible alternatives, between which one was forced to choose arbitrarily, and one's having chosen the film needn't have elevated it to a status of superiority. Nevertheless, once one has decided upon the film, one's decision stands as a premise from which the rational way to proceed is to figure out how to get to the film. The decision therefore exerts a rational force that isn't evaluative.

Although intentions are reasons for acting, then, and have normative force that influences the will, that force is not necessarily evaluative. I shall therefore say that they are *procedural* rather than *evaluative* reasons. Similarly, the step of reasoning that consists merely in fulfilling or adhering to an intention is a procedural rather than an evaluative step.

Often deliberation mixes procedural and evaluative steps together. The case that I discussed at the end of chapter 9 was one in which the agent's long-established plans exerted a force contrary to that of other reasons. I find this description of the case to be realistic. That is, we often find that a past intention exerts a purely procedural claim upon us—the simple demand that we follow through—and this claim competes with evaluative considerations about the best thing to do here and now. Some will object that an allegiance to past intentions on purely procedural grounds is irrational if it deflects us from the optimal

---

[1] This paragraph draws on the work of Michael Bratman, especially "Taking Plans Seriously" and "Intention and Means-End Reasoning."

course of action. My reply is that reflection on our practices of reasoning reveals that we aren't rigorous optimizers, since we do in fact respect the procedural claim of plans without thinking that it is accompanied by any evaluative force.

Some philosophers would claim that the force of intentions is indeed evaluative. They point out that our susceptibility to the procedural claim of intentions helps us to do what's best on many occasions, by making us respect the outcome of earlier and possibly sounder deliberations, and that it must therefore be tolerated even on those occasions when it deflects us from doing the best thing.[2] I agree that intentions do have this indirect evaluative force, but it is not always exerted and must in any case be secondary to their procedural force. Sometimes we do stick to a plan out of a reflective appreciation for the benefits of fidelity to plans, but often we stick to a plan simply because it's our plan and, as such, has a claim to be carried out. In the latter case, the plan has no evaluative force for us from our perspective within practical reasoning, even though there are evaluative arguments, from another perspective, that support our recognizing the plan's procedural claim. In any case, those evaluative arguments are arguments in favor of recognizing the procedural claim of our plan, and so their evaluative force can bolster but never replace that claim. They would never get started unless we were capable of practical reasoning in which some considerations were treated as procedural rather than evaluative.

The Distinction between Evaluative and Procedural Claims

My theory of practical reasoning draws the distinction between the evaluative and procedural force of reasons by distinguishing between their appeal to our desire for self-understanding and their appeal to our desires for self-awareness. An intention or plan exerts its procedural force, I say, by making the intended action attractive to our desire for the ability to name what we're doing or what we're going to do. Other reasons for acting exert an evaluative force by making an action attractive to our desire for the ability to explain what we're doing. And sometimes a plan can exert an evaluative force as well as its procedural one, when considered in conjunction with an appropriate desire, since considered in that light it can make our adherence to the plan seem intelligible and hence a means to self-understanding as well as self-awareness.

---

[2] This theme is prominent in Elster's *Ulysses and the Sirens*, as well as in some recent work by Michael Bratman.

OTHER DIMENSIONS OF EVALUATION

Even if evaluative reasoning coincides only with our pursuit of self-understanding, it still encompasses more than just consequentialist reasoning. For according to my account, our pursuit of self-understanding leads us to take the action that makes the most sense in light of all our dispositions, including not only our desires but our customs, emotions, and traits of character as well. If we judge an action's value by its intelligibility, as I claim, then customs, emotions, and character traits must reflect on what's best, by our criterion, in the same way as desires.

How Other Dispositions Recommend Action

Once again, I regard this consequence of my theory as a virtue rather than a flaw. For I think that accurate observation of ordinary discourse—observation unbiased by consequentialist philosophy—reveals that we do evaluate actions in light of dispositions other than desires.

Here I must review briefly some arguments that I laid out at length in chapter 9. There I argued that not all dispositions recommend the actions that would manifest them, since some dispositions are in themselves hard to understand, while others face opposition from our desires to suppress or eradicate them. Actions manifesting these dispositions would not be especially intelligible, and insofar as these dispositions fail to make action intelligible, they fail to recommend it. The action that makes the most sense is the one whose incorporation into our current self-conception would yield the best overall self-understanding, and dispositions recommend an action only to the extent that they lend it this sort of intelligibility.

Thus, when I say that we evaluate actions in light of dispositions other than desires, I do not mean that every habit, emotion, or character trait is taken as reflecting favorably on its potential manifestations. Rather, those dispositions which sit comfortably and understandably in our personality and can thus lend intelligibility to their manifestations thereby reflect on the value of those manifestations, given our criterion that the best thing to do is whatever makes the most sense.

What's more, our customs, emotions, and character traits must themselves be regulated by long-term self-inquiry. Surely, information about these dispositions must appear in our standing self-conception, together with information about our desires, and the quest for an intellectually satisfying self-conception must entail modifications in all of its components, and hence in all aspects of ourselves.

Indeed, the intelligibility of any one of these aspects is relative to the others. If our personality is to make sense as a whole, then our desires and emotions must make sense in light of our character, customs, and plans; our plans must make sense in light of our desires, emotions, character, and customs; and so on. Self-inquiry is therefore a process of mutual adjustment among these parts of our personality—all within the constraints imposed by those aspects of our psychological makeup which cannot change.

Hence the customs, emotions, and character traits whose manifestations are likely to make the most sense for us are the ones that we have integrated into our way of life because they belong to the most coherent standing self-conception. Quirks of character and behavioral tics are unlikely to carry any weight, since what makes them quirks and tics is precisely that they aren't integral to our way of life. The dispositions that carry weight in reflective practical reasoning will be the ones that harmonize with all our other dispositions and therefore reside in the core of our personality, as we conceive it.

Of course, different situations call different dispositions into play. In some situations, what makes the most sense is for us to act as pursuers of desired ends and hence to do whatever makes the most sense in light of our desires. In other situations, however, the main order of business is to maintain a custom, express an emotion, or be true to a trait of character, and desires then recede into the background of our deliberations.

I am confident that if the reader will only reflect on the whole of his practical life, rather than on that portion in which the pursuit of goals is most salient, he will find himself evaluating options in light of all of his core dispositions. When you deliberate about how to initiate a conversation, how to respond to an insult, what role to play in your office or extended family; when you plan a vacation or a dinner party; when you choose your friends or your words or your wardrobe—in all of these cases, I'd wager, your evaluative reasoning encompasses more than the means to desired ends. You evaluate the alternatives by the standard of what makes the most sense for you, for all of you, in light of your entire way of life.

Let me examine one of the examples that I have just enumerated: planning a vacation. The consequentialist school of evaluation would teach you to plan a vacation as follows. First, identify the desired outcomes of a vacation: rest, relaxation, entertainment, edification, a good tan, whatever. Next, gauge the degree to which each of these outcomes is desired, or worth desiring, and the degree to which it is likely to be achieved by each of the available vacation packages. Finally, compute the degree of rational-desire satisfaction to be expected from each package and choose the one that scores highest. Voilà: the ideal vacation. (If the foregoing computation is too difficult, the consequentialist method of evaluation has several shortcuts to offer. For a start, try imagining each vacation in its entirety, as a single, complex outcome, and figure out which of these outcomes you desire most.)

Well, I don't plan a vacation by any of these methods. And with some reservations, to be explained momentarily, I'm willing to bet that you don't, either. Naturally, I have various goals for a vacation, and these goals loom large in my deliberations. But other considerations come into play as well. There are my emotions and moods—how carefree or sober I've been feeling this year. There are my traits of character—how frugal or extravagant I am, how phlegmatic or energetic, how cerebral, spiritual, or sensual. There are also my customs—say, my having visited a new country every year, or my having returned every year to the same spot. Such customs don't necessarily override competing considerations, of course. If I'm sick of that same old spot year after year, or of the annual trial-by-novelty, I may consider breaking my custom. But the custom to be broken isn't just a pattern supervening on my past calculations of expected desire-fulfillment, a pattern to be broken with indifference, as the next calculation dictates. A custom has evaluative significance in its own right and is to be broken only on the grounds of significant countervailing considerations.

When I plan a vacation, in short, I work with a complete conception of myself, and I try to find a vacation that fits. When I picture myself touring the Louvre, or cruising the Caribbean, or climbing the Rockies, I'm not just asking myself how much enjoyment or enlightenment or melanin I can amass by these means. I'm asking myself, "Is this *me*?"

How Consequentialists Plan Their Vacations

You plan your vacations likewise, I say—provided that you haven't been corrupted by consequentialist philosophy. And I'm serious about that qualification. For if you think of yourself as a consequentialist, then that component of your self-conception will naturally affect how you deliberate. Whenever you are aware of deliberating—that is, when you deliberate self-consciously—you will be inhibited from considering any reasons that you wouldn't understand considering. And if you think of yourself as given to consequentialist calculation, you will regard nonconsequentialist reasons as making no sense for you to consider, and you will shun them accordingly. You will take only consequentialist considerations into account, as the only ones that make sense for you.

In so doing, of course, you will be engaging un-self-consciously in reflective practical reasoning, and perhaps even in a nonconsequentialist form thereof, since you may well be evaluating ways of thinking in light of your self-ascribed habits of thought. You will be trying to do what makes the most sense for you, as a whole person, although what makes the most sense for you as a whole person, in light of your self-ascribed habits of deliberation, may be trying to do what makes the most sense solely in light of your desires.

Thus, alternative modes of evaluative reasoning can take place within the larger framework of reflective practical reasoning. I am therefore ready to acknowledge that my theory of evaluative reasoning doesn't describe how everyone always reasons about what to do. But I do insist that insofar as you may reason differently, you do so only because you also reason in accordance with my theory, and only within the framework of the latter reasoning. Reflective reasoning is the tide in your evaluative reasoning, I say, even if it stirs up countervailing eddies.

PERSONAL MORALITY

In some of the examples I've enumerated, your evaluation of alternative actions involves moral considerations, and I have not yet explained how my account of evaluative reasoning can encompass morality. My explanation, briefly, is that the dispositions that emerge from long-term self-inquiry tend to include the dispositions that are fundamental to morality. When you ask, about a particular course of action, "Is this *me*?", you are asking in part whether the action would be true to dispositions of yours that are distinctively moral. How self-inquiry yields these dispositions will be my topic for the remainder of this chapter.

I want to avoid taking sides in the controversy over the correct conception of morality, either as it is actually practiced or as it ought to be. Rather, I would like to identify a theme that is common to most conceptions of morality and then to consider the rationality of incorporating that theme into our self-conceptions; the differences among particular variations on the theme will not concern me.

The Theme of Morality

The theme in question is impartiality. Most moral theories enjoin us to treat others on a par with ourselves in some way and to some degree, though the ways and degrees vary among theories. One theory requires us to love others as we love ourselves; another requires us to promote everyone's welfare, not just our own; a third requires us to permit ourselves to do only what we could rationally permit to everyone; and so on. The differences among these theories don't interest me at the moment; what interests me is the similarity, which is that they all prescribe impartiality of some kind.

Focussing on impartiality as the theme of morality will enable me to follow philosophical tradition by comparing the rationality of being moral to that of being prudent. Insofar as morality requires us to treat others on a par with ourselves, it is comparable to prudence, which requires us to treat our future selves on a par with our present self, or future occasions on a par with the present. This similarity has led some philosophers—most notably, Sidgwick[3]—to argue that the same rationality attaches to morality as to prudence. I concur, although I have a different view of rationality from Sidgwick's. My view is that impartiality among persons, like indifference among times, is rational because it gives one access to an unqualified self-conception and hence to a powerful and perspicuous account of one's conduct.

The impartiality of sympathy. Consider, for example, the impartiality that is embodied in universal sympathy for other persons. Sympathy is a trait of character—that is, a disposition to have prevailing desires of particular kinds. A sympathetic person responds to other people's feelings by wanting what he would want in response to the same feelings if they were his own. Encountering pain, he wants to alleviate it; encountering loneliness, he wants to fill it; encountering joy, he wants to prolong it. And these desires are usually strong enough to govern his behavior toward the subjects of these feelings.[4]

(Many people are selectively sympathetic, since they are moved only by the feelings of some people, such as their close family or friends. I am assuming, however, that moral sympathy is unselective and universal, a sympathy for other people as such.)

The presence of universal sympathy in a person affects his self-conception in much the same way as the presence of timeless values such

[3] *Methods of Ethics.* See also Thomas Nagel, *The Possibility of Altruism* (Princeton, 1970).

[4] Here I am ignoring the question whether sympathy requires a measure of empathy—that is, whether a person must vividly imagine or somehow participate in another's pains and pleasures in order to respond as he would to his own. This question concerns the psychological basis of a sympathetic disposition rather than the nature of sympathy itself.

as prudence. Recall that prudence and other values are desires that a person can attribute to himself without indexing their occurrence or their objects to particular times. Similarly, sympathy is a tendency to be moved by various experiences in ways that needn't be indexed to particular persons as the subjects of those experiences. A sympathetic person can therefore conceive of himself as disposed to be moved in various ways by various feelings, irrespective of whose feelings they are—as disposed to want pain alleviated, loneliness filled, enjoyment prolonged. And these universal responses will account for his behavior toward others as well as toward himself. In short, sympathy enhances a person's intrinsic intelligibility, and so it is the sort of disposition that gets cultivated in the course of self-inquiry.

Here I am offering a precise content for the vague suspicion we have that the immoral person, in failing to treat other people as he does himself, is being somehow illogical or inconsistent. Moral philosophers have long struggled with the problem of pinpointing the immoralist's inconsistency, since he certainly isn't guilty of any obvious self-contradiction or deductive fallacy. My proposal is that the immoralist's inconsistency can be diagnosed only by the standards of inductive logic, as formulated in our canons of theory-choice. The immoral agent, in his treatment of persons, makes himself a special case, an exception; and although he doesn't thereby transgress any law of deductive inference, he does transgress a principle of theory-choice—namely, the principle that for the sake of generality and simplicity, a theory should avoid having to provide for special cases and exceptions. In harboring special dispositions toward himself, the immoral agent becomes resistant to a fully general and simple description, thus depriving himself of an intellectually satisfying self-conception.

The inconsistency of someone who lacks sympathy is much like that of someone who lacks prudence: it's an offense to good reasoning in the sense that it prevents him from knowing what he's about. Just as an imprudent person is said not to know what he wants, so an unsympathetic person might be said not to know where he stands on various aspects of human experience—not because he has a stance and doesn't know it, but rather because he has no consistent stance.[5]

[5] Literally speaking, of course, a person whose stance is inconsistent can still know where he stands. I am using this phrase in the same spirit as it bears in the claim that a person of chaotic desires doesn't know what he wants. I explicated this usage in chapter 10, pp. 278–79.

Samuel Scheffler says, "A person whose deepest and most powerful desire is to inflict pain on others, and who acts accordingly, may succeed in establishing a coherent personality" (*The Rejection of Consequentialism: A Philosophical Investigation of the Con-*

I am not claiming here that self-inquiry is what leads people to become sympathetic. People become sympathetic in many different ways, under many different influences. All I am claiming is that being sympathetic is an intrinsically rational state, in the sense that it's a state that self-inquiry would favor. I am not explaining why particular people are moral; I'm explaining why it's rational for them to be so. My guess is that very few people are moral on account of its rationality.

Impartiality toward kinds of behavior.   An agent can also gain intelligibility by cultivating impartiality in his plans—or rather, in a particular kind of plan, which I call policies.

Many plans are not suitable for inclusion in our standing self-conception because they lack the requisite generality. Our standing self-conception is a permanent repository of information that will continually come into play in our reflective reasoning, whereas many plans simply schedule a particular act for a particular date and therefore need to be remembered only on that date, whereupon they are fulfilled and immediately retired from service. Such plans have no place in a lasting theory of ourselves.

Only two kinds of plans, that I can think of, are likely to be worth including in our self-conception. One kind is what some philosophers have called life-plans—that is, overarching plans whose fulfillment will take years, if not a lifetime, and will entail much subsidiary planning. Our life-plans may include long-term commitments to a career, to a family, or to a way of life. Because such plans must enter into our deliberations repeatedly over long periods of time, they belong in our standing self-conception.

Another kind of plan worth including in our self-conception are standing plans of a kind that I call policies. These are plans to the effect that we shall act in a particular way on every occasion of a particular kind. They may include standing plans of always responding to invitations, of never drinking and driving, of turning the other cheek, and so forth. No matter how often we fulfill these plans, they still commit us to future fulfillments, and so they are never completely fulfilled. Being thus perpetually in force, they belong in our standing self-conception, too.

Policies are to plans in general what values are to desires in general.

---

siderations Underlying Rival Moral Conceptions [Oxford, 1982], 18). This is precisely what I am currently denying. I say that a person who profoundly desires others' pain cannot establish a truly coherent personality because he cannot wholeheartedly desire his own pain and hence cannot make his stance toward others coherent with his stance toward himself.

That is, they are plans without temporal qualifications. A policy is a plan that one always has, and it's a plan of doing something always, or never. Self-inquiry therefore favors the development of policies for the same reasons that it favors the development of values—namely, that they enhance the agent's grasp of himself. Just as a stable and coherent set of values enables a person to comprehend what he wants, so a stable and coherent set of policies enables him to comprehend how he behaves.

An agent can gain even more intelligibility by adopting impartial policies toward various kinds of behavior, irrespective of the agent. Rather than adopt one policy of always or never behaving in a particular way and another policy about how to respond to such behavior in other people, an agent can adopt a global policy of favoring or opposing the behavior in question, no matter whose it is. He can have a policy of standing up for truthfulness, say, or never tolerating lies. Of course, such a policy would be rather vague, given its reliance on phrases like 'standing up' and 'not tolerating'. But most long-range plans are vague, in that they commit the agent to a course of action whose precise specification will require subsidiary decisionmaking, and a policy of never tolerating lies would be vague in precisely this way. The agent who adopted such a policy would be leaving open precisely how not to tolerate particular lies on particular occasions. Such openness about the details of execution would not rob the policy of its informativeness or practical force.

Global policies, like impartial responses to feelings, simultaneously enhance the generality and simplicity of one's self-conception. Herein lies the rationality of doing unto others as one would have them do unto oneself. Someone who will tolerate from himself what he won't tolerate from others, or vice versa, might be said not to know what he's willing to tolerate—just as the person without values is said not to know what he wants, and the person without sympathy might be said not to know where he stands on human feelings.[6] Self-inquiry can thus favor cultivating many different kinds of impartiality that are recognizable as moral.

Once again, the foregoing is not intended as an explanation of how particular people become moral. Various people adopt impartial policies of behavior for various, idiosyncratic reasons. All I'm claiming is that the adoption of such policies is rational in that it promotes the

---

[6] As I said in note 5, these people do, literally speaking, have the knowledge in question. A person who is said not to know what he wants does, in fact, know what he wants. He just wants many incompatible things or different things at different times (and he knows it). My point is that the phrase 'not knowing what one wants' seems to reflect the impact that disorder has on a person's grasp of himself.

agent's self-understanding and would therefore be favored by self-inquiry.

The Limits of Impartiality

The question naturally arises why self-inquiry should stop at favoring the aforementioned kinds of impartiality. To be sure, impartial attitudes toward human feelings or to kinds of behavior may give one access to a simpler and more general self-image, but one's attitudes toward feelings or kinds of behavior are not the only dispositions in which impartiality could be cultivated. Why doesn't self-inquiry favor generalizing one's personal ambitions, for instance, to the point of wanting everyone, and not just oneself, to become, say, a world-famous philosopher?

My answer to this question—as to a similar question in the preceding chapter—is twofold.[7] On the one hand, self-inquiry does favor cultivating impartiality wherever one can intelligibly do so. On the other hand, self-inquiry wouldn't lead one to purge oneself of partiality altogether. The reason is that some person-specific dispositions, like some time-specific dispositions, are impossible to shed or make sense for one to keep, because one would be hard pressed to eliminate them or positively wants to retain them. Self-inquiry requires that one become amenable to concise generalizations, but only insofar as one can understand doing so. One's desires for self-knowledge will account for one's introducing some degree of generality into one's motives and policies, especially where the changes required would be otherwise acceptable, but a thorough purge of person-specific attitudes is out of the question.

The Lone Conscience

The account of morality given thus far fills a significant need in the phenomenology of moral life, in my opinion. It explains the rationality of the intensely personal, almost private morality that we sometimes find in people of an original and uncompromising stamp. These people are highly moral, deeply moral, and yet their morality seems to be neither the result nor the cause of any active socialization on their part. They are self-made moral agents who keep their principles to themselves. What marks them as moral is that they know just where they stand, what they'll stand for—and consequently, who they are.

Another mark of such lone consciences, as I call them, is that they are completely innocent of moral theory, or at least of any theory stated in the vocabulary of moral philosophy. They have no need for

---

[7] Pp. 284–85.

high-flown terms like 'right' and 'wrong'. Their moral knowledge is formulated entirely in personal terms, as self-knowledge. It's the knowledge that they just don't do certain things or stand for them from others.

Obviously, not all moral agents fit this mold, and my treatment of morality would be inadequate if it couldn't account for the rationality of a morality that was more social in its motivation and manifestations. However, I think that being unable to account for the rationality of lone consciences would be an equally serious failing. I am skeptical of any metaethical theory according to which the rationality of being moral requires an interest or participation in social conventions, practices of justification, or the like.[8] Some people are intensely moral, in their own way, and yet couldn't give a damn about participating in society or justifying themselves to others.

Having explained the possibility of a lone conscience, however, I shall turn to a more public form of morality. And in order to account for the rationality of public morality, I shall first have to expand my theory of agency.

PUBLIC MORALITY

Thus far in this book I have portrayed the rational agent as a solitary figure, pursuing self-knowledge in isolation from other people. I have thus neglected the phenomena of social decisionmaking and interpersonal coordination. This neglect, which may have troubled the reader all along, must by now have raised an urgent objection in his mind. For how can I suggest that the rationality of our being moral has nothing to do with our sociality?

Well, I haven't really meant to suggest any such thing. My reason for neglecting social interaction until now was simply that I couldn't discuss the relations between agents until I had said enough about agents in isolation, and there has turned out to be so much to say—so much, in fact, that my discussion of interpersonal relations will have to be unduly brief.

Understanding Others

Suppose that a person wants to understand other people as well as himself, and to understand them not just here and now but in the long run. This person will have a motive for developing standing concep-

---

[8] One of the theories I have in mind here is the one sketched by T. M. Scanlon in "Contractualism and Utilitarianism," in *Utilitarianism and Beyond*, ed. Amartya Sen and Bernard Williams (Cambridge, 1982), 103–28.

tions of other people's desires, habits, and traits of character. He'll be moved to develop, say, highly specific conceptions for the people he knows best; general conceptions for various types of personality to be found in the populace at large; and a single, even more general conception applicable to everyone, insofar as universal generalizations are possible.

These conceptions of other people, together with the agent's self-conception, will jointly constitute a theory of human behavior, and this theory will be subject to the same criteria of cognitive merit that I have been applying thus far. That is, the agent in question will seek to maximize simultaneously the generality, simplicity, accuracy, and precision of the potentially explanatory information that he stores about people, including himself.

Naturally, the virtues attainable in a person's theory of human behavior will depend on the intrinsic intelligibility of the phenomena. The more random and incoherent the phenomena of human behavior, the more unwieldy, imprecise, inaccurate, or narrow the agent's theory will have to become. When trying to understand other people, of course, the agent will have little power to influence the intrinsic intelligibility of his explananda, since he can hardly coerce others into making sense to him. Nevertheless, he will retain some influence over his own dispositions, and insofar as these may introduce irregularity or incoherence into the phenomena of human behavior overall, he will be interested in reforming them.

But can a single person's dispositions make a noticeable difference in the overall intelligibility of human behavior? I cannot help but think that the answer is no. Even the most eccentric personality will add only a drop to the ocean of human eccentricity, thus adding only an imperceptible complication to one's overall theory of human behavior.

Yet I cannot help but think, too, that one's overall theory of human behavior is not suited for everyday use. Each of us has compiled personality sketches of innumerable individuals and types—people real and fictional, past and present, intimate and remote. But for the purposes of daily life, we don't need a theory that can encompass the differences between St. Francis and Fagin, Napoleon and Hamlet, Emily Dickinson and Cher. In our workaday intercourse with the people around us, we can dispense with much of what we know by making many simplifying assumptions about what people are like. There are some dispositions that we can be confident of finding in anyone we're likely to encounter, and others that we needn't bother to look for at all. Which of these simplifications we can get away with depends, of course, on which people we are most likely to encounter, and we must have a means of suspending any simplification as soon as we encounter an exception. In the absence of exceptions, however, we work with a specific yet simple—and admittedly false—conception of human nature.

In this latter conception of human nature, I think, the degree of detail and simplicity that we can attain may indeed be significantly affected by the degree of our own eccentricities. Potentially useful rules of thumb may founder on a single exception if it's sufficiently salient; and what could be more salient than ourselves? We therefore have a motive against making ourselves the exception to any regularity found in the personalities around us. For insofar as we participate in those regularities, we can better hone the theoretical tools that serve our daily needs.

Thus, the desire to understand both ourselves and the people around us—the desire for social self-understanding, as I shall call it—favors social conformity. In particular, it encourages us to conform ourselves to any regularities to which the people around us already conform. It doesn't encourage us to become carbon copies of one another. After all, acts of self-reform undertaken for the sake of social self-understanding will have to be intelligible, lest our efforts to understand everyone prevent us from understanding ourselves. And each of us has many motives in light of which undue conformism wouldn't make sense. Hence the desire for social self-understanding, like the desire for individual self-understanding, will oppose our going overboard in pursuit of its object. Nevertheless, it will move us to enhance the intelligibility of human nature in our social vicinity by not diverging from regularities that we can sensibly follow.

Attaining Joint Self-Understanding

Now consider a group of people each of whom seeks to understand the members of the group, himself included. Each person in the group will feel a moderate pressure to fall in with any going regularities, and all are likely to recognize their mutual interest in getting some regularities going. The desire for social self-understanding will therefore provide the members of a group with a motive for finding dispositions on which they can converge. They will have a common motive for developing a shared way of life.

Since a shared way of life is to provide the members of the group with a common understanding of themselves and their fellows, their desire for a common self-understanding will favor a way of life that's intrinsically intelligible. That is, they will have a motive for converging on dispositions that can be represented in a general, simple, accurate, and precise conception of what members of the group are like. These dispositions are likely to be of the same kinds that are favored by individual self-inquiry—that is, unqualified desires, general policies of behavior, and perhaps even life-plans.

Intersubjective good.   The unqualified desires on which a group converges will constitute the group's shared values. And the kinds of shared values that social self-inquiry favors can be called socially rational.

Like any dispositions favored by self-inquiry, socially rational values will tend to have the formal structure of rational beliefs. That is, they will tend to be stable, consistent, coherent, and so on, since values possessing these formal features will enhance the social intelligibility at which social self-inquiry aims. Unlike individually rational values, however, socially rational values will be intersubjective—that is, shared—and so they will bear an additional similarity to rational beliefs. Whereas individual self-inquiry may lead different agents to cultivate different values, social self-inquiry, by its very nature, will lead different agents into evaluative agreement.

Socially rational desires will therefore be especially easy to mirror in beliefs that afford all the intellectual satisfactions that are indicative of truth, by our standards. If the group accompanies every desire developed through social self-inquiry with a belief attributing goodness to the object of that desire, then their beliefs will seem to bear witness to a property that is not only stably and systematically distributed in the world but also publicly observable. The members of a rational group will thus tend to desire as if in response to a real property of things.

I think that the point of divergence between social and individual self-inquiry is the point at which intersubjective goodness and subjective goodness diverge as well. Insofar as we can understand ourselves in terms of a socially developed self-image, we regard ourselves as desiring objects whose goodness is absolute and publicly observable. Insofar as social self-inquiry has fallen short of inducing complete agreement, and we understand ourselves by means of a self-image that isn't shared with those around us, we regard ourselves as desiring objects that are good only for us or only from our perspective. In either case, however, we desire as if in response to a stable and consistently distributed feature of the world—and hence as if in response to a property that's real.

Mutual benevolence and sympathy.   Among the dispositions on which a rational group might converge, mutual benevolence and sympathy are likely to be universally favored. One reason is that each member of the group will stand to gain more from the benevolence and sympathy of others than he stands to lose through his own; another reason is that these are dispositions in which members of the group can be somewhat impartial, and so they can enhance the intrinsic intelligibility of the group's social self-image.

Of course, each person's selfish, nonintellectual motives will favor his becoming a free rider on any convention of benevolence and sympathy by exploiting others' goodwill without reciprocating. But if the people around him have developed conventions of benevolence and sympathy, his desire for social self-understanding will favor participating in those conventions. And if such conventions haven't yet developed, the idea of them will probably occur to most people as suggesting additional dispositions on which they can sensibly converge, thereby enhancing their joint intelligibility. Mutual benevolence and sympathy are therefore likely to become part of the group's solution to a shared epistemic problem—namely, the problem of social understanding.

Here, then, is a rough sketch of another argument for the rationality of being moral. If the members of a group enhanced their joint intelligibility by jointly satisfying some simplifying assumptions about human nature, they would be engaged in a social analog of individual self-inquiry. The dispositions that they would jointly cultivate for this purpose therefore deserve to be called rational, in a social rather than an individual sense. And those dispositions are likely to include the dispositions of morality.

As before, my arguments are not intended as an explanation of how morality actually comes about. They are intended to show that morality *could* come about by a form of practical reasoning and hence that it *is* rational, no matter how it actually emerges.

Mutual trust.   Note here that the social rationality of being benevolent and sympathetic goes hand in hand with the rationality of assuming that people in general are similarly disposed. The members of a social group seek to converge on a set of dispositions so that each of them can understand himself in terms of a theory that accounts for the others as well. The point of developing conventions of mutual benevolence and sympathy, then, is partly to make the social phenomena susceptible to explanation by the simple and general proposition that people are benevolent and sympathetic. There is no point in joining the affective conventions without adopting the theory to which they give application.

Thus, to say that mutual benevolence and sympathy are rational is to tell only half of the story. What's rational is a convention of mutual goodwill and trust—a convention in which everyone expects everyone to be well-intentioned, and everyone lives up to these mutual expectations.

The pursuit of social self-understanding thus helps to account for the familiar interactions between a person's character and his conception of others. It helps to explain, for instance, why trust of others is often a sign of virtue, and suspicion of others, a sign of vice. The reason why people tend to conceive of others in their own image is not just that they lack imagination. It may be that they positively hope for others to be like them, so that their own dispositions may be rationalized—that is, conceived as being in harmony with the social environment and, to that extent, intelligible.

Similarly, the desire for social understanding helps to account for the corrupting influence of vicious company. People are continually molding themselves in the image of others, in order to make the social scene more intelligible. Consequently, if one lives in a dog-eat-dog world, the only way to attain social understanding may be for one to act like a dog.

First-Person Plural Policies

The dispositions on which a group converges may include not only values, such as benevolence, and traits of character, such as sympathy, but policies of behavior as well. Each agent has policies expressed in the first-person singular, specifying how he behaves, and generalizations, expressed in the third-person plural, describing how others behave. But each agent may also realize that he belongs to a group that is seeking common modes of behavior, and so the group may be able to converge on first-person plural policies, specifying how all of them behave. One can then avoid distinguishing between what "I" do and what "they" do, since there will be a simpler representation of what "we" do. The result is a better grasp on how people, including oneself, behave.

Insofar as the resulting descriptions refer to everyone's behavior in the first-person plural, they are not straightforwardly self-fulfilling; their status as intentions is therefore problematic. Although an agent can get himself to do things by adopting a policy of doing them, he cannot exert similar control over the behavior of those around him, unless he occupies a recognized position of authority. In that case, a single agent can indeed decide how everyone is to behave, and he can therefore frame his policies in the first-person plural without hesitation. What I have been imagining, however, is a leaderless group, in which coordination is achieved by each member's efforts to converge with the others. And the question is how any member of such a group could think of himself as deciding how "we" are going to behave.

Part of the answer is that each member of the group can indeed exert a very slight influence on others, insofar as they are attempting to coordinate their policies with everyone's, including his. No policies will ever get adopted if everyone waits for the others to go first. Each person must adopt the policies that he expects others to adopt and can then abandon any one of those policies if it fails to gain sufficient adherents. Since each member of the group knows that a policy will be generally abandoned if its constituency is too small, he can regard his adopting the policy as helping to bolster the constituency needed to keep the policy in place. To that extent, he can think of himself as helping to decide how the group is to behave.

What's more, formulating one's policies in the first-person plural can be appropriate even if one isn't in fact deciding on behalf of the group. The plural form can represent one's intention of affiliating oneself with the group rather than any pretension of guiding it. One's policies about how "we" behave can embody one's decisions to join the group in adhering to particular patterns of behavior.

Among the policies that are most likely to gain a critical mass of adherents are policies of mutual self-restraint and mutual aid. Of course, a group might conceivably converge on policies of mutual interference and neglect, but each member of the group will want to avoid such a convention, simply because he wants the others to treat him with respect and charity. Alternatively, the group might contemplate policies reflecting each member's egoistic inclination to demand respect and charity from others without reciprocating, but such policies would lead everyone to treat himself as an exception, and so they would constitute a less intelligible way of life for everyone than impartial policies. The group is therefore likely to converge on policies of favoring mutual aid and self-restraint, or opposing mutual belligerence and neglect, irrespective of the agent. Everyone will then be able to understand himself, and everyone else, as being for various kinds of civil behavior and against various kinds of incivility.

Beliefs attributing rightness and wrongness to the actions favored or opposed by socially rational policies will, once again, afford all the intellectual satisfactions by virtue of which beliefs pass for true. Rightness and wrongness can therefore be regarded as properties projected onto actions by socially rational policies. A rational group will adopt shared, impartial policies for or against various kinds of behavior as if in response to real properties of that behavior. Rightness or wrongness can be regarded as the properties to which the resulting policies seem to respond.

I therefore regard principles of morality as beliefs corresponding to the impartial policies on which a rational group would converge. Adopting those policies, both jointly and individually, would be a step in social self-inquiry, and so the policies, and the beliefs corresponding to them, are rational.

Here I think that my theory does offer not only an ideal reconstruction of how morality could occur but a realistic explanation of how it does. I believe that much of a child's moral education consists in assimilating first-person plural policies of behavior. My own memories of childhood, I know, include very little discussion of right and wrong and a lot of instruction in how "we" behave. I believe that my instructors were encouraging me to adopt a particular self-image—an image of myself as part of a group that held conventional policies of behavior. They were doing so, I believe, in the knowledge that my self-inquiry would lead me to embrace those policies and to act accordingly. For as I sought to understand my practical and social worlds, I was inclined to retain and fulfill any policies of behavior that enabled me to understand my own behavior on the model of how everyone around me behaved. And like my fellows, I preferred the existing conventions of self-restraint to any conventions of mutual interference.[9]

---

[9] Here is another way to apply the resources of my theory to questions of interpersonal rationality.

Suppose that we sometimes understand social groups in a way that doesn't depend on a prior understanding of their individual members. Suppose, in fact, that we sometimes understand individuals only by regarding them as components of a social unit that we antecedently understand. In that case, we may even understand ourselves, at times, in terms of the groups to which we belong. That is, our self-understanding may be based on our social understanding.

Now, if the members of a group share the same conception of the group, and if they understand themselves in terms of their membership in it, then their self-conceptions may lead them to act in concert. Each member of the group will be inclined to do what he can understand, and what he can understand will be fulfilling his role in the group. Each member will therefore be inclined to do his bit. Here, then, is a possible explanation of how practical reasoning, as I define it, may yield interpersonal coordination.

The question, of course, is how our conception of a group might incorporate the fact that it is governed by a jointly held conception of it. I ought to be in a position to answer this question, since I have already explained how a person's self-conception can include the fact that he's governed by that very conception. Unfortunately, I don't have an account of how we understand groups independently of understanding their members, and so I can make no headway with this proposal at present.

The Status of Morality

Note, finally, that my justification of morality is a skeptical justification. I have explained why we are rational to think and act as if the happiness of others is good, or as if coming to the aid of others is right, whether or not goodness or rightness exist. My explanation is that our beliefs in goodness and rightness acquire the form of truth from the dispositions that they accompany, which acquire that form in turn from the reasoning by which we make sense of ourselves—the reasoning that constitutes us as agents. Being moral is the ultimate form of making sense, which is the foundation of our practical nature.

BIBLIOGRAPHY

Alexander, Peter. "Rational Behaviour and Psychoanalytic Explanation." *Mind* 71 (1962); 326–41.

Anscombe, G.E.M. *Intention.* Ithaca, N.Y.: Cornell University Press, 1963.

———. "Thought and Action in Aristotle." In *New Essays on Plato and Aristotle*, edited by Renford Bambrough, 143–58. London: Routledge & Kegan Paul, 1965.

———. "Under a Description." *Nous* 13 (1979): 219–33.

Aristotle. *Basic Works.* Edited by Richard McKeon. New York: Random House, 1941.

Audi, Robert. "Psychoanalytic Explanation and the Concept of Rational Action." *Monist* 56 (1972): 444–64.

———. "Intending." *Journal of Philosophy* 70 (1973): 387–403.

———. "Acting for Reasons." *Philosophical Review* 95 (1986): 511–46.

Aune, Bruce. *Reason and Action.* Dordrecht: D. Reidel, 1977.

———. "Castañeda on Believing and Intending." In *Agent, Language and the Structure of the World*, edited by James Tomberlin, 223–29. Indianapolis: Hackett, 1983.

Austin, John. *Lectures on Jurisprudence; Or the Philosophy of Positive Law.* London: John Murray, 1911.

Baier, Annette. "Theory and Reflective Practices." In *Postures of the Mind: Essays on Mind and Morals.* Minneapolis: University of Minnesota Press, 1985, 207–27.

———. "Act and Intent." *Journal of Philosophy* 67 (1970): 648–58.

Baier, Kurt. *The Moral Point of View.* Ithaca, N.Y.: Cornell University Press, 1958.

———. "The Social Source of Reason." *Proceedings of the American Philosophical Association* 51 (1978): 707–33.

Beardsley, Monroe. "Intending." In *Values and Morals: Essays in Honor of William Frankena, Charles Stevenson, and Richard Brandt*, edited by Alvin I. Goldman and Jaegwon Kim, 163–84. Dordrecht: D. Reidel, 1978.

Benn, S. I., and Gaus, G. F. "Practical Rationality and Commitment." *American Philosophical Quarterly* 23 (1986): 255–66.

Bentham, Jeremy. *An Introduction to the Principles of Morals and Legislation.* 1823. Reprint. New York: Hafner, 1948.

Binkley, Robert; Bronaugh, Richard; and Marras, Ausonio, eds. *Agent, Action, and Reason.* Toronto: University of Toronto Press, 1971.

Boër, Steven E., and Lycan, William G. "Who, Me?" *Philosophical Review* 89 (1980): 427–66.

Brand, Myles. "Intending and Believing." *Agent, Language, and the Structure of the World*, edited by James Tomberlin, 171–93. Indianapolis: Hackett, 1983.

———. *Intending and Acting: Toward a Naturalized Action Theory.* Cambridge, Mass.: MIT Press, 1984.

Brand, Myles. "Intentional Actions ańd Plans." *Midwest Studies in Philosophy* (University of Minnesota Press) 10 (1986): 213–30.

Brand, Myles, and Walton, Douglas, eds. *Action Theory*. Dordrecht: D. Reidel, 1976.

Brandt, Richard, and Kim, Jaegwon. "Wants as Explanations of Actions." *Journal of Philosophy* 60 (1963): 425–35.

Brandt, Richard B., "Traits of Character: A Conceptual Analysis." *American Philosophical Quarterly* 7 (1970): 23–37.

———. *A Theory of the Good and the Right*. Oxford: Clarendon, 1979.

Bratman, Michael. "Simple Intention." *Philosophical Studies* 36 (1979): 245–59.

———. "Intention and Means-End Reasoning." *Philosophical Review* 90 (1981): 252–65.

———. "Castañeda's Theory of Thought and Action." In *Agent, Language, and the Structure of the World*, edited by James Tomberlin, 149–69. Indianapolis: Hackett, 1983.

———. "Taking Plans Seriously." *Social Theory and Practice* 9 (1983): 271–87.

———. "Two Faces of Intention." *Philosophical Review* 93 (1984): 375–405.

———. "Davidson's Theory of Intention." In *Actions and Events*, edited by Ernest Lepore and Brian McLaughlin, 14–28. Oxford: Blackwell, 1985.

Bricker, Phillip. "Prudence." *Journal of Philosophy* 77 (1980): 381–401.

Campbell, C. A. *On Selfhood and Goodhood*. London: George, Allen & Unwin, 1957.

Canfield, John. "Knowing about Future Decisions." *Analysis* 22 (1962): 127–29.

Castañeda, Hector-Neri. "Intentions and Intending." *American Philosophical Quarterly* 9 (1972): 139–49.

———. *Thinking and Doing: The Philosophical Foundations of Institutions*. Dordrecht: D. Reidel, 1975.

———. Replies to Michael Bratman and Bruce Aune. In *Agent, Language, and the Structure of the World*, edited by James Tomberlin, 395–409, 435–40. Indianapolis: Hackett, 1983.

Chisholm, Roderick M. "Freedom and Action." In *Freedom and Determinism*, edited by Keith Lehrer, 11–44. New York: Random House, 1966.

———. "The Structure of Intention." *Journal of Philosophy* 67 (1970): 633–47.

———. *The First Person: An Essay on Reference and Intentionality*. Minneapolis: University of Minnesota Press, 1981.

———. "Human Freedom and the Self." In *Free Will*, edited by Gary Watson, 24–35. Oxford: Oxford University Press, 1982.

Churchland, Paul M. "The Logical Character of Action-Explanations." *Philosophical Review* 79 (1970): 214–36.

———. *Scientific Realism and the Plasticity of Mind*. New York: Cambridge University Press, 1979.

———. "Eliminative Materialism and the Propositional Attitudes." *Journal of Philosophy* 78 (1981): 67–90.

Cramer, Konrad. "Hypothetische Imperative?" In *Rehabilitierung der praktischen Philosophie*, edited by M. Riedel, vol. 1. Freiburg, 1972.

Danto, Arthur C. "Action, Knowledge, and Representation." In *Action The-*

ory, edited by Myles Brand and Douglas Walton, 11–25. Dordrecht: D. Reidel, 1976.

Darwall, Stephen L. *Impartial Reason*. Ithaca, N.Y.: Cornell University Press, 1983.

Davidson, Donald. *Essays on Actions and Events*. Oxford: Clarendon, 1980.

———. "Reply to David Pears." In *Essays on Davidson*, edited by Bruce Vermazen and Merrill B. Hintikka, 211–17. Oxford: Clarendon, 1985.

Davis, Lawrence H. *Theory of Action*. Englewood Cliffs, N.J.: Prentice-Hall, 1979.

———. "Wayward Causal Chains." In *Action and Responsibility*, edited by Michael Bradie and Myles Brand, 55–65. Bowling Green, Ohio: Philosophy Documentation Center, 1980.

Davis, Wayne A. "A Causal Theory of Intending." *American Philosophical Quarterly* 21 (1984): 43–54.

Dennett, Daniel C. *Elbow Room; The Varieties of Free Will Worth Wanting*. Cambridge, Mass.: MIT Press, 1984.

Dent, N.J.H. *The Moral Psychology of the Virtues*. Cambridge: Cambridge University Press, 1984.

Donnellan, Keith S. "Knowing What I am Doing." *Journal of Philosophy* 60 (1963): 401–9.

Elster, Jon. *Ulysses and the Sirens: Studies in Rationality and Irrationality*. Cambridge: Cambridge University Press, 1979.

———. *Sour Grapes: Studies in the Subversion of Rationality*. Cambridge: Cambridge University Press, 1983.

———. "The Nature and Scope of Rational-Choice Explanation." In *Actions and Events*, edited by Ernest Lepore and Brian McLaughlin, 60–72. Oxford, Blackwell, 1985.

Fleming, Brice Noel. "On Intention." *Philosophical Review* 73 (1964): 301–20.

Foot, Philippa. "Reasons for Action and Desires." *Proceedings of the Aristotelian Society, Supplementary Volumes* 46 (1972): 203–10.

Frankfurt, Harry G. "Freedom of the Will and the Concept of a Person." In *Free Will*, edited by Gary Watson, 81–95. Oxford: Oxford University Press, 1971.

———. "The Problem of Action." *American Philosophical Quarterly* 15 (1978): 157–62.

Friedman, Michael. "Explanation and Scientific Understanding." *Journal of Philosophy* 71 (1974): 5–19.

Gauthier, David P. "How Decisions Are Caused." *Journal of Philosophy* 64 (1967): 147–51.

———. "How Decisions Are Caused (But Not Predicted)." *Journal of Philosophy* 65 (1968): 170–71.

Gibbard, Allan. "A Noncognitivistic Analysis of Rationality in Action." *Social Theory and Practice* 9 (1983): 199–222.

Gilbert, Margaret. "Vices and Self-Knowledge." *Journal of Philosophy* 68 (1971): 443–53.

Ginet, Carl. "Can the Will Be Caused?" *Philosophical Review* 71 (1962): 49–55.

Glover, Jonathan. "Self-Creation." *Proceedings of the British Academy* 69 (1983): 445–71.

Goldman, Alvin I. *A Theory of Human Action*. Princeton: Princeton University Press, 1970.

———. "The Volitional Theory Revisited." In *Action Theory*, edited by Myles Brand and Douglas Walton, 67–84. Dordrecht: D. Reidel, 1976.

Grandy, Richard E., and Darwall, Stephen L. "On Schiffer's Desires." *Southern Journal of Philosophy* 17 (1979): 193–98.

Grice, H. P. "Intention and Uncertainty." *Proceedings of the British Academy* 57 (1971): 263–79.

Hamlyn, David W. "Unconscious Intentions." *Philosophy* 46 (1971): 12–22.

———. "Self-Knowledge." In *The Self*, edited by Theodore Mischel, 170–200. Totowa, N.J.: Rowman and Littlefield, 1977.

Hampshire, S[tuart]. "Fallacies in Moral Philosophy." *Mind* 58 (1949): 466–82.

———. *Thought and Action*. London: Chatto and Windus, 1959.

———. "Reply to Walsh on Thought and Action." *Journal of Philosophy* 60 (1963): 410–24.

———. *Freedom of the Individual*. Princeton: Princeton University Press, 1975.

Hampshire, Stuart, and Hart, H.L.A. "Decision, Intention and Certainty." *Mind* 67 (1958): 1–12.

Hare, R. M. "Wanting: Some Pitfalls." In *Agent, Action, and Reason*, edited by Robert Binkley, Richard Bronaugh, and Ausonio Marras, 81–97. Toronto: University of Toronto Press, 1971.

———. *Moral Thinking; Its Method, Levels and Point*. Oxford: Clarendon, 1981.

Harman, Gilbert. "Practical Reasoning." *Review of Metaphysics* 29 (1976): 431–63.

———. *The Nature of Morality: An Introduction to Ethics*. New York: Oxford University Press, 1977.

———. "Rational Action and the Extent of Intentions." *Social Theory and Practice* 9 (1983): 123–41.

———. "Logic and Reasoning." *Synthese* 60 (1984): 107–27.

———. *Change in View: Principles of Reasoning*. Cambridge: MIT Press, 1986.

———. "Moral Explanations of Natural Facts—Can Moral Claims Be Tested against Moral Reality?" *Southern Journal of Philosophy* 24 (1986): 57–68.

———. "Willing and Intending." In *Philosophical Grounds of Rationality; Intentions, Categories, Ends*, edited by Richard E. Grandy and Richard Warner, 363–80. Oxford: Oxford University Press, 1986.

Hempel, Carl G. *Aspects of Scientific Explanation, and Other Essays in the Philosophy of Science*. New York: The Free Press, 1965.

Hofstadter, Douglas R. "Can Inspiration Be Mechanized?" *Scientific American* 247 (1982): 18–34.

Hornsby, Jennifer. *Actions*. London: Routledge & Kegan Paul, 1980.

Hume, David. *A Treatise of Human Nature*. Edited by P. H. Nidditch. Oxford: Clarendon, 1978.

James, William. *The Principles of Psychology*. 1890. Reprint. New York: Dover, 1950.

————. "The Will to Believe." In *Essays on Faith and Morals*, edited by Ralph Barton Perry, 32–62. New York: New American Library, 1962.

Jenkins, John J. "Motive and Intention." *Philosophical Quarterly* 15 (1965): 155–64.

Jones, O. R. "Things Known Without Observation." *Proceedings of the Aristotelian Society* 61 (1961): 129–50.

Kant, Immanuel. *Groundwork of the Metaphysic of Morals*. Translated by H. J. Paton. New York: Harper and Row, 1964.

Kenny, Anthony. *Action, Emotion and Will*. London: Routledge & Kegan Paul, 1963.

————. *The God of the Philosophers*. Oxford: Clarendon, 1979.

Kierkegaard, Søren. *Either/Or*. Translated by Walter Lowrie. Princeton: Princeton University Press, 1946.

Kim, Jaegwon. "Intention and Practical Inference." In *Essays on Explanation and Understanding*, edited by Juha Manninen and Raimo Tuomela, 249–69. Dordrecht: D. Reidel, 1976.

Kneale, W. C. "The Idea of Invention." *Proceedings of the British Academy* 41 (1955): 85–108.

Kolnai, Aurel. "Deliberation Is of Ends." In *Ethics, Value, and Reality*, 44–62. London: Athlone, 1977.

LePore, Ernest, and McLaughlin, Brian, eds. *Actions and Events: Perspectives on the Philosophy of Donald Davidson*. Oxford: Blackwell, 1985.

Lewis, David K. "Attitudes *De Dicto* and *De Se*." *Philosophical Review* 88 (1979): 513–43.

Locke, Don. "Reasons, Wants, and Causes." *American Philosophical Quarterly* 11 (1974): 169–79.

MacIntyre, Alasdair. "The Antecedents of Action." In *Against the Self-Images of the Age; Essays on Ideology and Philosophy* (New York: Schocken Books, 1971), 191–210.

MacKay, D. M. "On the Logical Indeterminacy of a Free Choice." *Mind* 69 (1960): 31–40.

Martin, C. B. "Knowledge without Observation." *Canadian Journal of Philosophy* 1 (1971): 15–24.

McCann, Hugh J. "Rationality and the Range of Intention." *Midwest Studies in Philosophy* (University of Minnesota Press) 10 (1986): 191–211.

McGinn, Colin. *The Character of Mind*. New York: Oxford University Press, 1982.

Meiland, Jack. *The Nature of Intention*. London: Methuen, 1970.

Melden, A. I. *Free Action*. London: Routledge & Kegan Paul, 1961.

Mele, Alfred R. "Intentional Action and Wayward Causal Chains: The Problem of Tertiary Waywardness." *Philosophical Studies* 51 (1987): 55–60.

————. "Are Intentions Self-Referential?" *Philosophical Studies* 52 (1987): 309–29.

Milligan, D. E. "Reasons As Explanations." *Mind* 83 (1974): 180–93.

Mischel, Theodore. "Concerning Rational Behaviour and Psychoanalytic Explanation." *Mind* 74 (1965): 71–78.

————, ed. *The Self: Psychological and Philosophical Issues*. Totowa, N.J.: Rowman and Littlefield, 1977.

Mitchell, Dorothy. "Deviant Causal Chains." *American Philosophical Quarterly* 19 (1982): 351–53.

Morton, Adam. *Frames of Mind: Constraints on the Common-sense Conception of the Mental.* Oxford: Clarendon, 1980.

Mullane, Harvey. "Psychoanalytic Explanation and Rationality." *Journal of Philosophy* 68 (1971): 413–26.

Nagel, Thomas. *The Possibility of Altruism.* Princeton: Princeton University Press, 1970.

Nisbett, Richard, and Ross, Lee. *Human Inference: Strategies and Shortcomings of Social Judgment.* Englewood Cliffs, N.J.: Prentice-Hall, 1980.

O'Connor, John. "How Decisions Are Predicted." *Journal of Philosophy* 64 (1967): 429–30.

O'Shaughnessy, Brian. "Observation and the Will." *Journal of Philosophy* 60 (1963): 367–92.

———. *The Will: a Dual Aspect Theory.* Cambridge: Cambridge University Press, 1980.

Oakeshott, Michael. *Rationalism in Politics and Other Essays.* New York: Basic Books, 1962.

Oldenquist, Andrew. "Causes, Predictions and Decisions." *Analysis* 24 (1964): 55–58.

Passmore, J. A., and Heath, P. L. "Intentions." *Proceedings of the Aristotelian Society, Supplementary Volumes* 29 (1955): 131–64.

Paton, H. J. *The Categorical Imperative: a Study in Kant's Moral Philosophy.* Philadelphia: University of Pennsylvania Press, 1971.

Peacocke, Christopher. "Deviant Causal Chains." *Midwest Studies in Philosophy* (University of Minnesota Press) 4 (1979): 123–56.

———. "Intention and *Akrasia*." In *Essays on Davidson,* edited by Bruce Vermazen and Merrill B. Hintikka, 51–73. Oxford: Clarendon, 1985.

Pears, David. "Predicting and Deciding." *Proceedings of the British Academy* 50 (1964): 193–227.

———. "Comment" [on R. M. Hare, "Wanting: Some Pitfalls"]. In *Agent, Action, and Reason,* edited by Robert Binkley, Richard Bronaugh, and Ausonio Marras, 108–27. Toronto: University of Toronto Press, 1971.

———. "Intentions as Judgements." In *Philosophical Subjects; Essays Presented to P. F. Strawson,* edited by Zak van Straaten, 222–37. Oxford: Clarendon, 1980.

———. *Motivated Irrationality.* Oxford: Clarendon, 1984.

———. "Intention and Belief." In *Essays on Davidson,* edited by Bruce Vermazen and Merrill B. Hintikka, 753–88. Oxford: Clarendon, 1985.

Perry, David L. "Prediction, Explanation and Freedom." *Monist* 49 (1965): 234–47.

Perry, John. "Frege on Demonstratives." *Philosophical Review* 86 (1977): 474–97.

———. "The Problem of the Essential Indexical." *Nous* 13 (1979): 3–21.

Powell, Betty. *Knowledge of Actions.* New York: Humanities Press, 1967.

Railton, Peter. "Moral Realism." *Philosophical Review* 95 (1986): 163–207.

———. "Facts and Values." *Philosophical Topics* 14 (1986): 5–31.

Rankin, K. W. "Critical Notice" [on G. E. M. Anscombe's *Intention*]. *Mind* 68 (1959): 261–64.

———. "The Non-Causal Self-Fulfillment of Intention." *American Philosophical Quarterly* 9 (1972): 279–89.

Rawls, John. *A Theory of Justice.* Cambridge: Harvard University Press, 1971.

Raz, Joseph. *Practical Reason and Norms*. London: Hutchinson, 1975.
————. "Reasons for Action, Decisions and Norms." *Mind* 84 (1975): 481–99.
Regan, Donald. "Against Evaluator Relativity: A Response to Sen." *Philosophy and Public Affairs* 12 (1983): 93–112.
Robins, Michael H. "Deviant Causal Chains and Non-Basic Action." *Australasian Journal of Philosophy* 62 (1984): 265–84.
————. *Promising, Intending and Moral Autonomy*. Cambridge: Cambridge University Press, 1984.
Roxbee Cox, J. W. "Can I Know Beforehand What I Am Going to Decide?" *Philosophical Review* 72 (1963): 88–92.
Ryle, Gilbert. *The Concept of Mind*. New York: Barnes and Noble, 1949.
Salmond, Sir John. *Jurisprudence*. London: Sweet & Maxwell, 1930.
Sartre, Jean-Paul. *Being and Nothingness: An Essay on Phenomenological Ontology*. Translated by Hazel E. Barnes. New York: Philosophical Library, 1956.
Scanlon, T. M. "Contractualism and Utilitarianism." In *Utilitarianism and Beyond*, edited by Amartya Sen and Bernard Williams, 103–28. Cambridge: Cambridge University Press, 1982.
Scheffler, Samuel. *The Rejection of Consequentialism; A Philosophical Investigation of the Considerations Underlying Rival Moral Conceptions*. Oxford: Clarendon, 1982.
Schiffer, Stephen. "A Paradox of Desire." *American Philosophical Quarterly* 13 (1976): 195–203.
Searle, John R. *Expression and Meaning: Studies in the Theory of Speech Acts*. Cambridge: Cambridge University Press, 1979.
————. *Intentionality: An Essay in the Philosophy of Mind*. Cambridge: Cambridge University Press, 1983.
Sellars, Wilfrid. *Science and Metaphysics: Variations on Kantian Themes*. London: Routledge & Kegan Paul, 1968.
————. "Action and Events." *Nous* 7 (1973): 179–202.
————. "Volitions Reaffirmed." In *Action Theory*, edited by Myles Brand and Douglas Walton, 47–66. Dordrecht: D. Reidel, 1976.
Sidgwick, Henry. *The Methods of Ethics*. Indianapolis: Hackett, 1981.
Sorensen, Roy A. "Uncaused Decisions and Pre-Decisional Blindspots." *Philosophical Studies* 45 (1984): 51–56.
Stich, Stephen P. *From Folk Psychology to Cognitive Science: The Case against Belief*. Cambridge: MIT Press, 1983.
Stoutland, Frederick. "The Logical Connection Argument." *American Philosophical Quarterly Monograph Series* 4 (1970): 117–29.
Strawson, Peter F. *Individuals*. London: Methuen, 1959.
————. *Studies in the Philosophy of Thought and Action*. Oxford: Oxford University Press, 1968.
Sturgeon, Nicholas. "Brandt's Moral Empiricism." *Philosophical Review* 91 (1982): 389–422.
————. "Moral Explanations." In *Morality, Reason and Truth*, edited by David Copp and David Zimmerman, 49–78. Totowa, N.J.: Rowman and Allenheld, 1984.
————. "Harman on Moral Explanations of Natural Facts." *Southern Journal of Philosophy* 24 (1986): 69–78.

Taylor, Charles. "What is Human Agency?" In *The Self*, edited by Theodore Mischel, 103–35. Totowa, N.J.: Rowman and Littlefield, 1977.

———. "Responsibility for Self." In *Free Will*, edited by Gary Watson, 111–26. Oxford: Oxford University Press, 1982.

Taylor, Richard. "Deliberation and Foreknowledge." *American Philosophical Quarterly* 1 (1964): 73–80.

———. *Metaphysics*. Englewood Cliffs, N.J.: Prentice-Hall, 1983.

Thalberg, Irving. "Intending the Impossible." *Australasian Journal of Philosophy* 40 (1962): 49–56.

———. "Do Our Intentions Cause Our Intentional Actions?" *American Philosophical Quarterly* 21 (1984): 249–60.

Tomberlin, James E., ed. *Agent, Language, and the Structure of the World: Essays Presented to Hector-Neri Castañeda, with His Replies*. Indianapolis: Hackett, 1983.

Toulmin, Stephen E. "Reasons and Causes." In *Explanation in the Behavioural Sciences*, edited by Robert Borger and Frank Cioffi, 1–26. London: Cambridge University Press, 1969.

———. "Self-Knowledge and Knowledge of the 'Self'." In *The Self*, edited by Theodore Mischel, 291–317. Totowa, N.J.: Rowman and Littlefield, 1977.

van Fraassen, Bas C. *The Scientific Image*. Oxford: Clarendon, 1980.

Vermazen, Bruce, and Hintikka, Merrill B., eds. *Essays on Davidson: Actions and Events*. Oxford: Clarendon, 1985.

von Wright, Georg Henrik. *Explanation and Understanding*. Ithaca, N.Y.: Cornell University Press, 1971.

Warnock, G. J. *The Object of Morality*. London: Methuen, 1971.

Watson, Gary. "Free Agency." *Journal of Philosophy* 72 (1975): 205–20.

———, ed. *Free Will*. Oxford: Oxford University Press, 1982.

Wiggins, David. "Freedom, Knowledge, Belief and Causality." In *Knowledge and Necessity*, edited by G.N.A. Vesey, 132–54. London: Macmillan, 1970.

———. "Deliberation and Practical Reason." *Proceedings of the Aristotelian Society* 76 (1975): 29–51.

Wilkes, K. V. *Physicalism*. New York: Humanities Press, 1978.

Williams, Bernard. "Deciding to Believe." In *Problems of the Self* (Cambridge: Cambridge University Press, 1973), 136 - 151.

Wilson, George M. *The Intentionality of Human Action*. Vol. 31 of *Acta Philosophica Fennica* (Amsterdam: D. Reidel, 1980).

———. "Davidson on Intentional Action." In *Actions and Events*, edited by Ernest LePore and Brian McLaughlin, 29–43. Oxford: Blackwell, 1985.

Winters, Barbara. "Believing at Will." *Journal of Philosophy* 76 (1979): 243–56.

Wittgenstein, Ludwig. *Philosophical Investigations*. Translated by G.E.M. Anscombe. Oxford: Blackwell, 1967.

INDEX

absentmindedness, 27, 52n, 71–72
acting with an intention, 110–11. *See also* intention
action: causes of (*see* psychological causation); as conclusion, 92–94, 198; individuation of, 16n, 28n; metaphysics of, 101n
akrasia. *See* weakness of will
Alexander, Peter, 193n
Anscombe, G.E.M., 5, 16n, 18–22, 23n, 25, 69–70, 93n, 99n, 102–5, 109n, 113, 130, 132n, 191n, 194n; doctor example, 61–62, 64, 65n, 89–90, 99–100, 104–5, 155–58
Aquinas, Thomas, 102
Aristotle, 92, 136, 258n
Armstrong, D. M., 102n
Audi, Robert, 113n, 193n
Aune, Bruce, 99n, 201n
Austin, John, 113n, 121n
autonomy, 7–8, 173–88, 235; and foreknowledge, 9, 81–82; over one's future, 9, 226; over preferences, 9, 75n, 178–86, 246–47, 248–49, 255–56, 258–59; over traits of character, 9, 248–49, 251–53, 255–56, 258–59

bad faith, 82–83, 170–72, 173, 251–53
Baier, Annette C., 112n, 159n, 290n
Baier, Kurt, 193n, 206n
Beardsley, Monroe C., 113n
beliefs: as reasons for acting, 192–96, 199–200, 209–11; complexity of, 88, 125–26; how recognized by subject, 3n, 67–69, 126n; self-fulfilling, 63–64, 85n, 128–36; self-referring, 88n. *See also* motives
believing at will, 66n, 127–36
Benn, S. I., and Gaus, G. F., 62n, 113n
Bentham, Jeremy, 289n
book of life, 153–58, 162–63
Brand, Myles, 114, 125–26, 142n, 229n, 273n

Brandt, Richard B., 16n, 243n, 244n, 269n, 287n
Bratman, Michael, 111, 114n, 115n, 124–25, 126n, 200n, 201n, 232n, 233n, 299n, 300n
Bricker, Phillip, 284n

Campbell, C. A., 144n
Canfield, John, 164n
Castañeda, Hector-Neri, 99n, 112n, 114n, 121n
causation, psychological. *See* psychological causation
character traits: as reasons for acting, 249–50, 255–57, 301–4; defined, 243–44; explain desires, 245; sympathy, 253, 305–7, 313–14; undesirable, 248–49, 251–53, 255, 301
Chisholm, Roderick M., 97n, 113n, 144n
Churchland, Paul M., 16n, 273n
"cognitive psychotherapy," 287, 288
commands, 61, 99–100, 103–4, 191
commonsense psychology, 3–4, 16n, 136, 223–24, 242–45; as a theory, 272–73
conditioning, as an explanation of desires, 243
constancy, 221–22, 224–29, 254–55
Cox, J. W. Roxbee, 164n
Cramer, Konrad, 176n
custom. *See* habit

Danto, Arthur C., 19n, 95n, 102n
Darwall, Stephen L., 190n, 193n
Davidson, Donald, 16n, 97n, 101n, 109n, 114–24, 192–94
Davis, Lawrence H., 18n, 97n, 113n
Davis, Wayne A., 113n, 115n
deciding to believe. *See* believing at will
decision, 144–45, 166–67
deliberation: creative, 9, 257–59; about the future, 236–40
Dent, N.J.H., 193n, 282n
"desirability characteristics," 194n

327

Hamlyn, David W., 18n, 38n
Hampshire, Stuart, 5, 18n, 61n, 98n,
113n, 121n, 127n, 129n, 164n, 223,
258n; and H.L.A. Hart, 18n, 25n, 61,
164n
happiness, 38n, 285–86
Hare, R. M., 99n, 287n
Harman, Gilbert, 61n, 69n, 94n, 97n,
108n, 109, 112n, 113–17, 121, 124n,
126n, 131–32, 132n, 231n, 293n
Heath, P. L., 140n
Hofstadter, Douglas, 242n
Hornsby, Jennifer, 101n
Hume, David, 31n, 44, 160–61
hypothetical explanation, 5–8, 76–77,
241–42, 270–71

insomnia, 132–34
intention, 109–42; acting with an intention, 110–11, 112, 115–16, 126;
agent's knowledge of, 137, 141, 181n;
conditional, 117–21; content of, 86–
90, 96–98, 121n, 140–41, 181, 200,
201, 209, 218; defective cases of, 136–
40, 184–85, 252–53; defined as state
of being decided, 111–13, 115–17,
126, 143; defining features of, 94–98,
136–37; entails belief, 113–21; ineffective, 137–38, 201–2; and intentional
action, 110–11, 116–17; as locus of
self-awareness, 98n, 102–5, 141–42,
174, 200, 209, 237; a mental state?
109–13; negative, 96n; as reasons for
acting, 124–25, 200–202, 208–9; reasons for, 122–24; reflective command,
99–100, 103; as reflective description,
180–81, 246, 252–53, 255; as reflective expectation, 9, 12, 94–100, 121–
42, 147–58, 170, 171, 173–74, 215–
16; is self-referring, 96–98; unconscious, 137, 149n, 252–53; versus
goal, 112, 115–17, 126, 137n; versus
prediction (see predicting versus deciding). See also plans
intentional action, 110; versus foreseen
consequence, 113. See also intention
intention to act out of habit, 138–40
intention to adopt a preference, 180–85,
246–47, 248, 249, 251, 255–56
intention to alter one's character, 251,
252–53, 255–56

intuitionism, 268

James, William, 63–64, 71n, 72n, 140n,
142, 258–59
Jenkins, John J., 140n
Jones, O. R., 19n, 103n

Kant, Immanuel, 175–76
Kenny, Anthony, 18n, 25n, 99n, 102n
Kim, Jaegwon, 16n, 113n
Kneale, W. C., 91n
"knowledge without observation," 18–
22, 102

Locke, Don, 193n

McCann, Hugh J., 114n, 115–16, 121n
McGinn, Colin, 114n
MacKay, D. M., 164n
Martin, C. B., 19n
masochism, 288–89
mauvaise foi. See bad faith
Meiland, Jack, 113n, 121n
Melden, A. I., 18n, 25n
Mele, Alfred R., 97n
Mill, John Stuart, 287n
Milligan, D. E., 193n
Mischel, Theodore, 193n
Mitchell, Dorothy, 97n
monomania, 283–85
morality: impartiality as theme of, 304–
5, 306, 308; and mutual trust, 314–15;
projectivist theory of, 10, 291–96,
316–17, 318; rationality of, 305–7,
308–9, 310, 314, 316–17
Morton, Adam, 273n
motives, 16n; for acting versus for getting
oneself to act, 75; as causes of action,
(see psychological causation); for expecting an action, 65–66, 150; explain
actions, 40; as reasons for acting, 192–
96, 199–200, 209–11, 238–40, 247,
265; recognized by agent, 23–24, 30,
37–38, 67–69; unconscious, 33–35,
138, 179, 184, 192–93
Mullane, Harvey, 193n

Nagel, Thomas, 305n
Nisbett, Richard, and Lee Ross, 17n
normativity, 6–8, 189, 190–92, 196,

normativity (*cont.*)
   197, 204–8, 209–11, 238, 248, 264,
   299

O'Connor, John, 164n
O'Shaughnessy, Brian, 18n, 127n
Oldenquist, Andrew, 164n

Passmore, J. A., 140n, 141n
Paton, H. J., 176n
Peacocke, Christopher, 96n, 97n, 114n
Pears, David, 64n, 85n, 93n, 96n, 99n,
   113n, 115–16, 164n, 170n, 233n
Perry, David L., 114n, 164n
plans, 111–12, 215–38, 307; how constrained by evidence, 222–25; content
   of, 218, 230–31, 238; how filled in,
   229–32; how formed, 232–34; as
   long-range reflective expectations,
   216–34; as reasons for acting, 237–38,
   254–57, 299–300. *See also* intention,
   policies
policies: defined, 307–8; as moral principles, 315–17; rationality of, 308–9,
   316–17
Powell, Betty, 16n, 18n
Promises, 63n, 93n, 105n
"practical knowledge," 24–25, 102–5,
   185–86
practical reasoning, 81–108, 174–75,
   198, 210, 270, 280; as constitutive of
   agency, 100–101, 197, 206, 263–64;
   as creative, 257–59; involves no special
   logic, 108, 121n; long-range, 236–401;
   two modes, 236–38, 253–57, 298–
   300; topic of, 100–101, 197, 207–8,
   263–64, 265–68, 296–97, 298, 301–4;
   unconsciously articulated, 88–90, 106–
   8; versus theoretical reasoning, 82–83,
   90–108
"practical truth," 93n
predicting versus deciding, 81–82, 98n,
   99
preferences: defined, 178; second-order,
   182–85
principles. *See* policies
procrastination, 95
promises, 93n, 105n
pronoun, masculine, 4n
prudence, 238–40, 285–86

psychological causation, 3, 4, 7, 10–11,
   54, 58n, 77, 102n, 160–61, 165, 167–
   72, 173, 176, 189, 192–96, 208–11
psychology, commonsense. *See* commonsense psychology

Railton, Peter, 287n, 295n
Rankin, K. W., 62n, 95n, 105n, 113n,
   121n, 135n, 137n
Rawls, John, 287n
Raz, Joseph, 200n, 201n
reasons for acting, 6, 189–211; character
   trait as, 249–50, 255–57, 301–4; defined, 198, 204–5, 264; emotions as,
   250, 301–4; essential features, 190–92,
   205; future motives as, 238–40; habits
   as, 202–4, 301–4; intentions as, 124–
   25, 200–202, 208–9; must they involve desires? 250, 264, 302–4; plans
   as, 237–38, 254–57, 299–300; as
   premises of practical reasoning, 125,
   197–98, 264; present motives as, 192–
   96, 199–200, 209–11, 247–48, 256–
   57, 265; procedural versus evaluative,
   236–38, 253–54, 298–300; strength
   of, 256–57; versus causes, 189, 192–
   96, 208–11
reasons for desiring, 279–80; not essential to rationality of desires, 280–81
reasons for intending. *See* intention, reasons for
reductionism, 10; about intention, 109
reflective descriptions, 176–77; as intentions, 180–81, 246, 252–53, 255; why
   self-fulfilling, 75n, 180–81, 182, 246,
   252
reflective expectations: causes understood, 74–76, 86–90, 96, 106n, 137,
   140–41, 164; constrained by evidence,
   56, 57, 59, 95, 151, 158, 219, 222–25,
   232; content of (*see* intention, content
   of); effects recognized, 57n, 60n, 65n,
   66, 73–76, 86–90, 96, 137, 140–41,
   164, 169–70, 218, 219–20; formed,
   64–66, 74, 87–88, 95, 150, 152–53,
   232–34; grounds versus occasion, 61–
   62, 68, 132n; as intentions, 94–100,
   121–42, 147–58, 170, 171, 173–74,
   215–53; justified, 49n, 55–64, 103–5;
   as long-range plans, 216–34; as a